Falling Away from You

One Family's Journey through Traumatic Brain Injury

Nicole Vinson Bingaman

ISBN-13: 978-0692255926
ISBN-10: 0692255923
Library of Congress Control Number: 2015931575

Convurgent Publishing, LLC
4445 Corporation Lane, Suite #227
Virginia Beach, VA 23462
www.convurgent.com
www.nicolebingaman.com

Full names of medical professionals have been changed to protect their privacy.

Acknowledgments

The story you are about to read is ultimately a love story. It is about the love of family, friends, and a community that helped one person as they fought to survive despite surmountable odds. It has been a painful story to write, and at times difficult to share. Throughout the process there was never a moment when I felt I couldn't continue, but there were times when I wanted to stop because reliving it all hurt so deeply. The reason I was able to write it in the first place was simply because of love and the belief that telling our story was something I needed to do.

Before you open the book and begin to delve into our journey, I want to take a moment to thank some people who helped me gain the courage that I needed to complete this process. And I want to thank you, the reader, for choosing to discover what this book is about.

First of all, I would like to thank my mom for being a dynamic, unyielding force of love and light in my life. To my dad and Miss Connie: thank you for always believing in and seeing the best in me. To my grandmothers: thank you for the legacy of love you gave to me. To Eric, who has stood with me in the times when I have felt most afraid and alone: I treasure the fact that I am your baby sister. To Keith: your loyalty, trust and abiding love has been a constant over the past 25 years; thank you for all that you have done to create a better life for our family and the love you have shown to me. To Tanner, Avery, and Taylor: when you were first placed in my arms, I knew that being your mother would change me in many ways. Loving you taught me the depths and heights to which love will go. I am proud of each of you, and stand in awe of the inner strength you show. I am so fortunate to be your mother.

To Ruth Murphy: thank you for planting the seed of a dream inside the heart of a little girl; you are among the finest of teachers. To Jenna, who made this project possible and supported it every step of the way.

To Dr. Shelly Timmons, Dr. Randy Fulton, Susanne Hill, Kristine Longo, and Marissa Luskin: thank you for sharing your knowledge with me and your understanding of traumatic brain injury in your respective fields; your compassion remains your finest gift, but your knowledge is a most valuable tool.

To all our friends and family members who have helped us get through the past two years, thank you. Thank you for being present, for offering support, and for recognizing that some roads are not meant to be traveled alone.

To the survivors and families affected by traumatic brain injury: I am so proud to call some of you my friends. Your courage, bravery, and commitment are inspiring to me.

Finally, to Christy, one of the most loving mothers I have had the opportunity to meet. This book is written for our sons, who started their journey together. I will never forget either you or Dustin. Your memory is   forever   stamped   on   my   heart.

Love Wins.

Contents

Journal Entry

Day 7, November 29 (one week after the fall)

Watching you be still
Seeing you quiet
Resting in the midst of great turmoil,
With chaos all around.
You are quiet
And you are here.

It is enough
To see you,
But my heart longs to hear you.
Every touch matters,
Every moment heals.

My heart is weeping
And aching for you
Asking you to come home, to me, to us,
To yourself.
And yet all I can do is
Watch you
Be still.

Love,
Mom

Preface

The book you have just opened tells the story of a subject that I knew nothing about until I was forty-two years old. I had been familiar with people who have traveled the path that I would come to share with them, but in reality my knowledge of the topic was no more than what you see by looking through a tiny keyhole into a room. My view was at best limited. I had heard the stories of famous people like Gabby Giffords and Bob Woodruff who have also walked this road, but seeing them on television or reading articles about them would tell me so little about what they had endured. During my forty-second year of life, I became a student in the classroom of traumatic brain injury, or TBI. My mind and heart would begin to know and hold things I never knew it was possible for them to endure.

Prior to having an understanding of what the term *traumatic brain injury* means, I was living a fairly uncomplicated life. I lived in a small Norman Rockwell-type town in Pennsylvania. I had been married for twenty-two years, and had three sons aged twenty-one, nineteen, and sixteen. I was employed with the Pennsylvania Department of Public Welfare[1] as a caseworker and had a fairly close circle of friends. The fact that I enjoyed being a mother is an understatement, but I was also appreciating the fact that my children were growing up and that some of my life's focus was shifting. My life was far from perfect, but now I would give every cent that I have to go back to less complicated days.

Things would forever change on Thanksgiving Eve 2012, when my twenty-one-year-old son Taylor fell down the stairs in our home. What started as the evening of another holiday has led us down a road that has yet to end. This journey changed each person in our family from the inside out. Since that day, I have often repeated the phrase to myself, "Never again." By that, I mean never again will I take one breath, one moment, one skill, or one person I love for granted. Through this

---

[1] Renamed the Pennsylvania Department of Human Services in November 2014.

experience, I have learned in a brutal way that death is not the only thing that can steal someone you love away from you. It is not the only thing that can make you long to be with your loved one again.

In sharing my story, I hope that you can hear my heart. I hope to give you a glimpse of what life is like for traumatic brain injury survivors and those who love them. I hope to give you some inspiration and strength in your present journey or those to come. I hope to educate you about some of the many things that I did not know, so that you may better understand what TBI actually means. I also hope that bits and pieces of my broken heart are healed in the process. When you are done reading these pages, I hope that instead of feeling like you are peering through a keyhole into our world, you are able to see the whole house, with light filtering into every room.

As you will discover in these pages, traumatic brain injury is a slow-moving process that takes on a life of its own; and just when you think things have settled down, they can change. This journey is full of fears, hopes, friends, dreams that come true, and dreams that die. It has its highs and lows. It has been my greatest pain to share this journey with Taylor, but it has also been my greatest honor to be by his side.

In this book there are many, many heroes; and while Taylor is the central focus of this story . . . there are those who brought compassion, bravery, and courage to him when he needed it most. You will meet many of these heroes in these pages. Some of the most important ones are those who share a home with Taylor and who have stayed beside him every step of the way. They include my husband and the father of my sons—Keith—and Taylor's younger brothers, Avery and Tanner. Without them, this story would not have been written and would not be possible to share. I believe all of us had a part in saving Taylor.

Another group of extraordinary people that cannot go without mentioning are those who brought something that defies definition to us when we needed it most. Ultimately it was the gift of themselves. Many of these individuals were also broken, sad and struggling and yet they found a way out of their darkness to lend some light. They are my friends, who have been through the unimaginable death of a child, who reached beyond their pain and helped me sort through mine. There is the friend whose brother lost his life after falling down the stairs, when I was a young girl, who has cheered me on from afar and reminded me of why I need to give our story a voice. As a child I shared a special bond with her parents, and remember their grief. I hear their voices every time she speaks encouragement to me. There is the couple in our community, who first extended their concern to us by way of a bingo fundraiser, that have now become treasured friends. Each one of these people, and many more, have been nothing less than inspiring to me. I write for them, for those they have lost and for every tear they have shed.

Five centuries before Christ, the ancient Greek playwright Euripides said, "No one can confidently say that he will still be living tomorrow." I have learned that both the brevity and frailty of life is a constant and undeniable truth, a truth that at some point we all must come to terms with.

Part I: Danville

Chapter One
The Loneliest Place on Earth
November 22, 2012

The turkey was stuffed and another pan was filled for the feast that would take place. The carrot soufflé was not yet made, the baked corn was done, and the desserts were waiting to be thawed out from the freezer. The potatoes would have to be peeled, but I was certain everyone's Thanksgiving food wishes would be granted at the table. That was one of our family traditions: each person got to name a dish they desired and I would do my best to make it. As I fell asleep on Thanksgiving eve, I was running through the list in my mind, checking it again and again. The Thanksgiving to come would be special, because we had unfortunately not all been together the previous year and there was some extra stress in our world. I was feeling the pressure that comes with wanting everyone to be happy. I wanted a Hallmark holiday, but I know they seldom exist. I was excited for everyone, especially Taylor, to taste the pumpkin roll that I had made for the first time as my "something extra" to add to the table. I had gone over to my friend's house the week before to learn how to create the rolls from scratch. It was fun to be her student in the kitchen, and it also felt good to have something new to share with my family. I could hardly wait for my boys to taste the roll. It is a simple thing, but cooking on the holidays was another way for me to say "I love you" to my family. As the mother of three growing sons, I found that the opportunities to cook as an expression of love came often.

On occasion, other family members would be present for Thanksgiving, but this particular year, 2012, it would be just our immediate family. My husband of twenty-two years, Keith, and our sons Taylor, Avery, and Tanner would be gathered around the table to feast on the meal I prepared. Of course I missed the rest of our family, but I was looking forward to sharing the day with just the five of us. Taylor had mentioned earlier in the week that he did not know whether he would be around for Thanksgiving because some of his buddies were tossing around the idea of driving to Pittsburgh to hunt for the second year in a row. Taylor and I had a discussion by way of texting about the holiday and I had to be firm. Being the bad guy, I told him that he needed to be home because we were going to have Thanksgiving together . . . as a family. Feeling relieved, he did not put up any kind of argument.

Almost a year later, I found the Thanksgiving meal preparation list on my desk at work. It was a list that had not been touched or moved in almost 365 days. Like everything else on my desk, it had remained untouched in my absence. It sat with my half-empty coffee cup, which was next to my water glass. On the large desktop calendar, written in bold letters, it read November 2012. The pages on the calendar had not been turned in over a year, but everything else in our world had been turned upside down. Sitting at my work desk, I felt like I was taking a step backward in time. A step to a place where I wished I could return, before the chaos, before the sadness, and before the fall.

Everyone's name was invisible on the list because like any good mother, I knew each one's wishes by heart. Avery would want baked corn and an apple dessert; Keith and Taylor would request mashed potatoes and gravy; Tanner would demand carrot soufflé; and I wanted stuffing. My stuffing had taken on a life of its own and I felt so accomplished when I made it. Having been brought up in the South, I thought of good stuffing as an important contribution to the Thanksgiving table. Since we didn't have a lot of opportunities throughout the year to prepare a big feast, my taste buds were already watering that Thanksgiving eve. When I found the list a year later in 2013, I immediately felt heartbroken and bitter. The day had come—but never in the way that I had intended.

While I was in a deep sleep on Thanksgiving Eve 2012, no longer caring about my cooking list, I was suddenly awakened by my two younger sons. I heard Tanner and Avery in the hallway outside my bedroom, right outside the door. I had no idea what time it was—and to this day, I am still not certain. I just heard them whisper, "Mom, it's us . . . we need to turn the light on." I tend to scare easily in the night, and they are keenly aware of how jumpy I can be. By the tone in their voice, I knew it was important and took a deep breath, and answered them with, "Are you okay?" I was in the place between being fully awake and half asleep. For some unknown reason, I thought my sons had wrecked one of their cars. Earlier in the evening, they had gone to play guitar and jam at a friend's house, as everyone was home from college for Thanksgiving break. They were both safely in the house, however, and I felt an immediate sense of relief. Over the next sixty seconds, they explained that Taylor had fallen down the stairs; an ambulance had come; and Life Flight had been called. My oldest son was in a helicopter and I was in my bedroom, frantically throwing on clothes. *I had no idea what was happening.*

To this day, I am still perplexed by my reaction on that night, but I remember it vividly. I yelled, "Damn it, Taylor!!" in an angry tone. I will probably never understand why my first response was some strange outrage. As Taylor's mother, I sensed some sort of immediate danger, but I had no thought as to what we would be facing. I did not cry and I wasn't full of dread. *I was unclear as to what was happening.* In fact, in light of what was going on . . . I was fairly calm. Keith's reaction was much different, and in some ways worse. He felt sick immediately, with a sense of undeniable dread in his stomach. My husband developed a pale washed-out complexion, with a look of absolute fear on his face. He was very quiet, and clearly aware, even in his physical body, that something horrible had occurred.

As we left the driveway, Avery, our middle child, was acting so grown-up—which is something I am still thankful for. He did not want his dad or me to drive, and he was trying his very best to take care of us. I didn't want him to drive too fast or too slow, but I myself needed to fly. Remembering back, I was telling him to get there as fast as he could but not to speed. The panic was evident in my voice as I spoke aloud. *I don't think that any of us knew at that moment what we were feeling.*

I would later put the pieces together that not only had Taylor gone through hell in his body, but his younger brothers had to witness something far worse than anyone should ever have to see. Avery and Tanner had responded immediately to the crashing sounds of Taylor's body. They were in his room adjacent to the stairs, and heard him tumble down those stairs. I have gathered bits and pieces of what happened afterward, but that part of the evening in its whole raw form has never been my story to tell.

On the way out of our long driveway, we passed the ambulance and stopped to question the driver. Taylor had to be driven far out to an open field where the helicopter could land, and the ambulance was returning. The driver stated, "The things that we were concerned about seem to be cleared up." Feeling relieved, I suggested that we take two cars instead of just one, so Taylor could be comfortable for the ride home . . . *thinking he would be coming home that night*. We quickly got into two separate vehicles. Avery and Tanner rode in one car, with Keith and me following in the other. Now rambling, I explained how grumpy Taylor would be if we all had to be crammed in the same car. During the forty-five-minute drive to the hospital, I was remembering a time when he was twelve years old and had to be rushed to the emergency room. That story had a happy ending, even though there were a few rough days involved.

As we traveled through our small town of Mifflinburg, Pennsylvania, something began to awaken in me. I felt a sense of dread, and suddenly it hit me that if Taylor had been flown in a helicopter, he might not come home . . . *ever*. With this recent feeling of panic, I felt an immediate need to call my dad, and as soon as I started to speak, some truth came into my heart. As he answered my call, I said the words aloud: "Taylor may not be okay. He fell down the stairs and had to be taken to the hospital by helicopter." *It was the first of many times that I would break down.* I wanted to scream into the phone. My mind felt hysterical, but my words and body did not give that away. Instead my voice trembled gently with fear, but did not indicate the alarm that my heart felt.

We walked into the completely empty waiting room of the ER at Geisinger Medical Center in Danville, Pennsylvania. Tanner and Avery had already arrived. They were standing, and although they appeared to be calm, I could see that they were clearly frightened. As soon as Keith and I came in and told the lady at the reception area that we were here for our son Taylor, a gentleman came out. He calmly said, "I am a chaplain and we need to talk about your son." My first instinct was not to follow him. *I was afraid of what would happen next.* I knew in my heart how these circumstances end, and I wasn't about to listen to some stranger say that my son had died. At first I told the chaplain that I didn't want to go back. I felt that if I could avoid going into the room where they were ushering us, this situation would be less real. But we were summoned to a room anyway, and as I crossed the waiting area of the emergency room . . . I knew my family's lives would be changed forever.

The room was fairly empty with the exception of four or five chairs. They were the older-style metal chairs with minimal padding. If I recall correctly, the colors were black or blue. No pictures hung on the walls, and there were no magazines on the tables to read in your spare time. This was a room in which information was passed along, and judging from the information we were receiving, it was generally a room most people hoped to avoid.

I can still recall the feeling of anxiety that hung in the air of that room, and I have passed by it many times since. I sat across from it one day about a year ago when a family was told their loved one would not survive. If the walls of that room were to speak, they would tell us horrible things.

I was so grateful for the realness of this chaplain. Through our facial expressions, he could see that we were in incredible pain and he simply told us the facts. Our son, the big brother of Tanner and Avery, friend to many and so much more, had suffered a horrible injury. The doctor was coming in and Taylor would be in a fight for his life. At one point, the chaplain confessed that he could not begin to understand how we were feeling. He said, "I won't tell you some meaningless words to try to make it better. I am sorry, and I am here if you need me." He said it perfectly—no one could make this situation better.

A gentleman by the name of Dr. Kirkland came in wearing a down jacket and eyeglasses that stood out. The jacket was a metallic gray and he had on blue jeans with a dress shirt. The glasses he wore were a distinguished rectangular shape. They were the kind of glasses that made you think he was both interesting and intelligent. He looked awake and alert, but we knew he had just walked in the door from being soundly asleep at home. We have always been glad that he was the neurosurgeon on call that evening. He proved to be not only a skilled surgeon, but also a doctor who carries true compassion in his heart. A small female doctor was with him; her name escaped us at the time, but we would later learn to appreciate Dr. Towley. Dr. Towley was the trauma doctor and Dr. Kirkland was the neurosurgeon. We would come to know and trust them well. Our son's life was literally in their hands, and we had to allow them to be there if he had any chance of coming back to us.

What I am about to say may sound silly, but after a lifetime of watching shows like *House, ER,* and *Grey's Anatomy,* I thought I had watched this scene many times. This was not NBC or Fox . . . *this was real and this was my son.* I felt as if I were watching a movie. All that was happening seemed very surreal. I looked at Dr. Kirkland and felt compelled to say something that would let him know that the twenty-one-year-old man lying on his table tonight was so much more than he could imagine. And at that moment, the most important aspect was that he was my son; he was part of each of us standing there and his care was not to be taken lightly. I would speak words that I hoped would fight for him. I held the doctor's hands in mine and I looked at them. These hands could bring our Taylor back to us. I said what my heart needed for me to say and hoped against all the fears invading me that the words had been heard.

After speaking with the two doctors, we were led into an empty room. I have no idea what part of the emergency area we were in that night. I have made several trips to the emergency room with three rambunctious boys, but this area was different. We were somewhere in the back of the emergency room. It was quiet and there was a lot of space and silence that surrounded us. It seemed very large, sterile, and empty. The silence of the room was haunting. There was no rushing around, no fixing anything. The chaos must have settled and the emptiness of life in the room was chilling. It seemed cold and sterile, and this was not the place where I wanted Taylor to take his last breath.

And then I saw him . . . my Taylor. My strong, beautiful son was lying on a stretcher. The son that my mom and I always said looked like a prince still had that look, but death was trying to steal him away. He looked to be sleeping, but otherwise perfect. He was still; he was so still, in fact, that you knew he could not be stirred. Taylor had not shown any signs of consciousness since his fall. *And that is the last time I saw the Taylor I knew and recognized in body.* Everything about him was quiet.

The hospital team revealed all of the things you see on television—but we were experiencing it in real life. Nothing about the situation felt real at the time. It felt like we were out of our bodies, and I prayed this was a dream. The staff told us to say good-bye; they told us that this surgery might not work; and they allowed us to stay until the moment Taylor had to go into the operating room . . . which would happen very quickly. That very moment was a gift and something for which I would forever be thankful. Why was this horrible moment something I would consider a gift? It was the chance to say good-bye. I had previously lost my stepbrother and half-sister, both in tragic events which were brutal and unexpected, and I regretted not having a good-bye. I would not take this moment for granted. But how do you say good-bye to someone who can't hear you, who is just twenty-one years old, and who just hours before was living and enjoying his life? You don't, but you have to try. I had to believe that Taylor could both hear and feel our love.

There was nothing about the accident that felt real. There was nothing in it that felt as if it fit or belonged to us. But as much as we did not want to feel, acknowledge, or accept this truth, Taylor was lying on the stretcher, having had his clothing cut off just moments before and being flown by helicopter, as he unknowingly began the fight for his very life. I have no idea what occurred on that flight; I have never asked and no one ever told us. As Taylor lay still on the stretcher, we all told him that we loved him. We told him to be strong. I told him to fight and that I did not want him to leave us. I whispered in his ear, "Please don't go. I love you."

In my heart, I told him what I could not bear to say . . . *if we lost him, we would lose ourselves.* We all knew what this meant, but not one of us knew how to say it. Keith spoke more than the rest of us and I was thankful for his voice and words. I kept looking at my other sons,

19

reminding myself that they were okay and they were alive. I had never been so scared in all my life. But I would learn to face many, many moments of fear. I would learn how to control my fear instead of letting it control me.

Over the next several hours, we called family, friends, and those closest to us and to Taylor. I remember a few of the calls that I made, but most of them I can't recall. The worst calls that I had to make were to my parents and brother. I struggled with how to reach my mom, who lived alone. What do you say? I kept it simple and as scared as I was . . . I did not want to frighten others. If I did not allow panic and hysteria, then on some level the crisis felt less real. I don't really remember what was said because we knew so little, but we knew enough to know that Taylor might not survive.

Some of my friends have recalled those conversations with me. I think I sounded like a robot. *Taylor fell down the stairs. Taylor may not be okay.* I have no recollection of my words that day.

Several hours passed by and we would receive updates, but no *real* news. Taylor was in surgery and he was surviving this first part. I kept being thankful that no doctor was heading toward us looking grim, ready to tell us that Taylor was gone. We were on the third floor of GMC; the waiting rooms were rotated through by all of us. There was a sweet housekeeper who kept offering us tea or coffee. She had seen this kind of situation before, but she would not ignore us, especially on Thanksgiving Day. After several hours, Dr. Kirkland came out and announced that Taylor had survived. He spoke in what seemed like a foreign language; none of his words made sense or had any authority in our world. He asked us questions about Taylor's fall and the moments after the fall, and assured us that Taylor had been well tended to in the moments afterward by Tanner and Avery.

This is what we knew at that time. Taylor's skull had suffered massive blows. The right side was crushed, the left side was fractured, and the front was damaged. In those early days, that description meant nothing. *Taylor's survival was the only thing that was on my mind.* We were told that the first 72 hours are crucial. It was clearly explained to us that Taylor was in no way safe and his life was still in grave danger.

Taylor had intracranial pressure that resulted in his brain swelling. His brain was bleeding, and that needed to be stopped immediately. At a certain point of swelling, the brainstem[2] is affected and then the person dies if the pressure is not released. The intracranial pressure needed to come down. That was all we knew. We were scared and although we were together, we felt alone.

The waiting room was full, but it was not packed. It was still Thanksgiving Day. People were getting ready to celebrate, eat, drink, and be merry . . . but news was also traveling and many of our dearest friends and family were beginning to hear that Taylor Bingaman had suffered a fall. Later, I would feel regret and sadness about the way in which some of those who had been part of Taylor's life for years heard the news. They would come to share with me how their Thanksgiving table was full of tears, fear, and sadness. The only regret I had that day was that I could not allow myself the ability to release the emotion I held inside. I wanted to scream, run into the operating room, and somehow make this horror end. The clock did not stop, but it felt as if time itself were a form of torture.

With Taylor being an avid outdoorsman, gossip quickly spread that he had fallen from a tree stand while hunting. But Taylor had always been a safe hunter and took great caution regarding his surroundings. He was safety-conscious and he liked for his friends to be safe. Taylor cared about his life and he cared about the lives of others.

Taylor fell down the stairs in our home.

We had always dreamed of living in a log home. When a friend was selling this one privately, years ago, we snatched it up before anyone

---

[2] The brainstem is the lowermost portion of the brain, next to and continuous with the spinal cord. It regulates the central nervous system as well as the functioning of the heart and lungs, and thus is crucial to survival following a head injury.

else could. It was a great place for three adventurous boys. When they were growing up, one of their favorite movies was *Wild America*. They liked to live out this movie, always finding something fun to do in the woods around our home. I think between their adventurous hearts and their constantly moving imaginations, they wanted to be their own version of the *Wild America* brothers . . . and they were.

On one of our earliest days in living in our log home, I heard a lot of wild yelling from the boys. I had been in the bathroom and quickly ran outside. What I saw was a group of boys chasing a bear. Yes, they were chasing the bear! They were fearless and loved the wild. Later, we had to speak with one of the local game wardens to explain the dangers of humans interacting with bears.

Our home was a safe place, but a busy one. Footsteps could always be heard running to and fro, up and down, and all over the house. At the time, we had two open staircases, which had both been made from simple, thick, unfinished wood. These parts of the house caused us great concern when the boys were younger, but as they grew older there was nothing to be afraid of. It was nothing at this point in our lives to hear commotion on the stairs or underneath our bedroom. Our house lent itself to hearing everything; and in time, you could block out the noises. The acoustics were made for people who were far quieter than our boys.

Taylor and one of his friends had returned to our house after a night of catching up and hanging out with some of the local gang and other friends who were home for the holiday. Lots of kids gathered together at local establishments and caught up on Thanksgiving eve. Avery and Tanner were in Taylor's room playing video games when they heard Taylor and his buddy come into the house.

The rest of our large home was quiet. It was late, and all the Thanksgiving Eve happenings were coming to an end. We had crossed into what was technically Thanksgiving Day. And after dropping everyone else off, Taylor was the last to go. His friend lived just a couple of miles down the road from us, so Taylor had been the first to be picked up and the last to come home. After a few seconds in the kitchen, Taylor went into the bathroom. He said something to his friend about going to the bathroom before going to bed.

When Taylor emerged from the bathroom, instead of walking toward his bedroom . . . he headed for the stairs, which were straight ahead but in the opposite direction from his bedroom. His friend noticed Taylor standing at the top of the stairs, and he said it looked as if Taylor had suddenly stepped off a ledge into the air.

We have no idea why Taylor even headed down the stairs. Sometimes late at night, he would go to get something to eat from the freezer before going to bed. There was also a light on, but I doubt he was worried about turning it off. He was exhausted; according to his friends, he had been excessively tired all evening. In our minds, he did not actually intend to go downstairs.

Who knows where he was heading or what he was doing? But when he did it . . . he fell. At the moment of his fall, Tanner and Avery heard a loud crash and immediately ran to the stairs. Taylor was at the bottom of the stairs unconscious. They tried to awaken or arouse him, but had no luck. They said that when they initially looked at Taylor, he appeared to have simply passed out. As they took a closer look, they noticed that there was a small area on the back of Taylor's head that was bleeding. They immediately called 9-1-1. While waiting for the ambulance to arrive, Taylor began to tremble and his body began to tense and become rigid. As soon as the ambulance crew arrived, the EMT did a quick assessment of Taylor's eyes. He opened them, looked at the pupils, and immediately called for Life Flight. Avery went through the process of telling the crew where the closest field was, and as the ambulance drove off with Taylor, Tanner and Avery had the painful task of waking us and letting us know what had happened.

Every time I think of it, I don't have to work hard to imagine what the fall looked like. Taylor weighed close to two hundred pounds, and fell and crashed in just the wrong way. There was nothing right about the way Taylor fell. The force of the brutal blows met my strong, six feet tall, brave, beautiful, and sweet son with undeniable power. He had tumbled down thirteen stairs, each one delivering some type of blow

23

or beating to his head. For some reason, Taylor's head was the object that seemed to guide the fall. It was as if his head had protected the other parts of his body. No other part of his body was hurt, but the part that was injured would affect his entire being. These things were not noticeable right away to the human eye, but within a few hours, the initial force of the impact would be revealed.

I have always believed that the sequence of the horrible events that took place in the moments right after the fall occurred in some way as they should. I have played and replayed it in my mind and run through more than a thousand scenarios. The truth regarding the impact was very clearly explained to us, and for that reason, I will always believe that the decisions that were made that night saved Taylor's life. I have often thought if Keith or I had been present, would we have acted with the same response? Would we have made the same judgment? The boys did the right things for Taylor and it saved him. One of the first things that Dr. Kirkland would tell us, which would later be reinforced, was that if Taylor had not been brought to the hospital, *he would have died.* It was also explained to us that the fall itself caused every bit of damage to Taylor's brain on impact. It did not have time to progressively get worse.

Since Taylor's fall, the stairs have been carpeted; a door has been put in the place that used to be open; and an extra light switch installed. The stairs still make me feel sick when I go up or down them, but the cosmetic changes have helped make using them more bearable. When they were in their original condition, all I could ever picture was Taylor falling and not being able to catch himself. I am told that people came and cleaned up the blood. I am also told his brothers tried to clean it too. It makes my heart race and my mind enter into an absolute panic when I think of it.

Within twenty-four to thirty-six hours after his fall, Taylor's friends came and talked to us. They said that his behavior and mood had been somewhat "off" the entire evening that led up to the fall. That week Taylor had worked four twelve-hour shifts in a row, which was nothing new for his work schedule. He often pushed his need for sleep to the limits. But he was young and could run on empty. His friends explained that from the time they all met that night, which was around 7 p.m., Taylor was moody and excessively tired. He was acting out of character, somewhat grumpy and preoccupied. He also had to be awakened several times as they went from a friend's house to a local establishment, then to another place. His friends all said the same thing to us. They explained that Taylor was different than the usual "Bing" in ways that they could not pinpoint at the time, but would later cause them to ask whether something had been going on.

His friends wondered whether Taylor had had a bad reaction to something, or if he had started a new medication that they weren't aware of, or if something else had been going on. They had as many questions as we did. The biggest questions of all seemed to be "Why?" and "How?" Taylor's blood work showed that there were no surprise demons in his system. He and his friends had been out and they had been drinking, but by the accounts of those who were with him, Taylor was in control after he was awake. But there was discussion regarding how much alcohol had been consumed.

We asked whether there was any possibility that something else could have occurred. I wondered if he had suffered a concussion on the job. I wondered if he had had an aneurysm. I wondered whether I was getting the full story. I wondered if I had been close by . . . if this event would have come out differently. But all the wondering in the world did not change the fact that Taylor was in a coma with a large piece of his skull removed, and that doctors were constantly reminding us that *he might not make it.* The doctors reminded us again and again that there was not one specific thing that caused this outcome. Often tragedies happen as the result of a cluster of events. No one was to blame. There was no divine punishment involved. This was not some warped lesson that we somehow deserved. As Taylor's mother, I found it hard to have unclear answers. The reality was that Taylor's brain was so badly damaged that if there had been anything affecting his brain previously, it would now be undetectable.

Taylor had ridden his new Harley-Davidson without a helmet. At times, he drove faster than he should have. He was not reckless, but he was young and naive. He felt invincible; sometimes, I think he lacked the time and careful regard for his own life. I am sure I did the same thing when I was twenty-one. But Taylor was also a safety-conscious and cautious individual. He practiced safety on his job and in the woods. He was aware that being careless is not a good plan, and I don't think he practiced living life on the edge.

Thirteen stairs. Probably thirteen seconds. Thirteen moments in which twenty-one years were changed and much of them erased.

———

Taylor's first day in the hospital is difficult to remember. The memories are raw and vivid, but they feel far away, and much of what happened remains difficult to recall. All of Keith's family lives close by, so the waiting room was filled with two of his brothers and their wives and children. Some of Taylor's friends came just to sit with us, and there was such a pain and thickness in the air. Each of us was filled with fear, uncertainty, and wondering how to fill the new roles we had been given to play. No one could understand the kind of pain that we all felt; and at times, even being surrounded by people could feel like the loneliest place on earth.

A few days later I wrote in my journal, *"The hours in waiting were agony; not one of us believed our Taylor could leave us, and yet in our hearts we knew it was a strong possibility. Agony isn't even the right word. Sheer terror does not even define our emotional state. But what words can?"*

At one point, my youngest son, Tanner, said to me, "Mom, I need to eat, I can't help it, and I am hungry." It was okay to be hungry and it was okay to need to get out of the waiting. I still remember the way Tanner looked that day. Those hours not only changed Taylor forever, but they also changed those who loved him most. People were praying. Sometimes people were chatting and trying to be normal. This situation was all new and there was nothing predictable about any of it.

There was talk of miracles and everything being okay . . . but my heart was neither hopeful nor shattered. *It was numb.* I was in so much shock that I did not know how to behave, and I could not even entertain the thought that Taylor might not be okay.

Eventually the medical staff told us that we could come in to see Taylor. We were warned that Taylor was hooked up to a lot of things, a ventilator, and other devices. What had happened to Taylor's head during the fall was explained to us. He had crushed the right side of his head and that piece was no longer there. He also had damage to the left side of his head; and there was bleeding along the frontal lobe. There were large and small bleeds throughout Taylor's head. The large piece of Taylor's skull bone that had been removed was referred to as a bone flap. The piece that was taken was about the size of my hand. The missing piece had fallen from its normal location above his right ear to the place above his right eye. Taylor suffered multiple brain injuries and multiple brain bleeds. The skull was no longer there as protection, and the staff had to be extremely cautious.

Taylor was bandaged up; initially, he did not look as horrific as one might imagine. The most difficult part of looking at Taylor was seeing the intracranial pressure reader in his head. At the top of his head, Taylor had a very small gauge that came out. It looked like something you would see in a space alien. The staff measured the pressure and swelling when he came in to the ER on November 22; Taylor's pressure reading at that time was 50. At that number, the brain begins to push against the brainstem, causing the brain tissue to die. Dr. Kirkland initially told us that the normal healthy brain has an intracranial pressure that ranges from 5 to 15 millimeters of mercury, or mmHg.[3] This number had to go down and stay down. If the pressure was not relieved, *Taylor would not survive.* Taylor looked like a Martian. He also looked fragile. Along with the pressure gauge at the top, there was a bulb that collected fluid at the bottom. This bulb was a drainage tube and it was full of blood. Was he in there? Was he going to be okay? Would Taylor get through this? And if so, how long would it take?

---

[3] This is the same unit of measurement used in blood pressure readings.

Taylor's head and face were noticeably swollen and he was very puffy. His face was so swollen that he could not physically open his eyes if he had wanted to. His head was wrapped in white gauze. He still looked like Taylor, which was something that would come to change. Over the course of the next several days, his swelling would continue and his looks would begin to alter. People would say, "He looks good!" and I never quite knew what those words meant, but I agreed.

He was eerily still and it was quiet. In his room, there was a neon sign above his bed that read:

"Your family member has suffered a traumatic injury to their head. PLEASE NO STIMULATION INCLUDING: talking, television, radio, cell phones, or touching. You may sit in the room quietly."

We followed the instructions as best as we could. At some points, we were permitted to touch his hand and whisper the words we wanted to say aloud. Any time that waves of grief would come, it would be my practice to step out of Taylor's room and allow myself the freedom to really cry. We did not anticipate that Taylor would show any signs of stirring for a couple of days. He was sedated and given large doses of pain medication. He was being kept comfortable, in the way that you keep someone comfortable who is somewhere else in his or her mind.

In the hours that followed, no one slept. At some point in the early evening, my big brother Eric arrived. This was the man who grew up with me; one of my lifelong protectors. This was one person that I knew would do anything in the world to stop this from occurring. Eric stands 6 feet 3 inches tall and is one of the most intelligent and witty people I have ever known. We call him the Gentle Giant, and yet this giant was powerless to change anything. Eric's presence brought me incredible comfort. There was something about having my big brother there that made me feel safe and sane. I felt like there was a person here who had been through life and death with me, and that somehow he could maybe make it all right. Eric is calm and thoughtful, and his quiet presence brought me a sense of peace in those endless grueling hours that would continue for days to come. After his arrival, I remembered my very first Mother's Day. We happened to be in Virginia for Eric's college graduation. I remembered bringing Taylor and his outrageous reaction when the audience of a thousand erupted with clapping in the enclosed auditorium. And I remembered that on Mother's Day, next to the potted flower Eric bought my stepmom, was something for me. It was a dandelion in a glass of water; in childlike writing, Eric had written, "Happy First Mother's Day, from Taylor."

I cannot remember the night of the accident because we came to the hospital at such an odd hour. The days still seem jumbled to me. It was almost like having jet lag. One day led into another and so did the hours. I know that at some point Avery and Tanner went home to sleep. I know we spent our first night in the ICU, and in the waiting room with hospital blankets and pillows.

The day after the accident, we met with the head of the ICU. I cannot recall her name, but she was a wonderful woman who had just the right amount of compassion and professionalism. She reminded us that because Taylor was young, there would be a lot of curiosity about him. She suggested we set up a care page online or make use of social media. Avery said that he would share what was happening via Facebook. I was aware that I needed people to know that our world had been rocked. I just don't think any of us knew what to say. Looking back, I think we could have shared more, but none of us knew what those messages might have looked like. How do you explain what you don't understand? How do you express the fact that your whole world has been shattered and the pieces are still lying all around you? How do you put into words, "We might be watching our son die?" Social media of any kind was the last thing on my mind, but I knew they would help people understand the course of events. Those who cared about Taylor deserved to know what was happening.

The doctor also explained what would become a theme; *this was going to be a long and slow process.* Taylor's healing was going to take much longer than we liked. Our lives would be changed from here on out because Taylor would not be the same. All these words could be understood and comprehended, but as I look back, they meant nothing

29

without the knowledge they carried with them. What was this traumatic brain injury? Did we ever know anyone else who had this type of injury? What did all these words mean?

The doctor met with each of us privately as well. My mind was convinced that I could have somehow stopped this crisis from happening. I began the blame game with myself. I had been Taylor's protector since his birth, and now I had somehow failed him. How could I have not seen or felt this heinous event coming? How could I not know ahead of time that this accident would occur? It was a horrible feeling to be so out of control of the life and destiny of your child.

Information was fed to us slowly. It was an enormous amount to process, and so it was given to us like baby food. I think the staff started off by telling us simply what we needed to know. They would come to be our teachers and in some ways, our friends. Everyone from the multiple doctors to the numerous nurses, nurses' assistants, and other personnel would feed us little bites at a time. Most of them handled us with tenderness and undeniable care.

On November 23, 2012, the day after the accident, Avery posted the following message on Facebook:

> *For those who express love and concern for Taylor, we thank you as a family. The most we can share at this point in time is he has a rough few days ahead of him. We ask that you continue to keep him in your thoughts and prayers; don't be afraid to have a conversation with the man in charge. Many of you have shown concern and wish to be by his side; however, unfortunately he is not allowed visitors that aren't direct family until further notice. The best thing you can do for him is hope, pray, and let him know you are with him spiritually. Many of you have contacted my family or me, and while we've done our best to keep everyone informed, please realize our main concern is giving Taylor our love and support. Anyone who really knows him knows he's a trooper, and will not back down to any fight. Today, I give*

thanks for the power of love, and express my appreciation for those who have shown it to my big brother.

Later that day, my dad arrived. He had flown from Atlanta, where he was living with and caring for my 94-year-old grandmother. My dad is a quiet but strong man, and his presence carries a lot of weight. He is deeply religious and finds comfort in his faith. He was a rock for me over the next several days, but the first time he saw Taylor . . . he openly wept. I had seen my dad suffer the loss of one daughter and a stepson, both of whom he deeply loved, and I could not stand to see him lose again. I had seen his strength when our loved ones were both taken from our family suddenly and unexpectedly. I was confident that his faith would see him through this trial, and I hoped that he had some special favor with God that would allow our prayers to be answered.

Having Keith's brothers and their wives present, along with his mother, my dad, Eric, and some of our nieces and nephews was comforting. It gave me a sense of being less alone; and the notion that maybe all of our love combined could bring Taylor back crossed my mind more than once. There were prayers, there was concern, there were questions, and there was a lot of love. Moods fluctuated from hopeful to hopeless fairly quickly; it was a roller coaster we would have to learn to ride. In those early days and hours, we would ride the coaster together.

But the ride never seemed to end . . .

Chapter Two
No Singing Allowed
November 22–24, 2012

Day One felt like an eternity, and before it ended, we would have another few hours of feeling more fear than we already did. At some point late in the evening, we walked, tired as we were, to the cafeteria; and Keith, Avery, Tanner, and I attempted to eat. I took one bite and knew food was not something my body was ready to digest. The potatoes and stuffing sat in my mouth unable to be chewed. I pushed the bowl away and could not fathom eating one more bite. As we were leaving the empty cafeteria, Avery's cell phone rang. We had not left the waiting area once, but the moment we did . . . something bad happened. On the line was Taylor's doctor; they needed permission to place a central line in him. Feeling confused, I had no real idea of what a central line entailed. I have since learned that a central line is a long fine catheter with an opening (sometimes multiple openings) at each end used to deliver fluids and drugs directly into one of the large veins in the body. *This line would be the first of many permissions and decisions I would have to make for Taylor.* In a crisis, there is often not time to wait it out or jump on Google to research the best answer. There is simply a yes or a no. I am not even sure whether this conversation was the staff's being informative or if it was actually to obtain permission, but it had to happen.

We went back to the hallway to wait as a family. The regular ICU waiting room was closed, and we found ourselves in a makeshift waiting area in the hallway right outside the unit. The staff told us about other available waiting areas, but they were too far away and we wanted to be as close to Taylor physically as was allowed.

For whatever reason, having Taylor out of the initial trip to the operating room gave us a short minute's sense of safety, which would quickly disappear. As we returned once again to wait for the procedure to be completed, we sat in silence. There was a constant feeling of time standing still. My mind was in panic mode as if it needed me to run like wildfire—and yet we sat still for hours and hours. *What more was there to do?*

When procedures take place in the ICU, the staff closes the unit to all visitors. There are partitions placed up and signs that read "Procedure In Progress—Do Not Enter". No one is allowed in or out of

33

the entire area in order to keep the environment as sterile as possible. If your loved one is really in a precarious spot, the staff will tell you that you may stay in the room but you won't be permitted to leave until the procedure is over. The wait for the line to be placed seemed much longer than it probably was. It is amazing how slowly two hours can pass by, but the fear of what may happen is almost paralyzing.

When the doctor came out to speak with us after the procedure, there was more bad news. During the placement of the chest tube, Taylor's lung had been punctured and as a result, it had collapsed. A resident had placed this particular line. A resident is a medical school graduate undergoing on-the-job training and Geisinger is a well-known teaching hospital. This particular resident seemed to have an attitude that we did not care for. To him, Taylor was merely a young man who occupied a bed. Shortly after the incident with the central line, which was due to a mistake he had made, he was cracking jokes in the ICU. *This discourtesy was part of that roller coaster ride.* It was also a lesson in what to and what not to expend a lot of emotion on. Taylor was in the fight of his life and someone was telling jokes.

As a result of the collapsed lung, a chest tube was placed in Taylor's body. This tube added to the numbers of plastic tubes that ran to and from his body as well as to his growing list of medical conditions. A collapsed lung is referred to as a pneumothorax. The tube was placed between his ribs and the space around his lungs. The tube's job was to drain the air between the lung and the chest wall, thus allowing the lung to re-expand.

Both knowing and trying to familiarize ourselves with these terms was important to us as Taylor's ultimate caregivers. The doctors held rounds every morning. Rounds are a part of medical education as well as patient care, in which the team of doctors go from room to room and discuss each case with the family. In this situation, there were both specialists and students present. We started attending rounds the day after Taylor's fall. The head of the ICU explained that it would be vital for us to hear every detail of the plan for Taylor's care.

On our first day, the team came at its typical time, which was somewhere between 7:30 and 8:00 a.m. A medical student began by explaining the basics. He started with, "Bed twenty-nine is a twenty-one-year old," when he was interrupted by his teacher. The doctor said, "Excuse me, students, this is Taylor's mother. You will each say 'Good morning' to her when we start rounds." They all looked at me and I could see that the patient they referred to as "bed twenty-nine" was suddenly someone's son and not just a body. Some members of that team became very special to me, and I was always grateful when they could answer any questions I had regarding Taylor.

Avery posted the following to Taylor's Facebook page on Friday, November 23:

> *As a family we've decided to clear up some of the haziness about what has happened. We will do our best to keep you updated daily. Tayl suffered a traumatic brain injury and had surgery Thursday morning. Everything the surgery was meant to do was accomplished. We know you all want to visit him and send him your love; however, we ask that you continue to pray and send love spiritually, as only relatives are to be with him for the next several days, possibly weeks. At this point we have no timeline, we know that he is essentially in "cruise control" for the next 5–7 days. Doctors are unable to predict the outcome because we all react and heal differently. Many of you have tried to contact members of our family for information, and we apologize for not answering them in a timely fashion, or sometimes at all. Just know that Taylor is in the best hands faith can buy: God's. We sincerely thank you for the love and support you've provided for him and us. Please continue to pray for Tayl. Hope changes everything.*

The posts on Facebook would not come often in the beginning, but it was our way of keeping in touch with the outside world. We knew that it was important for friends to know Taylor's progress; and just because of the way things can go, we wanted the truth about what was happening with him to be shared . . . by us. Obviously there were details that we had to refrain from sharing publically, but we allowed ourselves to share what we could as best we knew how.

Going in to see Taylor during the first couple of days seemed as if there was always a new piece of equipment added to his body. His head was wrapped in white gauze, which covered up the long stapled incision that ran upward from his right ear and made a large C-shape toward the upper portion of his head. On the left side of his head was a smaller incision that was close to three inches long. Days would pass before we would see anything underneath the gauze. In the back of Taylor's head toward the bottom, there was a small hole that fed into a clear drainage pouch. You could see the blood-tinged fluid very slowly filling the bag. There was also another large fluid collector that came from the back. Taylor's face was swollen and his eyes could not be opened unless a doctor pried them open . . . and even that sometimes did not work. His eyes went from being red and swollen to turning black and blue. He had the usual blood pressure cuffs on one of his upper arms and a pulse oxygen reader on his arm and finger. On top of his head coming out from the gauze was the alien-like pressure gauge that monitored the level of swelling in Taylor's brain. His mouth was held open by the large ventilator tube; and the doctors hoped that the ventilator would be one of the first pieces of equipment they could disconnect. The machine attached to the tube did all of the breathing for Taylor. When the ventilator took a breath, so did Taylor. Taylor had the newly placed chest tube that came out of his right side. His legs were covered up to his calves with pneumatic compression devices, which filled with air from time to time to keep Taylor's circulation moving. Taylor was motionless and unaware of everything that was happening to him. All these machines were helping to sustain his life.

Before we knew what had happened, Thursday had turned into Friday, Friday into Saturday, and more people began to arrive. We all had different feelings about people visiting. It was an extremely raw, emotional time. I am a person who is generally very real with her

36

emotions, so it was most challenging for me. I think our family came together in a beautiful way, but with a silent understanding of some strange new rules that we would need to follow. Many of our friends were growing restless and needed to see us and hear from us themselves. We were caught up in our own emotions as a family, but there were many others who cared deeply about what was going on with Taylor. We were trying to keep them informed.

Avery posted the following on Facebook on Saturday, November 24:

As I attempt to ease your mind, please be aware that we've had requests to give a bit more detail. If you would like to share a bit of the nausea we've all experienced, read on. Taylor had a good night last night, he showed a lot of good signs and his reactions were right where we need them to be at this time. The pressure in his brain has remained low for the most part, aside from when he's being agitated by nurses, doctors, therapists, etc. The pressure has improved significantly; especially considering it was in the 50's when he arrived via Life Flight. To give you an idea of the seriousness, the pressure in your brain as you read this is likely between 0 and 10. Today is the first time we've been able to recognize him as the Taylor we know and love, as he's been extremely swollen throughout his entire body. A feeding tube was put in around lunch time and he's done well with it so far; however, he's held a strong fever all day and we've just seen a drop in the past two hours. The reason for the fever being so high is currently unknown as we await test results. At this point we have no idea what the outcome of any of this will be, because right now the only person who knows what will come of this is upstairs. We've had some absurd stories make their way to us, and while we appreciate concern, we ask that you don't pass on information that you've not heard from Taylor's direct family. Taylor is in a coma and will be for the next few days, and we will inform you when he may have visitors. We ask that you respect this and be patient, as we're all anxious and awaiting good news.

The most important thing right now is that you offer Taylor up to the healing hands of God through prayer.

Some of my closest girlfriends were part of the first visitors to come; they brought muffins and two large carafes of coffee. One of them, Kelly, had been our neighbor when we first moved to the small town of Mifflinburg over seventeen years ago. At the time of our move, Taylor had just finished kindergarten, Avery was three, and Tanner was only a few months old. Kelly's stepson and Taylor were the same age, and had been friends over the years. They had not been as close in recent years, but they certainly shared a lot of memories. I had known Kelly for a long time, and now we worked and sat together every day. Kelly was a person in whom I always confided about my kids. She knew what was happening in their world and she genuinely loved them. Over the years, she often told me what nice boys I had, and she was really invested in their growing up. Kelly has a special place in our lives and her presence at the hospital was comforting.

Over the last few months before Taylor's accident, he and I had been in a tough spot. Taylor was twenty-one years old; and for the first time ever, we hit a wall in our relationship that had been present over the last several months. Taylor was struggling with many issues, and he had distanced himself from our entire family unit. Throughout the struggle, Kelly had been the one to encourage and remind me of how fortunate Taylor was to have me as his mother. One day, a few weeks prior to the accident, she said to me, "Do I need to talk to him? He is so lucky that you are his mom and he needs to be reminded of that." In the days right before Taylor's accident, he sent me a long message with an apology and recognition of our relationship. These things happen in relationships, and when they do, they can make a parent feel terrible. Now I was left with a guilt that at times . . . *almost consumed me.* I had let Taylor down through my imperfections, and all I wanted to do was cook him a dinner that would make him smile and have him tell me one more time that he loved me. *Would I ever hug my son again? Would I ever be able to let him know how much I love him?* Memories were flooding back, and I kept wondering if they would be all that we would ever have of Taylor. My last e-mail from Taylor had concerned his résumé. He wanted to make some changes in his life and was even exploring the possibility of relocating. So many things had been left open-ended, and so many words had not been said. I felt robbed of my son and robbed of just one more moment with him. The last text I had sent to him was about Thanksgiving Day and my wishes for it to be a good day for our whole family.

On both Friday and Saturday, things seemed relatively quiet. *Taylor was still.* We were all under the impression that because of the trauma that Taylor had endured, he was hiding somewhere in a cave of healing. And yet we still anticipated more than absolutely pure stillness from him. The silence in Taylor's room was draining; and as we sat with him, so many of our memories with him flooded back. That was the day when my sadness and fear began to feel very real and present. It was the start of many days in which the agony inside would suddenly come spilling out like a river. *There was no way for me to silence the cries that ripped through my heart.* I had no knowledge of how horrible this process was going to get, but what I did know is that my son, who days before had been healthy, strong, and breathtakingly handsome, was somehow being taken from me. The idea that Taylor might not return in the same way was slowly introduced to us. The doctors and nurses did not tell us a great deal about what was to come, but in retrospect they worked hard to educate us.

As I mentioned earlier, my dad had flown in from Atlanta on Friday, and his presence gave me a feeling of security and peace. I had always been a "daddy's girl," and I knew that he would bring some sort of calm to the chaos that surrounded my heart. I also knew how much his presence meant to Avery and Tanner, who deeply admire and adore their "Pawpaw." He wore a sweatshirt that read "Hope" on the front and on the back, "Changes Everything"—the phrase that Avery referred to in his November 23 Facebook post. The shirt came from an awareness campaign I had created in honor of my stepbrother's life that told the story of his cruel and untimely death. He had been murdered several years before; we then learned as a family that sometimes hope itself is the only thing you have to hold onto. Avery had brought one of my "Hope" hooded sweatshirts into Taylor's room and we kept it there on a chair. He said to me, "Don't you think this shirt should stay with Taylor?" We were somehow hoping that the words that had come to mean so much to our hearts would penetrate Taylor's body, mind, and spirit, and that something good would begin to occur.

We would stand at Taylor's bed for hours on end, simply watching him. Sometimes I wanted to be alone with him and at other times, I could hardly stand to be alone. I can still remember sitting in the room with my dad, looking at him while he watched Taylor. He and Taylor shared a special bond when Taylor was growing up, and although Taylor was not one to say it, he loved my dad—his Pawpaw—very much. In fact, Taylor loved both of his grandfathers. In some way, I felt a sense of relief that Taylor's paternal grandfather was no longer here to see him suffer.

One of the memories I thought of as my dad and I sat in silence was of a time when I was just a little girl. He had taken me out to an abandoned beach for the day, just the two of us. The water was high on the inlet and he had a certain spot he wanted us to reach. I was too short to make my way across without the water coming up to my shoulders; I would not be able to walk across on my own. My dad carried all of our stuff across by holding it in the air, and then he came back for me. He hoisted me up on his shoulders and led me safely across the small body of water. That moment is something that was etched in my memory. I felt so safe and secure with him. *Would my dad be able to bring us safely to the other side of this?* I was becoming more aware of two harsh realities. The first frustrating reality was that there might be nothing that I could do to fix this situation for Taylor, and the second was that my own parents might not be able to fix it for me. My heart cried out to both my dad who was present and to God in heaven. I begged both of them to fix this.

During the day on Saturday, I found my way to Geisinger's chapel. When you walk into the chapel at Geisinger Medical Center, you

40

see areas that represent different faiths. There are four main areas and each represents a major world religion. As I sat in that room, I felt conflicted. Everything that I thought I knew had been brought into question. But I did not come to question that day. I came simply to say *thank you* for the gift of bringing Taylor through days one and two, and for allowing us the chance to have the time with him that we did . . . even if it was one-sided. I was keenly aware that the outcome of Taylor's accident had come very close to being different. I also knew that in a single moment, things could change for him. I would always be grateful that those who loved him most did not have to endure his sudden death, but instead we were able to express our love and care for him. I sat in the chapel and said a few simple words because my heart was fearful of saying more. I quietly murmured, "Thank you, and please bring Taylor back to us." Afterward, I sat for several minutes in silence wanting to have some sort of reassurance that things might be all right.

It was probably sometime on Saturday when I asked the doctor what I had been afraid to say. We had had long and strenuous nights of sleeping in the waiting room of the ICU, and the hours were all beginning to blur together. I had to go home on some type of regular basis; I needed to shower and I needed to sleep. We all had fears about leaving Taylor, so I had to know if and when he died . . . *how would it happen?* The doctor explained that it would not be sudden, and that we'd have time to make the forty-five-minute trip if Taylor began to decline. She said, "Nicole, I can promise you that if you go home and sleep for five hours, Taylor will not die while you are gone." I trusted this person that I had known for close to seventy-two hours. I allowed her assurance to make my choice for me. We made a decision as a family that one of us would be with Taylor at all times, but we also recognized that rest and routine would be important for us to continue to have in our own lives. A series of words began to be quoted to us repeatedly "This is not a sprint, it is a marathon"; and "This is going to be a long road, it is important that you take care of yourselves." *We were reminded again and again that nothing was going to turn around quickly for Taylor.*

When my friends recall those early days to me, I truly have only bits and pieces in my memory. From time to time, someone will mention their visit to the hospital or how their family stopped by. My response is usually a puzzled look, followed by asking, "Was I there?" The answer is always yes, but I have no recollection of many of those hours. Recently, a friend recalled to me how her sweet daughter, who was only thirteen at the time, had desperately wanted to see Taylor. Our families had been friends for years and she loved the "Bingaman Boys." I had apparently explained to her that she could not go back to see Taylor, but I don't remember any part of that conversation. I asked her, "How was I? Did I seem like I was holding it together?" And she said, "You were not all right—you were a mess." I have very vague memories of long hugs with Tanner or Avery and finding tremendous comfort in them, while not wanting to let them go. I also remember certain moments and a few individuals who evoked strong emotion in me, but for the most part . . . *this period was a blur.*

One morning, which I think was on day three or four, I went in to sing softly to Taylor. He was in such a fragile state and the nursing staff was trying to let us love on him without harming him. When the boys were little, they each had a song that I would sing to them, and then there were songs we all shared. One that I used to like to sing as they were falling asleep was called "Sleepy Town." I think I learned the melody and adjusted some simple lyrics along the way. It went:

Mommy loves you, Daddy loves you, Jesus loves you, go to Sleepy Town. PawPaw loves you, Nina loves you, and Jesus loves you, go to Sleepy Town. Avery loves you, Tanner loves you, Jesus loves you, go to Sleepy Town.

I would run through the long list of all those who loved them, and eventually they would fall asleep. I was ever so softly singing that song, and I also sang, "You Are My Sunshine." My three sons are the sunshine of my life, and if one of them was taken, *I was certain the sun would never shine again.* As I sang the song, I could see my blond-haired blue-eyed little boy, looking back and singing with me. Later, I was told to refrain from speaking, praying, singing, or anything aloud along those lines to Taylor. Taylor's brain required rest, and part of our challenge was to give it to him. But I was so hurt and stunned by those instructions. I was singing to Taylor to heal him and to heal myself. To be told not to sing was another form of torture. The staff members were protecting Taylor, but it felt as if no one could protect us. *I sang in my heart to Taylor and hoped that some part of him could hear my song.*

During harsh times like that, I could not help thinking of how different the real story of someone in a comatose state is from how it is portrayed on television. I think in part that that is why I was singing to Taylor. We all were waiting for that magical moment when Taylor's body would respond to our presence. The only responses that seemed to come were the reading of his blood pressure numbers and the level of swelling in his brain. This was nothing like the Lifetime or Hallmark channels, or *House* had portrayed.

The reality of our situation was heavy, real, and unmoving. It constantly felt as if an elephant were sitting on my chest, crushing all the life inside me. I was sad. I was tired, and I knew somewhere in myself that I could not afford to fall apart. I knew that Taylor needed me, Keith needed me, and Tanner and Avery needed me. I also knew at some place within myself that I needed to take care of my body in order to help others.

One of the helpful things that the head of the ICU did for us was to set up various times to meet with her. We could ask her any questions or talk about our fears and uncertainties, and she could help us understand as much as our minds would allow us to take in. She explained that we needed to allow one another the freedom to do what we had to do to cope with all of this and get through it. She said that each one of us would react and respond in a different way. She offered a lot of reassurance, and I was relieved when she could answer our questions. There was a heavy blanket of guilt in the room surrounding us. I think we were all battling our own inner monsters as to whether we could have made a difference in Taylor's fall happening. She took time to meet with us often over the next several days, and our confidence and trust in her grew.

Keith and I had been through many things together. We had shared life's greatest joys in both having and raising our three sons, and we had also been through many sorrows together. As I watched Keith, my heart felt broken for him. I could see and feel how afraid he was. He was pale and quiet as if this crisis was taking every ounce of energy he had. I knew the accident was something neither one of us would have ever thought could happen to our son. In fact, we were still very naive about what traumatic brain injury meant. We did not know that Taylor's injury would change the entire course of our lives.

The weekend would soon end, and it felt like an eternity had already passed. Many days felt like years. What were we going to do about work and school? How could life move forward for any of us when Taylor was lying in the hospital all day? I stayed as much as my physical body would allow me. For the time being, I was frozen there, but I was also taking baby steps to allow myself what I was going to need to survive this ordeal.

True exhaustion was setting in; eventually, I would have to give in to the fact that my own body needed rest and rejuvenation. I would have to figure out a way to make it acceptable to leave the hospital physically and trust that Taylor would be in good hands. Within our family, each of us would figure out his or her own way to negotiate the endless days at the hospital. We would do what we felt we needed to do for Taylor, for each other, and for ourselves. There was a lot of sacrifice involved and a lot of time spent looking out not only for Taylor, but for each other as well.

The first time I left the hospital, I went to Avery's apartment with him. Since it was Thanksgiving break, his roommates were gone. He had a wonderfully comfortable bed, and as soon as we got there, I tucked myself in it. His bedroom had an old oil-heated radiator, and he cranked it up. The warmth, coupled with the quiet and comfortable bed, allowed me to drift off successfully. Avery and I both fell asleep for a few hours. It felt difficult to be out of physical proximity to Taylor, but we were both so exhausted that as soon as our eyes closed, our bodies allowed us the rest we so desperately needed. The challenge was to turn off all the wheels that were spinning inside my head long enough to shut them down and rest.

I was not only afraid that something sudden would happen and Taylor would be in dire straits, but I was aware that his life continued to hang in the balance. I was also battling the continued questions that seemed to scream from somewhere inside me, questions that said, "How did this happen?" "Is this my fault?" and "How in the world can I fix this?" There was a certain amount of desperation that filled my mind. It was like being in a state of absolute despair, but having to learn how to calm your heart in order to function.

When I awoke from my first hours of uninterrupted rest, my eyes opened quickly and I was in a panic. It would be the first of many times and countless days when I would awake from sleeping only to remember what had happened to Taylor. *A fall down the stairs was threatening to take him away from us.*

People often remind each other to live as if today is their last day on earth. The truth is we never really allow ourselves to do that. It is often in the hours where we are faced with the unthinkable that we begin to wish we had spent our days and our time a little wiser. My head and heart were constantly wrestling with the fact that no matter how hard I wished or tried, I would not be able to rewind a clock to the time prior to this event and make sure it never occurred. There were moments when I wondered whether what was happening might all be some form of an unbelievable nightmare, but the more minutes that passed without being shaken awake from it, the more I began to understand that this situation was all too real.

One thought that recurred over and over again was that I wanted to be able to hug Taylor. I wanted to be able to remind him of what a precious gift his life was to me. I wanted to tell him that I was proud to be his mother, and that having him for a son had given me incredible joy. The thought of never again hearing his voice, never hearing him say "Mom," or never watching him consume his favorite meal in a rush with little regard for others at the table, almost brought me to my knees in sadness. To this day, I do not know how people can physically stand up

45

in a time of such great crisis and pain. It seems like it took all of my energies to be able to exist and survive. *If humans can die of a broken heart, I was certain I would be among them.*

Chapter Three
Without Taylor

As I have already stated, Taylor was an avid outdoorsman. From a very young age, he took a strong interest in hunting, fishing, and just being part of the outdoors. It was a way in which he and Keith connected from the time Taylor could walk and talk. The love that Taylor had for hunting grew to far exceed the interest that most people have in it. When Taylor was a little boy, his favorite bedtime stories told by his dad were stories from Keith's life about hunting.

Taylor also loved fishing. He fished for native trout in local creeks. He loved going out on the big river in Virginia to catch cobia. He loved watching the yearly competition for the big blues. The bottom line is that Taylor lived for hunting and fishing. More importantly, it was a way that he chose to connect with people of all ages.

When Taylor was twelve years old, he had an incident right before his first-ever hunting season. He was standing in our kitchen rolling around a small aluminum ball in his hands. Suddenly he coughed, and when he covered his mouth, the piece of aluminum flew down his throat. Taylor had fairly bad asthma and his breathing was immediately compromised. We called 9-1-1 and ended up going to the emergency room. We were dismissed within a few hours and assured that the reaction had nothing to do with the aluminum, but was instead an asthma flare-up.

He returned to school the following day, but as a couple of days passed he got much worse. After constantly being told it was his asthma taking on a new level of severity and trying to treat it with multiple medications to no avail, I decided to call my own doctor, whom I deeply trusted. She saw him right away and ordered a quick CAT scan. The scan revealed that Taylor had actually aspirated the foil and it was now embedded in his lung. The foreign object was causing Taylor great difficulty in his breathing. Taylor was immediately admitted to Geisinger Children's Hospital, but surgery had to be postponed because he had just eaten dinner. The following morning he was immediately sent into surgery. It was a frightening time and it was the first real medical emergency we had dealt with as parents.

One of the key matters on Taylor's mind through the entire ordeal was whether he would be able to go hunting. The big opening day was just seventy-two hours post-operation. Taylor had been a trouper and the members of the hospital team were exceptionally compassionate. On Sunday, the kindly doctor pulled me out into the hall and explained that in his opinion, Taylor would expend a lot more energy and frustration if he were not discharged and allowed to go hunting the next day. His advice was that Taylor be allowed to do as he had planned and go into the woods with his dad. The first day of that deer season, Taylor, who was worn out and tired, trekked into the woods and shot his first deer. I knew then that nothing would hold him back from doing what he loved.

The following year, Taylor got one of his first jobs and he could not have been happier. He would spend every Tuesday night loading the targets for trap shooting in the machine at the local sportsmen's club. The older members of the club enjoyed this weekly ritual of shooting practice. Through this job, Taylor developed relationships with many older gentlemen. He enjoyed listening to their stories as much as they enjoyed telling them. He didn't get paid much, but he didn't care. He always came home with a soda and a candy bar, and an increased interest in the sport.

Taylor was chosen for a write-up about fishing in the spring edition of the school yearbook in his senior year of high school. Taylor was so proud of himself and being chosen was a fine honor for him. He selected an impressive photo of himself with a huge bass, which is still framed and displayed in his room. Many mornings in his last year of high school were spent lying in a blind, hunting for geese or waterfowl with his brother Avery and their friends. They would wake up at the crack of dawn and head out into the freezing fields. I never knew much about what happened on those mornings, but I know they are some of Avery's most cherished memories of his big brother.

When Taylor was closing in on high school graduation, we encouraged him to explore any career opportunities that involved the outdoors. I arranged for him to job shadow for a day with a game warden, which he thoroughly enjoyed. At the time, Taylor was more interested in making money than pursuing his passion as a career. In the back of my mind, it was always something I wish he had executed.

Taylor loved the thrill of the hunt. Scouting for deer was a common hobby in our neck of the woods in Pennsylvania, but he seemed to enjoy the process more than anyone I'd ever met. We used to tease him that his closet looked like a mini-Cabela's store. Hunting deer, whether with a bow or a rifle, was easily Taylor's favorite pastime. It was an obsession that I felt kept him out of trouble as he grew up. He was a regular country boy; he loved being outdoors, country music, pretty girls, and his truck. He is the definition of a country song. He was extremely intelligent but at the same time, very down-to-earth and enjoyed the simple pleasures in life. Many of the walls of our log home were decorated with various trophies from hunting adventures, and Taylor's bedroom was the epitome of a wildlife-themed "man cave."

On the Monday following the accident, Keith still had time off from work. It was deer season in Pennsylvania. Monday, November 26, was the big day for deer hunters in our area. Most of the surrounding schools and many businesses would be closed.

Over the past several years, Keith and his three brothers would gather together with their sons and sometimes others to have their annual deer camp. The deer camp of 2012 would never happen for the Bingaman bunch. This loss was heartbreaking in itself for multiple reasons. Hunting season was by far the time of year that Taylor most enjoyed. It was a time that the guys reconnected, whether or not they were really into hunting.

Deer camp was about making memories, getting out in the woods, eating endless amounts of junk food, sharing traditions, and living however the group wanted for a few days. I could easily hear the laughter in my mind as I thought back over previous years. There were countless memories involving hunting that had been shared, and it was a time to reflect and remember events from years past. It had already been decided that the gathering for camp could not take place without Taylor. And I know that was a great source of pain for everyone. I could not, however, imagine a pain greater than that of his dad or brothers

50

regarding hunting camp. We would silently tell Taylor what day it was and reassure him that we hoped he would be out in the woods again soon.

Taylor had planned to take Tanner out on the first day of hunting season that year, which made it particularly heartbreaking. Tanner was fifteen years old, and though he had gone hunting many times, he had never had a successful hunt. Taylor had worked hard to find Tanner the perfect hunting location. He obtained permission to hunt on a local farm, placed a tree stand in just the right spot, and told everyone how much he was looking forward to being the guide as Tanner took his first deer. Tanner did not share the same enthusiasm for hunting, but he was more than happy to have that time with his big brother. Taylor was essentially the only reason Tanner was going to hunt, and Tanner was one of the reasons Taylor worked so hard at finding the perfect spot. Before anyone knew what was happening, all these opportunities for memories to be made were ripped away from them. As the deer season passed, I felt a sick, empty feeling in the pit of my stomach. My son should be out being able to do what he loved, not lying in a bed and kept alive by machines. He and Tanner should not have been robbed of the time together that they were both looking forward to. One of Taylor's friends kindly offered to take Tanner hunting for the day, but there was no way Tanner could muster the courage to attend without his big brother.

Some of Taylor's closest friends chose not to hunt that year out of respect for him. Others made the decision that they would dedicate their hunting season to him. This particular time was difficult for his buddies, and I respected the ways they thought best to handle it. Knowing Taylor, I doubted that he would want anyone to stay away from the woods on his account. Over the next few days, some of his buddies sent us pictures or posted them on Facebook. The captions said things like, "This one is for you, Bing." It was a way these young men could express their sadness about Taylor and their love for him.

On November 28, one of his best friend's fiancées posted a picture on Facebook that included her husband-to-be and the buck he successfully shot, with a caption that read: *Bing, this is for you. Brett*

51

knew you were with him this morning and he knows you're proud. We BELIEVE in you always and love you so much. Slow and steady wins the race."

A few months before the accident, one of our nephews, Evan, had written a paper in school about hunting with Taylor. Evan truly admired Taylor, especially in regard to hunting. Taylor was always more than happy to help a younger fellow outdoorsman increase his love of the sport.

Evan's paper was a fictional story about a particular day that he and Taylor had gone hunting. One evening he came into the hospital carrying the folded pieces of paper with the story in his hands. Evan was really young and had a hard time understanding the severity of the situation. He was clearly concerned for his cousin, and I admired his ability to come and sit with us at the hospital, sometimes for hours. His mother said to me once, "I wish you could hear Evan praying for Taylor. He is praying with his whole heart." It was hard for me to juggle my own pain and seeing others that I loved hurt too.

Evan's story was passed around the waiting room of the intensive care unit, and we were all silent as we took turns reading it. Later on, Evan's mother took the story into Taylor's room and read it to him softly. Each of us longed for that story to be real and wondered what the next hunting season would bring. For now, we had to manage the emotions of the current one.

Evan was in fifth grade at the time. He wrote:

When I get up on a special day like today, I get up before the rooster crows because my cousin, Taylor, is taking me archery hunting for a massive buck in my woods that he caught on his deer camera. I have to get ready before Taylor comes, so I go to the bathroom and out the window I see the delightful fall-colored trees. I don't have time to admire the trees because I have to get ready. So I throw water on my face to completely wake me up, and I put my gear on, and Taylor arrives! Some people like to spend their Saturdays reading, some people like to spend their Saturdays watching TV, but I like to spend my Saturday hunting.

The story goes on to tell a tale of hunting and eventually finding and killing a big buck. It ends with Taylor mounting the deer and hanging it in his room. Evan's story had a happy ending, and I longed for it to replace the reality of what we were dealing with. On December 1, Evan took his first deer in hunting season and we all knew that he did it with Taylor on his mind.

After long days in the hospital, I would come home in the evening tired and exhausted, but I would peek through photos of Taylor doing what he loved most, spending time in the woods. As I looked at Taylor's photographs, often sitting in his room on the computer, I felt closer to him. One of the pictures that caught my eye was of Taylor high up in the air in his tree stand with his bow drawn. He looked strong and invincible. *I did not know at the time, but I would never see that person again.* The man who had always worn a safety harness and practiced great caution in the woods had fallen down the stairs in his own home. The fall had taken so much from him already, but there would be more losses to come.

As deer season continued, there was an undeniable sense that Taylor was missing something he loved and that hurt us, but more importantly, we knew it would bother Taylor. At one point Keith and I were sitting by Taylor's bed, and Keith said to Taylor, "You aren't going to believe when you wake up that you missed deer season, but you will get out there again."

Just nine days before the accident, Taylor had posted some hunting photos to his Facebook page. He talked excitedly with friends and family about the upcoming season. He was full of the anticipation and excitement that the month of November always held for him. That had been just a few days ago, and now he could not even open his eyes or sit up.

With every passing day, we felt as if Taylor was drifting further away from us. We would have settled for him to come back just for a moment, but instead he continued to lie still, eyes closed, body completely unresponsive, and his mind unaware of all that was happening to and around him. He was on the longest hunting trip of his life—the hunt for himself—so that he could return to us.

Chapter Four

Love Wins

November 30–December 3, 2012

As a family, we were becoming increasingly attached to the ICU staff and felt a certain kinship with each of them. Avery and I were always present for rounds. This protocol had developed in the first days after Taylor's accident. I was feeling insanely tired and worn down; I had come to the place where I could feel the fragility of my emotional state. Avery's fragility was becoming more acute as well; we were running on empty. Our bodies had had little sleep and little food. Avery was becoming progressively more protective of his big brother and he needed more information. Early one morning, we had a moment when we snapped at each other. In retrospect I cannot recall the conversation, but what I felt as a mother was helpless and hopeless. My oldest son was in a coma fighting for his life, and my other sons had to try to be some sort of glue to hold him together. I tried to imagine how Avery and Tanner felt as younger brothers, but it was hard for me to grasp even my own feelings.

After the moment of anger, I simply came unglued. Several minutes passed by and I lost control of all my emotions. Morning rounds had started and the hospital team arrived to discuss Taylor. I was feeling pressure to know more, to ask more questions, and to have some sort of magic formula that would shed light on how Taylor might recover faster or more completely. As the doctors were talking, I began to sob. They were the kind of sobs that make you stop to catch your breath—the type of tears we never want to have to cry. It was the first time since the accident that I lost control of my emotions in front of the doctors, and it did not feel good. Two young female residents sat with me when the rounds regarding Taylor were complete to ask what was happening. As I sat beside them with tearful eyes, I explained that I felt as if I were responsible for all of this. It was my job to fix it, to make this nightmare end . . . as Taylor's mother. The reality was that I could not help Taylor, and I felt powerless in regard to Avery and Tanner. Avery needed more answers than I was equipped or educated enough to give him. At that point, they suggested that Avery become more involved with rounds, and they reminded me that any of us could meet with a doctor at any time.

Avery needed to understand his brother's condition from a scientific viewpoint. That would be the only way he could make sense of anything.

The residents hugged me and comforted me with their touch and their words. These young, precious, highly intelligent women reminded me that I am both capable and strong. They emphasized that no matter how much I might want to, I do not have the magical power to make this tragedy go away. Many elements involving Taylor were out of my control, but I had to continue to remind myself that it was not my fault and that I didn't have to carry the weight of the world on my shoulders alone. At the end of the conversation, they reinforced the point that each person in our family would react differently from others and that these differences are normal.

The residents' idea to include Avery in the morning rounds was a wise one. Avery's questions were challenging and difficult; but it helped him to be there. He wanted to understand how the physical challenges would play out in the long run for Taylor. He wanted to see any images or scans of Taylor's brain, so that he could identify the location of the damage. He needed to hear everything that he could firsthand whenever the hospital staff would allow it. He required more specific medical detail and his questions often alerted the staff that we were committed to learning as much as we could about traumatic brain injury. Intellectual curiosity was one of Avery's coping mechanisms.

Taylor would have to go back into the operating room on November 29, one week following the accident. We had been informed of the decision early the night before, and the procedures were to take place immediately the following morning. We were surprised by the number of procedures that Taylor's body needed in order to remain stable.

We were still unfamiliar with much of the terminology used for the medical procedures and all that being a patient in critical care entailed for Taylor. Taylor's body grew in its delicate weakened state. He had taken in nothing but fluids for seven days, and he continued to be fully dependent on the ventilator. He had tubes running all through his body and we didn't want more equipment added.

The doctors informed us that Taylor was going to need a tracheostomy[4] and a PEG (feeding) tube. Both of these are fairly common procedures in the medical world in regard to people in a comatose state, but they were new and frightening to our family. Because of Taylor's frailty, the procedure was not routine for his team of doctors either. It was reassuring to know that Taylor's team understood and respected our apprehension. As a family, we were learning to entrust Taylor's well-being to people who days before had been absolute strangers.

Tracheostomies are performed when there is an ongoing problem getting air into a person's lungs, and it's the safest way for oxygen to be delivered. The procedure requires an incision from the outside of the neck below the area commonly referred to as the Adam's apple and then making the opening a direct airway, specifically into the windpipe, which is also known as the trachea.

When the tracheostomy was initially mentioned, I wrestled with a lot of questions, but I still had faith that it was the best decision. *Did a tracheostomy mean that Taylor would have a hole in his throat forever? Would he be able to speak normally again? How would he ever be able to breathe on his own if this procedure were needed to open his airway?* Keith had his own set of questions that he wanted to have answered. It was interesting to see a pattern between us beginning to unfold. I was more trusting and less apprehensive about these matters while Keith was extremely worried. It was the difference between being momentarily paralyzed and forging ahead. Neither reaction was better than the other; it simply was how the turmoil would play out within each of us as individuals. It was carefully explained that this procedure was not optional if Taylor were to survive and be comfortable in his ongoing physical condition. It was explained that in most cases similar to Taylor's, the tube is simply removed when it is safe, and then the opening closes on its own. At this point, there were no other options. We

---

[4] A semi-permanent or permanent opening made through the front of the neck into the windpipe, either to serve by itself as an artificial airway or to allow the insertion of a tube to assist the patient's breathing.

read the materials provided for us in pamphlet form and finally gave our permission to perform the tracheostomy.

The placement of the PEG tube, which is more formally called a percutaneous endoscopic gastrostomy, and informally referred to as a feeding tube, was also essential to Taylor's ability to survive. The PEG tube is a tube placed into the mouth through the esophagus, going down to the stomach and exiting through the abdominal wall. This tube is a way to provide long-term nutrition or supplemental feedings for people who have difficulty eating or swallowing. In Taylor's case, not only could he physically not swallow due to his unconscious state, he would also have to learn how to eat again. We really did not understand the process in which he would relearn the simple things, and nobody was willing to jump ahead into that scenario.

Both these procedures were critical to Taylor's short- and long-term recovery, but in no way did we want him to have to go "under the knife" again. If there had been a way to avoid the surgery, we would have. It was something that each person in our family handled in a different way. One of the qualities that I admire and appreciate about our immediate circle is that none of us are dramatic or hysterical in our expression or acceptance of matters like these. Things went well in the operating room, and before we knew it, Taylor came out with two new attachments. *Taylor was becoming increasingly unrecognizable to us.*

The next day Taylor was clearly exhausted from the events of the day before. Even though he was in a coma, he still had to have anesthesia and the general line of procedure that accompanies having surgery. He seemed more deeply asleep, if that were possible.

On December 2, I posted on Facebook:

Many of you are so kind in asking how we are as a family. We are strong, we are sad, and we are not complete right now. We miss our Taylor being with us the way we want him to be. We find happiness in the little things, and yet we are deeply saddened by the larger picture in this moment. Thank you for all of the little and big things you have done for us . . . making us

59

food, bringing laughter to the waiting room, running errands, understanding that Taylor is healing in his resting, gas money, phone calls, texts, coming to spend time with our other kids. Every ounce of love shown to us strengthens us to love each other and tend to Taylor.

Taylor had another quiet and restful day. His vital signs continue to be good, with some small exceptions, which the doctors are working out. The neurologist who examined him today commented on his strength despite being in a coma. The (outer) swelling has gone down significantly and we hope the same thing is occurring inwardly. There was one tube removed, which is good. They are taking excellent care of Taylor here. Dr. Kerr, who I am told is a genius, reminded us today that this is a painfully slow process. And it is. We can handle that process in order.

Someone in our immediate family was with Taylor twenty-four hours a day, with the exceptions of quiet periods or times when no one was allowed in his room. If we weren't in Taylor's room, we were in the hospital. We all learned to sleep in random places in the hospital and developed some type of routine. One day, I went upstairs to sleep in the waiting area on another floor. The area nearest Taylor had finally been opened, but the seating was anything but comfortable. It seemed to be a deterrent for families who might be tempted to camp out in the room.

I found my familiar spot, which was in a room full of seating that was similar to sectional type sofas. I had my own pillow and blanket. Utterly exhausted, I laid my head down, stared off into space, and began to weep. The tears just ran down my face, silently, without recognition. I did not move in response to them nor did I try to wipe them off. I looked at the grey fabric that was inches away from my face and I cried. No one in the room knew I was crying, and they each had their own battles to face. In these early days, I often fell asleep crying and woke up doing the same. I don't know whether it was my body's way of releasing its turmoil, but it felt very natural. On this particular day, I woke up to a

60

long-time friend's whisper, "Nicole, it's Gisela. Do you need anything?" *I was so scared and felt so alone.* Since Gisela is an oncology nurse, I already knew that she had been with families who were facing the unthinkable. I felt comfortable with my sadness in her presence. Placing my head upon her lap, I let the tears flow as she rubbed my back and stroked my hair. We were both still in shock, and I was appreciative of her touch and presence more than anything. There was nothing she could have said or done to make the situation better or less frightening. Her gift to me was simple . . . it was coming and allowing me to rest my tired head on her lap and feeling the love she held for my family. I was keenly aware then of what the simple power of something as small as sitting with someone can mean.

My mother joined us on day nine of Taylor's residence in the ICU. My mom is a very tiny woman and has been all of her life. She is under five feet tall, her shoes are a size five, and she weighs less than a hundred pounds. Her nickname throughout her life had been Bunny, so when she became a grandmother she decided that the name Grandbunny suited her perfectly.

My mom was not the first person I called in the early morning hours after Taylor's fall. I wanted to call her and I needed to call her, but I was actually worried about giving her the terrible news. She lives alone, and for some reason, I was not sure she could handle what I had to say. She would not only have to bear the weight of what was happening to Taylor alone, but she would also have to bear the weight of my pain. I did not want to have to tell her until she was with someone else, but after a matter of time, I made the call that I had been avoiding. The conversation as I remember it, started by asking her where she was and if she was sitting down. I explained that I had something bad to tell her and continued to say that Taylor had fallen down the stairs. I explained that he was in surgery because his brain was bleeding. I wanted to communicate with her that his life was in danger, and somehow I did.

Most of my mom's response was silence. She expressed her disbelief and how she couldn't believe this was happening to me. Her first instinct was toward me, her daughter. *She knew that losing Taylor would mean losing me in many ways.*

Instinctively, I knew that my mother would want to come to us, but I needed for her to wait. Each day of waiting in New York City, where she lives, was very difficult, but I was trying to take in what I was learning. People kept telling me they were amazed that she had not come yet, but her honoring my wishes was part of her expression of love to me. It would be the first of many times when my mother would place my needs and wishes before her own. We were constantly reminded that Taylor's recovery was going to be a lengthy process and that we had to keep our reserve support in mind. The social workers and care management team had seen families go through this ordeal, and they knew we had a long road ahead. My dad had come the first full day and he had gone back to Atlanta after a week. My brother had come and returned to his home and children in Richmond.

Prior to my mom's arrival, we kept her up to date twice a day, and more often if need be. Avery and Tanner were great about keeping their Grandbunny in the loop of Taylor's progress. She was remarkably brave and calm. I don't know whether I imagined that she would have some type of hysteria, but that never came to fruition. The evening that she walked into the waiting room after a dear friend had picked her up, I could see the heaviness in her heart and the look of both fear and relief on her face. After a round of hugs, I took her back to see Taylor. She was not nervous in the normal understanding of the word; she was trying to be strong and she succeeded. She looked at her first grandson and felt thankful for his life. My expectation of her weakness was met instead by her quiet strength.

Having my mother present was one of the greatest gifts during the journey. She is a retired registered psychiatric nurse with close to forty years of experience, but she understood my need for her to put the role of nurse aside and be my mother. My mom understood my feelings, and knew that if I needed advice in reference to her nursing knowledge, that I would ask. She sat with me endlessly in quiet. She listened to my tears and fears, and allowed me to get angry. She fielded visitors when I

62

did not have the courage or strength to see them, and she gave me company in hours when I could have felt extremely isolated. In the middle of a frightening storm, when it felt that every wave was raging against me, my mom gave my heart the shelter and protection it needed. She constantly reminded me that she was proud of me and she let me handle things in my own way.

It was around this time that Taylor developed his second round of pneumonia. We were all aware of what this infection could mean for him, especially the second time. Pneumonia is an infection of the lungs that must be treated with antibiotics. Taylor did not have the traditional cough that usually accompanies pneumonia, and he had no real way of getting it out of his lungs. He developed fevers, and the hospital staff would attempt to cool him with blankets and a fan, but then he would shiver. The shivering was a concern because it was not good for his body to be in that state. The shaking was not good for Taylor's brain; he needed to lie as still as possible. The movements also depleted a lot of his energy and exhausted him in ways that we were unable to see, but became evident in his vital signs. The fever was dangerous because it could cause further damage to his brain past a certain point. There were all these medical tightropes we had to walk, and it was exhausting. The ICU staff had to find the right balance in treating Taylor.

One night at about day thirteen or fourteen, I was wandering down a long corridor that I often traveled, just to think. It was early in the morning, probably around 7 a.m. The hospital was quiet except for a few voices that could be heard through an open door. The doctors were meeting before rounds and they happened to be discussing Taylor. Taylor had specific teams, but at this point the most involved folks were those on the infection control, trauma, and neurology teams. Taylor had developed so many infections and it seemed like he constantly had to fight off yet another one.

The doctors summarized his previous day and announced, "Taylor is clearly not out of the woods. His family needs to know and understand that his life is still in danger." *Well, now we did.* They had unknowingly told his mother. It was not as if I hadn't been aware of what they were saying, but now they emphasized their words. I stood in the empty hallway and felt isolated. I wanted to run into the meeting and ask them how we were going to get Taylor out of the woods, but I didn't. I waited until it was my turn during their morning rounds.

Taylor was still on a ventilator, and he now had a tracheotomy and feeding tube. Infections hit his body, one after another. It felt like things were spiraling out of control on some cruel level, at some incredibly slow pace. He continually battled high fevers and infections.

I began to have a sense of fear about his visitors and protecting him from germs as much as we could. The staff was concerned as well, and we constantly had to tighten the reins. The critical care unit does not really have time to monitor who goes in and out, but they tried to help us navigate this new problem. I was struggling with this challenge. Deep down, I really did not want anyone outside our immediate family unit going in to see Taylor, at least until his current infection passed. It felt like I was battling for my voice to be heard, and often I did not have the strength or courage to say to anyone, "Please do not go in to visit Taylor today." At that point, the visits were really more about the person going into the room than they were about Taylor. I shared my feelings with my mom and Keith, but at times I felt like no one else heard them. *It was a very dark and lonely place.* I knew that our community loved Taylor and wanted the opportunity to see him, but my instinct to protect him was strong.

On December 6, I addressed some of my feelings on Facebook:

As Taylor's mother and protector since birth, I have an important request. Since I am at GMC most of the day from morning to evening, I know that what I am about to mention has occurred a lot. The AICU staff is very busy; they in no way have time to monitor the traffic that comes in and out of Taylor's room. The unit that Taylor is on is for family only, and sometimes at the family's discretion, a friend. Taylor is fighting his second bout of pneumonia in two weeks, and it is important that he not be exposed to any unnecessary germs. Please do not walk into his unit or his room. It creates awkwardness for me and it is not best for him. We do enjoy having visitors come, especially those with contagious joy, or who want to see us. But we do not want Taylor exposed to any more germs, so we ask that your visiting be kept to the waiting room. Much appreciation, and thanks for the support.

Writing that post took so much energy and courage, but it was one of the few ways I was able to express what I was feeling. I was afraid that I would turn people off or make someone angry at me. What I did not explain was that so many well-intentioned caring people had come, but they had created a flow of exposures to contagious illnesses that Taylor did not need. The doctors and nurses continually reminded us that visitors now had to be limited to immediate family.

In the few days prior to that, one of my former students was waiting for me in Taylor's room when I returned from getting a coffee. Some of Taylor's close friends and co-workers had simply walked in his room without anyone's knowledge. Along with our large family, there was too much traffic that was going in and out. I felt as if I was going to explode and no one really knew it. People were coming because they loved us and they cared about what was happening. I think it was hard for them to understand that even though some days had passed, *Taylor was not in the clear.* The volume of visitors and the germs that each one of them brought were both concerning.

One particular day, Pastor Number Three showed up when I had my head lying on the rail next to Taylor. I was silently crying and begging God to bring my son back to me. I lifted my head to find a stranger standing above me and I became very angry. I told him he needed to leave, and when he said, "I am here to pray for Taylor; someone asked me to come." I told him that he could pray in the hallway or somewhere else, but Taylor could not be exposed to any more germs. Later that day another pastor came, and he knew me. I joked with him that I was going to be put on some enemies list among his crew because I was not allowing all of them to come in. He understood that I was

65

protecting my young. *I felt like a lioness.* I was certain my "claws" would come out toward anyone who put Taylor in danger. I was learning to find my balance as his mother, advocate, and bridge between him and the outside world. In protecting Taylor, I was going to hurt others' feelings, but that is something that I had to accept.

After several days of undeniably excellent care, Taylor began to emerge from the place of critical danger. The roller coaster was constantly running, and you never knew when the bottom would fall out again. Baby steps became the way to measure progress. A friend had shared a quote with us that read, "Let him sleep for when he wakes he shall move mountains." I printed it and hung it in his room. Tanner and Keith made a sign that said "Love Wins." Our hearts held on to the words that each sign said and we tried our best to believe them.

I remember a particular evening when I stepped out into the hall to catch a breath. There had been a blue curtain closed for most of the day in the room two doors down from Taylor. There had been a steady flow of people to and from that room throughout the day, but it did not appear as if things were in crisis mode. Suddenly I heard the cries that come with someone's death. I knew that whoever was in that room had gone. They had in a matter of moments left this earth. I felt their loved ones' cries in every ounce of my body, mind, and spirit. I knew that family could be us and I wondered whether we could survive losing Taylor. I was in no way ready for the story of my son's life to end—it had hardly been written. Taylor had to keep moving ahead. He needed constant forward motion. We had to be strong for each other, but more importantly . . . *we had to be strong for Taylor.*

It was my perception that as a family, we were most impressed with the young male nurses who took care of Taylor. They seemed to want to connect with him. They seemed to do their job with an eye to excellence, and from my perspective, it looked as if they were giving Taylor the kind of care that they would want for themselves. They were also wonderful and kind to our family. Many times, they were free to offer hugs and encouraging words. They constantly told us that we were just as important as Taylor; they were caring for all of us.

I hung a few pictures in his room, one of him and a big buck, which grabbed a lot of the nurses' attention, and another of our family. I wanted the hospital team to see who Taylor had been before his fall; I wanted them to see our family as we once were.

A person who is in a coma is defined as having the following characteristics: they cannot open their eyes; they are not able to follow instructions; they do not speak or communicate in any way; and they have no intentional or purposeful movement.[5] The state of being in a coma is hopefully followed by a vegetative state, which is a more responsive state of recovery.

On December 3, Dr. Taggart, who was now the neurosurgeon directly involved with Taylor's care, told me that it was time for the sleeping giant to stir. We were twelve days out from the accident, and the responses were not at all where they needed to be. The swelling on the outside of Taylor's head and face had come down significantly, and everyone was hopeful that the same thing was occurring inside. I came home that night and wrote in my journal, "'Sleeping Brutey' needs to wake up." *I believed in his strength and will to fight, and it was time to reveal it.* The more days that passed when Taylor was unresponsive meant that his recovery could be less successful. We were always aware that Taylor could reach a certain stage and not be able to move past it. None of us believed that would happen.

December 4 was a big day for all of us. It started by having over 80 staples removed from Taylor's head. It was the first time that I was with him when I was not certain I could stay in the room, but I did. It was my "shift," and the staples had to come out. I was afraid, but it was one of many times I discovered a strength I did not know that I possessed. I whispered words of comfort into his ear and took deep breaths that allowed me to continue to stand. Once the staples were removed, the doctors determined that the incision had not healed enough for them to be taken out. It was a long incision that looked painful.

---

[5]BrainLine.org,
http://www.brainline.org/landing_pages/categories/coma.html (accessed January 29, 2015).

Taylor would have to have sutures put in so that the incision would not reopen. Everything that happened to or was done to Taylor's body required a lot of unseen energy on his part. By eight that evening, he was clearly wiped out, and the nurse assured us she would tuck him in and disturb him only when necessary.

A family whose daughter had suffered a traumatic brain injury approximately two years prior came to meet with us; that was the other significant part of the day. Their story had been highly publicized in our area, and I had made donations to the account that had been set up for their daughter and the other teenager who had been hurt in the accident. I thought I had followed their story, when in reality I knew only a small part of it. I remember thinking how incredibly naïve I had been concerning what they were dealing with. They were very gentle people, and they did not overwhelm us with a lot of their story or facts about it. They came to offer support and critical advice.

We all hugged; and they continued to tell us that we were now part of a club that we would never have imagined joining. Their daughter too had been unresponsive and not progressing as quickly as they had hoped, but she had made tremendous strides since then. I could see the sadness etched on the mother's face. I could tell that this situation had hardened her and changed her, even though I had no idea who she had been before.

They told us about the importance of choosing a rehabilitation center, and educated us about one that we were being pointed to that they had clearly found unimpressive. They also explained that recovery would be an incredibly long process, and that the mother had spent every step of the journey with her daughter, encouraging her in recovery, bringing her back to them. I knew that I was prepared to do the same. I also knew that Keith, Avery, and Tanner would support and respect my decision to be with Taylor. The one thing this family said to us over and over again was, "Never give up. Never, ever give up." We were determined to have as much of Taylor back as we possibly could, but we needed to hear those words from a family that fully understood the seriousness of the situation.

The moment that stood out to me the most was when the mother spoke about the first time she knew her daughter was still "in there." The daughter was in a children's rehabilitation hospital in Philadelphia. Part of the program was music therapy. One day, the therapists were playing music and her daughter began to doodle a smiley face. Her baby girl was somehow reconnecting after endless weeks of silence. I felt a sense of hope, and yet I was hoping for such a small thing.

It was so refreshing to hear something positive, but I also kept being reminded that they had lost the daughter they once had. A new daughter had emerged in her place. I was caught up in the fact that Taylor might actually speak to us again or open his eyes. It was hard for me to understand their sense of loss, because that is not at all where we were in the process. They knew how parts of our story would unfold, and they tried to prepare us as best they could in an hour.

My post that evening on Facebook read,

> *In the midst of dealing with a traumatic brain injury, there is also a lot of work to be done. Several things were accomplished today; and since each task can feel overwhelming, completing them feels good. One of the most touching things that happened today was a family who dealt with the same type of devastating injury came to talk with us. Keith and I found them to be realistic, hopeful and encouraging.*
>
> *We continue to give thanks for every little step and all of the love being poured out and then back into Taylor. The family said to us tonight over and over again, "Do not give up." And we won't.*

Later that night, I received the most heartfelt message from a friend. It said, *"There are people living in the midst of unattractive circumstances, amid hardships, toil and disease, whose daily life breathes out most gentle music that blesses others about them"* (J.F. Miller). She then wrote, *"This reminds me of your family. Even though you are going through a time of unspeakable horror, you still emit the sweetest spirit that calms those around you.*" Life had felt hard before Taylor's fall; as a family and individuals we had had our struggles, but I was determined that this struggle would not destroy Taylor, myself, or anyone else that I loved. Just as Taylor had to fight . . . so did we.

Eventually a very big step was taken in Taylor's recovery; the staff began to wean Taylor from the ventilator. When the ventilator is running, you can see how many breaths per minute the machine is performing, and how many the patient is taking on his or her own. The machine also displays how large the breaths are. Some quiet partners in Taylor's care had been the respiratory specialists. These specialists came in and read the machine, changed the settings and tubing, and carried out other tasks.

There is a balance to the weaning process because long-term care like Taylor's can lead to dependency on the ventilator. Taylor had struggled with severe asthma his entire life, so the additional strain of his injury added to the dependency. I had not previously been aware that taking a patient off the ventilator is one of the most critical and dangerous things that occur in the ICU. As the physician explained the process, he reminded us that they were being as certain as they could that Taylor could breathe on his own. The large tube that was in his throat was successfully removed, and the tracheotomy tube allowed for pure oxygen to be delivered to his lungs via another avenue.

Eventually, Taylor progressed to the point at which a team of physical therapists came in to work with him, with the goal of starting physical therapy. Taylor was lifted out of his bed into a chair, using a large lift, and he was placed in a sitting position in the chair for about an hour once a day. The plan was to progress to twice a day as soon as he would tolerate it. The therapists also worked with his arms, legs, feet, and hands in efforts to stimulate the muscles and parts of his body that he was not able to use.

The therapists noted that Taylor's use of his right side was far greater than that of his left. His left side seemed to forget it was there. It was lifeless and generally gave no indication of naturally reacting to the responses that one's reflexes automatically give. This is a condition called hemiplegia, which is the technical term for someone's inability to move one side of their body. It was frightening to dwell on the questions to which we did not have answers, and it was equally frightening to see that Taylor's left side was so still and unresponsive. Because the greatest amount of damage had occurred on the right side of Taylor's brain, it was the left side of his physical body that was impaired.

After weeks of not being permitted to touch Taylor often and having to remain in a state of constant silence, it was nice to feel like we were actually doing something to help him. We could even talk to him about what we were doing, even though he was unresponsive. We learned a lot from the therapists. The best ones came in and introduced themselves to Taylor and to us. If they did not identify themselves to Taylor, I would request that they do so. Most of them always explained to Taylor what they were doing and we had to believe some part of him heard them. There were times when it was hard to watch Taylor tolerate the sessions, seeing your son with no response felt just as awful as seeing him in pain. Eventually, after we became familiar with the therapy team, they kindly asked us to leave during the therapy sessions, which was often a welcome break for us.

Most of the leg exercises were to be done once an hour. We would gently turn Taylor's feet in a circular motion. We would do something that simulated pressing down on the gas pedal of a car and releasing it. We would flex Taylor's feet upward toward his upper body. We would even wiggle his toes. The tightness occurring in the muscles of his upper body was far more noticeable. His arms were often extremely stiff and hard to bend. We would bend his elbows and rotate his upper arm and shoulders. We spent many minutes of many hours flexing and bending Taylor's arms.

Taylor had to be handled with great care. There was a sign in his room that said, "BONE FLAPS ARE MISSING." This warning meant that underneath Taylor's bandages and the surface of his recently shaven head, there was now no bone to protect his already fragile brain where there used to be a complete skull. It was what might be considered an extremely large soft spot, like the fontanelles that babies are born with.

71

One day toward the end of the time in the ICU, I remember noticing that the sun was shining outside. We had been in the lower level of the hospital for most of the previous three weeks. It was as if the world had been a constant shade of grey. I rarely walked outside unless it was to get in my car, but the whole world looked darker to me. Taylor had a simple shade in his room that had been drawn for so many days. Now we were permitted to open the shade and let the sun shine in. And to my surprise, the wider world continued to turn despite the feeling that ours had stopped.

My Personal Journal Entries

I did not keep a journal consistently through Taylor's ordeal. It was something I was incapable of doing, but I did try, however. These were some random thoughts that I kept on my Kindle in a specific journal app. I sat by Taylor's bed in the intensive care unit to attempt to put my thoughts into words. I just never had the energy to do it for long.

December 4
This has been such an emotionally charged situation. There truly are no words to describe it. We are learning to celebrate the smallest of joys while fearing the largest of setbacks. It has been easy to feel hurt or disappointed, and yet that cannot be our focus. There is a constant flow of learning how to balance the little and the big things. We have to take in the words that are told to us and put them on a scale that somehow balances what we hope for and what is our truth. There are endless new terms that require explanation and understanding, and finally accepting them. We are trying to learn what we can; right now, it feels like that is all we can do.

December 5

How sweet it is to feel your hand in mine. I am amazed as I watch you wiggle and move slightly. Even as you rest, you are strong. I have recently been allowed to exercise your limbs. It feels wonderful to do something for you. I only wish I could do more.

When I think about making you dinner again, I weep. It is silly, Taylor, but I miss cooking for you. I am ready to peel potatoes for hours if necessary. I will even make whoopie pies[6] from scratch.

It is day fourteen. You are still battling a fever. This is a constant battle, unending and draining. You had 86 staples removed the other day. Then your brain fluid leaked and your head had to be stitched again. This broke my heart. But then again, everything breaks my heart these days.

December 6

Last night, around 10 o'clock, Grandbunny and I came home. Tanner was here and I was looking around your room. Tanner told me that it was okay for me to cry. I miss you, Taylor, so very much. This hurts in places that I didn't know I could hurt. Ginger [our family dog] misses you too. She has been chewing your sheets, constantly whining and tearing up your mattress pad. She is worried and anxious, and wonders where you are. My days at the hospital are not full but they are busy and tiring.

Tanner and Avery miss you too. Your dad is hurting and so quiet. As a family, this is the hardest thing we have ever endured. It is excruciatingly slow and painfully frightening. So, wake up sunshine—I want to see your beautiful eyes again soon.

December 7

I wish people would stop telling me that everything is going to be okay. I feel like they are ignoring our pain and our reality. Not everything in life offers sunshine and moonbeams. Some moments are nothing but dark.

---

[6] Whoopie pies, sometimes called black moons in the Pittsburgh area, are cakes made from two mound-shaped layers of chocolate cake with a sweet, creamy filling in the middle. Food historians trace the origin of the whoopie pie to the Pennsylvania Dutch region of southeastern Pennsylvania.

People who say, "Everything is going to be okay," need to know that right now it isn't okay. It may not be okay again, ever. As my beautiful son lies in a hospital bed fighting to live, telling me that it is going to be okay gives me nothing. It does not comfort me.

December 8

Today you opened your eyes briefly for the first time. It was very slow, but you did it.

No one can take your place in my heart. Come back to us, my sweet son. Come home.

December 9

My precious son,

Soon you will turn twenty-two years old. Please come out of this darkness so we can share in your light again. I have been filled with many questions over the last 18 days, but most of them I can't even ask at this time. All I know with certainty is that this did not have to happen to my bright, strong, and beautiful son. I thought before that my life had known immeasurable pain, and nothing could have prepared me for this. Nothing.

I will be strong for you. I have no other option. I will do what I have to do, and all that I can do for your life to be returned to you. There are things that will change and we will work through them one day at a time. A family is like this: when one unravels, all unravel. When one hurts, everyone hurts. We are not the same, Taylor. Our lives have been shattered. We want you back. Come back to us, Taylor.

I want you to be whole again. I miss you. I miss the way you tore into a bag of gummy candy with no regard for others. I miss your love for mashed potatoes and meat. I miss how you got so excited over venison sticks. I miss the way you did things without anticipating a 'thank you.' I miss you. It makes me sad, mad, and every emotion in between when you are not here.

Mom

Chapter Five

Transitions

December 9–December 14, 2012

After several weeks in the ICU, Taylor was moved to the Special Care Unit. In general, the transition to the Special Care Unit means that the patient is in a less critical state in terms of blood pressure, heart rate, and overall stability. Another major indicator that a patient is ready for the change is when they no longer require the ventilator to do all their breathing. Coming off the ventilator was one of the first big steps in Taylor's recovery, and so was moving to the Special Care Unit. Typically, when a patient is moved to special care, their status is changed from "critical" to "stable."

The idea of death or people being too close to it surrounded us, and the feeling that it could be Taylor who was dying was always in the forefront of my mind. The ICU staff prepared us as best they could for the transition; however, it was anything but an easy adjustment. Taylor was placed in a room with a large window next to the nurses' station. The nursing staff had a constant view of him, which gave our family a sense of security. The room was much larger, and lent itself much better not only to Taylor's comfort, but to the comfort of visitors as well.

Taylor had been extremely fragile in the ICU, but now his physical body was not as delicate. Many of the tubes that had been connected to him in one fashion or another were no longer needed, which was a terrific step in the right direction. Each piece of tubing or foreign object that was in Taylor's body opened a route for infection; less equipment meant fewer risks.

His head was still covered in white gauze, leaving his injury unexposed. We rarely saw it and had not yet had to adjust to the drastic change in his appearance that we would see later. In many ways he still looked like Taylor. His brothers teased him that he was growing a nice beard.

The first day that we came to the Special Care Unit was difficult at best. Before we left the house that morning, the staff called to let us know that Taylor had been moved while we were sleeping. My mom and I had no idea where we were going as we walked into the hospital and had to take a different route than we had since the day of Taylor's fall.

The room that Taylor had been assigned to was a much brighter room than the ICU. The light came through the windows and we could actually see him better. Something about the presence of light made part of the gloom that seemed to hover in the ICU . . . disappear. In addition, his new room had a spacious bathroom.

The nurses here were unfamiliar with Taylor's accident, and as they did not know our family, it was an adjustment for all of us. We had come to love the nurses in the ICU. They had shared so much of this journey with us, and we were not prepared to let go of the assurance and comfort they had provided. This transition was not going to be the first time that we would have to adjust to new faces and new personalities.

One of the first things that the Special Care Unit nurse said to me was, "We have to be careful; I don't want him falling on his head." *I felt myself coming unhinged.* We could not afford to feel worried about the hands that cared for Taylor. Later, we discovered that this nurse was one of the most tender-hearted and compassionate people on the unit. I have come to the conclusion that she was very nervous about caring for Taylor, and she simply spoke out of fear, which was completely understandable.

This transfer was supposed to be a step in the right direction for Taylor, but it did not feel that way. I was afraid that he was going to get hurt and wouldn't be given the same level of care. I was beginning to feel once again as if everything had been removed from my control, and I was unsure whether we were heading in the right direction. I wanted to unhook Taylor's machines, grab his bed, and roll it back to the place where they knew and cared for Taylor so beautifully. Feeling like every wall was caving in on me, my anxiety level was shooting through the roof. I was ready to tell the team when they came for rounds that this move had been a mistake. In reality, even if I would have begged to go back to the security of the ICU, Taylor no longer needed that level of care—which was something we were all grateful for. I simply needed to come to grips with our new surroundings. Part of this journey is being able to deal with change easily, and I was beginning to really understand that.

We had been on the unit for only a few hours when the team of doctors and nurses came in, along with the social worker who had been assigned to us. Some of the team members were familiar and others we had never met. My nerves were shot and I felt like I needed to speak up about how concerned I was. An unfamiliar doctor examined Taylor as I closely watched. He began, "Good morning, Taylor, can you open your eyes for me?" Taylor's response remained the same. *There was no response at all.* Keeping a close eye on this new doctor, I decided that once he was finished with the routine exam I would voice my concerns.

I asked the social worker whether I could say something to everyone while we were all gathered together. In moments like this, my mind would flash back to one of the most powerful scenes from the old movie *Terms of Endearment*. Shirley MacLaine played the role of Debra Winger's mother in a story that centered on Debra's character's battle with terminal cancer. At one point, Debra's character needed pain medication and the staff was taking their time bringing it to her. Her pain was increasingly visible to the audience. Shirley, who played the role of her mother, absolutely freaked out. Her hair was wild, her skin was pale, and she screamed frantically, while banging her hand on the nurses' station, that her daughter needed her pain medication NOW!

One of the aspects of that scene that made it both powerful and memorable was the true emotion that was shown. Any mother who watched it understood that whether or not she would act that way, she would relate to and fully understand the desperation this mother was feeling for her child. I would say to my mom when I felt that kind of emotion in myself, "I may have a Shirley MacLaine moment." We would laugh or smile, but we both knew that I meant my internal pot was about to boil over. My mom understood and would remind me that it is easier to hear a calm, reasonable person than one who has lost control of all their emotions. You don't have to show the whole world how crazy everything feels to you in the moment; however, you do need to speak in a tone of voice that lends itself to being heard. With a trembling voice, I spoke up; I had to make it clear what was important to us in regard to Taylor's care.

My fears, frustrations, and anxieties came from a place deep inside me. This private place was not the nursing staff's issue and did not represent any flaws that they had. I had come to have a standard of expectation for Taylor's care, and I was not willing to watch any of it fade away. This expectation was one aspect of this nightmare that I had some control over. I looked at all these professionals and felt intimidated, but strong. I introduced myself as Taylor's mother and began to speak about our expectations.

I calmly explained that I was clearly apprehensive about the transition, and I needed them to understand our position as Taylor's family. Knowing the staff would be taking care of a hundred different patients that day, I did not want Taylor treated like part of a mass. He was a son, a brother, a friend, a grandson, and so much more to countless people. He was an individual, and attention to the details of his care mattered to us. We not only expected excellence; we required it. In my mind no one should be just a number, but Taylor was my son and my sole focus. *I had to speak for him when he could not.*

I said that it was important that Taylor be greeted and addressed. We expected the staff to tell Taylor what they were doing with every interaction, and to always use his name. I requested that when they perform personal care for him, no one other than his father or brothers should be in the room. There was one incident in the ICU when Taylor had been shifted and cleaned up while another family member was present and actually participated in helping the nurse. That was not okay with me because I knew Taylor would not be comfortable with anyone outside our immediate family being present during those times. Most importantly, I said that even though Taylor was not awake and interacting with others, we still felt he was aware of what was going on in the room around him. Last, I wanted the team to always speak as if he were listening. When all my requests came spilling out, I wasn't exactly sure what the response would be. I did not cry, nor did I yell. I spoke my piece, and the doctor answered with, "Thank you. I think we all needed to be reminded of that today." *I felt relieved.* As the team left, I looked at my mom in the corner of the room who fully knew if she hugged me, the dam would break, so instead she blew me a kiss and made a silent clapping motion. She would become one of my greatest cheerleaders.

After my "speech," I really felt like I had not only been heard but also understood. It would take time for our trust to rebuild, but we accepted Taylor's new environment. I was learning more about advocating for Taylor. If I intended to be with him every single day, I would have to speak up when I felt it necessary.

Taylor's body received most of its exercise through others moving his limbs for him. We continued to move and massage his legs often. We would exercise his arms. We would rub his feet and put lotion on his body. We trimmed his fingernails and toenails. For a couple of hours a day, he was placed in a chair to sit upright. He sat and wiggled around enough that we always had to shift and adjust his body. These were the baby steps of bringing him back to our lives and world. We were allowed to stimulate him within the parameters set for us by the staff. Taylor had yet to open his eyes for more than a second or two. We were initially told that day eight or nine would mark his waking, but those days had passed with no sign of wakefulness. We were into week three and Taylor was still very unresponsive. We needed the sleeping giant inside Taylor to stir.

One afternoon, I was standing alongside Taylor's bed as I normally did day in and day out to watch him simply lie still. I rubbed his arm, bent over to hug him, and said, "Taylor, it's Mom." We often stood on his right side when trying to elicit a response from him because even if he wanted it to, his left side might not cooperate. On this afternoon, Taylor reached around my body, began patting my back, and played with my hair. *I was too elated to cry.* I experienced a moment of joy and a glimmer of hope. This was the most purposeful movement we had seen up until now. It was not command-driven, but it had an appropriate path and purpose to it.

Later that day, he opened his eyes for the longest time that anyone of us had seen so far. In fact, it was the first time I saw it. The movements of his eyelids made it look as if each one of them were somehow weighed down. He looked like an extremely exhausted child who opens its eyes for no more than three seconds and then drifts back to sleep. To see Taylor make those movements was astonishing. It was not long enough to make any kind of contact or connection, but it was exciting to see him take a new step. You could tell that something that is small and so simple to most of us required a huge effort from Taylor's body and mind.

This occasion marked a beginning of a new pattern with Taylor. His movements were not predictable, but rather spontaneous. He seemed to like patting people on the back or the bottom. We joked when he would do it to the female nurses that he was fully aware of his actions. He did not open his eyes on command, but from time to time he would open them just for a few seconds. These kinds of responses were automatic to his brain, but they were progress nonetheless. It felt good to have him respond and interact with others even on such a small scale.

One of the goals and hopes for Taylor was that he would become more aware and that his responses to various stimuli would increase. Although he opened his eyes, he was not aware of his surroundings. Taylor simply could not move forward in his recovery in the state he was in. For a person in a coma, everything is unpredictable. Brain injuries have similarities and comparisons, but they are also as unique as an individual's fingerprints.

At this point, Taylor continued to be given commands. They started with the neurologist or physician assistant in the morning. They would stand to his side and say in a loud voice, "Good morning, Taylor, this is Dr. Taggart. Can you move your feet for me this morning?" Then there was a period of waiting for Taylor to process the command, followed by a second command, "Taylor, can you squeeze my hands?" Next, the neurologist might say something like, "Good; now, Taylor, can you open your eyes for me? We need you to open your eyes." Every day it was the same process. Sometimes there was what may have been a response, other times the doctors weren't certain. The timing of these examinations was important. The doctors were not ready for us to give Taylor commands. As a family, we just talked with him unless we were asked to do otherwise. The staff encouraged our interaction with Taylor, but giving him commands or asking him to do something like wiggle his toes or squeeze our hands was something they wanted to have a therapist or physician present to observe. One of the reasons for the restriction is that if progress occurred, it would need to be documented, which would be important information to relate to any rehabilitation facility. Another reason that the staff wanted us to refrain from commands is that Taylor was not giving consistent responses. This inconsistency indicated that if and when he did respond, it was taxing on him. The timing and frequency of verbal commands had to be limited in order to get a true picture of Taylor's progress in this area of recovery.

The daily assessments and stimulation exercises began to increase for Taylor. One day, a bright, bubbly woman, probably in her early forties came in and introduced herself as Laura, the speech pathologist. Laura had a bright countenance and contagious smile. She illustrated a positive vibe, and seeing her would become a bright spot in our days.

I immediately liked and felt a bond with Laura. She told us that she would be doing various actions to alert Taylor and help awaken him. I admit that I wondered how speech therapy would work for someone who rarely even opened his mouth. Laura encouraged me to stay and watch, and announced that eventually I could help her.

The process began with simple short statements. Laura introduced herself to Taylor. She explained that he had been in an accident, and that he was in Geisinger Medical Center getting better. Most importantly, she clarified that she was there to help him.

After being at the hospital for a couple weeks, we learned that Taylor should be made aware from time to time of where he was and what was going on. As soon as we were given approval to speak to Taylor, a couple times a day we would say something like, "Taylor, this is Mom. You had an accident and you are in the hospital. Everyone is okay. Your brothers and dad are okay. You are getting better." It was important to keep Taylor oriented and calm even if he offered no response. It was important to assure him that no one else had been hurt, and it was important to remind him that he was progressing. Laura knew the value of that too and I liked the fact that she spoke to Taylor as if he were awake.

Taylor progressed to holding onto washcloths; he seemed to like having something in his hands to touch or keep busy with. Laura placed dry, wet, hot, and cold washcloths, small balls, and other textured items in Taylor's hands. She would tell him what each object was, and he seemed to enjoy it. Something about Laura was magical and comforting. I felt like she may be able to pull a reaction out of Taylor that others may not be able to do.

Another technique that doctors and therapists used was to speak very loudly to Taylor or clap their hands at the side of his head. This technique was done in a controlled setting and not something they wanted anyone else to perform. When Laura did these exercises, they seemed a lot less startling. The loudest auditory stimulation occurred when Laura slammed one of the cabinets in Taylor's room. His body gave an automatic startled response, which was a good sign. Laura was soft-spoken and gentle, and she seemed very comfortable interacting with Taylor and us. One day, when I told Laura that I thought she was amazing at her job, she smiled and said, "Just wait until you get to the rehab hospital . . . that is where you will see amazing therapists and techniques." *This speech therapy was the beginning of a much longer road.*

After a few days, Laura came in with a basin of ice-cold water. She explained that she was going to put each of Taylor's hands in the water. When both hands were placed in the basin, the left one did not respond, but the right one performed what is called a raking motion. Taylor's hands were like small rakes meant to move the ice back. For anyone watching, it felt exhilarating to see this step.

One of the doctors within the neurology department came in to observe Taylor during the exercise with the ice basin. I thought he would be as happy as I was to see the progress; instead, he said something that left me feeling as if I had been sucker-punched. He cautiously announced, "You need to be aware that this may be as far as Taylor progresses." He explained that Taylor had been stuck for some time at the same spot, and that while all of these responses were good, they were not enough to get him into a rehab program. If Taylor improved physically but did not become more responsive, we might have to look at another type of setting. He was referring to a nursing home. *I was furious.* I wanted to blame the doctor for delivering this news. I thought, he does not know us and he does not know Taylor! The reality, however, was very much present. Taylor's progression could peak at any point and all forward motion could come to a screeching halt. Taylor's life was not saved so that he could sit around raking ice cubes and touching washcloths. Although this doctor did not know Taylor, he did know how cruel and unrelenting an injury like Taylor's could be.

Laura began to enlist my help in Taylor's therapy sessions. She told Taylor that I was going to help her and explain things that we were going to do. He responded well to a slightly dampened lukewarm washcloth; he liked to put it on his face and up to his lips. His favorite activity appeared to be the sponge; Laura would take a tiny sponge and put tiny droplets of water on it. She would wet his lips and he would open his mouth like a baby bird. Taylor was not allowed to have water to drink, but this little amount was something that his body language indicated he liked. During these exercises Taylor's eyes would remain closed, and there was no evidence of any awareness on Taylor's part beyond his immediate physical reaction. He was still in a coma, therefore his reaction to physical stimuli was limited.

Taylor was making very small steps, but those steps counted. Later that day, when speaking to the social worker, I told him that Taylor would not be going to a nursing home. Whether I had any control over that remained to be seen, but I was not just going to let that happen. The social worker tried telling me that Taylor might have to stay in a nursing home-type setting for just a few days or until he progressed, but in my mind that seemed like a death sentence. The staff needed to see Taylor respond to a command, as distinct from an automatic or reflexive response.

As a family, we did not discuss these issues with Taylor in the room, but we did tell him that he needed to fight. We told him that coming back would be work. We reminded him how very much we believed in him. And in turn, our friends and family reminded us that they were by our side supporting us on the road we traveled for Taylor. Avery continued to spend most nights from about 9 p.m. until 1 or 2 a.m. with Taylor. The nursing staff understood and welcomed our presence. We were not disruptive but felt a need to be near Taylor at all times. We also believed that he needed to be near us. On December 12, Avery sent our family a public reminder via a Facebook post. He wrote,

> *Dr. King once said, "We must accept finite disappointment, but we must never lose infinite hope." Many storms have come our way, but none as wicked as this one. If [we] were alone we may have been swept away by now, but together we'll hold strong.*

I accepted those words and refused to give up the hope I held for Taylor's recovery. I had to believe that he could somehow, some way, find his way back to us. It was clear that Taylor had to reach a certain level of responsiveness in order to move to a rehabilitation center that specialized in traumatic brain injury, instead of a nursing home. *I felt as if I could not bear any more disappointment.*

Brain injury rehabilitation . . . those words had never meant anything to me earlier, but they would come to consume many hours of our thoughts over the next several days.

There are scales that measure progress as the body moves through brain injury recovery, and we would learn to live by them. The scale that we were led to focus on was the Rancho Los Amigos Scale.[7] This scale is one of the most widely used tools in teaching families about their loved one's progress. There are ten levels on the scale. Taylor was, unfortunately, still at Level I after close to three weeks.

---

[7] The Rancho Los Amigos Scale, also known as the Rancho Los Amigos Level of Cognitive Functioning (LOCF) Scale, was first developed in the 1970s and later revised. It is named for the Rancho Los Amigos National Rehabilitation Center in Downey, California. The name of the center means "The Friends' Ranch" in Spanish.

The scale was introduced to us, and we learned that in order for Taylor to be accepted into a rehabilitation facility that specialized in traumatic brain injury, he would have to indicate in more ways than he had done that he could hear and follow some type of command. We also had to figure out exactly where Taylor would be going.

There were a few options, but with Taylor's lack of progress, the choices would be very limited. The choices were Health South, which is adjacent to Geisinger Medical Center. Its advantages were simple; it is close to home, which held a lot of importance. Dr. Taggart wanted us to be clear about the role that she felt family and friends would play in Taylor's recovery. The second advantage is that Taylor would be close to one of the best hospitals in the state and a hospital that had already successfully treated him, should anything go wrong. Dr. Taggart wanted Taylor within her reach, and Health South allowed her that advantage. It was unclear, however, whether Health South would take Taylor as a patient at his present level of functioning.

The second choice was the Penn State Hershey Rehabilitation Hospital. This hospital was further away, but it was associated with a successful program. It was only a few years old, but it had modeled itself on other successful programs and was connected to a medical center with an impressive track record. Dr. Taggart said that she had a colleague who would work with her if Taylor were to go there.

Finally, there was Bryn Mawr Rehabilitation Hospital in Malvern, one of the suburbs in the Philadelphia Main Line. This facility was the furthest away from our home, but it had a solid reputation. The track record for the program appeared to be very successful, and the methods used seemed to be based on what had proved valuable in both new and old research regarding traumatic brain injury. If Taylor were to go to this hospital, Dr. Taggart would not have the access to him that the other facilities allowed. Taylor (and we) would also be three hours away from home.

A great deal of thought, research, and various factors would go into making this decision. We believed that it would be one of the decisions with the greatest effect on Taylor's recovery in this beginning stage. We came up with a strategy for choosing the right place. First, we asked whether the hospital could put us in contact with other families who had been to or used any of the specific programs we were looking at. Next, we talked with any personal friends or acquaintances who had connections with or knowledge of the field of traumatic brain injury rehabilitation, and we gathered their opinions. Many of the medical staff at Geisinger shared their thoughts with us in a way that was helpful and not pushy.

We also watched videos of the different programs online and read as much as we could on the facilities' own websites. Last, we set up appointments to either speak by phone or tour the places that would (hopefully) offer Taylor a new home and a place where he could progress. One night I came home from a long day at the hospital and looked on YouTube, of all places. There I found videos that families and professionals had posted regarding various methods, facilities, and other glimpses into the world of traumatic brain injury rehabilitation.

Who would imagine that YouTube videos would give us the first glimpse into what Taylor's recovery might look like? I tried to envision Taylor performing the activities that I saw the patients in the videos doing. Some of them walked with assistance. They spoke, but many of their faces seemed to droop. *Would Taylor walk? Would he speak? Would he eat again?* Finally, we were left with the most difficult and baffling question of all—*Would he emerge from this coma?* Anyone who had any experience with a traumatic brain injury as significant and devastating as Taylor's knew something that we had been told, but had not yet understood. They knew that the Taylor who fell was gone; and that if the body that he now lived in allowed him to emerge . . . he would be a very different person.

Chapter Six
The Scale That Everyone Was Watching

In the appendix at the back of this book is the Brain Injury Association of America's reference tool, the Rancho Los Amigos Scale. In order for Taylor to be accepted into a rehabilitation program, he had to show signs that indicated Level II activity was present, at the bare minimum. Many programs will accept a patient only when they meet the scale's Level III criteria. Everyone involved in Taylor's care would reference this scale, and we would learn to live by it. It was a concrete tool that we could understand in gauging Taylor's recovery progress.

The Rancho Los Amigos scale was one of the most effective and powerful tools that we were given in order to understand traumatic brain injury and its effects on the human body. The scale is incredibly accurate and gave our family ideas and goals that we hoped Taylor could attain, as well as the gift of understanding the normality of his behavior as a result of his injury.

The scale was introduced to us shortly after Taylor was transferred to Geisinger's Special Care Unit. It would become increasingly important. There are two different interpretations of the same scale. When Taylor had first come to the Special Care Unit, his eyes remained closed and gave very few indications of purposeful response. During the nine days he was there, he progressed from Level I to Level II, according to the scale. I believe Taylor's moving forward was based on a few factors. Since November 22, Taylor's body had been in a state of total and absolute rest. All his energies and reserves were used simply to keep him alive. His brain would not allow his physical body to respond.

Taylor's time in a coma had lasted for a month. We were so fortunate that he even began to emerge. The day of his accident, we had been informed that he should begin to wake up in eight or nine days— but that did not happen. Every brain injury is different, so it is very difficult for doctors to be exact. It is critical to remember that Taylor's progress could have come to a sudden halt at any given point in his recovery. This fact meant that we had to be prepared at any point in this entire process for Taylor to stop growing and progressing. No one knows when that might be.

The care team that Taylor had surrounding him, along with his family and friends, and their efforts to slowly lead him back into the world, was something that I felt he was aware of. We talked to Taylor; his brothers teased him about his facial hair that was growing out of control. We cut his fingernails and his toenails. He was given daily bed baths and treated as if he were simply asleep, but also handled with the intention of gently waking him. His doctors and therapists worked hard to elicit responses. His speech therapist in particular was very creative and determined to promote him to Level II.

Chapter Seven

Our Hearts Have Fallen

December 9–December 17, 2012

The search for the right rehabilitation hospital continued, and with each day that passed the anxiety involved in the decision intensified. Avery was back in university continuing his studies, and Keith had returned to working full time. Our family's primary focus had become finding the place that would be Taylor's and my temporary new home. We made plans to visit two rehab hospitals in person; both were within two hours of our home. We would research the facilities that were further away online and through word of mouth.

My mom accompanied me to explore the one closest to our home town, which is in a rather rural area. Upon arrival, we were given a very basic tour of the facility, which felt extremely impersonal. The tour was conducted by one of the heads of administration; and although I do not think that was the way he intended the tour to feel . . . that was simply my gut reaction. Our time there was unimpressive, shadowed by the absence of light and warmth in the air. The environment appeared very sterile. The gentleman who was with us kept comparing the program's success to patients who suffered a stroke; *Taylor did not have a stroke*. I knew that traumatic brain injury and stroke were both conditions of the brain, but the differences between them are vast.

The administrator also made several references to the hospital's standing with JCAHO[8] (pronounced JAY-co), which meant nothing to me as a parent or as an outsider to the medical field. My understanding of this term was limited to the fact that it was some sort of accreditation within the health care field. I specifically asked the administrator how many people under the age of thirty with traumatic brain injury had been treated as inpatients at his facility within the past year, and he was unable to answer. That alone gave me a shock of anxiety.

It is also my recollection that the art on the walls of this facility was limited to generic mass production pieces that evinced little thought.

---

[8] JCAHO is the acronym of the Joint Commission on Accreditation of Healthcare Organizations, which began as the Joint Commission on Accreditation of Hospitals (JCAH) in 1951. The organization changed its name to JCAHO in 1987, and again to The Joint Commission (TJC) in 2007. It is now known simply as TJC.

The wall art was poorly placed and bland to my senses. It was not the type of art that communicated healing or happiness to me. I felt as if the mood of the facility was partially reflected in the items that covered the walls and common areas. Our family was sad and afraid; I knew that bright, colorful art is another element that is important to healing. I envisioned paintings of trees and flowers that symbolized growth, or children's art that would make a viewer smile inside.

The final aspect of the tour that left a bad impression was the fact that we were not allowed to go into the part of the unit where the brain injury patients stayed. *How am I supposed to make a solid decision when I can't see where my son will be sleeping and spending his time?* We were led instead down a hallway and shown some rooms that were typical of the patients who stayed there. That wasn't good enough, to put it mildly. I instinctively knew that this would not be a facility where Taylor would thrive. Taylor was only twenty-one years old in 2012, and I wanted him to be treated as a young person. My overall impression was that this particular place was for people much older. My spirits were low when we left, but I still hoped the other options would feel right.

In the process of seeking advice, I learned something from a younger friend who was just starting her career as a speech pathologist. Her opinion, as well as the opinion of her future husband, who was a physician assistant, was to consider some key questions. *Did we want a more modern and perhaps better-equipped facility connected to a well-known name with a successful track record, but not a real history of its own?* Or: *Did we prefer a place with a proven track record even though the facility might be less modern?* It was a monumental decision and felt like the hardest one I would ever make. Asking those questions made matters clearer for me. The right equipment meant nothing unless it was in the most skilled and capable hands.

Tanner accompanied me to investigate the second facility on our list. I welcomed his eagerness to be a part of the process and thought that he offered a lot of insight that I did not have. As a young male, Tanner was able to define what would be important to him in that type of setting. I really valued his perspective and what it represented. Tanner is the youngest of my children, and when he told me that he needed to have a sense of peace about the location where Taylor would be spending the next several weeks made me realize how grown-up he had become. As Taylor's brother, he needed to have his own confidence in our decision.

In the weeks since Taylor's injury, we had been gathering as much information as possible about rehabilitation facilities and the role that the right placement meant for Taylor. We learned about:

1. outcomes and results
2. treatment plans
3. ages of typical patients
4. funding options and insurance issues
5. equipment used

We learned that if a patient was accompanied by a family member through the entire process from the hospital to the acute rehabilitation setting, they usually had a better outcome. There was some discussion given to the matter, but in my heart I knew I would be with Taylor every step of the way. I could not allow him to face the journey ahead . . . alone. Taylor was still unable to communicate in any form at this point. It was evident that there was not going to be a moment when he would open his eyes and all would be well. I wanted Taylor to have the comfort of my voice frequently. I wanted him to know someone who loved him was close by when he felt confused or afraid. I did not want him to have a moment of reality and wonder where his family was. I was also struck by the vulnerability that had become associated with Taylor. I had fears of his being harmed, even slightly neglected and somehow hurt worse than he already had been. Taylor was helpless, and one of us had to be there to help him at all times. It seemed critical for Taylor to have a voice in his treatment, even if that voice belonged to one of his family members.

While driving to the second facility, Tanner explained something to me that I would always remember. He confessed that he could have some sense of peace at home and school knowing I would be with Taylor wherever he was placed. He made it clear that if I were not going to be with Taylor, he was not sure that he could handle the thought of his having to be alone. In essence, we both had a haunting unease that Taylor might wake up and not have any understanding of where he was, what was happening, or how he had come to be in an unfamiliar place surrounded by strangers.

I learned that my staying with Taylor was not only a benefit to him and his recovery, but also something that was important to our entire family unit. My being with Taylor allowed everyone the security they needed to know that he was being protected and cared for by one of the people who loved him most. I don't think that any of us could have functioned under the level of anxiety that would have been produced if Taylor had not had one of us with him. That being understood was one thing, but the reality that we had to have an income, Tanner needed to continue his junior year of high school, and Avery had to complete his college semester was something that we were keenly aware of. Keith would stay in Mifflinburg and take care of our home, our dog, pay the bills, care for Tanner, and continue to work full time. I knew his burden was also great; he was just as worried about Taylor as I was, and not being close to him physically would be challenging. He would visit Taylor on every possible weekend.

When we entered the second rehab center, it appeared at once to be an improvement over the first place. We were made to feel welcome right away, and the staff seemed more accommodating and prepared for our visit. Earlier in the week, I had spoken at length with a mother whose young adult daughter had spent her recovery there and she had positive feedback to offer about their experience. The building itself was aesthetically pleasing. Everything looked fairly new; it was extremely clean and obviously well taken care of.

Tanner and I roamed around on our own and found the cafeteria, main gym, and other areas of interest. Each of the rooms was the size that I had envisioned. The gym was especially impressive; it was open, uncluttered, and filled with bright natural light. The equipment that filled the gym was what one would expect to see in a rehabilitation hospital.

There were parallel bars, large balancing balls, exercise equipment, and what appeared to be small tables where various activities were under way. At one of the tables, a therapist and a patient sat intently working together. We watched from a distance; it was not clear exactly what was taking place.

Eventually, we encountered a new staff member who led us into the locked brain injury unit. At the time, we did not know that it is standard protocol to lock these units. We had to be buzzed in and out of the unit designated for brain injury patients. Because it was Sunday, the unit was quiet. There were hardly a handful of visitors in the building.

We were briefly introduced to some nurses gathered at the nurses' station. They all seemed friendly, and most of them appeared to be rather young and most likely new to the profession. As we walked down the corridor, I could see a group of people sitting together in wheelchairs down the hall. They were all brain injury survivors—and what I saw took my breath away. I wished that I could become emotionally numb at that moment, but instead I felt sick. *How was my strong, bright, healthy son going to look in a chair like that? Who had these patients been before this place? Is this what I can expect for Taylor?* The patients each had empty stares and very little control over their bodies. They were grouped together, but could not have been more alone. There were no interactions occurring among them. It was undeniable that they had very little if any connections to the world around them.

There was one particular patient who stood out among them. She was a woman who appeared to be in her late forties. She was in a hospital gown, unlike the others who were dressed in sweatsuit-type clothing. Her hair was disheveled and her eyes looked empty, but also frightened. She was not sitting entirely upright; instead she was slightly slouched over to one side. She appeared to have no bra, which made me feel as if I were invading some personal part of her. The image of her is something that would stay with me for a long time. I felt a sense of compassion toward her, and I wondered what had brought her to the building that Tanner and I were standing in. *How did she arrive at such a place?*

I began to ask the staff some simple questions. As I tried to ask about Taylor's safety at times when he was in bed or unattended, something inside of me broke. I could hardly say Taylor's name aloud. The sense of dread that often invaded me suddenly and without warning seized me. I had to work very hard to compose myself and to control what I would later name the silent scream. The silent scream was the loud outcry that so desperately wanted to escape from my mouth and my body. *How could everything seem so normal, and people be so calm when my entire world was sidelined by a sense of chaos and things that I had no control over?* There are powerful, dreadful emotions that this entire process and experience was teaching me to contain. The thoughts that ran through my head always started the same way: *"How did this accident happen to Taylor?"* I felt equally frustrated that I could not communicate with him about it. I missed him, even though I sat by his body for hours every day. Taylor's body was nothing more than a shell, without the person inside him responding. I think I was desperately in need of comfort and a release of all that was happening in our lives. I wanted to find a safe place to let out my sadness and pain, but if it did escape, I was very aware of what it might sound like.

As we finished the tour and found our way to the parking lot, both Tanner and I agreed that something about that particular place did not feel right for Taylor. Our feelings were not a reflection on the facility; it was a reflection of what we felt Taylor needed. We needed to feel some kind of life inside the four walls. We needed to see glimpses of youth, vitality, and hope. As Taylor's mother, I needed something that would somehow communicate to my innermost being that Taylor would thrive in his new environment. I was looking for something that would show me that Taylor's coming back, even in part, was a possibility.

We made the drive back to Geisinger and went to eat somewhere close to the hospital. Something in me was not only missing Taylor, but also the normalcy that life had once held. I used to love "dates" with each of my sons. I was beginning to realize that being with Taylor would also require being away from the rest of my family. I was worried about them without me, and I was also worrying about how I would feel without having them close by. I felt very close to Tanner; there was so much about his school, his sports, and being a part of his life that I enjoyed. He was my baby, and I wanted to be able to cherish all the "lasts" of high school sports, events, and everything that each of those activities involved. My heart began to feel heavier about the ripple effect that Taylor's accident was having on the other areas of our lives. Taylor needed to be our focus, but that need was not easily undertaken. It was a decision that involved considerable sacrifice on everyone's part.

After lunch, Tanner and I returned to the Special Care Unit, where my mom and Keith were anxiously waiting. Tanner and I had shared something together that I don't think either one of us will ever forget—the first glimpse of a brain injury unit. It had shaken me to my core, and Tanner was putting on a very brave face. He wanted the best for Taylor and he would do his part to make sure his brother got it. Being the youngest was no longer about a big brother taking care of Tanner; the roles had been reversed.

We needed to make a clear decision over the next few days. Coming to a conclusion was not optional. Many factors go into choosing a rehabilitation facility, including how it will be paid for. A major part of what the social worker did for us was to determine whether Taylor's insurance would pay for his therapy; how much the insurance would cover; and what might happen if the days allotted by the policy ran out. One of the first things that the social worker discovered was that Taylor not only had a good insurance policy, but one that also supported cognitive therapy, which would be a critical element in Taylor's recovery. Many insurance plans do not recognize cognition in the determination of the patient's need for ongoing care.

From the moment I heard the name of Bryn Mawr Rehabilitation Hospital, something felt right about it. The staff at Geisinger spoke of its solid reputation consistently from nurse to nurse, floor to floor, and among the limited number of therapists we had had interactions with. It was a place that we had strongly considered from the time we began to explore our options.

Bryn Mawr Rehabilitation Hospital is located in a semirural setting west of Philadelphia. It is close to the city geographically, but doesn't have a city feel to it. We were told that there is a pond and walking path on the hospital grounds, and that it is nestled in a private area away from a lot of outside noise. Having looked at two facilities that sat on concrete and were surrounded by parking lots and business complexes, the idea of a more tranquil exterior environment appealed to us, as we knew it would appeal to the country boy in Taylor.

I spoke with Dr. Taggart about networking with some other people who had had to make this choice. She put us in contact with a nurse who was employed at Geisinger whose daughter had suffered a traumatic brain injury when riding a four-wheeler. Her daughter had spent the first part of her recovery at Bryn Mawr. The injury had not been that long ago, so her advice and experiences there were of particular value. The fact that she was an experienced registered nurse was something that I felt qualified her to really understand some of the most important aspects of the whole experience that she too had endured.

We discussed in detail the positive aspects of her daughter's recovery. I heard what she said, but I lacked the life experience to process what all of her words and explanations meant. The main content that I was able to glean from our conversation was that she felt very good about the decision her family had made to send their daughter to Bryn Mawr.

Toward the end of our talk, I asked her to tell me the worst thing about the facility, its staff, or anything unpleasant that she could think of. Her initial response was that she could not think of one bad thing to say. She had done such a fine job of communicating the positive aspects, but I really needed to know of any negative observations. Finally, after some thought, she said that the only shortcoming she had experienced was poor cellphone reception on the hospital campus. That was something we could certainly live with.

The final piece of information that she gave me was that Bryn Mawr provides a place called The Laurels where families like ours can stay without charge. The free lodging was based on factors like the patient's age, condition, and the distance that the family had to travel from their home. We would be three full hours from our home, so it was crucial for us to have a place to stay. Lodging was going to be a huge expense; it was something we had been trying to calculate. The thought that we might not have to contend with this expense was a huge relief. I had done the math over and over again, and the idea of paying eighty to one hundred dollars a night was overwhelming.

Over the next few days, our family watched the YouTube videos that the rehab hospital had posted about their brain injury program; we called to discuss simple matters with their staff; and my mom spoke at length with the coordinator of family housing. The pieces were coming together, and they finally felt right. We never visited the facility. We believed that Bryn Mawr Rehabilitation Hospital was the place that would provide the best total care for Taylor. Part of the decision we made was based on what we instinctively felt was right, coupled with the knowledge that we had gathered. It was not easy to simply trust our instincts, but we did. *Our decision had been made.*

The next step was to see whether Bryn Mawr would accept Taylor as a patient. Taylor was consistently showing Level II responses according to the Rancho Los Amigos Scale. Many places require patients to be at Level III.

The referral was sent by the social worker to all three facilities that we had researched or explored. There was a lot of emotional pressure. We understood that for whatever reason, perhaps unknown insurance issues, Taylor's lack of progress, or other unforeseen challenges, he might be turned away. We hoped for the best and tried not to dwell on what could be the worst.

After a tense twenty-four hours, we got the good news that Bryn Mawr Rehabilitation Hospital was willing to accept Taylor as a patient. It was around December 10, and we were all ready for the next step. I am not sure that any of us had a real reaction to the acceptance, but I do remember my mom smiling and saying, "This is great, this is what we wanted." Coming to this conclusion had been a challenge for each member of our family, but in a different way. On some level we each had to be willing to let Taylor go, and that was scary as hell.

Taylor's progress slowed a bit, so we waited. "One step forward, two steps back" became a familiar phrase. Over the next several days as we anxiously prepared to leave, Taylor fought off a low-grade fever, which could be a sign of underlying infection. In order to leave Geisinger, Taylor had to be cleared medically for his next phase of recovery; he also had to be fever-free for twenty-four hours. Five days passed by and then Saturday and Sunday came; no one would be moving then. In the hours of those days, there was a lot of preparation; my mom and I had to be packed and ready to go within a moment's notice. The discharge could happen fairly quickly. It felt like a tug of war between some force wanting Taylor to stay and another force pushing him forward. Hospitals in general can be breeding grounds of infection, and with that knowledge, Dr. Taggart was eager to get Taylor out of there. On Monday, seven days after Bryn Mawr's acceptance, we were told Taylor would be discharged.

Finally, Taylor was released from the care of Geisinger Medical Center on December 17, and it was time for the next leg of this marathon. The baton was being passed. The change from the Special Care Unit of the hospital to a brain injury rehabilitation facility would not have happened without a lot of hard and creative work. Although Taylor's body was fairly unresponsive, his therapies continued. He was prompted and pushed as much as he could be to respond in the ways that mattered to those evaluating him. All the hard work had paid off. It was a beautiful illustration of a team effort. My heart was immensely grateful to the staff of Geisinger Medical Center for their determination and dedicated approach to Taylor's care.

The day before we left, the first nurse who had cared for Taylor on the Special Care Unit wrote him a farewell message in a journal we kept for visitors so that they could leave messages for Taylor. She wrote,

I hope one day soon you open your eyes and that you are able to read this on your own. I wish you and your family the best of luck for a full recovery. I truly believe with prayers, a positive attitude, and the love and support of your family you will be able to move mountains. Stay strong and don't ever give up. Your nurse from SCU, Amanda.

Two days before Taylor would turn twenty-two, we left for his new home. We packed his belongings from the hospital, which were very few, and brought along a bag from home. We had been told to pack comfortable clothing for Taylor, which included boxers, sweatpants, T-shirts, and socks. Taylor remained still; to our knowledge, he was totally unaware of what was taking place.

Taylor was loaded onto the gurney for the ambulance. I recall that the sheets that were wrapped around Taylor were pink for breast cancer awareness. The drivers were very professional and understood that we were worried about Taylor's safety outside the hospital walls. Keith and Tanner had said good-bye the night before, and Avery came over to see off his brother and me. It was a painful and tear-filled morning. Avery had been by Taylor's side every day since his fall. Avery had spent many hours with Taylor when everyone else had gone home to rest. I was going with Taylor, but his dad and brothers had to let him go and trust that he would be well cared for—not only by me, but by people who were strangers to all of us. I could sense their agony and felt a deep responsibility about the tasks that they had entrusted to me.

Avery wrote a post on Facebook the day that Taylor went to Bryn Mawr:

Sometimes a bittersweet goodbye is necessary in order to embrace a new beginning. Taylor is on his way to a rehab facility in Philadelphia right now. While another fragment of my already broken heart was torn apart, I know that with time all things heal- especially our loved one. Today is the first step in the 6–8 week chapter of Taylor's recovery; I continue to put my faith in Tayl and have had glimpses of his strength over the weekend. He opened his eyes and connected with all members of our family for a very brief moment; while he's still not awake this gave us something to hold onto for weeks to come.

I'm grateful for the strength we've had as a family, no strength is more powerful than that held in the heart and mind. I thank you all for the unending support and providing words of encouragement and love in order to help us dig deeper and find strength we didn't know we withheld. I'm confident that he will continue to beat the odds one step at a time and slowly work his way back to us. Another big week is in store for Tayl; keep him in your daily thoughts. While the past week has proved we live in a wicked world, we can still hold onto the love we have for one another, remember to hold those you love close, and remind them of the love you have for them that will never cease.

A big shout-out to the team in Geisinger's special care unit, as they fell in love with Taylor and want nothing but the best for him- as do all of us. I'll try to provide an update towards the end of the week. Until then our family will continue to hold our heads high, even when our hearts have fallen below our ankles.

The ride to Malvern was long, and many of the roads were full of twists and turns. I was far more exhausted than I had realized, and I was glad that my mom had decided to keep me company for the drive. We were traveling over a lot of back roads and unfamiliar highways. It was an overcast and especially cloudy day. Despite the fog, we tried to stay within eyesight of the ambulance, but eventually got separated. It felt good to be out driving and seeing the world again. With a few exceptions, I had taken the same roads daily for almost a month. I was ready for a change. *I was ready for Taylor to have a new beginning.* As scary as the unknown felt, I knew it was better than a nursing home and I was grateful.

We arrived at Bryn Mawr Rehabilitation Hospital in the early evening. When we were just a few minutes away, I said to my mom, "What if I made a mistake?" She said, "Then I guess we pack him up and go elsewhere," and smiled; and then she said, "You didn't make a mistake, honey." As soon as we walked through the automatic doors, we were greeted with the friendliest hello. The two women who were sitting in the welcome area both had beautiful warm smiles. We told them we were looking for Taylor, who we hoped was already there. We were told he was getting settled in, and they directed us to his unit. As we were leaving one of the ladies smiled and said, "You made a good choice in coming here." We both believed her.

One of the first things I noticed as we were walking toward the elevator is that there were bright, but different forms of art along each wall. There was something about the presence of art that felt important to me in regard to Taylor's surroundings. My first impressions of Bryn Mawr were very good.

Taylor's unit was called the Maple Unit. We went upstairs to find Taylor, who was getting settled in. He was to be situated in an ICU-like setting. He was placed in one of five rooms that had a glass area which provided a constant view. He was directly across from the nurses' station and could be watched at all times. The main reason for his placement in that area was that he still had the tracheostomy and still required being connected to oxygen at night. Everyone on the Maple Unit required special care and supervision, but Taylor's physical condition meant that he required more intensive care.

The first minutes of becoming familiar with the unit were terrible and hopeful all at once. A brain injury unit is not like other types of rehabilitation unit; it is quieter than one would imagine and even more so in the evening. The Maple Unit was a very unfamiliar place. I had a profound awareness of feeling like a fish out of water. I did not take time to take in my setting or truly look at any other patients; I looked down the corridor at Taylor and his nurses, and was unable to take in anything else. My vision and focus were limited; looking back, I think it was my mind's way of blocking out things that would have been too

104

overwhelming for me all at once. I felt as if most of my senses had been temporarily turned off.

As we came down the hallway, two nurses introduced themselves. These two women would come to mean a great deal to Taylor and our family. Their names were Dena and Kristine, although for all intents and purposes they could be called the "dynamic duo." It was the end of Kristine's shift, but she stayed a little late to meet her new patient, Taylor. She later wrote these words about that night:

> *I totally remember the first time I saw Taylor. He came at the end of my shift. His face and eyes were swollen but he was so handsome anyway. You were very quiet but I knew you "carried a big stick." I remember explaining to you guys the routine of the unit and you asked many great questions. I remember opening Taylor's eyes when I was doing the assessment. I needed to evaluate his pupils, and when I pulled up the right eyelid, he turned his eye and looked right at me. I said, "Look at that, he is in there. He is looking at us, he is so in there."*

She also commented on his beautiful blue eyes and handsome features. I did not know until later that she was also the mother of three boys, but I did know that she and Dena both made me feel that Taylor was in good hands. My mom's nursing experience also made her feel certain that Taylor was going to be well cared for. I had confidence in leaving Taylor to get myself settled in, and that confidence surprised me.

It had been a long ride. It had been a long day. It had been a long week, and we were just short of a very long month. I was so tired. My nerves were shot and I knew I needed a break. I was actually craving quiet. My mind had not stopped racing since I was awakened on November 22; twenty-four days had passed since then.

My mom helped me get settled into my room at The Laurels, Bryn Mawr's visitors' residence. She said her good-byes to Taylor and I took her to the train station. She had been with us for a few weeks, and it was difficult to let her go back home. There was also a part of me that needed solitude. I could not remember many times over the weeks since the accident that I had been alone for more than a few minutes. I was ready to simply be with my own thoughts and feelings, but I was also very afraid. At the time I felt like a baby bird that was ready to fly on her own, but uncertain of whether her wings would work. I would experience the first night of a deep type of loneliness that I have become accustomed to in the weeks and months to follow.

After seeing off my mom, I returned to the Maple Unit. I had just touched the surface of taking in the surroundings. I spoke with Dena, and was relieved to see that many of the beds were set up almost like playpens. The difference was that the beds were fully enclosed. There was netting and rails that completely enclosed the patient. One of my deepest fears had been that Taylor would fall out of bed in his unconscious stirring and be unprotected. It is interesting to note that one might be tempted to think, "What if Taylor stands up? What if he wakes up and wonders what is happening?" In Taylor's case, neither of those what-ifs were even concerns. Taylor was very weak. His left side could not be used; and his waking, when and if it came, would be very slow. I would come to learn that Bryn Mawr was a very safe place and that Dena was a safe person.

I went back to my room and became familiar with the lodging area as much as my state of mind would allow. The room I was in had two twin beds and two nightstands as well as a simple bathroom. There was a communal kitchen area. Having reached the point of absolute exhaustion, I fell asleep largely unaware of what the next few months would be like. I was about to learn more than I ever realized about a subject I had never even heard of before a few weeks ago. I would quickly become a student of traumatic brain injury and the sounds of silence that surround it.

Part II: Malvern

Chapter Eight
Where Tragedy and Triumph Coexist
December 18, 2012

I did not know much about brain injury rehabilitation before now, but what I knew so far I had learned through various sources. We had been given some reading material through Geisinger Medical Center, and we had looked up information online as well as having discussions with various people in the profession or with those who had experienced traumatic brain injury in a family member.

Once we had made the final decision about Taylor's new facility, we found out as much as we could about Bryn Mawr. I knew that Taylor would participate in a variety of therapies and that there was a team who would be with him each step of the way. The team included three doctors: Drew Lynch, the attending neurologist; an internal medicine specialist; and a neuropsychologist. Dr. Lynch was featured on the videos we had viewed, so I knew his name and I knew that he looked both wise and kind. Beyond that, I knew very little.

I woke up early the next morning, probably around 5 or 6 a.m. With my newly found habit of inefficient sleep, I had begun to take Tylenol PM[9] or melatonin[10] when needed to help me rest. The night before, I needed the extra help drifting off to sleep because I was in a new environment, and I awoke feeling thankful that I felt refreshed. At this point, anything beyond four hours of shuteye was good.

I called Dena, the third-shift nurse, almost as soon as my eyes were open. She informed me that Taylor had been given a protective net bed in the middle of the night. This bed was a regular hospital bed with four canopy-type poles. Playpen-type netting was attached between each pole, and there was a cover over the top. The patient was literally zipped in.

When I had left the unit the night before, Taylor had been placed in a standard hospital bed. Dena had noticed that Taylor was moving

---

[9] Tylenol PM is the trade name for a combination of acetaminophen (a pain reliever) and diphenhydramine (an antihistamine that makes people drowsy).

[10] Melatonin is a hormone that regulates the sleep-wake cycle in humans and other mammals. It can be taken by mouth in capsules or tablets as a sleep aid.

around frequently, and she was concerned that he might end up outside the bed. It would not have been possible for him to stand up or get out of the bed on his own; he did not have that kind of strength. He could, however, have unknowingly positioned his body in a way that ended with him on the floor. I was relieved that he was being watched so well and that Dena clearly felt good about the level of activity he was displaying. Dena had years of experience in nursing patients with traumatic brain injury, so she knew that Taylor's movement was a good step in the right direction.

Bryn Mawr wasted no time leading Taylor to the next phase of recovery. I had been told the night before that Dr. Lynch and his team would make rounds early in the morning, around 8 o'clock, and that I should try to come over to meet him. Feeling anxious, I showered and dressed quickly, grabbed a cup of coffee, and headed over to see Taylor. I was pleased by the idea of continuing daily rounds. It was a way that I felt helped everyone within the hospital staff to be on the same page. I felt positive about the team approach that I was seeing.

As I entered the Maple Unit, I was buzzed in through the locked doors and began to walk toward Taylor's room. I was astonished by what I saw—Taylor was sitting in his own wheelchair! The outdated and unpleasant-looking plastic helmet that he had worn at Geisinger Medical Center was replaced with something more pleasing to the eye. The new helmet was made of soft denim that was fitted over his whole head. The helmet was snug, but not tight. A Velcro strap was attached from side to side under the chin. The back of the helmet covered his entire rear hairline, and the center of the helmet came down to cover his ears and entire head. The helmet's top stopped just below the front hairline. Because I absolutely hated the plastic helmet he had been wearing, seeing the new helmet gave me immediate pleasure. Taylor's appearance was improving from what he had looked like during the early days following his accident.

Taylor's wheelchair was positioned similar to a lounging chair, as distinct from a standard upright wheelchair. Part of what I had learned in researching the rehabilitation center is that each patient is given a wheelchair customized for his or her body. Although sitting was not something that Taylor had achieved on his own, it was a step nonetheless, and it was nice to see him in the chair. *It represented progress.*

Taylor was not only sitting up in the wheelchair, but also his eyes were open. They remained open as I moved towards him. *One one-thousand, two one-thousand, three one-thousand, four one-thousand, five one-thousand, six one-thousand, seven one-thousand, eight one-thousand* . . . for at least the eight seconds it took me to walk down the hallway, Taylor kept his eyes open. His eyes were not fixed on anything. If he saw me coming, he did not give any indication. His eyes remained open as I bent down in front of him and said, *"Good morning, Taylor, it's Mom."* I gave him a kiss on the cheek. His normally clean-shaven face had not been touched with a razor in a month. His brothers had joked about it, but I also think that it bothered them that Taylor was not able to care for himself in this way.

Taylor's blue eyes were devoid of any expression or thought, but they were open. The eyes that had previously been bright and alert were now dim. The old saying, "The lights are on, but no one is home," took on a true meaning. I could not tell whether Taylor was looking at me, but I was certain that he was not *seeing* me. If he held any recognition of who I am, it did not show. His expression looked empty. I cannot explain how it felt to see Taylor in this new state. Wonder and astonishment were the primary emotions that I was feeling. I was happy to see Taylor's eyes open; I just wished that I could tell what he was experiencing. I don't think he was thinking or processing any kind of thoughts, but that is something we will never know. This morning was the longest amount of time that Taylor's eyes had stayed open since his accident. No one was forcing them to stay that way, and despite the fact that his expression was empty, *I felt a sense of hope.*

Something that I was acutely aware of is that these moments with Taylor were a gift. After sitting next to him hour after hour, day by day, week by week, and seeing very little happen, to see him open his eyes was quite incredible. I remained guarded about my ability to celebrate the moment, though. I chose instead to quietly cherish this small victory that I had witnessed.

One thing that immediately happens in a rehabilitation setting is that the staff begins to encourage consciousness in many ways. A person like Taylor would have been getting a minimum, but healthful amount of stimulation every day. He was also placed in a typical recliner for at least thirty waking minutes every six or so hours in the hospital. Taylor was slowly being beckoned back to life. It is like a far-off whispering of a gentle friend who might say, "I know you are tired, Taylor, but can you wake up for me?" There is an art and a science to the stirring of someone who has gone to another place for so long.

We were constantly referring to charts, not only to understand where Taylor was, but also to truthfully and effectively communicate it to others. If we said, "Taylor's eyes are open," the typical response would be, "Then isn't he awake?" At this stage, Taylor was coming out of the coma and entering a vegetative state. I became aware of the common misconception that once a person is in a vegetative state they can't come out of it.

I was slowly learning to stay in the moment at hand. If I wanted, I could expend a lot of emotional energy looking backward or forward, but it wasn't worth it. There were too many minutiae surrounding everything. It is hard to explain, but I learned to take in what was happening, and while always wanting more and trying to think ahead, I also had to be in the moment as it took place. My mind had to be as clear and present as possible.

Everything that had happened, was happening, and could possibly happen felt like an ocean of events, thoughts, and possibilities. I needed to see the ocean before us in the form of single streams leading to rivers that eventually lead outward into the sea. If I looked at it all as an ocean, I would not be able to swim in it. The streams and rivers were far more manageable to my thought process than the sea of unknowns that was in front of us.

I noticed at some point in the morning that in the room next to Taylor, there were a large bunch of balloons, Pittsburgh Steelers decorations, and lots of what looked like average high school boy stuff. The balloons said, "Sweet 16" and "Happy Birthday." There was nothing that felt sweet or happy about seeing the decorations in that setting; it felt only profoundly sad. Our family would come to know these neighbors; our sons would become roommates. Together we would share moments no one can or would ever want to imagine. We would also share in moments that made us smile.

What I realized while reading the words "Happy Birthday" on the balloons in the room next to Taylor's was that we were going to be celebrating Taylor's birthday here too. I could see this boy's mother and her sheer exhaustion. How did they get here? How did we come to this pain-filled place as mothers? *When people looked at me, did they see a person whose eyes spoke of the sadness and brokenness that I saw in this mother's eyes?*

All mothers have fears. It happened to me at some point shortly after my sons were born. You experience the euphoria and miracle of new life, but at some point (at least for me), you feel afraid. That is why new mothers sometimes say they watched their baby sleep, or they checked on him or her over and over again. It is the place of recognition that we are all vulnerable. Over the years, my mind has played out all kinds of scenarios. As a mother, I was endlessly aware that something could happen to my sons. There is a list of fears that lie in some place we hope we never have to explore. You learn to push aside thoughts of disease, death, harm, abuse, kidnapping, horrible accidents—on and on goes the list. Mothers could never live in that place where constant thoughts of the worst-imaginable things run over and over again. In all of my imaginings, in my worst thoughts that would sneak up on me as a parent, I had never explored traumatic brain injury. I did not even know what those words meant.

The day was full of assessments and periods of rest for Taylor. One of the first evaluations was finding out where Taylor was on the coma recovery scale. For this assessment, the physician evaluates whether the patient is able to track things with their eyes; whether they respond to sound; what kind of motor skills they have; and their response to various stimuli. Taylor was in a vegetative state. *It might not sound like it, but this was progress.*

It would be the first of endless hours and days spent with the special crew of the Maple Unit. Taylor would undertake what would look like very simple small tasks to you and me, but they were very challenging for him. Things like being placed in the wheelchair; keeping his head upright; and responding in some small way to simple commands drained him completely. Taylor was simply a presence in what was happening, but his mind was not there. Taylor was on this journey for the long haul, and how he would come out of it was an absolute mystery.

The extent to which someone recovers from an injury like Taylor's has many variables. We were told over and over again that every injury is different and so is every recovery. Some of the factors affecting recovery from a TBI are:

1.) How long was the person in a coma before entering the vegetative state?
2.) What is going on medically in other areas of their body?
3.) What was the extent of their initial injury?
4.) Is the present injury the patient's first traumatic brain injury?

Some of these factors cannot be known or identified initially, so as the person transitions from phase to phase—or in some cases, doesn't progress—more can be determined.

The rehabilitation plan is not simple. I looked at it like a puzzle, because I am the kind of person who needs to associate something I don't fully grasp with something that I do understand. In the beginning, a good therapeutic team breaks down the recovery process into bits and pieces that families can understand. Recovering from traumatic brain injury takes millions of tiny things happening, little by little, piece by piece. Recovery is similar to the jigsaw puzzles with thousands upon thousands of pieces. For now, we were simply being shown the corners. The four corners of the puzzle are: physical, occupational, speech, and cognitive therapy. All that can happen in recovery starts at these corners in the hope that the puzzle will be completed piece by piece. The fifth element in recovery is recreational therapy, which is introduced further down the road.

I had envisioned what I had known of rehabilitation. The times I had been in a rehabilitation hospital prior to Taylor's accident could be counted on one hand, and the visits were for issues like hip replacements. *There was no comparison.* I thought that rehabilitation meant a lot of pushing and challenging someone to go to their limits and beyond, but here all of those things were spoken quietly, tenderly, and with great patience. Every word was well thought out, and phrases were spoken simply, directly, and one at a time. Not only was Taylor treated with tenderness and gentleness, but so was I. The experience that the staff had at Bryn Mawr had given them the knowledge to know that most families coming here were living a new nightmare and had barely touched the surface of their pain.

I had no previous knowledge of the ways in which someone is stimulated in regard to coming out of a coma. My paternal grandmother had been in a coma when I was in college, and years later she recalled my singing "Amazing Grace" at her bedside. The memory still makes me laugh because she never really liked my singing. I was eighteen years old and truthfully did not retain any knowledge of how she emerged from her coma. Her coma had occurred under far different circumstances from Taylor's and so had her recovery, which had been full and complete.
Kristine, one of Taylor's nurses, best explained the process of stimulating or waking someone from a coma this way:

> We are always "trying" different ways to stimulate someone, and then we stick with which one we find for that person and use it. If someone is still in coma and not responding to verbal or touch, we can use noxious stimuli. *Noxious* refers to smells and annoying stimulation like nail bed pressure or sternal pressure, which is somewhat painful, but if it elicits a response we then have something to work with. If they are still not responding, we know that we are not there yet.

I had previously learned that for Taylor to just sit upright and breathe on his own was the equivalent of his body's running a marathon. Every tiny action was exhausting to his brain, and the body responds to what the mind has to say. Your brain is in charge of so much that takes place in your body. If you are ever in this setting, you will notice that before and after any physical exertion, the patient's blood pressure is taken. Taylor was coming back to himself in a more complete and aware way, but it was going to be a very slow process.

It would take days for my eyes to adjust to what I was seeing, and days for my ears to accept what I was hearing. But what would take the longest was for my heart to understand that this is the path for Taylor and many others that life had led them to.

Sometimes I tried to imagine myself as a journalist. I was imagining Lisa Ling from CNN walking through the halls of Bryn Mawr, trying to understand every person and every story behind their injury. There were so many different stages of recovery taking place. Some people were speaking while others' speech made no sense. Some people were walking with a slight limp while others were always in wheelchairs. Some appeared very confused while others seemed to be convinced nothing was wrong. There were fascinating bits of information and incredible transformations that I was going to witness. There was also an undeniable presence of heartbreak. There were stories of both tragedy and triumph in the halls of our temporary home.

On the far left of the critical care rooms was a man who had obviously been in the military. *He did not speak.* His feet were poised in a ballerina toe-like position and they seemed frozen that way. His arms were bent tightly against his chest, and his fingers curved in a rigid manner. He always looked as if he were inhaling, but never seemed to release his breath. His eyes were almost always wide open as if he were in fear. There were posters of him and his young lovely wife before the accident in his room. I later learned that she was balancing going to school full time and living far away. She often was his sole visitor, as it had been a while since his accident and they were far from home. I never knew what brought him to Bryn Mawr, but I found myself thinking about it a lot.

Next to his room was a young and lovely girl who was in an upright wheelchair. She had beautiful long hair. She spoke clearly, but the order and content of her words made no sense. Her physical recovery had seemed quick from the outside, but inside her mind there was obvious turmoil. She spoke in an angry tone, with a steady flow of nasty words. She wore puffy white protective gloves over her hands so that she would not harm herself when she thrashed about. She was highly agitated, and her behavior was tough to control. She sometimes caused her wheelchair to lift off the floor, but the staff member with her was always patient with her. My understanding was that her accident involved her photographing a train, and somehow the train struck her on the side of the head. Quite honestly, I found her behavior at the time frightening, and wondered whether my son would develop that type of emotional outburst.

One of my most distinct early memories of Bryn Mawr is that of a young man sitting in the common area. His friends were visiting and he was talking with them. It was not a conversation that held any depth or real meaning, and the only part of it that made any sense was the words his friends would say. They were playing a simple card game and he was merely trying to follow along. At some point during the game, the patient undid the strap on his helmet and took it off. The entire area above his right eye to the upper corner of his head was gone. Where his skull had previously been rounded and protecting his brain, there was a huge gap. It looked as if someone had completely crushed the right side of his head, or stepped on it and left a permanent indentation.[11]

I would come in time to know a few of these families by name and their stories in more detail, but for now they were all strangers. There was nothing in my life that could have prepared me for the devastation I was seeing. *It was a frightening place to be thrown into.*

---

[11] At this point Taylor's head was actually still quite swollen, and I had not been exposed to the sunken area of his skull in the same way.

The thought of Keith, Avery, and Tanner being introduced to these sights in a few days was difficult. I viewed each of them as emotionally mature, and they had always been defined that way, but this situation was different. I did not have to imagine how it would feel to them. When the brain is broken or damaged, the entire individual changes from the inside outward. There was no way to escape from Taylor's situation.

The first full day of rehab was winding down. The final activity of the day would be Taylor's bath. This would be the first time since his fall that he would have something other than a sponge bath.

Taylor had been assigned a new sidekick named José. José was a nursing assistant who worked in Taylor's section. He is a man who takes great pride in his work and his profession. One of the first things he said to me was that he was going to take care of Taylor as if he were caring for his own brother. He told me in his slight Spanish accent, "Don't worry, Nicole. I will take care of your son." I gave him the baby wash I had purchased to use for Taylor's shower. His skin had become toughened, and I hoped that gentle soap and lotion would help. Taylor had been the kind of guy who always wanted to smell good, and I hoped he would not mind the Johnson & Johnson baby soap. Soon his friends would ship Old Spice and more age-appropriate toiletries his way.

Taylor was placed in a special chair used for safely showering people in an inactive nonresponsive condition. José undressed him while making sure that the curtains were closed and that not even I could see Taylor. He had assured me that Taylor would be okay. He explained that he would not get the incisions all over his head wet, but instead they would be gently washed along with the rest of his body. I smiled, imagining how good it would feel to have warm water covering Taylor's body after so many weeks of sponge baths. I also liked the fact that Taylor's privacy was important to José. Underneath everything that was occurring, I knew it was important to remember to protect Taylor's dignity as much as possible.

My mind drifted back for a few moments to Taylor's return from work one day about a year before his accident. He had spent his workday in a small, hot, and dirty crawl space. He was covered from head to toe in black dust. Even his face was coated with grime. It had been a long and difficult day, and he told me he had to shower before eating, but also let me know how hungry he was, in a grumpy tone. A few minutes later, he came out looking and smelling fresh and clean. That memory made me smile. We get so caught up sometimes in the big events of life, I was thankful for the memory of this little everyday occurrence.

When Taylor was finished in the shower, I applied lotion to his arms and legs and then tucked him in. Taylor did not have to wear his helmet in bed, but he was given a pair of white protective gloves to wear during sleep. There was not only the danger that he might scratch or hurt himself; his head was also full of scars that were trying to heal, and the plastic piece of his trachea tube could actually be pulled out quite easily. The gloves were large mittens that covered his entire hands; there was a trick to getting them on, not having them too tight, and making sure they would stay in place. José took care of all that. After sitting with Taylor for about half an hour, my own exhaustion set in and I returned to my room at the Laurels.

Truthfully, I don't remember falling asleep that night, but I know that the fact that Taylor was turning twenty-two the next day weighed heavily on my mind. I always celebrated the birth of my sons by taking time to remember with them and sometimes just in my head, the day that they were born. I was keenly aware that this day could feel a lot worse than it did. Taylor was not "with us" in the sense that any of us wanted, but the alternative was that he might not have been with us at all. In death, there is no place of hoping or dreaming about what someone can do or become—and Taylor was alive. *I reminded myself of the power of hope.*

The phrase that hung above Taylor's bed at Geisinger read, "Let him sleep for when he wakes he shall move mountains" still felt true. But now he also needed to awaken more fully so that the mountains could be moved. I knew that Taylor had always been a person of determination and great resolve. I just hoped he would be able to reach those qualities within himself.

119

Chapter Nine
McChicken
December 19–December 23, 2012

Taylor had been delivered by cesarean section two weeks after his due date. He weighed 9 pounds, 11 ounces, and was 21 inches long. It was a long labor and did not go quite as planned, due mainly to Taylor's size. I was lying in a recovery room not really aware of my surroundings, when suddenly Keith bent down next to my bed, whispering, *"I can't stay in here long, but the nurse said I could come in and tell you how beautiful our son is."* Taylor would be the first of three sons, and we fell immediately in love with his gentle nature. He had beautiful rosy pink cheeks that filled out perfectly. We brought him home from the hospital on the date of our one-year wedding anniversary, two days before Christmas. We were in love with each other and our little boy. He was the best Christmas present we ever received.

For many years of my children's lives, I would tell them on each birthday the story of the day they were born. Twenty-two years later, Taylor's birthday brought me to a kind of day I had never imagined . . . a birthday when I could not feel an ounce of joy; however, I did feel gratitude. Taylor was alive, but I missed him more and more every day, and his actual birthday made those feelings more profound. I never imagined that December 19 could be filled with anything but happiness, but now it was full of ever-increasing sadness.

His nurse Kristine made him a sign that said, "I am 22 years old today," and hung it on the back of his wheelchair. The gesture that was made by creating and displaying that sign was something I don't think I could have done, but it was something that was needed. When I saw the sign, I felt grateful for Taylor's life. I also felt grateful for the acknowledgment of his birth. The haunting reminders of almost losing him were still very present, and the fact that he was alive was a gift. A large part of moving ahead is based on a theory that you cannot get stuck where you are. We had to keep on living and constructing ways for Taylor to live again as well. Acknowledging and in some small way celebrating his birth was important. It was one of the many ways this incredible nurse and team at Bryn Mawr would win our affections.

It is almost embarrassing for me to admit, but I wanted Taylor to be showered with love and gifts on his birthday. I wasn't exactly acknowledging the fact that he wouldn't realize someone had given him a gift, but I didn't care. Wishing someone would send him balloons or a card was just another way I was dealing with my emotions. I felt as if he had been forgotten, but that simply was not true. I was in a place of immense pain and the sadness was beginning to take over. In fact, on his birthday many people in our small community wore special shirts that said "Team Taylor" on the front, and on the back, "Beating the Odds, One Step at a Time." A longtime friend of Taylor's named Shelby had spearheaded the creation and sale of these T-shirts as a way for people to express their support for Taylor in his recovery. My own exhaustion and disconnection from the world outside Taylor's injury contributed to the loneliness and isolation that I was feeling. It had been only a matter of weeks, but I was yearning for some type of normalcy. The year before, I had stopped by an informal gathering that Taylor and his friends were having when he turned twenty-one. He was laughing and smiling; he was on the brink of adulthood and I knew he had so many exciting things ahead. I longed for him to feel the same way this year, but I also knew that wish wasn't coming true.

All day long, I thought about what I could do to celebrate Taylor. *How could I give something to him?* Although it could be argued that I was giving him the most precious gift I had to offer—my presence—I began to formulate a plan and was very much in need of a distraction. Since we were situated right outside Philly, there were stores nearby that I could venture out to.

Before leaving, like always, I would attend some of Taylor's therapy sessions. Upon arrival at Bryn Mawr, I spoke with the caseworker who oversaw much of the daily operations, and she helped with choosing the various sessions I could attend. The first of the day was physical therapy with a woman named Sue. This is how Sue would later recall it to me:

> *The first time I laid eyes on Taylor, our transporter (the person who brings patients who are not ambulatory to place A or B) had dropped him off in the gym. I knew who he was right away; he*

was young, he matched the description of what I had read in his chart. He was sitting up in a red tilt-in-space wheelchair, wearing a helmet to protect his skull, grey sweatpants, and a navy blue T-shirt. The chair had a note taped to it, which read, "Today is my 22nd birthday!" I recognized the handwriting as Kristine's (Taylor's nurse). She knew that I had him for therapy, and that I insist on the singing of a loud off-key enthusiastic Happy Birthday song whenever a patient or staff member on our unit is celebrating a birthday. Taylor's eyes were intermittently half-open, and he was just beginning to interact with his environment, I highly doubt he had much awareness of the fact that it was his birthday or that we were singing to him.

As we sang, I remember sizing him up; I noticed he was a pretty big guy, maybe about 5'10" or so, and that his upper body still had a lot of muscle to it. (When people have prolonged stays in the hospital, and are low-level for a longer period of time, they tend to lose that size, especially on their weaker side). Taylor was restless and moving his right side a lot, his left not so much. As we sang, I was mentally trying to figure out the safest and best way to transfer him. Meeting someone for the first time, you have to get that comfort level with him or her, as well as him or her feeling it with you.

I think I was getting ready to lift Taylor onto the bolster, which is about the size and shape of a barrel turned on its side. In therapy, we use it for a lot of different things; for Taylor, I wanted to see if the gentle rocking would calm his restlessness, see how he interacted with motion and changes in his environment. I wanted to check out his balance reactions, see what he would do. As we were preparing, I noticed a petite quiet woman about my age walk in, looking somewhat overwhelmed, but calm. I knew instantly that this was Mom. It can be a little intimidating to treat someone for the first time and have a family member present when you're trying to assess the patient and situation, not knowing what little surprises they may throw your

123

way. You don't want to be caught off guard. Part of therapy for brain injury is that it can be unpredictable at times, especially that first session, as you're trying to figure the person out, and decide on the best approach.

I introduced myself, and asked her if she had any questions. She didn't at that moment, but I knew the questions would come. I didn't want to frighten or overwhelm her, so I think I asked her something along the lines of how much education did she have regarding brain injury and where Taylor was in his recovery. I don't remember her exact response, but I remember telling her I'd explain what I was doing, and to tell me if it was too much. I explained to her what I was doing and why, I remember sitting behind Taylor as he sat on the bolster (kind of looks like riding a horse), and holding him, and while I was explaining things to Nicole, I remember thinking it's got to be so weird for her to see a stranger holding her son (who was intermittently sleeping or gently thrashing around while this was happening) in a way that's not safe for her to do just yet, or for a long time. I can talk a lot about brain injury and behavior and recovery, and sometimes too much information can be overload; and Nicole looked like she'd been through the wringer for the past month, so I remember trying to choose my words carefully.

In any situation, people hear with different ears than you do with the things you say. I think I told Nicole about the Rancho scale, that Taylor looked like a Rancho III, probably getting ready to transition into an IV. I remember hoping she'd be okay with one thing I felt it was important for her to know . . . that things at this stage are probably going to look a lot worse before they start to look better.

Then, I got him up off the bolster, wrapped his left ankle in an Ace wrap, and had him put his right arm around the tech that was helping us. I got on Taylor's left side and assisted him with taking a step with his left leg, then quickly blocking his knee so it wouldn't buckle, and then encouraging him to step with his right leg. He did. After several steps, which were taxing for all 3 of us, we sat him down in the chair and I looked at Nicole. I remember wanting her to see something positive, as I knew that the other stuff I had been telling her can be overwhelming and heavy. She had tears in her eyes.

As I read Sue's words about that day, each moment came back with force. I can see her holding and rocking Taylor. She was very strong and seemed confident in the role she played, which I valued. Seeing her interact with Taylor, I immediately felt like she was a good fit for him. Taylor would have liked her in another setting . . . *and I always wished we were in one.* To see Taylor "walk" in some sort of fashion on his birthday made me feel as if he had been born all over again. He was essentially going through the various developmental stages of a young child.

I wish I could paint a picture that would tell you how the assisted walking looks. It takes a lot of skill and strength on the part of everyone involved. Physical therapy is an art. It is an art that requires being in tune with patients and their needs and level of endurance even when they cannot tell you. It is a "one foot in front of the other" process, in slow motion and having to fully rely on someone else's strength and ability.

Taylor was exhausted after the therapy session and was taken back to his room to rest. As soon as he was settled in, I left. Setting my GPS to Target, I drove off on my mission. I bought some winter-scene wrapping paper, snowflake decorations, and a small silver tinsel Christmas tree about ten inches high.

My plan was to create a space in Taylor's room for photos of him and his family and friends, as well as a place to hang cards or words of encouragement that might come in the mail. I also wanted to remind Taylor visually of the time of year. I hoped that these things would reach some part of him and I knew they also helped me. If and when he could focus and his vision would allow it, I wanted him to see that he was loved. As I returned to decorate his room, I made sure to set up everything on the right side of his bed so that it was visible from where he lay. Along with my decorations, Bryn Mawr had provided an information-gathering sheet. It was similar to something you might fill out on your first day of school. The various areas read:

My name is . . .
My friends call me . . .
My hobbies are . . .
The people who live with me are . . .

Each area on the sheet allowed the staff to get to know a little bit more about Taylor. I put a few photos of him that I knew he loved on the poster board. All those things made me feel good and productive. Taylor's room looked and felt a little less like a hospital room and more like a personal space.

Sue would be with Taylor again the next day. Before heading to Bryn Mawr, we had been told to pack T-shirts and comfortable clothes as well as making sure that he had a good pair of sneakers. I tried to pack things that were well-worn and already broken in. Among the things I packed was a "Class of 2009" T-shirt that Taylor's high school graduating class had created. On the back was Taylor's nickname, "BING." Taylor had been wearing that shirt while heading into physical therapy. When Sue read it, she asked me if she could call Taylor "Bing." So many of Taylor's friends called him that, so I knew that he would approve. At this point, I was excited to see what this new session would bring, and I was really anxious about Keith, Tanner, and Avery coming on the weekend. The session was much the same as the previous day. Sue did a lot of maneuvering Taylor's torso into a more curved position by guiding his upper body. She also bent and stretched his legs. All his muscles were stiff and they seemed to welcome the movement.

As the days passed by, I was familiarizing myself more with the staff while also continuing to weave myself into the new surroundings. Taylor's nurses and therapists never changed much, so I was happy to build relationships with just a few people who were caring for my son.

They were creating a cocoon of sorts for us, but mainly for Taylor. In order to heal, he needed to relax and trust what was going on around him.

I met Donna, the speech therapist, who made me a bit apprehensive at first. She reminded me of a strict schoolteacher, and I was not always sure how to interpret her words. More importantly, I wasn't sure whether she and Taylor could establish a connection. The next therapist on the team was Kelly, his occupational therapist. Donna was experienced and middle-aged, whereas Kelly looked young and very innocent. There was also Lauren, a primary physical therapist whom I had met briefly but was away for the holiday; and Josh, who assisted in the therapy room. Each of these people had different approaches, but it was clear that they took their role in their patient's recovery very seriously. Learning so many new names was a challenge for me. I often felt embarrassed because I could not recall a nurse or staff member's name. They would get jumbled in my head, but the thought of putting them in the notebook I carried never occurred to me, although I might have needed a photo next to their name as well.

One evening I went down to the patient cafeteria, which was on another floor, as it had advertised a Christmas concert. The patients who were present in the cafeteria did not have brain injuries; they were on the units that served stroke patients, spinal cord injuries, or amputees. The choir that was singing was young and lovely. Their voices had beauty and a purity that was moving and exquisite. They did not sing many songs, but as they did, the tears fell down my face softly and quietly. The songs were all holiday selections, but they were perfectly chosen for the place in which they were being sung. There was seriousness and beauty in each of them. This concert provided a brief, but meaningful moment of reflection for me.

Numerous thoughts were running through my mind as I sat and listened. I knew I would be incapable of getting into any kind of holiday spirit, but I also had a sense of gratitude for the new beginning that Taylor had been given. One of the servers was a woman in her fifties or sixties. She had bleached blonde hair and wore a dark shade of lipstick. She noticed my tears and offered me a soda, which I gratefully accepted.

127

When it was over and she came to get my glass, she hugged me and asked whether I was okay. It was a simple but warm gesture. I would find out weeks later that her son had passed away a few years earlier. She never told me how he died, but she understood a mother's grief.

The rigors of therapy started without much delay. Three areas formed the primary focus at the beginning of Taylor's treatment: physical therapy, occupational therapy, and speech therapy. The cognitive sessions would come later as he made progress. Each of these therapies offered a different path for Taylor's brain and gave him direction on relearning much of what had been lost from the fall.

The primary focus of physical therapy is to build a patient's strength, muscle tone, flexibility, and balance. Much of the focus is placed on the lower part of the body, addressing specific issues with the legs and the person's core muscles. Taylor's gait was abnormal due to his overall weakness, loss of coordination, and just the fact that his brain had in a sense "forgotten" how to walk. He also had the impairment on his left side that seemed to throw off everything else.

Occupational therapy (OT) focuses on the physical person along with their cognitive and visual perceptual skills. Initially, Taylor's OT involved using his hands to pick things up and grasp or hold various objects. The occupational therapist works to help people perform actions that are common in their daily routine. Eventually the tasks would increase, but they started out small. When initial assessments are made, they are made in regard to activities like dressing or brushing one's teeth. Patients are measured on the percentage of these actions they can do on their own. At this stage, Taylor required maximum assistance in all areas.

Speech therapy was very interesting to me. I thought, *"How can someone have speech therapy when they cannot talk?"* But it is about so much more than talking. The speech therapist needs three qualities, on a level far beyond average; they must have skill, patience, and creativity. The speech therapist or speech pathologist helps individuals find various avenues of communication. They encourage communication in various forms, whether written, verbal, sign language, or keyboarding. They also evaluate how well the muscles in the patient's mouth and throat are working to help him or her swallow properly. Right now, Donna was evaluating Taylor's ability to swallow and make small sounds.

For the next several days, Taylor's schedule looked much the same. This was how most of his days looked for the last days of December 2012:

7:30 a.m.: Nurses/assistants would get Taylor up and dressed for the day. His teeth would be brushed, his face washed, and other routine things were done that he could not do for himself. These tasks included applying deodorant and putting on socks and shoes. Taylor was not eating by mouth yet; his breakfast was still given to him through his PEG tube.

8:00 a.m.: I would come over to the rehab after a quick stop for real coffee in the cafeteria. Most mornings when I came in, Taylor was already up, out of bed, and in his wheelchair. The request of the staff was simply that I come after the time allotted to get him up and dressed. I wanted him to have some interaction with me every morning before starting his day so he would know that I was there. From time to time, I would come in and help with something like brushing Taylor's teeth or putting on his shoes.

9:00–10:00 a.m.: Occupational therapy

10:00–11:00 a.m.: Physical therapy

11:00–11:30 a.m.: Speech therapy

11:30 a.m.–1:00 p.m.: Rest period. Taylor was put in bed, his door was closed, and he would immediately go to sleep. I would also come over at this time to help tuck him in.

1:00–1:30 p.m.: Occupational therapy

2:00–2:30 p.m.: Physical therapy

2:30 until sometime around 5:00 p.m.: Taylor would sleep again.

This schedule was subject to change, and it did several times for Taylor when he needed longer periods of rest. It was clear that the therapies were very taxing on his mind and body. Even though he could not speak, he was visibly exhausted. I would come over in the evening right around 5 p.m. I was usually eager to see Taylor even though I had stopped by throughout the day. We would spend a few minutes in his room and then take off to the lower level of the hospital.

Taylor was on the Maple Unit, which fully occupied the second floor. There was a kitchen on the unit, which was connected to a large dining room, a gym, an observation room, and a large comfortable area with a television, sofa, and chairs for family members. The unit had four main hallways, but it felt confining to me. I wanted to roam and think with Taylor.

I had permission to take him to the main/lower level of the hospital. At the time, there was an inspiring and interesting art show that was taking place. The display was called "Art Ability." The program featured the work of many artists who had faced various disabilities. Multiple forms of art were featured. There were photographs, paintings, sculptures, drawings, and jewelry; and the art had been created in various media. The pieces were on display and would be for sale in the near future.

As I pushed Taylor up and down the hallways, I looked at the art. I chose "my pieces," and thought about where I would display them in my house. I talked to Taylor about them and stopped to show him the ones that I thought he would like or relate to. There were several hallways and corridors to go down, and that is what we did. The art inspired me; and next to the pieces, there were often stories that told you just a little bit about the person who had created it.

One item that immediately caught my eye was a bronze sculpture of three lions. Of course it reminded me of my three sons. I also found a watercolor painting to be soothing and it was easy to get lost in wondering how each stroke of the brush had been made.

Some of the art was bright and uplifting, with enjoyable subjects like wildly painted animals or childlike themes. Other pieces were reflective of the loneliness that comes to some artists with being different or disabled. These pieces portrayed a tangible level of sadness. Each piece was unique and special, and it provided a gift to all of us who roamed the hallways.

Because it was evening, a lot of the staff had gone for the day. Other patients and families who were visiting occupied the usually busy areas of the building along with two receptionists and the housekeeping and maintenance staff. It would not take long for me to make some friends with the skeleton crew of staff members. The people who worked at Bryn Mawr were friendly. They said hello and gave lots of smiles. They had been exposed to many people like us, and their hearts were full of compassion. They were not shy, and I think they wanted to convey that they cared. I found that a lot of staff members on the evening shift wanted me to know that I was among people who noticed our struggle.

One night, I was walking by the reception area and three ladies were chatting at the welcome desk. I had passed by them a few times before on previous nights. One of the ladies had a wonderful laugh and as I came around the corner, I could hear it. It made me smile and it made me laugh a little, too. As I approached them, pushing Taylor, who was in a reclined position in his chair, I told them that the laughter was the nicest sound I had heard in a long time. They were so kind and said, "Your son is lucky to have you." It was a welcome affirmation.

On Friday evening, Keith and the boys arrived, and I was eager for them to see Taylor in action in the gym. I had told them about each exercise that was taking place, but I felt certain that my emotions held me back from sharing a lot. At the time, it was becoming increasingly difficult to explain Taylor's condition; it was almost something you had to see to understand.

The best way to describe Taylor's condition is by looking again at the Rancho Los Amigos Scale. Taylor was consistently at Level II, with occasional times when his behaviors were reflective of Level III. The next two paragraphs are excerpts from the scale itself:

Level II Generalized Response: Patient reacts inconsistently and non-purposefully to stimuli in a non-specific manner. Responses are limited in nature and are often the same regardless of stimulus presented. Responses may be physiological changes, gross body movements, and/or vocalization. Often, the earliest response is to deep pain. Responses are likely to be delayed.

Level III Localized Response–Total Assistance: Demonstrates withdrawal or vocalization to painful stimuli. Turns toward or away from auditory stimuli. Blinks when strong light crosses visual field. Follows moving object passed within visual field. Responds to discomfort by pulling tubes or restraints. Responds inconsistently to simple commands. Responses directly related to type of stimulus. May respond to some persons (especially family and friends) but not to others.

At times when Taylor's eyes were open, he would simply stare; and his mind did not seem to register a response to any stimulus or to a particular person. At other times, however, he would look at a staff member or me and we could tell that he was making visual connections. One of Taylor's therapists shared the following information about what therapists look for in evaluating a patient's eyes: *"I look a lot at eyes; sometimes there is this dull quality to the eyes that they don't seem to see what's going on. Do they fixate on an object? Can they visually track things?"* She remembered that when Taylor's eyes were open, they appeared dull and sleepy, but he did briefly fixate on objects and track them. This finding was evidence that Taylor could see—a huge relief to us!

We encountered a few traumatic brain injury survivors whose injury had either permanently or temporarily blinded them. At least one family did not find out about their loved one's blindness until weeks after the accident, when they came to Bryn Mawr. This late discovery results from the fact that someone in a comatose state does not perform actions like visual tracking and fixating. It can be difficult to evaluate all the results of the brain injury when someone is in a state in which they provide very few if any responses.

I remember the absolute devastation of one mother, who had been coping with and adjusting to the reality that her son had been severely damaged because of his brain injury, and then told weeks later that he was also blind. I thought a lot about Taylor and the various stages and patterns of his recovery, and I tried to imagine a person emerging from a coma and also being blind. Later, this mother would learn that her son's vision had been damaged beyond repair.

I found comfort in our family's being together on that Friday night. Keith, Avery, and Tanner acclimated themselves to the Maple Unit, and in a short amount of time they had learned its routine. We settled into our room at The Laurels. The room had two twin beds and cots with mattresses, which we took off and laid on the floor. It was a tight squeeze, but we made it work. We spent the weekend taking shifts with Taylor; sometimes all of us came over together for brief periods. We did a lot of walking around the hallways, pushing Taylor along in his chair.

I remember having a conversation with someone about Christmas miracles. They told me that they were praying for a miracle to happen with Taylor. At this point, I had come to know some of the other families casually, but enough to relate fully to their pain. I had even heard bits and pieces of some of their stories. Three of the mothers I had become acquainted with were there because their son or daughter had been in a motor vehicle accident. Two of the patients had been in rehabilitation for more than six weeks; neither of them was walking or making any sign of connection that could be definitively identified.

The young woman who occupied a room down the hall from Taylor cried out constantly. Her cries were loud, and they sent chills through me each time they echoed down the hallways. It was hard to know whether she was in pain or whether her body was releasing some sort of automatic response. Each outcry was sort of like a scream, but it had a raw and primitive sound to it. It seemed to come from a deeper place inside her. Her mother was exhausted. Her tired eyes spoke volumes to me and each time we passed . . . we said hello.

The other mother was with her sixteen-year-old son. His accident had occurred because of an adult's decision to drink and drive. His mother was quiet and reserved; she stayed with her son constantly and became a beautiful symbol of love, loyalty, and protection. The pain that was etched on her face haunted me. I wanted to help, and I knew the level of fear she was experiencing. It hurt me physically to see her in such pain.

When I would see these mothers with their children, I felt helpless with and for them. I knew the prayers they prayed, as I prayed them too. I knew how afraid they were, because I was that afraid. I wanted each of us to have our children back in a way that was whole and complete. I wanted the agony to stop for these mothers, as much as I wanted it to cease for myself.

Taylor was already progressing further than these two patients. He was able to sit upright; his eyes were open; and there was some type of connection taking place. Taylor was definitively and undeniably beginning to emerge.

As the person who was praying for me spoke of Christmas miracles, I snapped back in an angry and trembling tone, "If God is going to give Taylor a miracle, than I want Him to hand them out to the whole floor. Every patient here deserves a miracle." It became a habit for me, as I reflected on and prayed for Taylor, to mention also the names of the other patients I was getting to know. When I would look at Taylor and plead for him to come back, I would also do the same for the others I passed. I had to remember that everyone's brain heals at a different pace and in a different way. It was difficult to see so much suffering, not only for the survivors, but often even more so for those who loved them. Moments of happiness were shared among us and treasured.

Something remarkable happened on December 23. I had picked up a sketchbook and marking pens earlier in the week, and used them with Taylor. I would draw simple pictures for Taylor and show them to him. I would also write simple phrases or words. I wrote short sentences like "I love you," or "It is winter." Taylor had scribbled and colored a head of hair on one of the smiley faces that I drew. He also started to write a series of letters, and sometimes a word or two, but nothing that made sense. On the twenty-third, while Keith, Avery, Tanner, and I were all with Taylor in the patient dining area, he finished a thought that I started. He wrote down words that made sense within the context of his life!

I wrote the date on the top of the paper and then wrote, "What do you want to do?" He responded by writing underneath:

1. McChixeyix-nothingying
2. Go AHunting ☺
3. Halard a rest 7 to to wake
4. Mow

This list was awesome and amazing! We do not know where this sudden line of clarity came from, but we celebrated it. It was an indication to us that Taylor was still in there. Prior to the accident, he had often made lists. I had written only the question and the date on this paper—he was the one who made it into a list! He wrote both the numbers and the words. As we all tried to figure out parts of it, it didn't take long. All the things that Taylor had written made sense in one form or another.

1. McChicken (he loved these)
2. Go hunting
3. Have a rest
4. Mow

Life can feel overwhelmingly dark and unpromising in times like this, but the glimmers of hope also feel overwhelmingly lovely. I thought about the crocus flowers that I have often seen peeking through snow-covered ground. In times that feel cold and lifeless, I have always held on to the notion that every winter is followed by a spring. Taylor had to get through his present condition in order to get to the next stage. He was writing and starting to communicate in ways we could understand.

One thing that is important to understand about the phases and steps of recovery from traumatic brain injury is that recovery often follows the one-step-forward, two-steps-back pattern which I mentioned previously. One of the major first steps forward that Taylor experienced took place when he wrote out his list. This list was an indicator at some level of his cognition and growing ability to communicate.

We had been reminded of the words attributed to J.R.R Tolkien, "Little by little, one travels far." We could see some of Taylor's journey, but much of it was occurring in ways that we were not able to see.

Chapter Ten
Silent Nights
December 24–December 31, 2012

Oh, how I wish that I could write a beautiful holiday story that would reflect something that might appear on the Hallmark Channel or the Lifetime television network, but this story is raw and real. It is relentless, and actually grew more and more painful with each passing day. There are some breathtakingly lovely and genuine moments, but there are some that felt so brutal they felt like they could not possibly be happening. There were times over the first month of Taylor's injury that I was most certain I was dreaming some nightmare that eventually would end. I thought I would wake up and find that none of these horrible things had happened to Taylor, to us. But I never did wake up; and the more days that passed on the calendar, the more I understood that sleep was the only way I could escape the waking nightmare that had become our reality. As soon, however, as the sleep was over, the moment before my eyes opened every day, without fail, I had to remember it again.

Ultimately, the last several weeks of our lives reflected a family whose members came together when they most needed one another. And yet in the midst of coming together, there was an undeniable amount of pain brewing within each of us. We were brokenhearted and full of burdens and worries. There were many thoughts that we did share, but many of our feelings were buried inside some part of us that suffered alone.

I don't remember much about that Christmas Eve, but I do remember parts of it. Keith, Avery, Tanner, and I had spent the day and most of the evening with Taylor. We attended both his physical and occupational therapy sessions in the morning.

The physical therapy session stirred conflicting emotions in us. Seeing Taylor in a position where he could walk with maximum assistance was exciting, but also distressing. Everything that he was doing was also coupled with something he was not able to do. Only a few weeks before, Taylor had been strong, healthy, and vibrant. To see him fully dependent on others was a hard adjustment. The phrase we had adopted when referring to Taylor's recovery—"Beating the Odds One Step at a Time"—took on a literal meaning. The rehabilitation setting was where we learned to understand that very small accomplishments are

138

stepping stones to larger ones. *We just had no idea of how far the steps could or would take Taylor.*

The occupational therapy session brought us to the place of uncomfortable laughter more than once. It was hard to process the emotions involved in seeing Taylor in such an infantile state, and due to emotional overload, we laughed nervously. Kelly, the therapist, would place numerous bottles in front of Taylor. There were water bottles, shampoo bottles, and other small plastic bottles that he could hold easily in his hands. Taylor began by simply picking up and touching the bottles. Then he started taking the caps off and smelling the inside of them, and eventually placed them to his mouth. He wanted to drink. At this time Taylor was not allowed liquids by mouth, and it was intriguing to us to see how he interacted with the objects. He reminded me of a little bird when its mother is feeding it, but he was not able to take in anything by mouth at that point.

We left Taylor at lunchtime so that we could eat and he could rest. There was tension and irritability in each one of us. We were exhausted; and all the changes of the last several weeks seemed to be catching up to our moods. We were grateful for our room at the Laurels, but being packed together in such a small space was less than ideal. I could sense that people were beginning to unravel and that this was nothing like the holiday we had imagined.

Avery had actually been scheduled to be in Africa for Christmas 2012. A family member had planned to take Avery with him to celebrate his seventieth birthday. Avery had been anticipating this dream adventure for many months. Within days after the fall, one of the doctors met with us and asked whether we had any concerns. I mentioned Avery's trip; a lot of planning and money had gone into it, but more importantly I knew it was very special to Avery. The trip was discussed, but Avery knew even prior to the discussion that he could not go. He would not have a moment's peace in Africa knowing Taylor was in the hospital, and he was not willing to leave any of us behind. The doctor made Avery's decision very easy that day; she told us truthfully that Taylor might die and she did not think Avery should go. The trip was rescheduled; thankfully, the company gave no argument about rescheduling when they received documentation from the physicians clarifying Taylor's medical condition.

Instead of exploring the animals and villages of Africa, Avery was instead spending Christmas Eve in a rehabilitation hospital, pushing his big brother in a wheelchair. By this time, Taylor had various small soft balls that he would hold in his hands, but not do anything more with them. We took turns pushing his chair, which seemed to comfort and calm him, much like a baby being pushed in a stroller. *It was truly a silent night.*

Tanner and I said good-night early and headed toward the exit of the hospital. As we did, we ran into my new friend from housekeeping, and I introduced her to Tanner. She had a large basket full of soda, sweet and salty snacks, and various other goodies. It was wrapped and decorated beautifully, and she said she had won it through something the hospital did for their workers. Tanner and I said good-night and as we walked out, she followed us and called for us to wait.

She handed us the basket and said, "Merry Christmas. You folks can use this more than I can." Tanner and I were both stunned by the kindness of this person who barely knew our family. We were touched and humbled by her generosity. I knew she had a family because she had shared that with me in our brief conversations. As we walked away, we talked about how gestures and moments like that are what the holiday season is truly about.

Keith and Avery soon joined us in our room, and as we gathered, the tensions in the air began to mount between us. Maybe all of our emotions rising so close to the surface were too much in combination. As luck would have it, Avery had a friend who lived close by and was away for the weekend. She had already offered her house to us. Sensing that everyone needed space, Avery and I left to stay at his friend's house, and Keith and Tanner stayed at the Laurels.

Despite my best efforts to take care of my entire family, most of my energy had been poured into Taylor. I felt especially disconnected from Keith, Avery, and Tanner, so it was special to have some time alone with Avery. Then I received a wonderful Christmas gift, just for me.

The first night that I checked into The Laurels, I was so appreciative to be close to Taylor at no cost. It was an immense blessing that relieved a lot of financial pressure on us. As I made myself familiar with the room and setting, I realized it had no bathtub. One of the simplest and most frequent ways I decompress is by taking a hot bath. In the wintertime, I take a hot bath every night after work. That first night, I cried over the absence of a tub. Trust me—I knew this reaction was ridiculous in the overall scheme of things, but I felt I needed the relaxation that a hot bath brings to help me unwind.

Since that night, I had been craving that perfect healing soak. As we walked into Avery's friend's house, I about jumped for joy when I saw the bathtub. One of the first things I did was to fill the tub and soak. I felt like royalty. Avery's friend had not only given us a sanctuary— which we did use a few times—but she had also given me something I really needed . . . the relaxation that a long soak in a hot tub brings. I had not been able to sit in a tub, close my eyes and drift off since before the night of Taylor's fall, and it felt good. The gift of a long, hot bath was exactly what I needed.

Avery and I spent a little bit of time talking; it was nice to catch up with him in that way. We also sat and watched television—it felt normal and feeling normal was a welcome change. There was no way to make this Christmas any easier, but I did not want it to feel more agonizing either.

Christmas Day was quiet and uneventful for Taylor, and in general on the Maple Unit. The hospital provided a free breakfast for everyone who was visiting. In the afternoon, we tucked Taylor in for his rest and went to the one place that was open in the area. It was a restaurant just down the road with a pleasant atmosphere and Asian cuisine. Food had no flavor for me; I was eating because people said I should, but it was merely a function. It was a tense and awkward meal, and a difficult day to get through. None of us felt or had the holiday spirit; instead we looked for an empty table in an unfamiliar restaurant in a town far from home. We had been in a whirlwind since November 22, and we had to slowly get back on the ground.

We had declared a "no Christmas" policy, but our community and some of our family disagreed. After eating, we came back to our room at the Laurels and opened some presents. My dad and stepmom had sent us some things that at least for a few minutes made us laugh, smile, and feel their love. My mom also had sent some thoughtful gifts. Last, we opened some gifts from our generous community. A good friend had initiated a "Tree of Love" for us at her interior decorating store. She had provided a way for people to donate in both practical and thoughtful ways. Our electric bill for the month had been paid, and there were numerous gift cards for gas stations and grocery stores. Some people who knew Tanner and Avery personally had bought them gift cards to get something special for themselves. It was a powerful gesture and we valued the support of our home town. People had come together for us in the spirit of the holiday season, and their love gave us a little bit of fuel.

After the extended lunch hour and naps, we all went back to see Taylor. We stuck to our routine and began to wheel him down the halls. During the walk, we stopped, and Keith took a photo of the three boys and me. From time to time people have said to me over the years, "You are like the old television show *My Three Sons*." That comment always made me laugh. *I felt now as if I had lost a son.* I wanted to believe the best, but I was aware that things were very much changed. I still had three sons, but one of them was gone in countless ways. I missed Taylor. *I missed everything about him.*

In the photo, Avery and I are smiling, but Tanner looks sad. Taylor is in his wheelchair, wearing his denim helmet. He is held in his chair by a wide light-blue pelvic belt that from a distance could be confused with a diaper. His eyes appear crossed, and he is clearly in another world.

It would be a long time before we would hear Taylor speak, but within a few days he began to write more frequently. In fact, earlier that day Keith had written on a piece of paper. "Today is Christmas." Taylor wrote back, "We missed it!" These moments when he did write did not last long. Taylor was easily distracted and in no way showed signs that he could carry on a conversation by writing, but his short answer was a start. Keith and the boys returned home that evening, and I settled in at the Laurels.

In the beginning of the following week, the ear, nose, and throat (ENT) specialist came to the Maple Unit. Kristine told me that I should accompany Taylor to the examination. The appointment concerned the possible removal of his tracheostomy tube. Kristine, Taylor, and I went into the small room with the doctor. He had to look inside Taylor's mouth and examine his throat by using a long instrument. This examination allows the physician to understand how the patient's gag and swallowing reflexes are working. Taylor made a horrible noise. It was evident that he was not only in pain, but also afraid. *I kept telling myself to stay calm for him.*

It was hard to hear these first sounds come from Taylor. They sounded primal and unfamiliar; they were like nothing I had ever heard before. As I stood there watching, I reminded myself that one of the main reasons I was with Taylor was to truly be "with" him. I was going to have to learn to push my emotions aside and toughen up. I was glad that no one I knew well was around to witness this examination. If they had been, I would have run into their arms and let out the pain inside of me.

Eventually, Taylor's horrible noises subsided and the examination ended. It was determined that Taylor was ready to begin weaning from the trachea tube. This weaning was a big and important step because until the tube had been removed, Taylor could not be reintroduced to foods or liquids, and he would not be able to speak. Some patients who have long-term "trachs" do speak with them by using a special valve, but this option was not in the plan for Taylor.

This is how Kristine explained the removal of the trach tube to me:

Once the ENT doctor clears the patient for weaning, the process begins. A speaking valve is used at first, allowing the patient to get used to a partially closed trach stoma (the stoma is the actual incision at the base of the neck.) This piece has a one-way valve,

143

which forces the patient to breathe in via the trach but allows them to exhale from their mouth. This exhaling is what allows the air to pass over the vocal cords to make a voice.

During the day, a trach cap is used and this allows the patient to be closely monitored; once that is successful, it is transitioned into the nighttime hours. Oxygen is used to help with breathing and closely monitored at night. After at least three days of successful capping, the nurse will remove the tube and apply Steri-Strips[12] to the site. It is kept dry and clean, and most of the time closes up on its own.

Within about a week of the initial visit with the ENT doctor, Taylor became trach-free! This news was exciting because it meant that he could begin the process of oral stimulation. He was going to be able to taste again, and I felt certain he would respond well to that. This change would also be a big step in terms of what he could do in speech therapy.

A few days after Christmas, I bought Taylor a few gifts. I picked up the children's book *I'll Love You Forever*, and began a nightly ritual of reading it to him. I felt like I should keep words and phrases simple and easy to follow, so that is what I did. I sang songs to him like "You Are My Sunshine," and softly spoke of memories that I hoped he was able to hear.

I also bought him some of the Bright Starts Lots of Links for infants, and attached them to his wheelchair. Taylor had started to be busier with his hands; the brightly colored links kept him occupied and would not fall off the chair. His favorite item quickly became a small purple sock monkey with a patch of even brighter purple hair on the top of his head. Taylor was starting to put everything up to his mouth and often in it, so the items had to be safe. Taylor held on to the monkey as I silently pushed him through the halls.

---

[12] Steri-Strips are the brand name of paper-based thin adhesive strips used instead of sutures to close small wounds. The strips minimize tissue scarring and are easier to care for than stitches or staples.

I knew that Taylor was not an infant, but I also felt like his mind could take in stimulation only in small doses. These children's toys held Taylor's interest and I did not have to worry about their safety. When I went to buy them, I tried to stay unemotional about it. Taylor had just turned twenty-two years old, and no part of me had ever envisioned buying him baby toys for his birthday, but that is what I was doing. I hoped that he would progress past these things, but I was learning enough about brain injury to know that they might be the end of the path for him.

For now we continued to build on what Taylor gave us. He continued to write from time to time on the sketchpad I had given him. On December 24, he wrote:

> Who knows
> mipactststance urhrinch butter
> happy first

Later the same day I wrote down for him:
> Your friends are okay.
> Your friends love you.

He responded:
> He appantely shot having foot beside
> Your drug?
> Gitten me when :)

Another time I wrote:
> Who do you want to see?

He responded:
> Snoodooz wtf
> Scham MV
> TcaVadm, vary Eviby
> Back.

On another undated day in the same time period he wrote:

Sorry for every equipement,

but ok c ya

seriously move

LKA TTay sorry hate again

412-1695

And probably the most understandable sequence of words was:

Fair Enough

Dad I hate everything. It's a lot of work

Later

And once, in response to my writing "I love you" to him, he wrote back to me, "Love you." Trust me, I took it in and soaked it up.

Much of Taylor's writing had arrows pointing in various directions placed intermittently between the words. We continued to try to reach Taylor in this way. We would write questions or draw pictures of items that might trigger a memory for him. A good deal of what Taylor wrote came across like pointless ramblings, but it was a way of connecting with him.

On New Year's Eve, I made the drive home to Mifflinburg, and Keith came to spend the weekend with Taylor. As I came to the road that led into the main part of town, I could feel the emotion stirring in me. I had missed being among my friends, my co-workers and my community. I missed the things that happen in the normal world. Tanner and Avery were at home waiting when I got there. Taylor and I had been in Malvern only for close to two weeks, but I had missed my home, our dog, and doing simple things like cooking in something other than a microwave oven.

I was going to be home for a day and a half, and I appreciated the break. I was anxious and nervous about leaving Taylor, but I was confident in Keith's care of him, and I knew he was also under the care of a first-rate team of medical professionals.

Tanner, Avery, and I went out to eat and to a movie to ring in the New Year. We joked about what a wild bunch we were, but I didn't care about the ball dropping in Times Square, going to a fabulous party, or having some other elaborate plan. I cared about having time with my other sons, whom I missed seeing every day. As midnight drew closer, I wished with all my heart that our new year would indeed be happy. I was back home for less than forty-eight hours, but being somewhere other than in a rehabilitation facility or hospital was refreshing for me.

I returned to Bryn Mawr feeling rested and re-energized from being home. This rest was more important than I knew at the time because another storm was brewing inside Taylor's body. The storm would drain all of us of any reserves we had left. An impending struggle for Taylor also meant an imminent struggle for us.

Chapter Eleven
A New Year Begins

In Taylor's therapy sessions, he continued to show progress. The hospital's routines and schedules were easy to follow, and allowed me to come and go around Taylor's agenda. An exact schedule was provided for me daily, and it was fairly consistent throughout the weeks. I developed as much of a pattern as I could in my day-to-day routine, which allowed me to become more comfortable with having some space between Taylor and me. Taylor's therapy sessions took up three to four hours of time between 9 a.m. and 3 p.m., and he required periods of rest in between. The rests took place between sessions, over the lunch hour, and after the final therapy of the day. Monday through Friday, I would come to the hospital around 8:30 a.m. and usually stay for a therapy session along with some additional downtime afterward, typically leaving around 10 a.m. I would return close to noon for about an hour; and return for the last time in the evening around 5 p.m. On the weekends, Taylor didn't have as busy a schedule and would normally start therapy later in the day. These two days of rest were essential to his healing.

It was always a relief to see Taylor in the morning. He would be sitting in his wheelchair outside his door, ready for the day. Each morning he appeared clean, rested, and well cared for. His morning socialization started with the nurses and the patients who occupied the rooms around his. Taylor was not verbalizing or giving any other signs of obvious communication, but the staff interacted with each patient and formed relationships with them. They were getting to know Taylor and that was a part of their superb talent. Taylor looked at ease in the hands of his caregivers, and you could sense his peace of mind, which comforted me.

José shaved Taylor's growing beard, with permission from Tanner and Avery. Taylor looked thinner now; the toll that not eating food for several weeks had taken was even more evident. He was pale, and had lost twenty-five to thirty pounds, but he could have looked a lot worse.

The new nurses told me that Geisinger had taken very good care of Taylor. I wasn't sure at first what they meant by that, but they were referring to how nice his skin had been kept. When someone is in bed for a long period of time, they must be kept clean and dry. They need to be turned and adjusted on a daily basis to prevent skin disorders like bedsores from occurring. From all that I observed in the early days of his accident, Taylor had been extremely well cared for at Geisinger, but hearing it confirmed by the staff at Bryn Mawr made a difference to me, especially since I knew we would be spending more time there in the future. The excellent care was continuing at Bryn Mawr Rehabilitation Hospital as well.

Taylor's therapies typically started at 9 a.m. On rare occasions, therapy began earlier if an occupational therapist were present who needed to establish a baseline of how much dressing, grooming, and other self-care activities Taylor was capable of doing. He was obviously still in need of maximum assistance, but even actions like lifting your arms or legs to place them in the right holes of your clothing counted. Part of rehabilitation theory involves bringing back what the patient's life used to be like and establishing a routine. In the morning you wake up, you get ready for work, and you start your day. *Taylor's brain needed to reestablish this routine.*

Both occupational and physical therapies mainly took place in the Maple Unit gym. This was a large bright open space full of constant motion. There was stationary equipment, large matted tables, huge bolsters, and several other therapy tools that were always in use. Most of Taylor's work occurred in the gym, as long as his mood and attention span would allow it. It can be extremely difficult for someone with a traumatic brain injury to be in an environment where there is too much stimulation. The staff was acutely aware of what was happening with each patient, and if they needed to be moved to another setting, they were.

Many mornings, I would push Taylor over to his first session. His chair was positioned along the wall until his therapist was ready for him. There were always several other patients waiting too. The ages and sexes of the patients varied greatly, and so did the appearance of their injuries. *Taylor was somewhat fortunate.* When he fell, he did not break

150

any limbs or cause significant damage to any other areas of his body. There were patients at the rehab who had broken femurs and pelvic bones as well as wrist and arm breaks along with their brain injuries. Their bodies had to heal in some fashion before the depths of their physical injuries associated with their brain injury could be fully revealed. Their additional fractures complicated their recovery.

While waiting one morning for therapy to start, another young patient began talking to Taylor and me. Taylor was having constant movements in his right leg. He was restless and continuously moving his right leg in a shaking pattern. It was very fast and uncontrollable. For some reason, this shaking bothered the young man next to us. I remember his name and the angry look on his face.

One of the universal truths about brain injury patients is that they often have a flat facial expression, which makes determining their mood difficult. When they speak, the words often come across in an unfriendly way because the vocal tone lacks the appropriate affect. This young man's irritation with Taylor was growing, and he kept ordering him to stop moving his leg. Taylor was not responding to many commands at this point and gave no indication that he would respond to this patient. *I felt protective and perplexed.* The other patient abruptly asked me, "What the hell are you letting him do that for? He needs to knock it off!" He was agitated and angry.

I had not yet become accustomed to these types of outbursts. Sudden outbursts and speaking in an angry tone are typical of what some traumatic brain injury patients experience. These patients often cannot gauge or control their reactions. The emotion might be present and it might or might not be appropriate, but if it were felt, it would be expressed. This outburst was indicative of this man's level of functioning and how he was processing everything around him at that point in time. It was not something I was familiar enough with to identify at that point. I didn't have enough exposure to it. It frightened and concerned me.

It was hard for me to move Taylor further away because there were a number of patients present, and where we were stationed was out of the way of the therapy sessions taking place. I wedged myself between

151

the young man and Taylor so that my back was facing him and my front was toward Taylor. The patient seemed to be fixated on Taylor and that frightened me. I wasn't sure what exactly bothered him about Taylor, but he was expressing immediate hostility. I was relieved when their separate sessions started.

At this phase in Taylor's recovery, there were many factors that the therapists were investigating. Some of what they were exploring was how Taylor reacted to noise or pain. How would he respond to a stimulus? Would he turn toward it or try to push it away? *Taylor was growing increasingly restless.* Noticing this development, the team used a technique that involved using a matted table. Taylor was straddled between the therapist's legs with his back against her chest, as if she were mimicking a chair. She would gently rock him back and forth. This technique was an effective way to soothe him before the more obvious and strenuous tasks took place. With his left-side impairment issues, even sitting provided him with a lot of help, but even after several weeks, Taylor could not sit up straight by himself. He tended to lean to one side, and his trunk needed a lot of detailed attention to strengthening the muscles. Sitting itself requires the participation of many different muscle groups. This rocking was comforting for me to watch. Taylor would relax in the hold of the therapist, and I could see that he was experiencing a sort of tranquility. His body indicated less rigidity. It was clearly beneficial to Taylor and provided a form of soothing stimulation for him.

Along with the sitting technique, Taylor would be placed in a lying-flat position. Sue, the therapist, described it in terms of an infant's development. *Could Taylor raise his head? Was he capable of rolling over? Could he hold himself up by his arms while resting on his knees?* All these developments that had taken place twenty-one years ago would unfortunately need to take place again. Just like an infant, you must conquer certain skills before you can master the bigger things, like standing on your own, walking, balancing, and bending.

In terms of walking, the process appears somewhat simple, but it is far from easy. I was always very cautious about using the term *walking* with people who were not aware of what it actually meant for Taylor. His legs were moving; he was standing upright; but he was not walking. *He was being walked.* At this point, no one other than his attending physical therapist or assistant was permitted to do any type of walking with Taylor. He was at a very low level of functioning, and even though he could participate in the motions of leg movements, it required a lot of preparation to make it work. The risk of his falling was great, which is why he was always in a wheelchair except when he was with the medical or therapeutic staff. I was not worried about the risks when the therapists were present; they were always in tune with what was going on with Taylor physically. They gave full attention to what was happening with Taylor and they were focused on him.

Weight-bearing exercises alone helped strengthen Taylor's arms and legs. The internal sensors in Taylor's brain were not sending him the signals needed to use his left side as he normally would have done. His knee and hip were wrapped to give him the stability to work on his right side. Someone was always on one or both sides of him holding him up. He could not go far, but he could take several steps. Witnessing Taylor walk never grew old to me. I was both fascinated by and appreciative of what was occurring.

Repetition is a close friend to patients like Taylor. If they are going to walk again, they must repeat the motions over and over. One of the staff members at Bryn Mawr explained to me that simple motions that we perform on a daily basis, like sitting down or standing up, would require someone with a brain injury thousands upon thousands of repetitions of the same action.

There was not much happening that we could see in relation to occupational therapy. The occupational therapist helps the person get back to their routine; a term frequently used in this particular therapy is activities of daily living, or ADLs. On certain days, Taylor was awakened by the occupational therapist in the morning and started his routine. On other days, he worked with his nurse or nurse technician to complete these tasks. The routine was the same, but the person with him might change from day to day. Since Taylor was considered to need maximum assistance, someone was always with him, but he was not yet ready to work with the occupational therapist every day.

What *was* different is that he was being directed and led by another person. Just a couple of months previously, Taylor woke up to his alarm clock around 4:30 a.m. to go to work. Depending on the day, sometimes he drank a cup of coffee, grabbed his lunch, and headed out the door. He then met up with some co-workers to carpool to their job together.

A large part of what may happen with a brain injury is that individuals may have difficulty recalling the order in which events should occur. This order is called sequencing. For the brain injury survivor, remembering routine behaviors and patterns, and organizing in your mind the steps required to complete various tasks is suddenly nonexistent. Doing ordinary activities like brushing your teeth, combing your hair, washing your hands, and tying your shoes suddenly makes no sense. The order of the process is no longer part of working memory.

Helping with sequencing in early recovery might look something like this: The therapist comes into Taylor's room in the morning, with Taylor still in his pajamas from the night before. The therapist starts by assisting Taylor in taking off his pajama top and putting on a clean one. The same pattern happens with his bottoms, socks, and eventually his shoes. Then he will be led in brushing his teeth, washing his face, and perhaps applying deodorant. Taylor was not participating with awareness at this time, but he was assisting from time to time physically. The best way to describe what the process looked like might be as if someone were sleepwalking or performing an activity while remaining asleep physically. Taylor's memory recall might have been simply raising his arms or helping to guide the sock onto his foot for a second, but the memory recall was important and so was the physical action. As I stated earlier, Taylor was still at the level of maximum assistance.

The starting goal of speech therapy had been laid out simply, but certainly required considerable dedication and skill. There are two areas involved in speech therapy. Taylor was experiencing the early stages of a speech disorder, which meant that he was unable to produce sounds

154

fluently or effectively. His injury had also caused a language disorder, which meant that he was unable to understand or express thoughts, feelings, or simple communications.

Taylor's initial goal was to be able to safely swallow liquids without aspirating and to establish some form of communication. It was in some ways difficult for me to understand why Taylor could not have water or ice chips, but the doctors insisted that it was simply unsafe. If a liquid were not properly swallowed, there would be serious consequences because it might enter the respiratory tract and lead to a condition called aspiration pneumonia.

The speech therapist's initial goal was not for Taylor to speak. It was instead to have Taylor recover to the point at which he could safely take in food and liquids. For now, we would have to learn to pick up cues of communication in some other way. Communication had to be recalled and enhanced on two levels, receptive speech and expressive speech.[13]

In terms of safe swallowing, the plan was to introduce Taylor to honey-thick liquids, followed by nectar-thick liquids and finally, water-thin liquids. The first several days were spent giving Taylor one or two tablespoons of the flavored honey-thick liquid, and then Donna, the speech therapist, would evaluate his ability to swallow.

The flavored thickened liquids have two purposes. First, the flavoring that is added awakens the taste buds in a way that water can't because ordinary water is tasteless. Water is also thin in consistency, which means that the brain might not have time to react to its presence in the mouth. By the time the brain registers the presence of the thin, fast-moving liquid, it has already been swallowed. That is when trouble can occur. The flavoring in the thicker liquid acts to awaken the taste buds, and the thickness allows the liquid's presence to register in a way that is more conducive to a delayed reaction.

The therapist wants to see a full and complete swallow. In order to do so, Donna placed her hand on the front of Taylor's throat and felt

---

[13] Receptive speech refers to a person's ability to perceive and comprehend spoken language; expressive speech refers to the person's ability to produce meaningful speech.

for the complete swallow. This maneuver took a lot of guidance and it was very similar to feeding an infant. *I never thought Taylor would be in the position of an infant at the age of twenty-two.* Donna made her instructions clear and simple, and Taylor seemed to follow her lead. Donna would say, "Taylor, I need a full and complete swallow." Depending on how the swallow went, she would respond by saying, "Good job!" or "Let's try that again. Give me a complete swallow this time."

The first time Taylor was introduced to the juice thickened to the consistency of honey, he did not hesitate to show his enjoyment. Of course I wanted him to have more, but it had to be taken slowly.

It was the first week of January; Taylor had been a patient at Bryn Mawr Rehabilitation Hospital for eighteen days. He was making small steps of progress that we were not shouting from the rooftops, but we did feel hopeful about his development. Seeing Taylor have real movements; having him communicate by writing; and knowing that he had actual hours of waking and sleeping were all positive steps, but they did not mean that Taylor was back.

As a family, we found that explaining what was occurring and having it understood by those on the outside looking in was a complicated undertaking. I think in part it was that people's responses, which came out of love and genuine happiness, came across to us as exaggerated and misplaced. From the early hours of Taylor's accident, comments had been made like "He won't even have to go to rehab," "He will recover completely," "I just know he is going to wake up and be himself"; and in our hearts we understood that these remarks were meant to help, but instead they hurt. These words were also wrapped in the love that people had for Taylor and they truly wanted him to be okay. *But we had to protect our minds and hearts too.* People have a difficult time accepting how quickly life can change and steal someone from you. I imagine that Taylor's friends, our friends, and our extended family were all dealing with their own battles of acceptance and denial. I think also that everyone who knew Taylor and understood what had happened to

156

him had to look at his or her own mortality. If this accident could happen to Taylor, it could happen to anyone.

It's difficult to share your feelings about what was happening with someone and then have him or her respond with false hope. Platitudes like "There is a reason for everything," and "God doesn't give us more than we can handle" felt like knives in my heart. What I heard and felt as Taylor's mother in response to those remarks was part of a war raging inside me. "There is a reason for everything" translated in my mind to something like "You did something to deserve this." And "God won't give us more than we can handle" felt like someone was saying that there must be some sort of lesson that God was teaching me. These things sometimes kept me up at night. *How could THIS be part of the plan for Taylor's life? What did we do to cause this to happen? And if God would not give me more than I could bear, why did this situation feel like it was destroying me?*

I wanted my friends and family simply to be with me in my pain. I did not expect them to have perfect words. A simple "I love you" or "I am here" was enough. In fact, for me one of the most refreshing and honest moments I had along the way was with a longtime friend. She had not seen Taylor since his accident and came over to Geisinger when he had been transferred to the Special Care Unit. We had been friends for many years and she also had three sons very close in age to mine. When she walked in and saw Taylor, she began to cry, really cry. She held her hand over her mouth and could not stop her tears. She was not prepared for what she saw, and the rawness of her emotion showed. She said something to the effect of, "Oh, my God, I can't believe this is happening to Taylor." She wept with me; she said she was so sorry; and she did not candy-coat what I felt no coating could cover. She allowed herself to be sad and frightened with me. She also wept openly with me, which was something that was rare. There was a gift in her sadness shared with me. Her tears implied that because I was hurting so deeply, she was hurting too.

So much had happened over the six-week time frame since the accident, and it was a lot for our minds and emotions to keep up with.

157

We were not without hope, and we were certainly happy about Taylor's level of progress. However, we were surrounded at Bryn Mawr by families and people whose recovery seemed to have come to an abrupt halt. We were all wrestling with the stark reality that we had no idea who Taylor would be at the end of this part of his journey. We knew that our cautious optimism had served us well. Faith had been a deep thread sustaining our lives and family for many years, but we had also experienced some strong heartache. *Sometimes prayers were not answered the way we had hoped.* Avery often expressed to me that he was thankful that I am a realist. And I am. It is hard not to be when you are looking at your son whose skull was broken and many parts of his brain destroyed, and being told the best-, worst-, and in-between-case scenarios. It was also hard to take the pressure of feeling somehow as if I as Taylor's mother had control over the extent to which Taylor might recover.

Issues like this are what I refer to as walking the tightrope of brain injury. The phrase came to me before I had a chance to fully comprehend it, but I understood it now. As Taylor's mother, along with Keith, Avery and Tanner, I would have to find the balance that we needed to move forward. We would become unsteady along the way, and we would have to remain strong at our core to continue to keep our balance—but forward motion was necessary too. It required us simply to put one foot in front of the other the best that we could; and many times, when one of us was too exhausted, another would have to jump on the rope and take his or her place. This journey mandated the presence of strength and balance inside each of us.

Part III: Paoli

Chapter Twelve
A New Monster
January 5–January 15, 2013

"Grown don't mean nothing to a mother. A child is a child. They get bigger, they get older, but grown? What's that supposed to mean? In my heart it don't mean a thing."

-- *Beloved*, Toni Morrison

By now, I had a well-established routine of going to the rehab right away in the morning. I had acclimated myself well to the facility and my trust in their care for Taylor grew daily. My feelings of being in a constant state of panic or turmoil had subsided, and I was adjusting to Taylor's stage of recovery. We had been at Bryn Mawr Rehabilitation Hospital for over three weeks. Things were moving along in a way that allowed us to at least feel like we could catch our breath.

On Saturday, January 5, Keith and Tanner woke up at home, packed the car, and drove to see Taylor and me. I woke in the morning intending to stick with my normal routine of going to see Taylor right away, but changed my mind. Taylor's schedule was often more relaxed on the weekends, and I knew he might not yet be awake. I had called earlier to check on him and he was sound asleep. Looking back, I am not certain that a great deal of thought went into my decision to see Taylor later in the day, but I needed to get some food for the weekend because Tanner and Keith were visiting. The Laurels had a large common area with a refrigerator, table, and chairs, and a kitchen area with a sink and microwave, which helped us immensely. It was nice after a long day to be able to eat in our room or at the table in the common area instead of always having to eat out.

Before going to see Taylor, I drove to Wegman's and was enjoying shopping. Weekly tasks like going to the grocery store were no longer part of my regular schedule, which made shopping for groceries a pleasure. I never would have imagined grocery shopping to feel that way, but normalcy can be a gift in the midst of chaos. I distinctly remember thinking that it was challenging to feel normal in any kind of way. I got absorbed in looking at the fresh fruit and other produce, as well as the multitude of items that Wegman's offered that were so different from the grocery store in our little town of Mifflinburg. I found pleasure in

161

picking out things that I knew Keith and Tanner would enjoy, as well as "real food" for myself.

I was close to the last aisle in the store when I noticed I had missed a call. Reception inside the store was poor and I hadn't heard my phone ring. As I walked closer to the front of the store, I saw that I had a voice mail. The call was from Selasie, the Maple Unit's secretary. Her voice was calm on the other end requesting that I call the unit as soon as I got her message. Upon hearing her voice and message, I was not panicked; her tone had been calm but imperative. I stopped in an aisle of the grocery store to make the call; Selasie connected me to a nurse named Christine. I knew Christine because she had previously spent a few shifts with Taylor. She began to recount an incident involving Taylor. The emergency consisted of a series of seizures, and now he was being taken to the closest hospital. As I reflect back on this moment, I remember my reaction; in an instant I felt nauseated.

Immediately upon hearing Christine's words, every part of my physical body began shaking. Instinctively, I knew Taylor was in danger. I was on the edge of absolute hysteria; and a crowd of shoppers gathered around me. Nearing the level of screaming, I was trying to ask whether Taylor was okay while also trying to calm myself. I had very little control over my emotions. Christine spoke firmly and softly, "*Taylor is all right. We need for you to get to the hospital. The ambulance will meet you there.*" I could feel her compassion toward me and it calmed me. I was in an unfamiliar store in a strange town and was surrounded by strangers. If one of them had offered me any comfort, I would have graciously accepted it. I am almost certain that my level of emotion frightened them. I was in shock, but unlike the last terrible blow, I had some notion of what might be coming.

My hand was shaking so forcefully that I could not hold the phone to my ear or mouth for several seconds. The shaking affected my entire arm and caused my cheeks to vibrate. My heart was racing, and I was filled with absolute terror. The nursing staff made an extremely wise choice in limiting the initial details that they shared with me. They did not have to tell me that a seizure is a bad turn of events; I knew it was a dire situation and I knew that if Taylor was being taken by ambulance, it was extremely serious. The crisis felt worse than the night that Taylor fell; and my reaction to it was far more defined by absolute fear than before. Taylor was already in a hospital setting—for him to be sent somewhere else meant he was in definite danger.

Christine offered me reassurance by telling me that Taylor's nurse, Kristine, whom I trusted implicitly, was by his side. When I explained to her where I was, she told me that the hospital was a few miles up the road from Wegman's. It was a straight shot and I assured her that I would be fine behind the wheel. She had done a good job at deescalating my hysteria.

Right before hanging up, Christine informed me that Taylor was still being prepared for transport to the hospital. She thought it would be quicker and best if I did not return to Bryn Mawr but instead meet them at the Paoli Hospital. What she did not mention was that Taylor had experienced three brutal grand mal seizures[14] that piggybacked on each other and were difficult to stop. Taylor had to be stabilized before he could be transported. I imagined Taylor needing me and I was not there. *Why had I made the decision to come to the store?* I began to question myself. It would be a long time before I could let down my guard again. It would become more difficult to leave Taylor in the care of others.

I went to the store's customer service desk, explained that my son was having an emergency, and they clarified that the hospital was indeed up the road and easy to find. I left my groceries at the desk and called Keith and Tanner, who were en route to Bryn Mawr. When I arrived at the hospital, Taylor was not yet there, but they told me the ambulance would be arriving shortly. I sat in the emergency room

---

[14] Grand mal seizures are seizures that affect the entire brain, as distinct from seizures that affect only one side of the brain. Grand mal seizures are generally referred to nowadays as tonic-clonic seizures because they usually have two phases: a tonic phase in which the person's body tenses and they lose consciousness; and a clonic phase in which the patient's muscles contract and relax repeatedly, resulting in convulsions.

163

waiting area and wondered what all of this meant. I was alone waiting impatiently for Keith and Tanner to arrive.

Taylor had been relatively stable medically since arriving at Bryn Mawr; there had been no crisis or emergency situation. I am sure the risk of seizures had been explained to us, but because Taylor was weeks out from his initial surgery . . . *this crisis took us all by surprise.*

When Taylor came in on a stretcher, he was heavily medicated and sedated. I was glad. Taylor looked surprisingly peaceful, but I knew the seizures had taken a large toll on him. I was worried about his level of agitation and knew that it might be difficult to soothe him. The attending neurologist came in with questions about Taylor's initial injury and what had been happening up until this point. He stated that he was actually surprised that this was the first time Taylor had experienced any type of seizure.

A seizure occurs when there is a sudden electrical disturbance in the brain. A seizure that occurs more than seven days after a brain injury is called a late post-traumatic brain injury seizure. Seizures are not uncommon after the type of injury that Taylor had had, but they were certainly uncommon to us. The fact that they did not alarm the neurologist did offer us some sort of comfort.

Taylor was sent for a CAT scan, and blood was drawn to record the levels of various medications in his system. He had been taking an antiseizure agent, but the level in his system had not been high enough to prevent the seizures. We were advised that Taylor would be admitted to the hospital for a few days. The seizures that Taylor had experienced could have affected him for even a few days afterward. Unfortunately, his crisis had occurred in the middle of a heightened flu season; and although Taylor was supposed to be placed in the intensive care unit, he was placed instead on an observation floor.

Taylor was given an increased dosage of Depakote,[15] which represented a more therapeutic level better correlated to his seizures.

---

[15] Depakote is one of the brand names of valproic acid, a first-line treatment for the type of seizures that Taylor had.

This dosage would be given over the next three days, and Taylor would be monitored. The Depakote was given along with a long list of other medications. The list was exhaustive, and I was supposed to be keeping track of them as best I could. He was prescribed no fewer than seventeen medications at the time of his hospitalization in Paoli. The list included artificial tears, as his eyes were unable to produce enough water on their own; three asthma-related medications; drugs to help him go to the bathroom, sleep, relax, wake up, calm down, stop blood clots, prevent infection; antipsychotic drugs; antidepressants; and more. I felt overwhelmed by the responsibility of knowing and understanding what each of these medications was supposed to do. Most of them were given through his feeding tube and one was given through a shot in his thigh. It was then that I attempted to keep a record of the medications Taylor was taking and what they were for. It was a wakeup call to me that I had not been following closely enough. Each and every detail mattered, and I would have to become more aware of the larger picture. Knowledge is power in this kind of circumstance. Taylor's recovery depended in part on our knowing all that we could about every detail.

Keith and Tanner arrived, and we got Taylor settled in. In the midst of this incident, I was relieved that it occurred when Keith and Tanner had already been driving to see us. Dealing with this type of thing alone would have been more burdensome for many reasons. I returned to Bryn Mawr to gather a few of Taylor's things that we needed. One of them was protective mitts for his hands. The hospital at Paoli had mitts, but Taylor had managed to take them off in a matter of seconds. The mitts that the rehab provided were far more secure.

Kristine and José were there, and they were a welcome sight. I was feeling regret that I had not been there when the seizures took place. I thought Kristine was the next best person to have been with Taylor, but in reality, she was the first best person to have been present. She told me that one of her first thoughts after wondering where I had gone, was that she was thankful I had not been there. Kristine is a nurse but before that, she is a mother. She understood that if witnessing the episode were

165

troublesome for her, it would have carried a far greater degree of agony for me.

Kristine was one of the most professional presences at Bryn Mawr. I knew she cared about our family, but she maintained a healthy distance. I am sure that she couldn't afford to get too attached. She cared for and about Taylor. She admitted to me that the grand mal seizures that Taylor had had were difficult for her to see even after her many years of experience. She defined them as very bad episodes. She was thankful that I was not present because I think she knew that seeing them would have been too much for me. I never saw myself as fragile in this whole ordeal, and I think I was very strong for Taylor, but I am also now aware that I was delicate and it was obvious to others around me. Just imagining Taylor going through those things was horrible enough. If I had been there, it might have sent me over the edge.

Taylor stayed at the Paoli Hospital for four days. Each day was full of little rest and even more stress than we were accustomed to. Taylor could not be left alone even overnight. One of us would sleep in a recliner in his room. Keith stayed for the first night and I stayed for the next two. The nursing staff was unfamiliar with Taylor's needs and they were unprepared to handle him. On Sunday, when Tanner and Keith left, I was panic-stricken. I was truly worried for Taylor's safety.

One thing worth mentioning is that within a couple of weeks of Taylor's accident, a nurse at Geisinger spoke with us about an important issue. His brother had suffered a traumatic brain injury years before, and this man had watched his parents not only suffer but experience extra frustration in trying to navigate his brother's care. He approached us to suggest giving strong consideration to acquiring guardianship for Taylor, both legal and medical. We also needed to establish ourselves in the legal sense as having power-of-attorney privileges over Taylor's finances, business affairs, and decision-making. In order to become Taylor's guardians, we had to go to court and petition for these legal privileges. We went about twenty days after Taylor's fall. The judge was compassionate and fair. He did some things that helped reduce the expenses of the process as well as making it easier to navigate than we had initially anticipated. This guidance was something that became valuable to us in countless ways. In precarious times, like Taylor's hospitalization, guardianship and medical decision-making rights played a vital role.

One of Taylor's closest friends wrote the following message on the public page created in support of Taylor and our family on January 8:

> *You are stronger now than ever before, Bing. The size of the fight inside of you is inspiring to so many. Some people are strong, but you have proved to be the strongest. With that being said, keep on pushing forward, one small step at a time, we believe.*

They were words written to Taylor, which he could not have read or comprehended, but I did both for him. And I believed them.

Fortunately, Paoli had provided a net bed and much of the time we had to leave Taylor in it, completely zipped up. This confinement left Taylor acting very restless. On one occasion, a therapist came in to get Taylor out of bed and into a chair. I understood her to say that she would be coming right back, but she didn't. Taylor was still missing his bone flaps and his head was in a vulnerable position. At Bryn Mawr, safety precautions were always in place; there were protocols and they were carefully followed. For example, Taylor was never left unattended and any time he was moved or placed in a standing position, he wore his helmet. At this hospital, on this particular floor, matters like helmets, safety belts, and other items related to protection were not part of the routine or treatment plan. By the second day, I had spoken with the patient advocate twice.

Since the accident, I had never moved Taylor from a chair to his bed. At Bryn Mawr, only trained staff were permitted to do those things. There was a certain finesse to lifting him and letting him balance on you. But when the therapist left, Taylor attempted to stand on his own. He wanted to get back into bed. I knew he could not hold himself up or balance his weight, so I pressed the call button and tried to do what I had

167

witnessed numerous times at Bryn Mawr. I also called out for help, but I was worried about a reaction from Taylor, so I couldn't shout. Taylor had something like "sea legs"; even though he imagined that he could hold himself up, he couldn't. Taylor's safety was in my hands and that scared me. A fall could have been more than disastrous for him. I felt relieved when I was able to navigate him safely into bed. *I also knew that Taylor needed to get back to Bryn Mawr.*

On another occasion, I had to put Taylor's mitts on his hands. The mitts protected him and those around him. His behavior was getting out of control and the lack of routine, new medications, and untrained staff members were affecting him. Taylor had no ability to rationalize or reason with what was occurring around him. I unzipped his bed to put on the mitts—which in itself was tricky—and things went south from there. I could get on only one mitt at a time, and I had to secure Taylor's other hand, which was thrashing around. He did not like it and began grabbing at me and swinging his arms. Taylor was still relatively strong. I ended up getting smacked in the face a few times, and Taylor somehow got hold of my dangling earring and almost ripped it from my ear. As his grip tightened and he began to pull, I placed my hand over his and squeezed until he released. I did not want to be injured while trying to help Taylor. My face stung, my ear hurt, and my level of fear and frustration was growing.

It was a long set of days. On Tuesday my stepmom, Miss Connie, was coming in from Atlanta and I had to pick her up at a train station. It would take me thirty minutes to pick her up, so I arranged with a staff member to sit with Taylor while I was gone. I left with the understanding that someone would be in his room the entire time I was away. Fortunately, Taylor was asleep and he was secure in his bed. I had spent the morning discussing his safety with the head of the department. When Miss Connie and I returned, no one was with Taylor. I began a louder campaign to have him discharged; and later that afternoon, he was. My voice was finally heard. It was in everyone's best interest to get Taylor back to the rehab.

Reflecting back, I know that Taylor's level of care was not affected by nurses who did not care, because they did. Many of them tried hard to make it work. It was not about a lack of skill because skill was present. In my opinion, it was about the absence of exposure to and knowledge of traumatic brain injury. I was just glad that Taylor came through the stay unscathed; and the words "Home Sweet Home" now applied to Bryn Mawr Rehabilitation Hospital. The doctors at Paoli did manage to safely adjust Taylor's medication, and the seizures stopped for the time being.

The presence of my stepmother, whom I have always called "Miss Connie," was both sweet and supportive. Several years ago, her son Ralph had been shot and killed in a random drive-by shooting in Williamsburg, Virginia. Ralph was simply in the wrong place at the wrong time, and a group of angry, rebellious teenagers had started their five-hour shooting spree by taunting and then shooting him in the back of the head as he rode his bike home from work.

My sweet Miss Connie represented a lifetime presence of love to me. She embodies intelligence, sensitivity, kindness, and courage. She is also one of the most wonderful Southern belles in the world, our family's very own Steel Magnolia. The murder of her son, who was an identical twin, had torn her down in so many ways. I grieved the death of my stepbrother, but in all honesty, I grieved Miss Connie's suffering the most. It took a lot of reflection to accept what had happened to someone who had been such a beautiful source of good in my life. It was a process that would take me years. I hated to see someone that I loved so deeply in such absolute turmoil. I knew that Miss Connie understood my pain. I knew that her heart had been smashed, broken, ground up and beaten to a pulp when her son was killed. If there were a safe place to cry now, it would be on her shoulder.

A couple of years prior to Taylor's fall, she had written me one of the most heart-wrenching letters I think I have ever received. It is one of the times in my life when I felt I was seeing into someone's soul. Miss Connie handled her grief with grace and dignity, but those of us closest to her knew she was lost in much of it. She wrote to me that when Ralph was killed, so many things were taken from her. She no longer found joy in the activities that used to bring it to her. For years she had played the piano beautifully and now she could no longer bear to play. Gardening and growing roses had been one of her passions, and now, they just felt empty. She loved singing and had always been part of choirs even in her adult life, and now there was no joy in that. There was a hole and void caused by the senseless death of her son. I was at a different place in my grief and Taylor was still here in a different way, but we shared something I never want to share with anyone else. We shared the weight of what grief and loss can bring, and we understood each other. There are things that no mother's heart is prepared to deal with, and both of us were living out those things.

Taylor had always called Miss Connie, Nina, and my dad, Pawpaw. She had come alone to be with me, to see Taylor, and to help in any way she could. The timing was perfect. She and my dad were living with and caring for grandmother, who was in her nineties, several states away, so they were not able to be close by. Taylor was not yet speaking, but he tried to vocalize and he laughed a lot. He tried at times to speak, but his garbled utterances made no sense.

I could tell that he recognized Nina. At this time, no one outside of Keith, Avery, Tanner, or I had seen Taylor. Under the advice of the doctors and what we felt was best, we had not yet permitted visitors to come to Bryn Mawr. Miss Connie was the first one to see him when his eyes were opened and in his present stage. We were in Taylor's room, and I reminded him, "This is Nina, and she came to see us." Taylor grinned and then gave his Nina a big and exaggerated wink!!! *That* was communicating! Nina then lifted her hand to give Taylor a high-five, but instead he took her hand in his and kissed it. She later wrote in Taylor's visitors' journal that in that moment her heart totally melted. She also wrote that she was prepared for recovery to take time, but she desperately wanted Taylor to come back to us completely.

A year and a half later, if I close my eyes, I can still see Miss Connie making laps with Taylor around the Maple Unit. Her legs appeared tired and I know she was mentally drained as well, but she continued to push him along. In this moment, I could see both the sadness and love that was present in my stepmother's mind. This was her grandson, one of the loves of her life, and she expressed that love in a way that moved me, and will be etched forever in my memory.

Taylor would have to be readmitted to Bryn Mawr and reevaluated. The process was relatively smooth and the admissions person, who gave out pens and a T-shirt with each new admission, remarked that this was our second time coming around the admissions bend. It would not be the last.

On January 11, I provided the following update on Facebook:

After hearing from some of you, I need to clarify Taylor's progress. Taylor is still in what is termed a minimally conscious state. However, even in this state, in rehab life moves ahead. Part of emerging from a coma is getting the mind to understand the old, normal things. An example might be brushing your teeth; the mind does these things on autopilot. In rehab they are done with great assistance and special tools. Taylor is not awake in the sense that we are. He is emerging. It is hard to update and clarify where Taylor is. Traumatic brain injury is as different for everyone as each individual fingerprint. No two of either are the same.

If Taylor were to see you, he would not recognize you. He would not point at you. He would not say, "Hi" or anything else. When he attends therapies, his body actively participates and this requires great effort. I do not want to paint a picture that is not true. Many of the families I have talked with express that no one can imagine what we see and experience in here. I think sometimes in my posts I am protecting you, my family, and Taylor, but I am trying to be as honest as I can be about where Taylor is in his recovery.

Miss Connie stayed with me through the following week. Her company was a blessing in a time of such loneliness. On the Saturday a week after the seizure episodes, we drove to my home together, and Keith came to stay with Taylor. We spent a day and a half with Tanner and Avery. Miss Connie cooked a delicious, comforting meal for us, while Tanner and Avery played sweet songs on their guitar. I took advantage of a long hot bath, the comfort of my own bed, and the familiarity of my home. Miss Connie and I returned to Bryn Mawr later Sunday evening and she left the following morning. She filled me up with all of the good that was inside of her. She reminded me to hold on to hope, and I could not have been more thankful that she had been with me for those past several days. Saying goodbye to her was most difficult.

Time moved along in Bryn Mawr. The new monster, seizures, had reared its ugly head for the first time. It would not even begin to be close to the last. There was great relief that the adjustment in Taylor's medication was working and for now, it had made the monster disappear.

On January 15, I further explained what was happening:

Taylor continues in a minimally conscious state. Everyone asks, "Is he awake?" And that is a tricky question. Taylor participates in various therapies daily to make him more aware, but he is still technically in a coma. The things he is able to do at this point, he does from memory recall. He remains confused and totally unaware of what has happened. Taylor suffered a devastating brain injury and we will not know the true affects for several months. We have not been given a prognosis. There have been slow and subtle progresses. For now, your support helps in many ways and eases many burdens and we thank you.

Chapter Thirteen
Nothing Is Guaranteed

After the seizure episode, it seemed as if Taylor had hit a plateau. The staff warned us that this apparent lack of progress could happen, but fortunately the period of stillness quickly passed. Taylor was finally, thankfully trach-free; however, a lot of work had to take place so that he could eventually take in food and nutrition by mouth. The feeding tube would stay in, but the goal would be to use it less frequently. We didn't want the tube to be a necessity for Taylor. It had to stay in place for the time being because the bone flap that had been frozen was to be put back in his head in early February. Keeping the PEG tube meant less trouble if for some reason a setback occurred that left him again unable to eat. Taylor was also not yet taking in enough nutrition on his own; a feeding supplement had to be given.

Donna, the speech therapist, included me in her treatment plan as things progressed. Donna explained that it was vital to pick up on Taylor's nonverbal cues. Taylor had started to make gestures, like pointing in a particular direction when asked which way he wanted to go in the hall. He seemed to like being in charge of something as well as having some sort of input. As the first-born of three boys, Taylor was used to being a leader in our home, but he had been a quiet leader. Prior to his injury, Taylor was never one to draw attention to himself, but at times he could be demanding. He had high expectations of himself and of others. I never experienced him as being bossy, but he was clearly a person who had a plan that he intended to carry out. This type of thought process seemed to be present in therapy.

It was not difficult to understand what he was trying to express, which helped him to stay calm. Taylor's thinking at this point was very limited, which made interpreting his thought process easier.

Taylor did not welcome my presence in his speech therapy sessions. During physical therapy, however, he seemed proud to have me watch. As he and his therapists came walking around the bend, he often noticed me and stood a little taller. This positive response was not the case in speech therapy. After a couple of times witnessing him become highly agitated, I decided to put some space between us. If I watched at all, I stood behind a piece of glass at a distance or from a position around

174

the corner where I could hear what was happening even if I couldn't see it. The therapist explained that Taylor's agitation was not uncommon. The lack of communication was frustrating and on some level Taylor was aware of his limitations. When it was just the two of us, he willingly participated in the various communication exercises.

Another tool that the therapist suggested was making a set of personalized flash cards. The cards all contained items that both related and provided recall to Taylor. The series looked something like this, front to back:

Hometown—Mifflinburg
Age—Twenty-two
Brothers—Tanner and Avery
Work—Silvertip [an HVAC company]
Dog—Ginger
High School—Mifflinburg Area
Dad—Keith
Mom—Nicole
Team—Wildcats

We also crafted a photo album of the people who were directly involved in Taylor's life prior to his fall. There were one to two photos on each page, and each person was identified in clear, large print, as they would have been by Taylor. Some of the photos also included Taylor, and I felt a lump in my throat each time I viewed them. *I wondered whether I would ever really see again the person who was in those photos.*

Taylor was fortunate enough to receive a steady flow of get-well cards from family and friends. The cards were part of his recovery too. We looked at them together and I would read each one to Taylor. He allowed me to read only two or three cards at a time and then he was done with that activity. *He had a limited attention span.* And when he was done with something, his body language made it very clear. He would grow agitated and restless or completely zone out, either way I knew it was time to stop.

The evening hours allowed for a lot of makeshift therapy sessions with Taylor. As always, I pushed the wheelchair for hours around the rehab floors with Taylor as my passenger. These nighttime hours were a time when I was able to witness and participate in a lot of Taylor's gradual progress. In the early days, we simply walked in silence. The motion of the chair was soothing to Taylor and I knew when he needed calm and quiet versus having me chat. He rode along, leaning back with very little activity or participation.

As he rolled along, I would discuss the art that hung on the walls of the corridors. There were particular pieces that I thought he would enjoy or relate to more easily, so I would stop in front of them and talk to him about them. If a photograph or painting portrayed a simple concept, I would point that out. For example, one photograph was of bright green leaves with dew on them. I explained the photo to Taylor and reminded him of the fact that we lived in the woods surrounded by trees. Sometimes, I just talked about the colors in the art. There was a lovely watercolor painting of a sailboat, and I reminisced about our times on the water over the years. I used the objects around us as tools to connect to Taylor, and hopefully to help him reconnect to himself.

Each night, I tried to go to one particular window where cellphone reception was good. I would always call home and occasionally call the extended family. Imagining that Taylor missed the rest of our family, I would hold the phone up to his ear and let him listen to Keith, Avery, or Tanner. Taylor did not speak, but he did listen. Their words to him were short and to the point but always encouraging. I believed that keeping that type of connection mattered. The input that Taylor was receiving was just as valuable as the output that we hoped he would soon be able to return.

Slowly, Taylor began to make more complex movements. There were rails along the hallway walls, and he started to hold on to them with his right hand, sliding his hand along the rail as he rolled. He was not able to do the same on his left side, however. He also began to toss a

176

small foamy ball about four inches in diameter and attempted to catch it. We would spend ten-minute intervals every hour in a quiet, remote area playing catch until he got restless. Taylor did not sit still well, so most of the time I kept us moving.

Many of the moments in the hallway were spent in silence. Taylor had often been quiet before the accident, especially when he was in a thoughtful or pensive mood, but this silence was too much. I wanted him to say something to me. I wanted him to ask me something that he might have said before, like "Where am I and what in the hell is happening?" I would push Taylor along and quietly pray for him. I thought about where we were, and I tried to envision how far he could come. I became engrossed in the songs of Patty Griffin, and there were other songs on my iPod that touched my heart. The songs that I played over and over again were Patty Griffin's "Up to the Mountain," "I Don't Give Up," "Rain," "You Are Not Alone," and "Making Pies." Each of these songs had something in them that I related to, but mainly I was comforted by the gentleness that they offered. I came to grips with my sadness and freely let my tears fall, in a way that felt safe and comfortable to me. I related many of the lyrics in some way to Taylor, and the music helped to heal a part of me by allowing me to feel my pain. The song that spoke most to my confused, broken heart was Patty's version of "Don't Come Easy."

Red lights are flashing on the highway
I wonder if we're gonna ever get home
I wonder if we're gonna ever get home tonight
Everywhere the waters getting rough
Your best intentions may not be enough
I wonder if we're gonna ever get home tonight

But if you break down
I'll drive out and find you
If you forget my love
I'll try to remind you

And stay by you when it don't come easy.

Nothing was coming easy for us and it was not coming easy for Taylor. But we were surrounded by those whose stories were at times even more heartbreaking and hard to watch unfold. My heart was taken to new levels of pain and my spirit was continually moved to reach out to others. With every day that passed, my resolve to help Taylor progress increased, as did my care for the many others in our position. I was thankful for the fact that Taylor was showing progress even if it was in very small increments.

It was around the third week in January, nine weeks since his fall, that Taylor began to verbalize. He did not start by speaking sentences, but rather one or two words. His voice was not at all the same as it had been; instead it was raspy and could be compared to a weak whisper. You could easily see that speaking itself took a lot out of Taylor. He had not fully lost his language ability, but there were also many and obvious deficits. He knew that I am his mom and he called me that. He also had a clear recognition of his dad. As far as his brothers, it was not clear what was happening, but I was sure that he was happy to see them. He recognized them but could say only Avery's name, and not Tanner's. When he saw his dad on the weekends, there was happiness present in his eyes. I can't fully explain it because Taylor had hardly any facial expressions, but I knew he recognized the love of his dad. Keith brought Taylor a large pillow in the shape of a trout, and every night when I tucked him in in Keith's absence, I would remind him of how much his dad loved him.

The week of January 20, we made a decision along with Taylor's treatment team to allow people outside our immediate family to come and visit. There was a team meeting at the beginning of each week to discuss the continued plans for Taylor and his progress or lack of it. The team meeting was a time when everyone involved in his care could come together. A psychiatrist and a neurological psychologist became more actively involved in his routine. As Taylor emerged from his silence, it would be important to have some interpretation of his feelings. It was also essential for the staff to understand who Taylor was and what might have been going on in his mind prior to the fall. A patient's psyche plays an important role in his or her recovery. Taylor having visitors was something everyone agreed would be beneficial for him.

The first friends to make the three-hour drive to Bryn Mawr were two long-time buddies that he had known since elementary school, Trevor and Bobby. They had seen Taylor in a coma, but not since he had begun to emerge into consciousness. Taylor's mouth broke out in a huge grin when he laid eyes on his friends. He recognized them and made some correct word associations with them. Taylor and Bobby thumb-wrestled at one point in the visit. This game was something new that Taylor liked to do with his dad and brothers. Bobby purposely lost the match; when it ended and Taylor knew he had beaten Bobby, he called him a pussy. Trevor and Bobby both laughed so hard—it was a good moment. That comment came from the friend they knew, and it was something that Taylor would have said previously. It was a moment that would not be forgotten.

Their visit was good for Taylor and it brought happiness to each one of us to see him experience genuine pleasure. It was a bit awkward as Trevor, Bobby, and I strolled through the halls with Taylor. I was at a loss for words, but as Taylor's mother, I felt I had to say something. The rules required me to stay with Taylor, so I teased the boys by saying that they should just pretend I wasn't there. Taylor tired easily, so the boys and I chatted and shared our feelings when he went for his nap. It was a sensitive time for everyone. My thoughts churned endlessly. I was grateful that these young men, Taylor's dear friends, had chosen to visit instead of staying away. I knew that it was not an easy task for either of them. It spoke of their courage, compassion, and bravery. Once the visit was over, I fully understood its importance in terms of Taylor's recovery. *His friends reached a part of him that I could not.*

That week Taylor had four more visitors. His vocabulary and recall seemed to grow with each person who showed up. The next visitors to come were Taylor's Uncle Rick and Aunt Kellie. He recognized his uncle and was able to identify him as Uncle Rick. When

Rick asked if he could come back again, Taylor said "Yes." Taylor had a harder time identifying and connecting with his aunt, but her presence was still important to him and graciously accepted.

When his friends Brett and Shelby visited, Taylor was happy to see them, which was apparent from their smiles and laughter. At one point, Taylor took off his helmet and handed it to Brett. Brett put it on his head and Taylor laughed hysterically. His laugh was different and strangely animated, but we knew what he was expressing.

As the week progressed Taylor grew tired, and it seemed like the visits were becoming too draining for him, especially when visitors came back to back. Reconnecting required a lot of work on Taylor's part.

The clues that Taylor was feeling drained were not difficult to interpret: he simply would not make eye contact or attempt to communicate verbally. *He just shut down.* It was his way of telling us that we still needed to take it slow. His recovery was a balancing act for us. Taylor's friends, who were very concerned, wanted and probably on some level needed to see him. But consideration in Taylor's recovery meant that his needs came first and foremost. One of the factors that had been discussed with us from the time that Taylor was in the intensive care unit at Geisinger is that the healing of the brain is a slow and often tedious process. One point that was crucial for us to remember is that too much stimulation could bring a setback.

Matters started to improve during the final week of January. Taylor was taking in a larger portion of his diet by way of honey-thick liquids, and his swallowing was improving. He enjoyed the benefit of tasting the various liquids that came with his speech therapy. This enjoyment, coupled with more frequent communication, was a big step in the right direction. He began to ask for specific things. He repeatedly asked for "purple" and a "turtle." He also asked for a pair of scissors and his pistol. None of what he asked for made sense in that situation, but they were words and they meant something.

I also noticed that his body was becoming physically stronger. Taylor spent a good deal of time on a MOTOmed[16] in physical therapy.

This piece of equipment allowed him to stay in his wheelchair. His feet were placed on motorized pedals, and when the machine was turned on, it would move Taylor's legs around in a cycle. When Taylor began to pedal on his own, the motor would stop so that his leg muscles were doing the work. Taylor was also doing a lot of exercises on the mat and bolsters. He was still regaining the most basic strengthening tools. He walked every day with maximum assistance in his physical therapy sessions, and from time to time, he walked up and down the stairs. The stairwell that he used was in an enclosed hallway that no one other than patients and therapists had access to. This made completing the task at hand doable. Never once did I feel that Taylor's safety was compromised, the team gave full attention to his care.

In terms of cognitive improvement, he was at the point when he recognized some people and certain objects. He expressed attachment to a pillow that a close friend had made for him with a large blown-up photo of our dog Ginger on it. If I could have ordered one of those pillows for every patient with a dog, I would have! Taylor's pillow brought joy to everyone who saw it.

Taylor had moved to a consistent Level IV on the Rancho Los Amigos scale. We were not yet able to see the true inner workings of what had occurred as a result of the damage to Taylor's brain. Most of what we could identify was based on what we could see outwardly. Taylor's injury had been identified as having caused the most damage to the right side of his brain, which resulted in physical deficits on the left side of his body.[17] He remained incredibly weak and rarely used his left side for anything. *It was often motionless.* As far as mental functions like logic, personality, memory, and reasoning, we were still in the dark as to who would emerge.

---

[16] MOTOmed is the brand name of a movement trainer that can be used to move a patient's arms or legs passively; to move them with the assistance of a motor; or to provide active resistance that requires the patient to use his or her own muscle strength.

[17] Wilder Penfield, a famous Canadian neurosurgeon, discovered in the 1940s that the right side of the brain governs movement and sensory perception on the left side of the body, and vice versa.

On the practical front, insurance issues were mounting. I was spending several hours a day discussing Taylor's upcoming surgery. Taylor's insurance from his place of employment was coming to a close. I could transfer him to mine, but everything was in limbo. I was on FMLA leave[18] without pay, but with benefits. In time, I would have to change over to paying for our continued benefits. The case managers assigned to Taylor helped me to navigate these treacherous waters. They were busier than anyone I have ever seen in any business or medical setting. Their phones rang incessantly, and someone like me was forever knocking on their doors. They had to tell families bad news, good news, and anything in between. Often, they served as liaisons between physicians and the patients' families. The case managers made it clear that they would help advocate for me, and they did. They provided a place where I could say things that I didn't know whether anyone else could understand. I became particularly close to one of them, who managed Taylor's case for much of his stay. She had an incredible sense of humor. She was down-to-earth, and no matter what mood I brought to her door, she provided support. Our conversations would go from crying to laughing in a matter of seconds. It was a place to be open about all that was happening. Brain injury sucks—and that was a theme that we stuck with. She dubbed me a "firefly"; she saw me as a person who brought light wherever I went, and I so wanted to keep that light of hope burning.

I was getting closer to a number of families who occupied The Laurels and the halls of the rehab. I was there all week alone, and although there was minimal socialization, connections among us did form. We might chat in the waiting area or while riding in the elevator. Taylor had a roommate, and his mother and I became fast friends. Taylor and this young man shared a room for many weeks. David was just fifteen years old when an adult who was driving while intoxicated killed his girlfriend and left him in a minimally conscious state. I also met some parents who had received a call one day telling them that their daughter

---

[18] Job-protected unpaid leave for qualified medical and family reasons, provided for employees of covered employers by the federal Family and Medical Leave Act (FMLA) of 1993.

did not show up for work. Missing work was highly unusual for her, and when they arrived at her home, they found her unconscious. They never knew what happened, no medical reason could ever be identified, but she was in a comatose state. She offered very little if any response to them while she was at Bryn Mawr, and it was absolutely heartbreaking. I met a man and his fiancée, both of whose lives were forever altered when he made the choice not to wear a helmet and then was hit by a motorist who did not see him. The stories were endless and they matched the bottomless amount of pain stored within the walls of the rehab hospital.

Taylor's recovery was already surpassing that of many patients around him. It was agonizing to see people's children or loved ones fail to make progress. The fact that Taylor was able to get up and walk with assistance was much further than many others would get, but there were also many patients who were progressing. They filled the gym with movement. They would come and go in a matter of weeks rather than months. One day these patients might be talking with their family or eating takeout in the small cafeteria, the next week they would go home. And there were those like Taylor, who were making forward strides that could be measured from the time they had come to the facility, and yet they had much further to go. There were no predictable outcomes in the rehabilitation facility. There were guesses about what the future might hold and previous cases that suggested information, but nothing was promised and nothing was guaranteed. For some patients . . . time stood still and for others it passed. There was no way to know how quickly recovery would take place, or whether it would at all.

In the middle of all my questioning, I was inspired to write something of my own for Taylor. In mid-January, I wrote the following and titled it "Taylor's Song":

> *You are still my shining star*
> *You are still my deepest joy*
> *And even though you seem so far,*
> *You are here, my precious boy.*

I will wait for you to come
I will hope for you to wake
I will accept the smallest sum
Of every little step you make.

We will hold on to our hope
We will wait for life's full hour
We will not sit and mope,
We will trust in love's strong power.

I know you are stronger than this.
I know you are braver than this.
I know your future is brighter than this.
Come home, Taylor,
Come home.

The cry of my heart had not changed. I wanted Taylor to come home. I would sing the very last part of my song to Taylor over and over again as I pushed him through the hallways. Sometimes I would laugh, wondering if he wanted to say, "Hey, Mom, enough! Put on some country music. And *please* stop singing."

PART IV: Danville 2

Chapter Fourteen
Snails and Africa

My February 1 Facebook post read:

After hearing from a few of you and knowing how much you value the updates, I realize it is time for another. A friend said to me this week, "Even if nothing changes, we care and we want to hear how you all are."

We are entering week ten of Taylor's recovery, and although he has come so far, it is not far enough. I liken it to traveling to Africa by foot alongside a snail. It is painfully slow and at times we are unsure we will ever reach our destination. We anticipate much more, and wait with hope for progress to unfold.

In the real world we are dealing with insurance issues and frustrations, which have consumed hours upon hours, and have felt especially stressful. The magnitude of these issues is a lot to process, so instead of looking at the mountain, we look at the stones, removing them one by one, and eventually we hope they disappear.

Taylor continues to be at Level IV on the Rancho scale. His diet has been upgraded to include liquids that are a nectar-based consistency. This is thinner than the honey and is a good step. Taylor eats a simple puréed diet. If you know Taylor, you will not at all be surprised to know that he is enjoying chow time.

All in all, Taylor makes slow but continual strides in all of his therapies.

As a family we work continually to remind Taylor of his strength, progress, his circle of friends and how loved he is. For many things in life there are not quick fixes or easy answers. We just move through them the best way that we can. It always makes it easier when we don't have to do it on our own. Thank you for standing with us.

Later that same day, Avery came to visit. He came on Friday afternoon and stayed for the night. His college semester was moving ahead and he had to keep up his grades, but he made time to make the grueling drive to Bryn Mawr. I remember peeking out the window that Friday afternoon and seeing Avery be-bopping along. He was wearing the cutest panda bear winter hat. Oh, how I loved him, and how I cherished his presence in the midst of this. There is nothing that makes you value your children's lives more than almost losing them. The reality of knowing that they could be gone in an instant was always in front of me. The panda hat, which was actually made for a young child, brought smiles of delight to everyone who saw it.

Each Friday night, after tucking Taylor in, Avery and I would go and grab a bite to eat. After days of eating makeshift meals in my room at The Laurels, eating something fresh and delicious was a treat. We found a great local Thai restaurant. The first time we went, Avery was in sweatpants and I was wearing jeans and a sweatshirt. It was a fine dining establishment, but we chose it because we really wanted Thai food. When we entered, I immediately told the staff that I was sorry for our casual dress, but we were visiting a family member in the hospital and we were just trying to be comfortable. The restaurant staff was not concerned even though many of the tables around us were filled with well-dressed people. The staff was especially cordial to us that night and we instantly liked them. We savored the delicious food and shared a dessert of mango and coconut ice cream that was made off the premises. When I tell you it was some of the best food I have ever eaten, I am not telling a lie. From time to time, we would try another eatery, but that Thai restaurant quickly became our favorite place to eat in the surrounding area. The family who owned it also staffed it, and they continued to treat us with warmth and hospitality. On occasion, they would give us a free appetizer or an extra scoop of ice cream.

After dinner, we would come back to the room, talk, or sit together and watch television. It was a time when I grew even closer to Avery. He had to mature a lot faster than I had ever imagined and he was a wonderful leaning post for me. None of my sons had ever seen me cry so much or so frequently. I was thankful that they could handle my tears. I was also thankful for Avery's hugs. They had always been full of all that good stuff that hugs are made of, and I felt so grateful for them. My feelings were hard enough to contain day to day, and I needed a safe place to share them. One of the gifts that Avery often gave me, other than his time and his listening ear, was his willingness to share his own updates on Facebook. I really felt that it was important to hear things from a perspective other than mine. When Avery left that weekend, he posted on Facebook on February 4:

> *I haven't updated on Taylor recently because it's hard to find the right words that describe the situation without being too optimistic or pessimistic. Taylor remains at the Level IV and is beginning to do more things. He is eating small amounts, but everything he's eaten thus far is the consistency of mashed potatoes or similar. Essentially nothing he has to chew in order for it to go down; the therapists are making sure he's able to swallow before moving on to foods with greater substance.*
>
> *Taylor's physical therapy is going well, but it's a slow process. He's trying to regain his balance and ability to walk right now, and he's being held back by the inability to control his left side. Taylor has been talking, but keep in mind that the tone isn't what we're used to.*
>
> *Some of the things he says make sense and others are complete nonsense (at least in our minds, but in his they likely make perfect sense.) His unique sense of humor is still in place and we've seen shades of it in recent weeks; there's no doubt in my mind and the minds of those who have seen him that "he's in there."*[19]

---

[19] One of the things that Avery had set up for Taylor was an electronic tablet similar to an iPad. Avery had added an application that replicated farting noises when certain colors were touched. Taylor loved that application, and it reminded me of what having three sons often includes . . . joking about the sounds of farting, and then laughing. That tablet app was one way that we were able to see Taylor's humor.

Taylor's memory does seem to be intact, but sometimes he is just in need of reminders. The medical staff suggested reintroducing Taylor to friends and family who have been the most prominent in his life, since he's more likely to remember them.

Sometimes Taylor seems upset or extremely happy to see someone (his face looks like he's going to cry but he's physically unable to do so). Keep in mind that if you'd like to see him, it's not going to be a day off of school or work as a field trip so to speak. It will wrench at your heart, but if you can be strong for Taylor, that's what he needs most right now.

Looking back, I think that if Avery had been one-hundred-percent honest with others, he might simply have written, "Does anyone know how much I miss my big brother? Does anyone understand how hard and scary this is?"

But that would have been too painful to say or admit, let alone announce to others. So Avery did what we were all trying to do—paint a picture that was easier for other people to see and perhaps easiest for us to digest. Our family has never had a flair for the dramatic, and that worked in our favor. We did not have to create any drama; it was there in the situation itself and we did not need to feed into it or make it up. Our lives were a constant roller coaster of emotions, and very few of those emotions fell on the good side of the scale.

After the weekend ended, my mom visited Bryn Mawr. We had planned to have time together and of course, some time with Taylor. My mom was hopeful that she could relieve some of my stress, but matters changed fairly fast. We knew that Taylor's bone flap replacement surgery was imminent, but it had not yet been scheduled. My mom came on a Monday, and by Tuesday, we were being told that his surgery might take place that Thursday.

The last time my mom had seen Taylor was the night he was admitted to Bryn Mawr. He had not yet opened his eyes for more than a few seconds at the most, and had been completely unresponsive. This time when she came in, he was sitting in his wheelchair ready to face the new day. We took him into the dining room and I said, "Taylor, do you know who this is?" He responded, "Gram," then stopped and I gave him a clue: "Gran . . ." He thought and then said, "Grandbunny." That is a moment that my mom still remembers. She was so happy to see Taylor in the condition that he was then in, considering where he had been, but she also was sad to see him as he was. That was a conflict many of us were caught in. We missed the person we had always loved and known, and yet we felt relieved that some part of him was still there.

Taylor's interactions with others were perfunctory at best. If you caught a glimpse of a part of his former self, it was brief, lasting only for a fleeting moment. One of the hardest concepts to grasp was that he could not understand that you missed him. He had no idea of the world that was turning around him, the hell he was stuck in, and the agony that those he loved most were undergoing.

The day after my mom arrived, things started to get a little crazy. The team at Geisinger wanted the surgery to take place on Thursday, February 7, 2013. We were in between insurance companies and there was some difficulty in getting the procedure approved. Taylor's insurance from his place of employment had been terminated, so he was placed on the insurance we had through my employer. The transition was seamless, but that did not mean it was smooth. My insurance company had to be caught up on the past ten weeks. Bringing the new carrier up to speed on Taylor's health was an arduous task; it meant that a number of communications had to be transmitted through several sources, and I was at the center of all the communicating. I had the responsibility to pass requested information from point A to point B.

I was spending countless hours on the phone with the billing and scheduling staff; I felt like I had become an employee of the hospital and the insurance company versus being a patient's mother. I spent hour after hour on the telephone, back and forth, dealing with denials and frustrations. The team wanted the surgery scheduled. In order to proceed with scheduling, the billing department had to know it would be paid for. This process was a large part of what advocating meant. I had a big role in making sure things happened in a timely manner; if they didn't, Taylor's procedures were in jeopardy.

The financial costs were already piling up and taking a toll on our family, and I was reluctant to add more pressure on us if I didn't have to. I had been encouraged to sign a release saying that if for some reason the new insurance would not pay for the preliminary tests or the surgery, we would be responsible for all costs involved, which totaled several thousand dollars. *It wasn't a matter of whether we would pay for it.* It was a question as to why the new insurance wasn't going to sign off on the procedure. We were presented with all kinds of terms and ludicrous questions. At some point early one morning, I blew a gasket as my mom stood and watched. I had my cellphone up to my ear; I was dialing Bryn Mawr from the landline and looking up some insurance policy on the computer. The lady on my cellphone was telling me that I was going to have to jump through yet another hoop, and when she disclosed that information, I launched my laptop across the small room. I felt like I was some puppet in a cruel Punch and Judy show, and now I was embarrassed. My mom said in reference to my outburst, "Better out than in." Fortunately, the computer landed on the other bed and not on the floor.

I stood firm that until all the procedures and steps involved were approved, Taylor would be staying right where he was. One of the many problems at this point was that other matters like ambulance transportation, Keith's taking a day off, etc., had to be planned as well. I felt like I was going crazy trying to align every piece of the puzzle that needed to be fitted into place.

We kept up with business as usual, as much as possible. My mom's and my plan to help me unwind would have to be postponed. The day that we were scheduled to leave for surgery, Taylor was more alert than ever. He was telling his own form of jokes and remembering how my mom did not like him farting at the dinner table. He had a smile on his face that for the first time seemed like it was coming from within. Seeing him resemble the "old Taylor" made me very afraid of sending him into the operating room. He was making progress, and I did not want him to be set back even an inch. There were lots of theories as to what might happen, but the neurosurgeon, Dr. Taggart, was encouraging along with the staff at the rehab. They had gone through many similar situations, and generally the person who came out of surgery was improved from the person who had gone in.

The reason why Taylor's surgery was so important is that the skull acts as the brain's protection, like a soldier's armor. It holds everything in place and to an extent protects the softer tissues underneath. Once Taylor's bone flap was replaced, the physical structure of his head would be more nearly like it should be.

The decision came at the eleventh hour; the insurance company finally approved the surgery. It was late Wednesday morning and Taylor was loaded into the ambulance by late afternoon, accompanied by José. José was Taylor's constant sidekick. He and Taylor had multiple interactions on a daily basis, and I knew José would take good care of him. My mom and I would follow the ambulance in my car.

Taylor would undergo a cranioplasty and bone flap insertion on Thursday, February 7. Dr. Taggart would perform the surgery. The medical dictionary's definition of a cranioplasty is that it is a surgical repair of a deficit or deformity of the skull. In this case, the bone that had been frozen the night of Taylor's fall was to be reattached. This bone would first be put back in place; and then the surgeon would reattach it to the surrounding bone by using mini-screws. After the reattachment, the large skin flap that had been folded back would be sutured together. This time the surgical team had chosen not to use staples.

Dr. Taggart is a caring, skilled, and experienced neurosurgeon. She pursued Taylor's case with us and was excited about treating him. It was difficult for us to make the change from Dr. Kirkland's care to hers, but Dr. Kirkland was a specialist in pediatric rather than adult neurosurgery.

There were many obvious risks and concerns involved in this surgery, the main one being that Taylor's body might reject the bone flap. This possibility was explained to us as an uncommon, but not unexpected occurrence. For now, we had to push that worry aside.

Replacing the bone was not optional. And the best bet was to try to use Taylor's own bone instead of a prosthetic piece.

One of the hardest things for me to think about was the fact that Taylor would have his head cut open again. The previous incision had barely healed, and the small amount of hair that had regrown on his head would now be shaved again. I remembered the sutures, the staples, and the pain. *I was afraid.* I was afraid that Taylor would now recognize what was happening and be in pain. I feared what might and could go wrong. I feared that Taylor would resist the procedure that had to be done, and I did not want him to be further confused.

My mom and I spent the night in a hotel that was just a few miles away from the hospital. We didn't arrive until close to 11:00 p.m., and had to be at the hospital around 5:30 the following morning. And true to form, I took a long hot bath. I was too anxious to stay more than a few minutes away. Keith would come over right away in the morning, and he and I would be with Taylor in the time period before his surgery. Taylor was awake and alert, but very unclear about what was happening. He was not agitated or frightened; he simply accepted what the staff explained to him. His communication was limited, but it was a lot more frightening for us than it was for him.

The surgery went well. It took longer than anticipated, but Dr. Taggart was happy with the outcome. It was hard to see Taylor puffy, swollen, and confused; but all in all, we felt that the procedure was a success. Shortly after Taylor's accident, his head had swollen to the size of a basketball . . . I was thankful that it did not get that big this time. For the next few days, Taylor was groggy and had very short periods of wakefulness. He had been heavily sedated and was also given stronger doses of the antiseizure medication, which added to his grogginess. On the fifth day post-surgery, he (and I) returned to Bryn Mawr.

Kristine was waiting for us; she expressed concern over how swollen Taylor's face still was. His eyes were so puffy that he could not open them. His mood, however, was more relaxed at the rehabilitation facility than it had been in the hospital, and it was clear that he felt more comfortable at Bryn Mawr. It had become familiar to him and a second

194

home to me. I hoped those things would help to boost his recovery. Returning to Bryn Mawr felt like walking into a room full of good friends, being embraced and understood.

The highlight of the next couple of days was the consumption of some Magic Cups, which are nutritional supplements—frozen desserts fortified with extra protein. Something was not coming together properly in Taylor's recovery, and some people thought from the time he returned to Bryn Mawr that he had been discharged from Geisinger too quickly. The staff at Bryn Mawr kept a close watch on him, as did I. This careful observation meant that I would spend much more of both daytime and evening hours by his side. One of his friends sent him the most adorable camouflage-patterned teddy bear; Taylor held it close to his swollen face and puffy eyes. I worried, but trusted that he would be okay.

Three days after our return to Bryn Mawr, I wrote on Facebook:

> *Taylor has had a rough time bouncing back from the surgery he had a week ago. I am aware that the magnitude of the procedure was unknown to us. Things appeared more simplistic than they turned out to be. Today, as I looked at Taylor I could see the exhaustion. I began to reflect on what he has been through, not just in the past week, but also over the past month. He is an amazing fighter.*
>
> *Those of us who know Taylor know that he has always taken pride in his physical strength. Having that compromised would be agonizing for him. He is still not aware of the state he is in.*
>
> *Please understand that as Taylor's family, we are trying to bring him through this the best way that we know how. A dear friend wrote to me that she is "believing in a happy ending, that puts all fairy tales to shame," Having that ending will require a lot of hard work.*

Taylor spiked a fever one night that continued into the next day, so five days after he returned to Bryn Mawr, we had to turn around and go back to Geisinger. An ambulance transported him, and once again, I followed. My mother had already gone home, so the music of James Taylor kept me company. I laughed as James sang, "In my mind, I'm going to Carolina . . ." I wished I were going to Carolina myself! The three-hour trip was getting harder each time. I was depleted of any real energy and I felt it as I slipped into the rhythm of the road. Caffeine was a necessity, and I needed to remain aware of the potential need to pull over if I became too tired.

When Taylor arrived, he was taken to the emergency room. We spent the night in the ER because they did not have a bed ready for him in the hospital. Taylor was placed in an open bay area with about eight other patients, separated by only a blue curtain. There was a lot of commotion and chatter; this noise, combined with the fluorescent lights that were never turned off, made for a difficult place to keep Taylor's level of stimulation as low as possible. As the night went on, people were either admitted or sent home. I was frustrated and I did express that to the staff. We had been under the impression that Taylor would be admitted on arrival, but that was not possible at the peak of flu season. He also had to be evaluated by the neurologist on duty even though we knew Dr. Taggart was having him admitted. The staff understood my frustration and all parties maintained that conversations go better when approached by trying to understand the other party's perspective. The nurses were doing the best they could, and getting upset with them would not have been productive or beneficial.

Avery came in the late hours of the night to keep me company and to help me. One of us had to be right next to Taylor at all times, because he was in a gurney rather than a safe bed. In the early morning hours, the night shift nurses found a private room for us within the emergency unit before the start of Avery's school day. They brought in a comfortable chair, as the only one in the open area was a metal one. I grabbed some coffee and oatmeal before Avery had to leave; and now that Taylor was in a more comfortable bed, he was able to rest. I tried to sleep as much as I could, but my periods of rest were abbreviated versions of catnaps.

We were placed in the room across from where we had first learned about the severity of Taylor's condition—the room that we had been sitting in while the chaplain explained to us that we might be seeing Taylor for the last time. In some sense that was true. Taylor looked like himself that night of his fall. He appeared to be sleeping, and the ravages of his accident were not yet apparent. When Taylor opened his eyes for the first time for more than a few seconds, the light inside him had gone out.

I could see the empty room across the hall, the room where the beginning of this story unfolded. Being that close to it made my heart pound hard in my chest. Later in the morning, I heard the cries of a family who had to say good-bye to their loved one. The door was open as they made phone calls asking people to come to the hospital quickly, as the team was not sure much time they would have with their loved one. The sounds of their sadness led me back to the fear and shock we had felt that first night. I never wanted to see that room again; I had already gone back there a million times in my mind. Finally, a room opened up on the Special Care Unit, and it was comforting to be among people we felt familiar with.

Taylor's fevers continued over the next few days, but their origin remained unknown. It was classified as a "fever of unknown origin" or FUO. Taylor had several seizures and slight setbacks that played out physically. The forward progress that had taken place in such areas as walking, bending, and general movement was not coming along as easily in other areas. Taylor still needed time to recuperate. It was most fortunate that Taylor had been so strong before his fall, which meant his body had a bit more fight in it.

The reality of it all was hard. It was exhausting, day after day, and in the hospital setting, it was a chore to rest. The words "This is not a sprint, but a marathon" played over and over again in my mind.

I knew it was critical that Taylor's medical needs be met so that his rehabilitation could be maximized, but I missed our familiar faces. I missed having the same nurses, Dena and Kristine. I missed the Bryn Mawr therapists. All in all, I missed the idea of making progress. The staff at Geisinger was good to us, however, and there were a few special people that made the days easier. One of them was a nursing assistant, a young man, probably in his thirties. He had a calm demeanor and was always very pleasant to have around. He would often remind me to go grab something to eat when I left the room for a cup of coffee or just to see a change of scenery, and he would remind me that it was okay to take my time. Keith's brothers and their wives also came periodically, and seeing them was always good. Their presence was welcome and helpful during such a draining time. Keith's youngest brother is a registered nurse, so he would come and sit with Taylor to give us a bit of a reprieve.

Each day that I called the staff at Bryn Mawr, I would try to talk to Kristine or Dena; I really missed these special ladies. Dena and I had spent a lot of time together in the evenings. She was always busy, but never too busy to listen or chat. Dena had the warmest smile and genuine heart. She always asked how the rest of the family was doing and cared about all of us. Dena and I had shared some tough moments in recent days, and she had been such a source of comfort to me. I felt very safe with Dena; I felt that she was a longtime friend. She was the type of person who kept things real. Her heart shone through in everything she did. Over time, Taylor allowed her to tuck him in at night, and he enjoyed those special interactions. Dena referred to Taylor and his roommate as "my boys." When her shift started, you knew you were in for a smile and kind company.

Dena was also fiercely protective of me. There was an evening when one of Taylor's friends, whom I did not know, was sending me messages that were upsetting to me. Throughout the course of Dena's shift, these texts kept coming and Dena comforted me. Dena helped me to see that these messages were highly inappropriate, and that it was a cruel and unkind thing that this "friend" was doing. Dena has a terrific sense of humor, and she balanced what was happening with her insight and humor. There was another instance when Dena approached me about a negative interaction that had taken place with an unfamiliar staff member. I was visibly upset, and she wanted to know why. While explaining through my tears of rage what had taken place, Dena remained calm, reassuring, and professional. But the next morning, the nursing supervisor requested a meeting with me. Dena had gone to her in efforts to help me sort through a precarious situation. Dena was not only caring for Taylor, she was making sure that I was cared for too.

Taylor was cleared to return to Bryn Mawr after six days. This was the fourth time he had been admitted over a two-month period. For insurance and legal purposes, I had to go through the whole process again. The admissions advisor brought her cart into Taylor's room and we both laughed. She asked me if I wanted another pen, bag, or T-shirt.

Prior to returning to Bryn Mawr, I was told something that was supposed to be good news, but it did not feel that way at all. Kristine told me that when Taylor returned, he would be moving to a different part of the unit. Taylor had been in the area where the patients who were less medically stable were kept. These rooms had large windows and were in plain sight of the nurses' station. Now that Taylor was trach-free, he was ready to move to a new room. Another change that had happened over the last few weeks was that Taylor had been toilet-trained. This progress was part of moving to another room as well. Taylor still had accidents, but he was dry when he woke, and he was able to tell you when he needed to go to the bathroom.

I am sure that Kristine had experienced this scenario many times, but this move was our first. *I did not want Taylor to move. I did not want him to have a new team of nurses.* I wanted our little nest where we felt safe and secure. I wanted the familiar faces and voices. I wanted José, Kristine, Brian, and Dena. I had never really liked change before, and this one scared the hell out of me. There were two positives; one was that by walking the unit night after night, I had come to know many of the evening-shift nurses. Taylor's new nurse was the only male nurse on the evening shift. Taylor liked him and always enjoyed passing by his area. The other positive aspect was that this move meant that Taylor was doing better; he was less dependent medically.

We got Taylor settled in his new room and for the first few days, he was without a roommate, which helped. For several days and even longer, I could hardly bear to see Kristine. When I walked by her station, my eyes stung with tears and a huge lump settled in my throat. I felt a bit abandoned. She was the person I had trusted implicitly to care for Taylor. When I was not there in the daytime hours, she was. Her very presence gave me comfort and I did not want to let that go. I was afraid and I actually felt hurt.

I know that hurt may be a hard thing to understand, but Kristine, Dena, and José were our people. José had to give Taylor his shower. He knew that Taylor was impatient, and he knew that when Taylor gave the signal to go to the bathroom, he meant *now*. Kristine and Dena knew how to administer his Lovenox[20] shots in a way that he could handle. Dena was the one person other than me who tucked Taylor in and who else would know that he needed that? She and Kristine knew and cared about Taylor, and I wasn't sure that anyone else could meet those standards. Kristine told me that most of her patients transitioned to Freda and Nick, who would become his primary nurses. She assured me that they would take excellent care of Taylor. She reminded me that she was only a few steps away. I was angry with her for letting us go and more than that, I was furious that we had to be in this place with Taylor.

I told myself over and over again that we were fortunate to have people in Taylor's life that were so hard to let go, because that spoke to their excellence. While the staff did not coddle me in regard to my feelings about the move, they did offer understanding and comfort. It felt like another loss on top of a growing list of losses. I missed my son; I wanted him back, fully and completely. I did not want to deal with one more drop of pain or sadness in my bucket. I feared that another single drop would wash me over the edge, but it didn't.

Freda understood my apprehension and made an effort to keep the lines of communication wide open. Taylor quickly attached himself to Nick, the night nurse. Taylor called him Matt, and acted as if they were old friends. We would later learn that Taylor actually thought Nick

---

[20] Lovenox is the brand name of an anticoagulant drug given to prevent the formation of blood clots in the deep veins of the legs. Patients who are bedridden or unable to walk for long periods of time are at increased risk of these clots.

was a friend from high school whose name was Matt. This caused a lot of confusion for Taylor, but most of the time in his mind he just settled on the idea that Nick was Matt despite what we were telling him. Taylor would ask him about his parents and his house. We did not play along, but Nick had a gentle way of explaining who he was. Nick was a gift to our entire family. I called him "Nick at night" and I loved him. He had a sense of humor, and as a fellow male, he understood Taylor.

At the end of February, we were able to see notable progress. Taylor stayed at Level IV on the Rancho Los Amigos scale. That had not changed, which grew frustrating. There were, however, marked changes in terms of his therapies. From the physical standpoint, he went from a two-person maximum assist to a two-person minimum assist. This definition referred to walking, moving from his wheelchair, getting in and out of bed, and other similar changes of position. Every physical action still required a great deal of effort, but Taylor was doing more of the work on his own.

He continued on the nectar-thin diet in speech therapy, but had been able to add small amounts of ginger ale and water. He was permitted to drink one ounce of thin liquid at a time. He was now on a puréed diet and had eaten his first meal of puréed fish and mashed potatoes. His therapist was working to add blended foods to his diet, but that was not very successful. The feeding tube was still used to meet his caloric and nutritional needs.

Taylor was beginning to recognize and name objects. He had partial aphasia and lots of confusion. Aphasia is a group of language disorders caused by damage to the brain in people who had a normal ability to use language before their disease or injury. Their difficulties may range from problems in finding words to the complete loss of the ability to speak, read, or write.[21] Donna's role as Taylor's speech therapist was to break the cycle of Taylor's communication problems. She had to awaken Taylor's comprehension of what was said to him as

---

[21] Acute aphasia most often results from a stroke or head trauma, but may also develop in patients with epilepsy, brain cancer, or progressive dementias like Alzheimer's disease.

well as teach him once again how to produce his own speech. The thoughts, sound formation, and production of everything together in human speech are a complex process.

Another symptom of Taylor's injury was now apparent, and it was frightening. Taylor had seemed to have a hard time identifying his brothers as separate persons from early on. He would often use Avery's name. He would ask for Avery and express sadness that he wasn't around, but he seemed to dissociate himself from Tanner.

Tanner is the youngest of our three sons. He is a strong athlete and that was always how Taylor connected with him. Taylor loved to watch him as the running back at Friday night football games. Taylor rarely missed an opportunity to cheer Tanner on. We joked that Taylor was living vicariously through him, but it was awe-inspiring to see how proud Taylor was of his little brother. He wore clothing with Tanner's name and number on it, and rallied his friends around Tanner and his team whenever he could. Now, suddenly, it was if Taylor had only one younger brother; he did not distinguish between Avery and Tanner. If Avery was not around and Tanner was, Taylor either ignored Tanner or called him Avery. We had to remind Taylor of who Tanner was.

At the end of February, Taylor's attitude toward and recognition of his little brother changed. *It was not for the better.*

Chapter Fifteen
The Beast Within

It was sometime between late February and early March that Taylor became more expressive in his speech, but his ability to communicate was far from perfect. He called a number of things by the wrong names or terms; for example, he called mouthwash "blue." He called his slippers "sliders," and he sometimes asked for a "sucker" when he meant to ask for a straw. His thoughts took a long time to process and waiting for him to gather his scattered thoughts and then express them was a constant exercise in patience. I think that may be why he initially communicated by giving us the middle finger so frequently. Frustration mounts and then anger sets in.

Taylor held steady at Level IV on the Rancho Los Amigos scale, and yet some new changes were surfacing. When I use the term "held steady," that is not an indication of how we wished for things to be; *it is a description of how it was*. The days at Level IV seemed endless. It seemed as if he had been stuck there forever, but in reality it was merely a matter of weeks. Taylor was displaying more agitation, more frustration, and far less patience. We were told that it could take several weeks for him to move through this stage of turmoil, and that there was a possibility he would not move through it at all. It seemed as if his mind was clinging to the idea of not moving on.

I kept notes on the specific behaviors that Taylor was displaying in direct relation to the level he was at on the scale.[22] Taylor was now **making clear attempts to remove any restraints or tubes**. Taylor was never "restrained" in the sense the word is usually taken to mean; however, he did have safety belts and other devices that kept him from getting out of his wheelchair or falling out of bed. Had he even stood upright, he would not have been able to balance himself. He was also paying more attention to his feeding tube. If pulled hard enough it could have come out, but that seemed unlikely. He would also be **overly reactive to painful stimulus**, both before and after its occurrence. This reactivity mostly centered on his nightly Lovenox shots, but from time to time, he indicated that someone had hurt him if they "touched him too

---

[22] Wording specific to the scale is set in bold italics.

hard" in relation to his personal care. He was ***exhibiting aggressive fight or flight behavior***, which was increasing by the day. Along with that, his moods would switch from being extremely happy to extremely hostile, with no apparent reason for the change.

All these behaviors presented problems for everyone who interacted with Taylor, but they were not new to the staff at Bryn Mawr. In fact, in my discussions with other family members on the unit and just direct observation, I could see a lot of behaviors with similar patterns. They interfered with Taylor's participation in parts of his treatment. His level of trust was diminishing and his level of distrust was increasing. Tasks like showering Taylor became a huge chore. José was in a different unit, but he was worked into Taylor's schedule because he was one of the few hospital team members with whom Taylor felt safe. If Keith was there on the weekends, Taylor was willing to let him take the lead. The protocol around the shower routine was that patients were showered every other day, and it was necessary to keep this routine in place for Taylor.

The issue of showering in relation to cleanliness became even more important. Taylor's large incision began to look and smell strange. The incision had a new bright redness to it that was accompanied by a small but continual leakage of fluid. Clear drainage is normal, but an excessive or foul-smelling amount is concerning. After resting or in the morning, Taylor's pillowcase began to show evidence of a significant amount of drainage. A swab was used to take a sample of the fluid that seeped out, and the results showed that Taylor had a surface *E. coli*[23] infection. This finding would mean the addition of both a topical antibiotic and oral antibiotics. A bacterial infection was always something that could happen. Taylor was not aware of what he was touching, and even though he routinely washed his hands (always with assistance, particularly after using the bathroom), he could still carry

---

[23] *Escherichia coli*, abbreviated *E. coli*, is a rod-shaped bacterium ordinarily found in the digestive tract. Most strains of the organism are harmless, but some strains can cause food poisoning, urinary tract infections, and superficial skin infections.

germs to other parts of his body. The topical cream did not bother Taylor, but the oral antibiotics upset his stomach. He was just relearning his body's signals that he needed to go to the bathroom, so the drug made it more challenging for him. The origin of the infection was never found, but all signs indicated that it was gone. Blood tests would also confirm that the infection had cleared up.

On March 6, I posted on Facebook:

The long stage of Rancho Level IV continues. After the team met yesterday, they expressed that they are also ready to see Taylor move past this stage. This stage can be the longest part of the acute rehab experience. The days have turned to weeks, and the timeline is taking a toll on our hearts.

Among the many challenges that we face, perhaps the most challenging and difficult is that Taylor is not able to grasp the idea of what happened to him and why he is here. This means that we are constantly explaining it to him, only to have him forget the explanation and not comprehend it in anyway. Taylor has no concept of his injury, his need for safety, and the situation he is truly in.

On the brighter side of things, Taylor has been able to eat pudding and now can move to other foods. He has tasted every flavor of Handi-Snacks and Jell-O pudding on the shelf. I never knew flavors like ice-cream sandwich; vanilla sprinkles, and strawberry cream existed before now! The speech therapist has added some chocolate mint ice cream (without the chips), which used to be his favorite. He also tasted some crumbs of a chocolate chip cookie. Taylor is being introduced to a more extensive variety of textures and consistencies.

Little by little the doctors are removing Taylor's sutures. The lengthy incision area is super-sensitive and the removal of the sutures causes a painful sensation for Taylor. Two doctors accompanied by some other staff members work together to remove a few of the sutures at a time.

A friend who recently visited brought Taylor two things. She brought him some peonies in a glass vase for his room. She told me the story of how Taylor sent her flowers once just because he wanted to make her day brighter. She also brought a soft, cuddly stuffed English bulldog. Taylor has named him Sniper.

We thank you for your continued support and concern for Taylor and our family.

The posts that I wrote and shared were meant to give people a glimpse into our world at Bryn Mawr. There was much, however, that I did not feel comfortable sharing. There were good things happening and the visits from friends were certainly special, but there were day-to-day challenges and moments of extreme sadness. Feelings of absolute desperation were present and increasing every day. I wanted and needed to let people know how Taylor was and how we were, but it wasn't always easy.

When Tanner and Keith came to visit, we had to prepare for the cruel side of Taylor's personality that was now a part of how he related to others. Tanner is handsome, and one of his trademarks is his beautiful blond curly hair. Tanner's hair was long and Taylor became fixated on its length. When Tanner walked in, ready to see his brother, Taylor had suddenly begun to express hatred toward him. He called him a range of ugly names: "faggot," "dumbass," and "stupid"; and sometimes he used words that were far worse. Taylor's new vocabulary was filled with curse words and inappropriate terms. It was horrible and embarrassing to hear him say these things. The worst part of it was that Taylor was hurting Tanner while Tanner still missed his big brother and tried to help him recover. *I felt like someone was putting our hearts through a grinding mill.* They had already been battered and bruised, and it did not feel as if it would ever get better.

Another bad habit had also started. Taylor often lifted his body in such a way that he could pound his wheelchair on the floor in anger. He had moved to a standard upright wheelchair, which enabled him to shuffle and scoot around. It also, however, gave him more freedom to lift his chair and potentially hurt himself. Whenever I took him away from the unit, I had to use the tilting chair. *And soon I would not be permitted to leave the Maple Unit at all with Taylor.*

There were a few nights when I remember that I had felt particularly hurt, shocked, and embarrassed. There was a new patient on the unit who seemed to be doing very well, especially in comparison to everyone else. He was probably about sixteen years old and he appeared to be more present cognitively than the other patients. I used to laugh because he was always smiling and waving at everyone. He would ride around in his wheelchair, acting like a mayoral candidate of a small town. He was talkative and friendly. He was also fairly articulate and appropriate in his speech. Most of the people with whom I had interacted when they were initially admitted to Bryn Mawr did not have very good speaking skills, if any.

This young man always had a slew of visitors who filled up the areas designated for socializing with family and friends. I never knew what had happened to him, but my guess would be that it was a mild brain injury in comparison to the other brain injuries on the unit. A mild traumatic brain injury is still life-changing and calls for treatment. This young man's stay in the hospital was fortunately brief.

One evening, I was pushing Taylor along in his upright wheelchair. His behavior had been so erratic that I was not permitted to take him off the unit. As we passed by the visiting area, the young man was smiling and gave me what had become his typical "Hello," along with his mayoral-style wave. The contrast between his and Taylor's behavior was stark.

Taylor was in a foul mood that night and I was trying to get him back to his room as quickly as possible. He was thrashing around in his chair. By thrashing, I mean that he resisted my moving the chair in a particular direction, while at the same time using his body and his own strength to move in whichever way was the opposite of mine. We were not allowed to leave the unit that night, and Taylor did not like that rule at all.

As we passed the group of smiling visitors surrounding the young Mr. Mayor, I waved and conjured up a smile. Taylor began to lift his chair off the ground and shout, "You stupid whore. You are a damned bitch, and an ugly black-ass whore." We made it past the onlookers as the tears stung my face. Taylor was talking to me! Nick was working nearby and I said, "Well, it's a beautiful day in someone's neighborhood, but not mine." One of the things that I loved about Nick is that he constantly reminded me that Taylor was very lucky to have me there. He told me how much he enjoyed our family, and he made it clear that he knew this surly young man was not who Taylor really is. After Taylor's verbal tongue-lashing, Nick encouraged me to leave for the night and I did. There was a growing sense of concern inside me that this phase might not end. I was deeply hurt, but I was not ready to let anyone see that.

As soon as I entered the outside area, I called Keith, sobbing; I told him that Taylor's behavior was getting too difficult, and I felt like I couldn't stay anymore. *I wanted to run away.* I wanted someone to fix my son's broken brain and my shattered heart. I was pouring out all the love that I had to give to Taylor, and he was calling me names that I know he never would have used with me before. Leaving was not an option, but staying was excruciating. Keith encouraged me to do what I needed to do to get through it.

What if Taylor continued to hate me? What if he continued to hate Tanner? What if in the end he hated everyone and everything?

The following night I was helping Taylor get into the bathroom. At that time, I had been trained to get him safely from point A to point B. When Taylor said he had to go, there was not much time to waste. Often, Taylor did not actually need to use the bathroom . . . he just wanted to get up and out of his chair. I was not allowed to walk with him alone, but sitting still in the evening was hard for him. I had just situated him on the toilet when he became irate. He cussed and yelled, and shouted out all sorts of things that made no sense to me. Suddenly, he stopped. He just stared at me and I saw something flickering in his eyes. He was looking around, and I could tell that he had no idea where he was, why he was

209

there, or what exactly was happening in his world. He was afraid. As Taylor sat on the toilet, I got down on his level and asked him, "Taylor, are you afraid?" He nodded his head to indicate "Yes." I told him that he was in a safe place, that I was with him, and that he did not need to be afraid. He calmed down—and for a moment, I felt I had reached him. I hugged him as best as I could, despite the awkwardness of the way we were situated. He took in a deep breath, and with tears running down my face, I whispered to the air, "I am afraid, too. I am afraid you won't come back to me."

I felt like I was watching a movie of someone else's life, a life that was certainly not my own. My son was here; well, his body was here. But even that had changed. He walked differently, spoke differently, and his voice had changed. His head was sunken in, his smile was crooked, and the light in his eyes, the twinkle and the spark that summed up who he was, was gone. But he was Taylor—he was a new Taylor. I am his mother, and I knew that somewhere inside, my presence meant something significant to him.

I was standing in a bathroom with my twenty-two-year-old son who needed help to get on and off the toilet. He could not clean himself after using it, and he needed help washing his hands. When he did start to wash his hands, repeating the motions of lathering soap in his hands took minutes rather than seconds. And then he might want to do it over and over again. His hands were cracked and dry from constant washing. How did we get here? And would we ever go home?

Some days we felt like we were losing little pieces of Taylor, more and more often. To observe Taylor off by himself in some world that was far removed from reality, with little clarity or recognition of what is true and real, was agonizing. There was definitive activity in his brain, but it seemed to be a cluster of various factors that when combined equaled confusion. It was like a long, complicated algebraic equation that was far too extensive to solve.

That weekend I went home while Keith came to Bryn Mawr. Throughout the past week, Taylor had been begging Keith over the phone to come get him and bring him back home. Every evening, the phone conversation with Keith centered on when Keith would be coming and whether Taylor could go home with him. At times, Taylor pleaded with me to bring him home; and when that didn't work, he begged me not to leave him. Some nights he was very angry and frustrated. I knew that I had to leave in order for him to be able to calm down, but leaving him was hard.

Taylor was upset with me because I wouldn't take him home and now his dad also had to say no. Over the weekend when I was gone, two of Taylor's friends had come to visit and the visit was rough. Taylor was happy to see his friends, but he was increasingly fixated on the idea of getting home. Taylor's behavior was unpredictable; his state of mind fluctuated from happy to sad without apparent rhyme or reason.

Taylor tried to convince his friends that he could go home with them since Keith had told him it wasn't a possibility. All the while, Keith was growing concerned about Taylor's reaction to his friends' departure. The friends left and Keith took Taylor back to his room. When Taylor learned that he was not going home with anyone, he swung at Keith, hitting him in the jaw. Keith's reaction time was faster than the weakened swing, but it still stung and more importantly it stung Keith's heart. We all loved Taylor and gave him the best care that we could, and now he seemed to be in a constant state of anger and frustration.

The inappropriate behavior continued and we had to place extreme limitations on Taylor's visitors. He could become hostile and sometimes violent without notice. He could be physically dangerous to himself or others. This phase of his recovery was a nightmare within a nightmare. I prayed that we would wake up. This stretch became the hardest to get through because its end seemed uncertain. People had no idea what they might encounter when they did visit Taylor; his mood swings were all a "normal" part of brain injury and the recovery process, but his behavior felt cruel and often embarrassing. We also knew that Taylor would have been ashamed of his own behavior.

This scenario went on for days and days. On another occasion, Taylor was getting agitated and out of order and I was trying to get him in bed and settled before I left. I could see that the situation was turning ugly; the little bit of control that Taylor had was unraveling. I naively tried to negotiate with him. "It's okay, buddy, calm down." I leaned over his bed to get the covers to pull over him, and as I did, he kicked me with force in the stomach, while also grabbing at me and throwing whatever weight he had in my direction. Fortunately, only one of his legs was strong, but it still hurt. A wonderful nurse was with him that night, and she taught me an important lesson. Several people came in to get Taylor in bed and began the process of calming him down. It would have been nice to walk away from Taylor in the midst of these tirades, but he was still unsteady and leaving him suddenly unattended would be unsafe. He was also afraid, and that knowledge bothered me.

In my previous job, which had involved teaching at-risk youth with severe behavior issues, I learned the value of de-escalation. Taylor did not need anyone to add fuel to his fire. He needed someone to help him put it out. The nurse, who I think was named Marie, was an angel to me that night. I was trying to leave the unit but I was sort of frozen. *Was Taylor going to be all right? Could he calm down? Was his agitation going to harm him?*

Marie explained to me that what we were seeing in Taylor was part of his recovery. His aggressive behavior issued from a different part of his brain that was healing. Fight was better than silence. Frustration was better than no emotion. She promised me that the staff did not decide whether they "liked" a patient based on this kind of acting out. They knew that inside Taylor was a person who had existed before the fall, and that that person was still part of him.

Marie told me that I should give some consideration to limiting my nighttime hours with Taylor. She suggested I leave at least an hour earlier or whenever Taylor began to show an increase in his level of agitation. She also recommended that I begin to count the days. Starting now, she felt that within fourteen days Taylor would be past this stage that seemed to be defined by rage. I listened to her and I trusted her. She hugged me; she hugged me tight, while telling me that I would be okay and that Taylor would be cared for. One of the skills that Marie possessed was her understanding that I knew Taylor. She validated that as his mother, I understood him. But she also helped me understand that she knew about brain injury. The best staff at Bryn Mawr used an approach of compassion and empathy. Instead of talking to you, they talked with you. They allowed you to educate them about the patient; in turn, they taught you about brain injury and its effects on your loved one.

Marie gave me an extremely valuable piece of advice that night. She explained that in her experience with brain injury survivors, often removing the stimulation around them could calm their agitation. As Taylor's nurse that night, she turned off all the lights. The staff assigned to him sat in a dark corner of the room in absolute silence. Taylor then calmed himself. This removal of stimulation was a technique that proved to be effective time and time again. Even though I had been worried about any time that Nick was off at night, Marie had been the perfect person to be with Taylor. She was patient, firm, understanding, and highly intelligent. I thought that Marie is one of those special people who happens to be in the place where she is needed most at that time.

I continued to see Taylor daily, just not as often, and my stays were shorter. During the day, I limited my visits to when he was getting ready to rest or eat. He seemed more relaxed during those times. He enjoyed my rubbing his back or just sitting next to him right before his afternoon nap. *My heart was breaking for Taylor*. I felt as if he were some sort of crazed animal trapped in a cage. Taylor was always initially happy to see me in the evening, but at some point in the visit, he would begin to lash out. When I decided to leave, however, he would beg me to stay. It was horrible. Nick was great at reminding me that sometimes taking personal space is good. He wanted me to protect myself and he followed through on his promise to take good care of Taylor.

Other matters had to be adjusted as well. For example, Taylor became very particular about who could be with him for toileting. Nick, José, or another male that he knew and trusted could help. There were several females whom Taylor seemed to really trust, but he would often say that he did not want them helping him. When Taylor did not like someone, rotations were done when possible. The staff knew better than to take his likes and dislikes personally. One of the aides that he liked was a warm, tenderhearted woman from Jamaica named Bridget. Bridget has the loveliest dark skin and her smile stands out from her soul like a lighthouse. Her magical and soft accent made me want her to read me stories while I fell asleep.

Bridget's laugh, full of pure joy, can be heard from several feet away. It seemed to bubble up from the inside of her. Bridget was Taylor's companion for many nights, which meant she was mine as well. Taylor had been put on a one-to-one staff assignment, which meant we would always have someone with us. Bridget saw the best and the worst of Taylor, and something about her appealed to him.

Bridget has a motherly softness, but she also conveys authority. She would say in an authoritative voice, "Now, Taylor, don't you talk to your mother like that." He would listen to her, and I felt like I had a big sister. One night, Taylor fell asleep and Bridget came in to sit with him as I left. As I passed her, she stopped me, wrapped her arms around me and said, "My heart hurts for you and your family." Most of the time our conversation was about Jamaica, her home, or something wonderful she had made to eat, but in that moment, she let me know that she was my friend.

Bridget was not the only shining star on the Bryn Mawr staff. There was a wonderful man named Trevor, who reminded me a lot of my father. Trevor had a steadfast faith and an optimistic outlook. It was difficult for me to hear from Trevor that God loves Taylor (and me) and that He has a purpose for Taylor's life. But because Trevor was gentle and kind, his faith was something that was a blessing to me in a time when my beliefs floundered. There was also a young girl named Rachel, who was good-humored and soft-spoken, but had a way of reminding Taylor that he too was young. She was fun to be around. And there were the numerous staff members whom we passed by night after night, who always said "Hello," and who, simply by being friendly, made our world a little brighter.

The long days at Bryn Mawr Rehabilitation Hospital opened my eyes to a whole new world. Daily life for most patients and their families who were with us was the living epitome of the phrase "emotional roller coaster." One could go from feeling hopeful about the day ahead to experiencing immense frustration within seconds. There is an ever-present anxiety and fear looming before you as you witness new challenges daily. A rehabilitation hospital is a place where profound love coexists with extreme suffering. Those of us who had become friends both wept and celebrated together.

Taylor and I spent most of Sunday, Monday, Tuesday, Wednesday, and Thursday nights alone at Bryn Mawr. There were also the morning and daytime hours that I would visit. Taylor was healing, and his body and mind were fully attending to him. There was limited cellphone service, but truthfully, I found that talking on the phone was often exhausting. I seldom wanted to recount the events of the day and all that they involved. What I was living and experiencing was something that was hard to put into words. I was submerged in a world full of hurting families, struggling parents, confused children, and exhausted spouses. I witnessed people face the horror of being told that their loved one's insurance had run out and that their time in rehab was going to end. I watched as families saw no progress, no forward motion, and no improvement day after day. I heard mothers struggle to recall the names of their beautiful children because either they could not remember or their brain would not allow them to say the names. Good things happened and painful ones did too.

There were relationships among all these events and occurrences. There were mothers and fathers, siblings, children, friends, and members of extended families. There were even dogs who were brought in to visit. For those of us who had been at Bryn Mawr for several weeks and now months, a bond had formed. I was alone many times with Taylor, but at a moment's notice I could have had a friend. I was also willing to be that friend. Each one of us had a different fear, a different story, and eventually, a different ending, but we also shared a common bond. We became like family. The staff was also part of our family. They were the voices of reason, comfort, and reassurance. That held us up when, as Avery explained, "Our hearts had fallen below our knees." We had been brought together by unforeseen circumstances, and we knew that when we felt most alone, we still had one another.

Taylor could not move through this phase fast enough for me, and it would continue to take its toll on his recovery. But I was able to endure it with him because I loved him and knew that others loved me.

Chapter Sixteen
No Escape

To understand an injured brain, one has to have some knowledge of a healthy brain and how it operates. The Merriam-Webster dictionary defines the brain as the organ of the body in the head that controls functions, movements, sensations and thoughts. According to the National Institute of Neurological Disorders and Stroke (NINDS),

> The brain is the most complex part of the human body. This three-pound organ is the seat of intelligence, interpreter of the senses, initiator of body movement, and controller of behavior. Lying in its bony shell and washed by protective fluid, the brain is the source of all the qualities that define our humanity. The brain is the crown jewel of the human body.[24]

A brain is made up of nerve cells, also called neurons. Everyone is born with approximately the same number of nerve cells, but the widely accepted theory is that these cells, once damaged, cannot be replaced. Neurons form tracts that route throughout a person's brain, and these tracts serve to carry messages that allow our body to perform its various functions.

Think of the human body as an orchestra and the brain as its conductor. There are many parts to play, but everything must work together in order for body and mind to come together in the way nature intended. The brain sends the signals to the rest of our whole being to do everything that we do, including the multitude of things we give little or no thought to. Because of our brain, we blink; we know how to read and write; we know how to speak; and we follow a pattern that allows us to reason with, think about, and understand the world we live in. Our brain is also the processor of all the sensory stimuli that swirl around us.

The brain also serves as the regulator of all our body's systems; it controls and monitors our breathing, heart rate, body temperature,

---

[24] National Institute of Neurological Disorders and Stroke (NINDS), "Brain Basics: Know Your Brain," Introduction. http://www.ninds.nih.gov/disorders/brain_basics/know_your_brain.htm (accessed February 5, 2015).

metabolism, thought processing, movements, personality, sensory perception, and language ability, and those things are just the tip of the iceberg. Each part of the brain functions as the director of both simple and complex functions. In order for music to be read, comprehended, and played, every instrument has to be in tune, and operated by someone who knows how to play it. For the person who has suffered even a minor or mild brain injury, many instruments in their "orchestra" cannot even be tuned (in a sense), much less played.

Taylor's injury predominantly affected three areas of his brain, the left and right hemispheres and the frontal lobe. The most significant damage was to his right side, but there was marked damage in the other areas as well. *Any damage to the brain is bad.* We were beginning to see not only more of the physical effects of his injury, but we were also becoming more aware of the larger picture. As Taylor emerged from his coma and his minimally conscious state, his emergence revealed a new person to us. This new person had deficits in every area of his thought processes and emotional perceptions. This person was also profoundly different from the person we had known before the fall.

This transformation played out in a variety of identifiable ways. It was interesting to me that when I researched left- or right-side brain injury in its most generic sense, I was seeing clear reflections of Taylor. The left-side effects that were most apparent outside the more obvious physical effects were impaired logic and catastrophic reactions.

Impaired logic meant that reasoning with Taylor was challenging. For example, if he had just gone to the bathroom, voided his urine, and then was put back in his wheelchair with his protective strap on, within five minutes he insisted that he had to pee again. It was hard to explain to him that he had just gone to the bathroom and that his bladder could not possibly have filled up in such a short time. He did not understand the reasoning that if he had just emptied his bladder, there was nothing left to discharge. He was tested for urinary tract infections (UTIs) more than once, because he was constantly asking to go to the bathroom and became very upset if he were told he had to wait. We began to narrow his bathroom visits down to every fifteen minutes and then we moved to half-hour increments. Getting Taylor in and out of the chair was quite a process, and if he happened to be outside the unit, we were not allowed to get him out of the chair. This situation meant that we would have to take the elevator back up, find a staff member, and then take him to the bathroom when he actually did not need to go.

Taylor was also experiencing depression and anxiety. That mixture of emotions did not reveal itself in the typical sense, but it was there. The depression was more difficult to identify, but the anxiety manifested itself in his actions and behaviors. These symptoms were managed with medications that included Lexapro, Geodon, and Buspar.[25] The medications did not cure these symptoms, they simply made them manageable. Another aspect of treating these symptoms was addressing them. Taylor would spend half-hour appointments several times a week with Dr. Pollak, a wonderful neurological psychologist. Dr. Pollak worked with Taylor to help him grasp as best he could what had happened to him. She also took into account how Taylor might have been feeling about his life prior to his fall. That person was still a part of Taylor. Questions like: *Had Taylor been happy before the fall? What was happening in his life that was either good or bad? What kind of direction was Taylor heading in both personally and professionally? What was his sense of self? What kinds of things would he tell me about who he was prior to this accident?* The answers to these questions were significant, because as Taylor became more cognizant of his situation, he also expressed more feelings. The puzzle of Taylor's mental and emotional condition had to be pieced together with the limited amount of emotions that he was able to identify.

Dr. Pollak also played an important role in our lives as Taylor's family. She helped us learn and comprehend as much as we could about

---

[25] Lexapro is an antidepressant of the selective serotonin reuptake inhibitor (SSRI) class that can be used to treat generalized anxiety disorder (GAD) as well as depression. Geodon is classified as an antipsychotic, but is used off-label to treat both depression and anxiety. Buspar is another relatively new anxiolytic (antianxiety drug) that is considered safer for patients than either benzodiazepine tranquilizers or barbiturate sedatives.

traumatic brain injury and its emotional impact on each one of us. We were all in denial about the way in which Taylor's injury affected us as individuals. We could not see it. We felt it, but we were also still caught up in a whirlwind of many new emotions. Dr. Pollak did not focus only on Taylor; she was available to our entire family. I found Dr. Pollak very comfortable to be around and I felt I could always confide in her. She had years of experience with families in our situation, and she knew that what might not feel natural to us was actually typical for families like ours.

Some of the important topics that I addressed with Dr. Pollak were issues that I could not discuss with others. I carried a tremendous amount of guilt about what had happened to Taylor. As his mother, I felt it was my duty to protect him from something as devastating as his injury; I had been protecting him for his entire life.

I found myself at times getting trapped inside a cycle of questions that haunted me: *Was this accident my fault? Could I have prevented the fall? Why didn't I sense it coming? How did all of this happen? Did God hate me? Were we being punished?* As I have said before, people would make remarks to us like, "There is a reason for everything," and "God doesn't give us more than we can handle." I absorbed all of those words, and what I heard was that I did something that made this injury happen to Taylor. It was a huge, heavy, and horrific burden to bear. Most of the time I was able to balance my feelings with reason and a sense of reality, but sometimes I just could not do it. Being able to share these things with Dr. Pollak gave me comfort and reassurance not only about who Taylor was, but who I am and who we are as a family.

Dr. Pollak worked with Taylor to understand his raw emotions that had risen to the surface. Dealing with Taylor on this level had to be very basic. Taylor could identify emotions in their simplest form, but it was impossible for him to grasp the roots of his feelings or understand them. One time he whispered to Keith that he wanted his father to bring his pistol to the rehabilitation facility and shoot him. He said to him, "Please just shoot me, dad." This incident was a moment of sudden clarity for Keith, and it scared him. *How would Taylor feel about all that had changed for him? Would he be able to cope with the scope of the changes that would become part of his life?*

On occasion with visitors, Taylor would remember a time when his feelings had been deeply hurt by that person. The situation had occurred prior to his accident, and may never have been addressed. After the visit, he would replay the emotional response over and over again into the entire next day, and it took a lot of work to distract him from his negativity. His feelings of hurt, worthlessness, and sadness escalated, and produced more chaos in his already confused mind. This behavior is an example of a catastrophic reaction.[26]

The right-side impairments were also vast. One of the sad effects was that Taylor thought at times that someone at the rehab was an acquaintance he knew from home. Since Taylor could not recall the acquaintance's name and was also confused . . . it wasn't clear to us what was happening. An obvious instance of visual memory impairment occurred when he identified his nurse Nick as Matt, who was a friend from home. Because Taylor had made this misidentification with us, we could at least address it. But at some point, he described who he thought two other people were, and he also wondered why they had not been kinder to him or spoken with him more often. He confused Donna, his speech therapist, with the mother of his close friend Brett. And he confused another staff member whom he saw daily on the unit with the mother of another dear friend. He could not recall the names of these women—Janet and Dee—whom he had known for years, but in his confusion he thought they were passing him by every day and ignoring him. It made me sad to think that he experienced both sadness and confusion over this. In reality, neither of those women would have ever

---

[26] Catastrophic reactions are inappropriate and highly emotional outbursts due to a person's inability to cope with either real or imagined events. They can be triggered by painful memories of past events as well as by present tasks or instructions that the person finds too complicated. Catastrophic reactions may occur in patients with Alzheimer's disease as well as those who have suffered a traumatic brain injury.

ignored Taylor, but that is what was happening in his mind. He did not mention this confusion to us for weeks, so we did not even know it was occurring.

Taylor also experienced a decreased awareness of his physical deficits. He did not understand that he could not walk on his own or that his left side was basically acting as if it were asleep. He thought he was fine, and had to be told over and over again that he had had an accident; that he was in the hospital; and why he was there. It was painful to have to say the words to him over and over again, and to watch and experience his reaction.

Taylor struggled with multiple challenges in regard to issues that involved both sides of the brain. These included but were not limited to: a reduction in his thinking speed; confusion; lack of attention; limited ability to concentrate; mental fatigue; and impaired cognitive skills in all areas. If you asked Taylor a question, you had to give him ample time to answer. For example, it would have been unwise to say, "Are you hungry? What do you want to eat?" You had to allow time for him to process one question before presenting him with another. More than one question at a time was too many. One would have to say, "Are you hungry?" and then wait for several seconds to see whether he answered; sometimes the question had to be asked again. It helped for me to understand that Taylor's brain was like an older, slow computer processor. Sometimes I would even count to myself after asking a question so that I gave him sufficient time to answer.

Taylor lacked clarity in much of what he did comprehend. He saw other patients around him and recognized that they were sick or hurt, but he did not understand the seriousness of their situation. He also felt that he was "okay." No connection occurred in Taylor's mind that he was also significantly impaired. This dissociation was something that was evident in other patients at Bryn Mawr. It was as if Taylor were thinking, "I know why they are here, but why am I?"

One day, Taylor's roommate heard him being unkind to me, and when Taylor went in the bathroom his roommate declared, "You should leave. My mother would never stay if I talked to her like that!" It had

223

become increasingly obvious that Taylor really got on this man's already frayed nerves. In fact, I was becoming concerned for Taylor's safety and had discussed it with the nurses. I had witnessed what happened when Taylor was angry, and the fact that he was the object of this man's scorn concerned me. The roommate would lock his jaw and glare at Taylor with an angry, intense look. Often when Taylor spoke, the man rolled his eyes or let out an exasperated sigh. Granted, Taylor was in a most unpleasant state, and his roommate was coping with his own fragile situation.

The beds were equipped with sensory alarms, so that if by some chance a patient did get up, a loud alarm went off and help would arrive. Taylor was not in immediate danger, but my protective nature was alert. Taylor's roommate, who had been thriving just weeks before as a computer engineer when something went haywire in his mind, was still clearly a very intelligent man. His mother had been quiet and was understandably caught up in her own grief. We had spoken only a few times, when I told her where she could find the laundromat and some good restaurants. That day as we left the unit she confessed to me, "It is ironic that my son would tell you that yours shouldn't speak to you like that. Just last week he was telling me off!" We both laughed. It was a difficult confession for this quiet woman. I knew she was only at the beginning of something very harrowing. Her son had moved to Bryn Mawr within a little over a week of the discovery of some random malfunction in his brain. Taylor and I had been there for over three months. I could see and fully understand her pain.

Taylor's recovery was endlessly stressful for me. Not only did I feel as if Taylor were drifting further away emotionally, but also as if he were caught in a cycle of violent inner hurt and rage. His confusion also brought his progress to a halt. I did as Marie advised me to do; I counted the passing days. If Taylor did not emerge from this terrible space in a certain number of days, then I would panic. Until then, I had to trust that he would come out on the other side.

From time to time, especially at night, I would find myself feeling isolated and fearful. The person who loved to make people laugh, who was ever mindful of his words to others, and who would rather sit, stew and say nothing, had replaced by someone totally different. Taylor's mouth and eyes indicated his displeasure with everything surrounding him. He had no sense of empathy for his family; and as his only visitors or company at the time, we bore the brunt of his angst. If I thought about it too much, I would begin to experience the physical sensation of someone sitting on my chest. The air inside my lungs felt limited, and my heart felt like it might pound its way through my chest. I had to calm myself. I had to reassure myself. I had to learn to redirect my thoughts to a happier time or place. I took a lot of deep breaths, and I remembered an old technique that my own doctor had taught me a few years before. She explained to me that in times of stress I should close my eyes, quiet myself, and imagine a candle with one of my favorite scents. I should then take deep breaths, breathing in the scent of that candle, slowly and intentionally. After that, I should release my breath slowly and completely, as if I were blowing out the candle. It helped; it was a simple coping mechanism for a complicated period of time.

One weekend, Keith and Tanner were unable to come to see us. Avery came on Friday night and had to head back on Saturday morning. Taylor's behavior had both peaked and then plateaued at the height of his emotional frustration. The word I would use to describe myself at that time would be broken. It could have been worse; I might have felt more despair. Sometimes I felt like I was at the bottom, but I knew the pit was deeper still. I was at times ashamed of Taylor's actions. He could be cruel, often restless, and hard to control. I remained worried that this cycle would continue and that "our" Taylor would remain hidden from us, replaced by this person who lacked reason and self-control, and who would quickly disregard the feelings of others and see only his needs.

That weekend, I reached out to a family friend in the area, who is also a speech pathologist. She took me out for a relaxing dinner. She listened to me with open ears as well as an open heart. Afterward, she went with me to see Taylor. Because she was familiar with brain injury through her profession, I felt comfortable with her presence. Marissa is a beautiful young woman with golden hair, a petite frame, and a lovely smile. She is also the older sister of two of Taylor's longtime friends. It took Taylor a few tries to get her name correct and we helped him, but then he said something hilarious. As our visit was ending, I asked Taylor whether there was anything from him that he wanted Marissa to tell her little brothers. He winked, smiled, looked right at Marissa, and said, "Tell them about us!" I don't know whether this remark stemmed from some unspoken long-time crush or from that silly place inside of Taylor, but it was a gift. He made us laugh.

During those endless days that felt devoid of any hope, my big brother Eric came to spend a weekend with Taylor and me. The weight of the sadness I was feeling was palpable and I was thankful to have someone to share it with. The fact that I had someone with me who had known me for my entire life was healing and comforting. *I did not have to pretend for one second to be okay.* I was able to be honest and to release some of the agony I was holding inside. I knew that Eric was sad for me. As the father of two young children, he could imagine how he would feel if Taylor were one of his own. Imagining even for a second was enough. I often thought that I couldn't believe this disaster was happening to Taylor. For those who had spent most of their lives loving me, the thought that ran through their head was, "I can't believe this is happening to Nicole." Those people were some of my greatest comforters in the very dark hours that we found ourselves unable to escape.

Taylor's foul mood continued. Loving him through this period was an act of great compassion. Some days it was hard to get up and go back for more of the same. When Eric was there, we spent time with Taylor and we spent time together. My big brother was realistic in reminding me that in order for Taylor to succeed in navigating through his recovery, I had to be aware of my own needs. Not only did I have to tend to Taylor's care, needs, and planning, but I also had to make a concentrated effort to care for myself. There were moments in our weekend together that I was unable to hide the fraying of my nerves, and how the daily grind of it all was wearing me down. In some way, it was a relief to take the cork out of the bottle, and release some of the inner pressure. *I was hurting. I was terrified. I needed to be reminded that I could do this and that I could do it well.*

The days of March continued to move along. I had established friendships with others whose loved ones continued their recovery at Bryn Mawr. Over the course of the last several weeks, I had the privilege of watching other patients and their families experience both joy and sorrow. It seemed like a coin toss as to what would happen, but for those who were moving forward, it was something I would define as a joyous struggle. We celebrated the many things that happened in therapies and in the daily routine, but we also missed the persons we had known before their accidents. Experts call what we were feeling ambiguous grief. *What were we actually missing? How do you mourn the loss of someone who is still present physically? How do you know which parts of them will return?* The emotions involved in ambiguous grief are hard to understand, hard to explain, and hard to process, and that is why we were fortunate to have one another.

One family I had come to know fairly well was particularly special to me. They were an older couple, and their daughter Sarah was in Bryn Mawr due to an anoxic brain injury. This type of injury is different from Taylor's; an anoxic brain injury occurs when someone's brain is deprived of oxygen for an extended period of time. The cause of this woman's injury was unclear. She had been found unconscious in her home, and her doctors could not determine how long she had been unconscious. Her parents were gentle, soft-spoken, and kind. They were hurting so deeply, but yet so faithful in their visiting and caring for their unresponsive daughter.

One of the most gut-wrenching aspects of rehabilitation is that some people don't respond; they simply remain still. There were patients at Bryn Mawr who stayed the same day after day and their prognosis, though still unclear, became more and more frightening. This couple's daughter had given very little response to anything that occurred. She was unable to speak, and it was unclear whether any sort of processing was occurring in her mind. Her parents brought her dogs to visit, hoping for a response that did not come. Some of her old sorority sisters came

227

for a visit, and again there was no response. This couple was battling insurance issues to keep her in rehabilitation and had been struggling with the insurer for some time. Part of the reason patients are allowed to remain in rehabilitation is because they are showing signs of improvement. Many times these signs are invisible, but even small outward improvements like increased range of motion come into the assessment. During this time frame, the couple had been told that their daughter would soon have to leave Bryn Mawr, and they were in the process of looking at nursing home facilities closer to their home.

Keep in mind that to members of a patient's family, every hour in the rehab is a gift. The facility was teeming with life. It was a safe cocoon. It seemed that if good things were going to happen, the rehab was where they started. Therapies were given and hope was still present. Discharge often represented changes that were unpleasant, especially in situations in which there had been little response. One day I was coming through the doors that I had to be buzzed out of, and Sarah's father ran up to me. He was smiling and talking fast. "Guess what?" he said with great excitement. He did not give me time to answer, but I knew he was going to share something good. "Sarah gave us the finger today! She gave us the finger!" I hugged him and we cried together.

As I stepped into the elevator to leave, it occurred to me that we were celebrating something that would seem odd to most people. Sarah was communicating! I recalled the period when Taylor was first emerging and how he seemed to enjoy "flipping the bird" nonstop. These rude gestures are among the oddities of brain injury. Who knows? Maybe they are the patient's way of saying that he or she is unhappy about their situation. But any sign of communication is a major event, and that finger signal bought this couple's daughter a few more days in a place where perhaps she could move ahead even more. I knew exactly what we were celebrating!

On March 26, I posted on Facebook with great relief:

I feel thankful to provide some good news. After weeks of being very agitated and restless, Taylor seems to have reached some

228

sort of calm. He is still at a fragile emotional state, but he seems to have far less agitation and frustration occurring. This calm helps him focus more on his therapy and healing.

Taylor also no longer has to get nightly shots for blood clots. This is a BIG deal because the shots, which were given in his abdomen, were so painful and bothered him a lot. Taylor has been given these shots for months, and not to have them is a relief for all of us. Tonight, Nick, Taylor, and I are having a "No More Shots" celebration. We will celebrate with ginger ale and some sort of soft sweet food. Taylor's diet has also been upgraded to include soft foods, which has opened up a whole new world of eating for him. Bits and bits of Taylor's memory bank are coming back to him, as well.

The last month has been difficult; I have found my tears to be my closest friends. So today I am happy to give good news!

Taylor's emergence from his state of high agitation came to an abrupt halt. He still had moments of misunderstanding and frustration, but he was calmer and the level of rage and anger had subsided. This transition was a welcome relief. Hope peeked out toward the horizon and we found it to be a most beautiful sight!

Chapter Seventeen
Alarms, Pill Dispensers, and Rubber Sheets
Late March into Early April 2013

Taylor's mood had changed; and though there were still moments of unpleasantness, it was much easier to cope with his newly found attitude. The angry and frustrated person had been replaced by someone who was calmer and more reasonable. When Taylor emerged from the black hole he had been in, he was more determined than ever to work hard in his therapies.

In terms of physical changes and therapy, he was still walking with one person assisting him. I was now permitted to actually walk next to him at nighttime rather than just rolling him around in his wheelchair. We had to stay on the unit, but that didn't matter . . . we walked endlessly down the long hallways. During physical therapy sessions with Sue and Lauren, he was working on navigating the stairs, walking outside to get the feel of different surfaces under his feet, and gaining more balance on his own. He had to adjust to the uneven surface of the sidewalk and the feel of the grass versus the tiled surface of the hallway. He also went to carpeted areas in the rehab to practice walking. The nonstop dedication he was devoting to his recovery contributed to his improvements. His torso was strengthened and so were his legs. His perception and awareness had also expanded.

One of Taylor's favorite places to walk to was near a room he had previously stayed in so that he could visit a former roommate. This was the sixteen-year-old whose brain was shaken and rattled severely due to the impact of a motor vehicle accident. His girlfriend had died from her injuries in the same accident a few days after it occurred, and he presently remained in a nonreactive state. The driver who had caused the collision was intoxicated and walked away from it with no permanent physical damage. Her psychological trauma, however, was swift and severe. The young girl who had died in the car was the driver's very own daughter, and the mother's intoxication was the cause of her own daughter's death.

Every night Taylor looked forward to walking to the area for specialized care where he had spent his first two months. His former roommate had not moved out of that area since his admission. Taylor loved to pop into his room, say hello to his family, and chat with his grandfather, who was known as "Poppy." Poppy was a gentle man who had driven two hours almost daily to support his daughter as she helplessly watched her son make little progress. Her son was unable to speak, eat, or communicate, and it was unclear whether he understood what had happened to him. His eyes were open, but it was hard to read what thoughts he might or might not be having. His movements were limited and involuntary.

Taylor liked to cover his buddy's legs with the Steelers blanket that was displayed on his bed. His mother, aunt, uncle, and grandparents welcomed us with open arms; they loved us and we loved them. It was mostly unspoken that Taylor was progressing in ways their loved one wasn't, but it was something we were all acutely aware of. The situation was cruel and at times it felt extremely unfair. *Why were the recoveries of these two young men so vastly different?* One day the grandmother, who they called Me-Maw said to me through her tears, "I would give anything to hear my grandson say 'I love you' to his mom or just to be able to say the word 'Mom.'" I recalled the time when I so desperately wondered whether Taylor would ever speak again, and now he was doing just that. It was devastating to watch this family that I had grown to love come to terms with the lack of progress their sweet loved one was making. He was at a standstill and they were powerless in many ways.

There were many patients who progressed and regained skills that their injury had taken away, and then there were those who remained stagnant. These patients had reached a point that they could not move past. Therapies continued for each set of them, but the paths diverged widely. When progression occurred, the therapies could advance, but where there were no changes, new plans had to be formulated. Success achieved through one mode for one patient did not guarantee it for another.

When returning to the former area, Taylor also enjoyed seeing Kristine, Brian, and Dena, the wonderful nurses with whom he had become familiar as he emerged from his coma. They were part of the reason he had flourished as much as he had and that our family was coping as well as we were. Kristine worked the morning shift, so as we came around the corner, she would say, "Good morning, Taylor, how are you?" And he would answer with one word, "Good." Brian was an overgrown teddy bear with a loud voice, and he would greet Taylor with a booming and boisterous, "Bing! How are you, man?" Sometimes there were high-fives and handshakes. Brian brought out the masculine side of Taylor, so he always enjoyed their interactions. These interactions reminded Taylor that he was still one of the guys. I always loved to see the grin that surfaced when Taylor spotted Brian.

Dena worked the evening shift. Taylor and I both looked forward to seeing her. She always greeted us with her enthusiastic warmth and asked, "How's my buddy?" Sometimes after I left for the evening, she would come and tuck Taylor in. She was a precious person and an exceptional nurse. She was so kind to our entire family and made us feel loved. That is what gave Bryn Mawr such a special feel; you were part of a larger family. Dena was one of the most caring people we had encountered so far. She had a down-to-earth genuine nature that shone through everything she said or did.

Due to the changes in Taylor's mood, we could allow his friends to come and see him again. The interactions produced a positive effect, but those closest to him needed to be prepared for how drastically things had changed for Taylor. Taylor was delighted by these visits. He would laugh and relish the company of the circle of friends he had formed over the years. The friends spoiled him; they brought him yummy treats, T-shirts, magazines, and funny things to make him smile. People sent whoopee cushions and musical cards in the mail. All these gifts spoke to the level of love and support that Taylor had waiting for him at home. Taylor and I carried the whoopee cushion around the halls, and the nurses would play along as we "secretly" put it on their chairs. It was fun, and it felt like life was hovering over us more often than the dark cloud of loss and despair. Taylor would chuckle and the amusement that he expressed was contagious.

In occupational therapy, Taylor was finally learning to perform his ADLs more independently. Where he once required maximum assistance, he now needed only minimal assistance. This transition was, however, scary for everyone. As a family, we were trained in ways to help him with certain tasks at home. For example, we were taught how to help him get on and off the toilet. Taylor still leaned sharply to the left, which could lead to a fall from the toilet if he were not closely supervised. He needed guidance with self-care activities like brushing his teeth, putting shampoo in his hands, and washing his body. There was still nothing he could do entirely on his own, but he was working hard to gain as much independence as he could.

We encouraged Taylor to get dressed on his own, to remember the correct order of things, and to perform the steps in the correct chronological order. His left side had gained strength, but it was still much heavier and lazier than his right side. When putting on his socks, boxers, or pants, he would often require help to lift his left foot, and he could not balance on his own. He was mastering the skill of tying his shoes, which was thankfully not as challenging as when he had first learned to do it. The actions he had previously known how to do sometimes came back to him, albeit more slowly and less completely. While he had to relearn virtually everything, these tasks had bits and pieces that were already present in his mind—they just needed time to resurface.

Speech therapy was progressing as well. Taylor was now able to read and make word associations. He still had some aphasia and would often refer to or identify things incorrectly. He might call his blanket a "saddle" or his French fries a "fork," and we had to figure out what he was asking for or trying to say. His thoughts did not flow in a normal rhythm and we had to be patient and attentive when carrying on a conversation with him. His diet remained limited to soft foods, but items like meat and pasta had been added, and his chewing and swallowing were improving.

As things progressed Taylor began to recall his favorite foods, and his friends enjoyed supplying them. Everyone was delighted to see him do something he always loved to do . . . eat!

The first highlight was when he was able to chew a bite rather than just taste the filling of a whoopie pie, which had been made with great love by a dear friend. Intense supervision was required whenever he ate, but this was terrific progress. It had been about three weeks before when he basically rolled the filling around his mouth after it was placed on a spoon, then in his mouth, much like one does with a very young child. Many tears fell that day, because I knew the love that was in each spoonful, and this was something that we had not been sure he would be able to do again. Another special memory was when Shelby brought him homemade venison and noodles. This gesture made him feel like royalty, and she was his queen. He told the entire unit how much she loved him and he did not intend to share one bite. Every delicious morsel had his name on it. On another weekend, his friend Jayme drove up with Avery and they picked up dinner at an Olive Garden on the way. This was a well-thought-out choice, because the pasta was soft, and chewing it was not such a challenge. The food itself was such a treat and he devoured it. But the real treat was being in that moment, with Jayme and Avery. Taylor felt their love, and anyone in the room could see it. Food was not simply about eating. Food was connected with a treasure chest of memories and associations of happier times.

The feeding tube was still in place, and it would stay there until he was discharged. This precaution was still needed just in case a setback occurred and Taylor was unable to take in food in by mouth. We kept the treats in steady supply with things like Wendy's frosties and milkshakes. Taylor had lost around 50 pounds since his accident and he needed to regain some of that weight. Foods like raw vegetables, lettuce, nuts, or those that were otherwise difficult to break down completely when chewing were still off limits.

Taylor had been a patient at Bryn Mawr Rehabilitation Hospital since mid-December and now it was April. In a sense, we were fortunate that he had both progressed and been approved to stay as long as he had. On April 2, we received some news that was both frightening and positive. In the team meeting with his case manager, nursing team, therapists, and physicians, Taylor was given a tentative discharge date of April 17. There would be a lot that would need to occur over the next two weeks in order for Taylor to return home safely.

The case manager spoke to me before Taylor was informed of any date. Taylor had not stopped asking when he could come home. We decided that we would mark the date on his calendar further out than the date that we expected. We all knew that the date could not come and go because a delay would be both detrimental and devastating to Taylor. If his discharge had to be moved up on the other hand, he would be excited.

Over the next few weeks, our family attended multiple therapy sessions with Taylor. We discussed any concerns that we had about his safe homecoming and our sense of security in bringing him home. I was anxious, nervous, and terrified. I was not as happy as people might have imagined. *I was numb. I was sad. I was afraid.* Many things are taken into consideration when an insurer approves a longer stay for a patient like Taylor. Being discharged does not necessarily mean that someone is ready to come home; it means that the insurance company is not going to pay for them to stay in the hospital or rehabilitation facility any longer. The son, brother, and person we would be bringing home with us was not the same person who had shared our lives over the past twenty-one years. We had much to learn about living with traumatic brain injury outside the hospital walls. We were embarking on a new adventure—one that we hoped we were prepared for.

In physical therapy, we were taught exercises that Taylor should and could do at home. We learned how to get him safely up from the floor if needed. We learned about the limits and risks involved in caring for him. We learned about what to do if for some reason he acted in a way that was harmful to himself or one of us. We were reminded of the usefulness of the emergency response system (9-1-1). We were told to notify our local responders of the fact that Taylor would be coming home, and making sure they knew about his ongoing medical condition.

In relation to occupational therapy, we spent time in an apartment-type setting that the rehab made available. There was a kitchen, bathroom, bedroom, and living room. Families could spend the night there or for a designated period of time. Occupational therapy focuses on the tasks and routines of daily living, which encompass a broad spectrum. Kelly, the occupational therapist, walked Avery and me through each room, and discussed safety issues and concerns.

In our home, Taylor, Tanner, and Avery had a separate shared bathroom. We would need a safety seat for the toilet to prevent falls. The seat came with side rails for balance. Taylor was unable to hold himself completely upright; he also needed the rails for support when getting on and off the toilet. The bathtub would have to be replaced with a walk-in shower. The shower would also need to have safety bars and a bench that Taylor could sit on. We also needed to install a handheld shower device so that Taylor would not have to stand to wash and rinse himself. We had to make sure that the bathing products were within reach of the bench so that Taylor would not fall over when stretching to reach something.

Our front porch had two sets of stairs and another drop-off point. We would have to place lumber barriers across all but one set of stairs, so that Taylor would not inadvertently walk off them. The throw rugs in all rooms had to be removed as they were a tripping hazard. A door was installed to block the staircase where Taylor had fallen. The stairs were carpeted, and lights and switches were installed at the top and bottom of the staircase. This redesign was one of the most welcome changes. *I hated that stairwell*. I never wanted to see the raw wood or tile where Taylor's head had been all but destroyed. *I hated those stairs*. The tile floor at the bottom of the stairs was replaced with carpeting as well. The change had made it easier for me to look at the stairwell, and to walk up and down on it.

The furniture in Taylor's bedroom had to be replaced. All his furniture had been hand-me-downs . . . dressers, the chest of drawers, etc. Many of the drawers had to be jimmied and shifted to open, which made them unsafe. He needed a mattress that would provide firm support for his back and body, so a new one was purchased. The bed was placed with one side against the wall, and the other side had a safety rail attached to keep him from falling out. His carpeting was old and had several wrinkled spots, so it was replaced. His television was mounted on the wall, and the computer he had purchased before the fall was moved into another room. Taylor would not be able to use the computer on his

237

own. He was functioning without a mental filter, unable to recognize social standards and limitations as well as deal with a lower level of cognition. He had to be supervised when it came to things like social media, Facebook, surfing the Web, and other computer-related activities. At this point he showed no interest in the computer, but we felt certain the time would come. The gun cabinet that we had given him to celebrate his eighteenth birthday had to be moved out of the house. All the guns, ammunition, and other hunting-related items had to be removed as well.

In the general areas of the house, we had to create pathways that simplified navigating each room. We had to remove a lot of clutter and smaller pieces of furniture that might have caused problems. Some items had to be cleared from countertops and tabletops. One of the recliners was moved up from the den to Taylor's bedroom, so that either he could rest in it or one of us could sleep in it if necessary. We also purchased four door alarms: two for the entry doors; one for Taylor's bedroom door; and the fourth for the stairwell. An alarm would sound whenever one of these doors was opened. A lock was installed on the stairwell, with a key that was kept in a safe place hidden from Taylor. All our knives, medications, and other potentially dangerous items were stored in a safe or locked place. Previously we had a 17-, a 19-, and a 21-year-old in our house, and it had been a number of years since we had to safety-proof our home. Now we had to look at it through a new lens. We had a responsibility to give Taylor a safe, hazard-free environment.

We purchased a baby monitor with a camera device, allowing us to view Taylor at all times. We bought a bed alarm, which was a pad for the bed with an alarm that would sound when Taylor sat up. The list of safety measures continued to grow, including items like pill dispensers, rubber sheets, new cloth sheets, and lots of random pharmacy items. It took a crew of people to help us. One of Taylor's dear friends went mattress shopping; another organized the bathroom remodeling; three friends took care of all the hunting items and their removal; and I scheduled a time to come home and try to organize some of the chaos. Bringing Taylor home was going to be a group effort. Our friends and family were willing and able to help, *and we needed it.*

Keith was working hard on the home front. He called installers, set dates, and coordinated deliveries as well as working full time and making sure that Tanner was well tended to. Keith also had to be put on the schedule at Bryn Mawr to receive his training and session times with various physicians. The countdown had more than begun, and soon it would be time to leave the nest at Malvern and fly on our own. Ready or not, the time of Taylor's discharge was coming and we knew that we had to continue to prepare for that day.

Chapter Eighteen
Beef Lo Mein
Early April 2013

Taylor had been given some clear goals to achieve. He had a blue binder that he carried around named "Bing's Goals." Taylor needed to have things clearly stated, simply presented, and specific in terms of how to complete them.

Donna, the speech therapist, had made a chart for keeping a tally. The goal was to have a tally of zero at the end of every day. The goals were defined as "Behaviors that I am working to AVOID." They were as follows:

1) Interrupting people when they are talking to someone else.
2) Asking the same question more than two times.
3) Asking to go to the bathroom more than once in a half hour.
4) Asking to call Mom unless it is a scheduled time.

Underneath, there was a self-evaluation area. It read:

1.) I think I did_____ today.
a. Great
b. Okay
c. Poor

2.) Tomorrow I will work on:
a. Not interrupting
b. Not asking the same questions
c. Not asking to go the bathroom as often
d. Not asking to call my mom as often

These goals were a clear example of concrete thinking. They stated in specific understandable language what Taylor needed to focus on. They were reasonable expectations, but they made me sad and angry. *I did not want to be treating my twenty-two-year-old as if he were seven.* I appreciated the process, but I detested the circumstance. I hated to feel as if Taylor were "misbehaving." Each goal that was listed represented a problem area for Taylor. It was helpful to have a tool that identified what the expectations were, but that did not mean it was easy.

Taylor seemed to adapt well and tried to do what was expected of him. He was relearning the boundaries and parameters that are a part of the world we live in. Taylor's mind seemed to be in constant motion. He wanted answers to the questions that seemed to crash like waves against the shoreline: "When am I going home? Can I call my mom? Can I go to the bathroom?" The brain is a busy place, and it helped me to understand that busy-ness is far better than inactivity. Taylor's mental activity meant that his brain was trying to form new pathways to replace the old ones that had been destroyed so that his thoughts could be processed and acted upon.

Later in the week the medical team noted that:

Patient has shown excellent gains during the week. He has been very responsive to working with staff and it has helped reduce his perseverations. Patient is highly motivated in therapy. He is eating and his spirits are very good. He denies any acute depression or anxiety. One-to-one coverage persists as it helps him keep active and organized when he is not in therapy.

His perseverations[27] have diminished, but he continues to focus on going home, eating, toileting, and his family. Patient must be kept in a wheelchair when off of the unit. Limited attention span continues. Keep activities brief. Try to build in rewards for accomplished goals. Keep therapy sessions to thirty minutes. Provide education regarding why he is at the rehab. Remind him of his functional and cognitive limitations. Saying something as simple as, "You had a brain injury, you have difficulty walking and a poor memory, and you are here to get better." Patient continues to be a fall risk, reduce risks.

---

[27] Perseveration is the medical term for persistent repetition of a movement or verbal remark without the ability to shift easily to a different response when the stimulus is changed.

The team at Bryn Mawr was working hard to bring Taylor as far as they could before we brought him home. We were reading more and more information about living with a brain injury survivor, and I attended multiple informative groups. Keith continued to get the house in order to make the transition home as smooth as possible.

Other than his transfers and readmissions, we had not taken Taylor out of the hospital setting since the previous November. Some of the brain injury patients had been permitted to have day trips, home visits, or short outings, but that had never been advised for Taylor . . . *until now.* It was now Saturday and Avery had come the night before.

Part of the course of action needed to bring Taylor home was learning what life outside the safe cocoon of the rehabilitation facility would feel like to him. For me, the outside world had become unfamiliar. I felt strangely out of place and invisible everywhere I went. I wondered at times how the rest of the world could continue its life as usual when ours had changed so irrevocably. As much as our home town had embraced us, I had experienced the silence of those who were just not sure of what to say or do. I, along with Taylor, had been sheltered and protected. It was time to reenter life in the real world again and I was not sure I was ready.

Avery was there for his training period and Sue met with us together. Sue reminded us of various concerns that she had and gave us some tips on how to best approach the patient she called Bing. Sue had a heart the size of Texas coupled with extensive knowledge of traumatic brain injury patients. She reminded us that Taylor was unaware of his limitations and discussed ways to keep everyone out of harm's way. She talked to us about being aware not to push Taylor too hard, and recognizing when both his body and mind had reached their limits. Taylor still tired very easily and we would have to be cognizant of his verbal and nonverbal cues.

Dr. Pollak also met with Avery that Friday afternoon. She and I had had many conversations over the weeks, and she offered to speak with anyone else in our family who wished to do so. I was immediately comfortable with Dr. Pollak because she felt familiar, nonjudgmental, and accepting. She had rosy cheeks and her bright outfits always made me smile. Avery chatted with her for a few minutes, but it was unfair of me to think that he would open up to her in an instant. This preparation for discharge was still new, raw, and increasingly real territory. We were all venturing daily into areas we had never explored before. These areas were not limited to learning about traumatic brain injury; they were also about gaining insight into our own feelings, grief, and struggles concerning our loss and the person we now had before us.

The recreational therapist had arranged a short outing for Avery, Taylor, and me on Saturday's schedule. There was an Asian restaurant down the road, the one where we had eaten Christmas dinner. Because we had been advised that Taylor should not be taken too far from the rehab, we chose this place. I am certain it was an exhilarating moment for Taylor. We had discussed beforehand what might be both enjoyable and beneficial to him.

We talked with Taylor about options and thought about what type of environment would feel the safest and most comfortable to all of us. The restaurant we chose was quiet; "elevator music" was typically playing, and the lighting was dim. It was not a place with a lot of commotion and even when it was the most crowded, it did not feel overwhelming.

The sun was shining brightly and the air had a springtime feel to it. We left the Maple Unit and went down the elevator together. It was Avery and I, along with the therapist and José, one of our favorite aides. As we left the elevator, Taylor was walking with one of us by his side. We got outside and Taylor and I waited as the therapist and Avery brought the car around to the door. We walked to the car together; Avery and I had to watch and learn how to help Taylor in and out of the vehicle safely. Taylor would not always remember the steps involved in getting into the car, and his left side was still rather weak, which made the process tricky. We had to assist him with putting his head down so that he would not hit the doorframe, as well as getting his seat belt buckled. Taylor appeared to be both excited and nervous. This was his first time riding in a vehicle other than an ambulance since his accident. He was not particularly talkative, but rather seemed to be quietly taking it all in.

At this point in Taylor's recovery, it was clear that something was physically wrong with him. I was not sure how an outsider would identify or explain it, but it was evident. Having never knowingly been exposed to a traumatic brain injury patient, all I can say is that to me, Taylor did not look healthy or well. His body had suffered a severe trauma and several other physical difficulties, and his condition was apparent, just not in a blatant way. Taylor was excessively thin, his head was misshapen, and when he moved, he was slow and stiff. There was also the fact that on this particular day, he had four people hovering over him. If he happened to speak, it was clear to the listener that he had challenges when it came to communication.

Avery, Taylor, and I were seated in our own booth and the staff was seated at the table across from us. Part of the process that you learn when caring for a traumatic brain injury survivor is that you as a caregiver need to have a plan in place. It would not have been wise to place a menu in front of Taylor with twenty choices and expect him to choose one. We previously discussed with him what he might like to eat, and he knew what he was going to order. Avery and I were patiently coaching him the whole time. As the waitress came over, before she even had a chance to greet us, Taylor blurted out, "I want beef lo mein." He took a breath and then said, "And I want a Sprite." Avery and I got a case of the nervous giggles. I liked having Avery there with me.

My mind flashed back to a time when the boys and I had gone out on Mother's Day. Taylor wanted to drive his oversized Dodge Hemi truck, and he drove too fast on the way to the restaurant. I scolded him and told him I wanted to arrive alive at our destination and that he needed to slow down. He was proud of his large, loud truck, and I think he enjoyed being the driver for the day. When we arrived at Red Lobster, I was excited to share a new place with my boys where they had never been before. Taylor claimed to be starving (which was always the case). Right after we ordered, he began to complain and grumble about how long it was taking for the food to come. Taylor hated to wait! He especially hated to wait for food. His impatience was not funny, but it always struck a funny chord with me.

Waiting for the beef lo mein that day was an exercise in patience. It did not take long, but Taylor wanted it the moment he ordered it; that had not changed. When the dish came out of the kitchen, hot and steaming, he did not hesitate to take a bite. We had to help him to not eat too fast; to remember to blow on his food and thoroughly chew it. The danger of Taylor's choking was apparent to us. Avery and I recognized that Taylor was going to need a lot of help in the world outside the rehab. The meal was a success and also a learning experience. Overall, it felt good to be out of the hospital with Taylor, but it also felt good to return to the safe haven of an inpatient facility.

The rest of the weekend was quiet and uneventful. We were counting down to the moment when we would bring Taylor home. Avery wasn't sure whether he would be back before Taylor's homecoming, so he made his rounds of saying good-bye. The staff at Bryn Mawr had come to mean a lot to us, but we also meant something to them. Avery was a bright, intelligent young man and the staff valued his presence as much as he valued theirs. A mutual respect had been born. Over and over again, I was told what supportive and remarkable brothers Taylor had, and it was true. Avery and Tanner had become heroes in my eyes. I was immensely proud of them. People would later call Taylor "Superman," but his brothers were superheroes too!

As Avery left that evening, he told Taylor good-bye. Taylor told him that if he wanted to, he could stay with him in his room and they could have a sleepover. He said to Avery, "I like it when you are here with me." Avery replied to him in sincerity. His words were thoughtful, pure, and spoken with tenderness, "Buddy, you have to stay here for just a few more days. You can call me any time. Mom is here with you, but I can't stay. I have to go back to school." It must have been hard for Avery to leave that evening. He had suddenly become Taylor's "big" brother. He now shouldered so much of the role that Taylor had played in our family. The responsibility had shifted, and we all knew that the part of Taylor that was the older brother might not ever return.

Avery seldom if ever cried, but I cried for him. All the tears that he held inside ran down my cheeks and I wept. *I wept for Avery. I wept for Tanner. I wept for Taylor. I wept for Keith. I wept for me.* All our dreams seemed to have shattered somehow, like shards of sharp glass scattered everywhere. The pieces of our lives seemed to lie around us, and we each had to at the very least attempt to put them back together. This horrible accident had occurred in less than thirteen seconds as Taylor fell down thirteen stairs, and now all our lives seemed forever altered.

We had been unaware when Taylor fell that night that we too would fall. We would fall into despair, darkness, depression, and desolation. We would have to reach for hope in the midst of hopelessness. We would have to fight for faith when it seemed as if God had left our side. We would have to believe that something good could come of such horror. And in the broken pieces of our hearts, we would have to depend on one another in order to put them back together. I had never been so keenly aware of what our family meant to me. I had never known how strongly we could stand together and that the love we held could actually endure the unthinkable, unimaginable, and inexplicable, all with the hope of bringing someone who was either lost, stolen, or both back to us.

A few days later, Taylor and I had a scheduled meeting with Dr. Pollak. The plan was to discuss Taylor's thoughts, ideas, and expectations for his homecoming. Taylor was not returning to the same world. My leave from work had been extended until November 2013, and my role was to be Taylor's full-time caregiver.

Taylor would be attending occupational, physical, and speech therapy sessions three days a week in an outpatient setting. He would continue to rest and recover at home, and his life would be a well-planned routine. Taylor would not be permitted to be alone, drive, work, or do many of the things he was accustomed to doing before. It would be a drastic change for all of us. Taylor needed to have some idea of what lay ahead for him.

Dr. Pollak and I sat down that morning with Taylor and I was feeling positive about the meeting. I felt certain it would be a valuable experience for both of us. As we all sat down, Dr. Pollak began to explain to Taylor what we would discuss. Taylor was situated between her and I. As Taylor began to respond, I noticed a twitch in his lip and he began to speak in a way that was unclear. I knew something was wrong and I quickly stated, "I think he is having a seizure." I tried to stay calm because I did not want to alarm Taylor. Dr. Pollak jumped up and called a code. In a matter of seconds, we had Taylor on the floor and I was watching yet another horror unfold. Taylor's body was shaking all over and he was drooling. His mouth made a repetitive jerking motion, which looked as if a small fishing hook were in place at the edge where his lips met. It was as if an unseen puppeteer were pulling on the lip in some strange rhythmic pattern. Taylor's eyes remained open for the most part, but most of the time they were rolling back in his head. José was on the floor right beside him and had placed something soft under his head. Brian started an IV, medication was administered, and the seizing stopped. So many people were surrounding Taylor. I had come to love and trust these professionals. I looked around the room and I told myself to be calm. Taylor was going to be okay. He was safe and I was safe. And then I wondered to myself, "What happens when he comes home and I am alone with him?" Was Taylor going to survive all the changes that had occurred in his body? Would we be able to take care of him? Ready or not, it was happening and we would have to do our best and trust in ourselves.

The rest of that day was spent trying to convince Taylor to rest. We had originally planned a full day of activities, and he did not want to settle down. According to researchers as well as patients with epilepsy, it is common for a person to feel excessively tired after a seizure,[28] but on

---

[28] According to a group of three French researchers, about 50 percent of patients with epilepsy report extreme fatigue after a grand mal (tonic-clonic) seizure. See S. Hamelin, P. Kahane, and L. Vercueil, "Fatigue in Epilepsy: A Prospective Inter-ictal and Post-ictal Survey," *Epilepsy Research* 91 (October 2010): 153–160.

this day, Taylor was wound up. I, on the other hand, was exhausted. I was not at all ready to do this without the team of people that surrounded us. Taylor was begging to go home and I was almost dreading it. I was being thrown into a world of being the mother of an adult child with severe disabilities and challenges. The question on the agenda was whether I was ready. Taylor was coming home, and his life would now be in our hands.

Chapter Nineteen
Snapshot of My Heart
April 9–April 15, 2013

I hate to admit it even on paper, but I wasn't ready for Taylor to make the transition home. The reality was that whether or not I felt ready, he was going to be discharged. Sometimes that is how life is: you take a deep breath, you accept the challenge in front of you, and you embrace it. Resistance gets you only so far. Fear was not going to consume me. We could do what was needed and Taylor would be okay in our care. He was, after all, ours. Keith and I had been caring for him since he first bounced into the world: we had been there the first time he got sick, we had learned how to treat his asthma, and we had taken care of his boo-boos and broken bones. We had helped him sort through his teenage years, make good career choices, and enter the world of young adulthood. We had to trust in that and in ourselves. We would be raising Taylor for a second time in many aspects.

Keith drove to Bryn Mawr for one of our final weekends and for his time of training. It was not difficult to admit that we didn't know everything—how could we? Traumatic brain injury is a vast topic and you essentially learn something new every single day when caring for a TBI survivor. We had been integrated slowly into helping with Taylor's daily care, but its requirements were still very new to us. Helping your six-feet-tall, 140-pound son get dressed is far different from helping your three-year-old little boy. Learning to be more patient than ever was new because every task took more time. There were many moments that felt like an exaggerated time warp. Every second seemed to stretch into minutes. Taylor needed to process thoughts and then think about each action. *Life was running in slow motion.* A walk that might have taken five minutes before now took fifteen. These training and learning sessions reminded us of these new nuances. Advice like "Never rush Taylor," "Leave extra time to get to appointments," "Don't give him external pressure" (by giving him too many directives at one time), and "Be slow to anger" is really crucial to understand. Taylor was not only fragile physically; he was fragile emotionally as well. It was not unimaginable that setbacks might occur. Our comprehension of all that Taylor's brain injury would encompass was expanding daily.

When Keith came on Saturday, I drove back to Mifflinburg. We had a full schedule in terms of Taylor's homecoming. A group of my friends came to our home to help organize and sort things out. We had been told to simplify our surroundings and so we got busy doing just that. Room by room, the house was cleaned, reorganized, and emptied of any clutter. We had boxes scattered around that were filled with various piles. We had items to be donated, items to be thrown out, and still others to be stored. I was getting a bit carried away, but it reminded me of some sort of nesting instinct, similar to what happens right before a mother gives birth and she somehow knows and prepares her home for the newborn. I don't think I could have handled a busy, cluttered home any more than Taylor could have. Somehow this process of purging was therapeutic for me. During our consolidation gathering, one of my friends said to me, "Are you sure you want to get rid of all of this stuff?" I wasn't certain, but the clutter made me feel overwhelmed. Another dear friend suggested that I could simply store anything I was unsure about discarding at her house. I needed to have some sort of clean slate for Taylor's arrival and this cleanup day was one way for me to obtain it.

A group of Taylor's friends worked hard to make his room not only safe, but special too. They made sure the things he loved were hanging on the walls, along with some new decorations. One of his best friends ordered a set of camouflage sheets and a new comforter for him, knowing he would appreciate the outdoorsy theme. Pictures of fundraising events in Taylor's honor and cards of encouragement hung on the walls. The room felt more open and offered a sense of comfort and warmth.

On the other hand, many of the things that Taylor cared about were missing. We took down the fishing lure key rack where he used to hang his truck, car, and workplace keys. The gun cabinet and all his hunting gear had been removed, along with his work tools and anything that might be deemed unsafe. The room was redone for the new Taylor. Much of our old life had been redone as well. It was a fresh start, but not one that we had wished for.

That day at home was good for me. I had not been around a large group of people very much. These were people that I had known well before, but now so much inside of me had changed. My entire world had been turned upside down. *I was sad. I was afraid, and I was grieving a tremendous loss.* It was consoling to be with people who seemed to understand that I was not the same person I had been six months before. I was glad that they had not run away.

Before the weekend ended, several of the people who had offered to help us with Taylor when we brought him home gathered for an informal meeting. Many of these people had not yet seen Taylor. I had planned this time to help them understand some of the best ways to relate to Taylor and some of the changes that they could expect. Taking care of him would be an enormous responsibility. Taylor could not be left alone; he was confused and he had challenges in regard to his health that affected many aspects of his life. He lacked balance, strength, and coordination. He remained at risk of seizures; moreover, there were always the unknowns that were simply lying in wait, ready to reveal themselves when least expected.

I was honored by the presence of my friends who wanted to help us. Some of the strongest, bravest, and most compassionate people in our town would be by our sides, supporting us in any way that they could. I tried to believe that Keith, Avery, Tanner, and I would not be alone in our new responsibility of caring full time for Taylor.

I returned to Bryn Mawr that Sunday evening and Keith returned home. Once again, the only place we might have passed each other was the Pennsylvania Turnpike. I was tired. I was tired of the long commute. I was tired of not being able to eat dinner with my family. I was tired of missing my dog. More than anything, I was tired of missing out on the moments that were rapidly passing me by. I had missed almost all of Tanner's junior year in high school as well as Avery's normal weekend visits home. I missed being able to cry with Keith in person versus over the phone. I missed doing laundry in my own washer and dryer, and I missed the smell of coffee brewing as the day was about to begin. Even though I felt unsure of how all of the dust would settle, I was ready to take the leap. I might leap kicking, screaming, and resisting all that was ahead of us, but I was as ready and prepared as I could be.

Not only was Taylor coming home, but I too was coming home. We had spent December, January, February, March, and now half of April sleeping in a small bed in rooms that were not our own. We had awakened every morning and opened our eyes to unfamiliar walls and surroundings that were necessary, but lacked the coziness of our familiar log cabin house. It was time to return; and as anxious and apprehensive as I felt, I was beginning to realize how nice being home would feel.

My mom took the train from her apartment in Manhattan to spend a few days with Taylor and me before his discharge. My mom wrote to Taylor on April 9,

> *I came back to see you before you go home next week. I loved seeing you and how much progress you have made. I am very glad that I could be part of your journey.*
>
> *You have a lot of support from people who love you, both family and friends. Your mom has been on this journey through your recovery daily, and your dad and brothers came weekly. Your friends have been incredibly supportive and they are giving you back the love that you have given them.*
>
> *I take comfort in waking up every morning thinking of your mom and you together. I love you, Taylor.*
>
> *Grandbunny*

My mom and I decided together that a special celebration was in order. Over the months, I had come to have a favorite hangout. Whenever my friends came to visit, I would introduce them to the Dixie Kitchen. In fact, a group of college friends that I had not seen in more than twenty years all took the trek to Malvern, Pennsylvania, one day to remind me that we were not alone. We gathered and shared stories for hours at the Dixie Kitchen. They wanted to see Taylor but I was too reluctant. It would have been confusing for him and burdensome for me. I will always remember feeling such love and gratitude for old friends

254

who drove many miles—one for more than six hours—to gather around me and express their care for us.

The Dixie Kitchen was a wonderful restaurant that reminded me of my life in the South. The couple that owned it worked hard to make it a place that felt like you were going to lunch at a friend's house, and they had come to hold a significant place in my heart. Before the owner had opened this welcoming gathering place, she had been a nurse who worked in intensive care settings. The staff was always friendly, and over time they became familiar with our story. Coincidentally, they had a regular customer who had also suffered a traumatic brain injury years earlier. I was never able to meet him, but I was able to hear about how he had grown and readjusted back into society. His story encouraged me to always move forward.

For Taylor's going-home celebration, my mom and I ordered what the Dixie Kitchen called "upcakes." Upcakes are the restaurant's special version of a cupcake; they are made in all kinds of scrumptious flavors. An upcake is a small cake baked in the same shape as a cupcake, and then turned upside down. Instead of icing simply covering the top of the cake, it is also spread on the sides of the cake.

We ordered a total of fifty upcakes. Taylor ate three of them, which was a big deal at the time. We placed a book where some of the staff could write notes to Taylor and to us, and each note contained some of the kindest words we would ever read. The day of celebration was April 13, and we would be leaving on April 15. At the time, it felt like one of the most heartbreaking days in our entire ordeal. In my mind I saw myself as a small child, holding on with all my strength to someone I was not ready to be torn away from. The aides, secretaries, greeters, transporters, doctors, nurses, cafeteria and cleaning staff, therapists, social workers, and other patients and families had all become so precious to me. They gave me love, strength, insight and courage when at times I had none. *Why did we have to go?* It was time, but my heart was a long way from ready.

I pondered on the brilliant words attributed to Winnie the Pooh by A.A. Milne: "How lucky I am to have something that makes saying good-bye so hard." Dena and I talked the night before we left. My mom and I had given Dena a plant named Job's Tears.[29] To me, it was a reflection of the tears she allowed me to cry with her at the most difficult time up to that point in my life. Dena was representative of so many of those who had come to occupy a large space in our hearts. Her kindness gave me what I needed to get through another day. Her tender care helped to mend our shattered hearts and broken dreams. Oh, how I would miss my friends in this place! I did not want to experience or feel another loss or another ounce of pain.

Brian, our dear "teddy bear nurse," sat down and had lunch with me a few days before we left. I knew I could not forget this man. Brian candidly shared some insights with me about what families who get through a trauma like Taylor's must do. He spoke with me about embracing the changes that would happen instead of running from them. He encouraged me to accept what is without losing hope of what could be. He seemed to say that it is okay to look back, but not to do it so much that it hinders looking forward. Each moment like this with our friends who happened to be on the staff at Bryn Mawr reminded us that as alone as we may be tempted to feel, we are not. I captured these moments as best I could, like snapshots inside my heart. I repeated to myself, "Never give up." I promised to fight as hard for Taylor's recovery as I had been doing, and I resigned myself to the thought that no matter how dismal, challenging, and tumultuous the days ahead might feel, that I would fight on. I would not let fear be victorious over my determination.

The day of the party, I decorated the table and placed Taylor's special journal on it so that people could write down their thoughts. The upcakes had letters on them that spelled out "BING IS GOING HOME!!" On the additional cakes were tiny houses made of icing. I bought small gifts for those who had come to mean more than any gift could ever convey, and I watched Taylor try to wrap his mind around all

---

[29] Job's Tears, also called coixseed or tear grass, is an ornamental plant that produces hard white seeds which can be dried and used as beads for jewelry. The Cherokee Indians have made necklaces from Job's Tears beads for generations.

that was happening. He was so thrilled with the idea of his homecoming that it was hard for him to focus. It was also hard for him to understand that leaving Bryn Mawr might not be all sunshine and roses.

We took photos and we laughed a lot. I would not allow myself to cry. One of the younger male staff members pulled me aside and told me how much working with our family had meant to him. He asked me if I understood why the staff was so happy in regard to Taylor and his progress. Understanding that everything is about perspective, I encouraged him to tell me more. He explained that Taylor was a success story. Not all endings were this happy and we should know that as a family, we were part of Taylor's success. He hugged me tight and told me that Taylor was lucky to have me as his mother. My heart was full. Many of the staff that day expressed how much they had come to appreciate and care about our family as a whole, and the feelings were mutual.

Some of the sweet thoughts that were written in Taylor's journal were:

We at Bryn Mawr Rehab are all so proud of your hard work as you get better from your accident. I am impressed that you always remember to thank the nurses and therapists helping you! Your mom and dad are raising a wonderful young man. – Dr. Pollak

You came a long way, my friend. I am very much proud of you, and happy for you. – Nursing assistant

You have come a long way in your recovery and have worked very hard in all of your therapy activities. Keep working hard, we will be cheering you on. – Kelly, occupational therapist

BING!!! From the day I first saw you come in I could tell you were a fighter, and that you would be a lot of fun too! It has been a pleasure to work with you, watch your progress, and see you

rise over the obstacles in front of you, accept the challenges and finally, get to go home! Keep working hard, challenges will keep coming, but with your hard work and positive attitude you will continue to soar. – Sue, physical therapist

I am so proud of how hard you worked to get where you are today! What a journey! I am honored to know you. – Nursing assistant

As a physical therapy student I only knew you a short time, but seeing all of your work and dedication was very inspiring. – Physical therapy student

Taylor, you bring a smile to everyone you meet. – Staff member

It was an honor to watch all of your tremendous progress here at Bryn Mawr. You are such a strong, brave young man. Your mom and your family never left your side. I am honored to know all of you. Take it slow and be easy on yourself. – Case manager

As happy as I am that you are going home, I know that we will all miss you. – Nursing staff member

Taylor, I am profoundly going to miss you. I cannot say good-bye to you, but I can say good luck. – Nursing staff member

It was great to see you progress from the tube feeding to regular food. – Nutritionist

You have been such a friendly person to my daughter and I. We will miss seeing you, but we are so glad you have improved so much. – Mother of another patient

Even though a horrible accident happened to you I believe that God has been with you throughout this ordeal. It is hard to fathom how far you have gone in your recovery. You are a miracle. What a great family you have! I want to clone your mom, especially. I did not know you before this but you must be one in a million seeing all of the friends and loved ones who drove all the way here to visit you. We will be missing your sweet demeanor and your family. I will especially miss your mom. – Nurse

Do good at home and thank goodness you finally left the hospital. I am running out of wheelchair pieces to repair your chair with. Be well. – Staff member

Taylor, it has been amazing watching your progress and recovery. You've done so well, worked so hard, even through the harder moments. You are truly blessed to have a loving, supportive family and I am so glad that you will be home with them. Enjoy life, love and family. – Staff member

It was truly a pleasure to have met you and your family. I have never had such a wonderful patient or seen such a supportive family. I will miss you and your family very much. – Nick, nurse

You have come so far! Wishing you continued progress and a lifetime of happiness. – Nurse

This is it . . . and very soon you will be home with your loving family and friends. I fell in love with Avery the most. Your smiles are charming and I know where you get it from, your mum, dad, and even Grandbunny. You should hold dear to your heart how much they all LOVE you. Love is a strong thing. Your family and friend hung in there for you. It is time to make everyone proud that you made it. We are all happy that you made it! I pray that

259

angels watch over you every day. Keep smiling and don't let the past reflect when you are going. The future will be brighter. Enjoy life and embrace everything good that comes your way. – Secretary

I don't know where to start, but what a turnaround you have made. I was your first nurse when you came to us. You could not eat and you could not walk or talk. I thank God for how far you have come. You have a terrific family who love you very much. I have seen you work very hard and you need to continue that hard work. You are very special to many people. I have had the privilege of helping you and getting to know you. – Nurse

I am happy that you are finally able to go home, but I will definitely miss seeing your smiling face every day that I am here. Keep up the good work and I know you will just keep getting better and better. – Nursing staff member

As the day came to a close, I wondered whether we would ever get home. I wondered if anyone in the building knew that I was once again in sheer agony. The loss of everything familiar was becoming a sad song that played over and over again. I should have been shouting, "My baby is coming home! We are bringing Taylor home!"—but that is not how it felt . . . it felt uncertain, unpredictable, and scary. As I lay my head on the pillow that night, my thoughts churned in a million directions, the main one being, Why did everything have to feel so hard? Would I ever stop feeling sad? Would Taylor ever really come home to us?

PART V: Mifflinburg

Chapter Twenty
Welcome Home
Mid-April 2013

When a person like Taylor enters a rehabilitation setting, the outcome is always something that remains to be seen. Everyone had high hopes for Taylor when he was first rolled through the doors of the place that would become our temporary home, but we did not know which one if any of those goals would be achieved. Keith felt certain that Taylor would one day walk again, but no one really knew.

When Taylor was admitted, he had not held his eyes open for more than a few seconds. He had not spoken. He was unable to breathe without a ventilator for a full twenty-four hours. He had a tracheostomy and feeding tube. He could not stand. He could not lift his arms or legs on his own. He could not communicate, and he had little if any control over his body's own natural functions. It was unclear whether he would ever do any of those things again, as well as much more. These were only the physical problems; he also had an array of cognitive challenges.

Taylor's brain had been all but destroyed, and our spirits had been crushed. Bryn Mawr, its staff, and parts of the story that will never be able to be seen or explained in terms we can grasp, helped bring bits and pieces of our son, our brother, and our dear Taylor, back to us. For that reason, we will forever be grateful.

Traumatic brain injury in general is unbelievably complicated. Each person and each injury is at a unique point on the spectrum of what is and what could be affected. Much of it is impossible to pinpoint in regard to both the initial injury and the ultimate recovery. Oddly enough, our journey in many aspects had just begun. Taylor had achieved a lot in his recovery, showing improvement in many regards. But Taylor as a person had changed. There were all sorts of dimensions to this type of injury that seemed to be discovered daily. The brain affects everything about us; and true to that fact, almost everything about Taylor was different. The differences were evident in many ways, from the twinkle no longer present in his eyes to his uninhibited way of relating, his fear in doing small tasks, and his short-term memory lapses. His movements were different, his smile had changed, and the part of Taylor that perhaps cannot be defined but summed up his personality, seemed to have dropped into some abyss. In regard to cognitive development, we no

263

longer had a twenty-two-year-old son. His injury had shaved off years of thoughts, patterns, experiences, and knowledge that when combined had made Taylor who he was. Now he was someone who seemed far younger, and he had many new behaviors that we were still trying to figure out and adjust to. At this point, no one had pinpointed a developmental age for him, but we knew he was functioning at a far younger level.

As a family unit, recovery from a traumatic brain injury made us focus on what mattered most, as well as learning to prioritize how and what needed to be handled. There were going to be constant decisions and changes and we had to adapt to a general atmosphere of stormy seas. We also had to navigate Taylor through them with the thought of bringing him home to stay.

After the initial trauma occurred, we had had to wait for Taylor to move from the intensive care unit at Geisinger to a step-down unit within the hospital. Next, Taylor had to come to a point, physically and cognitively, where he could be considered for admission to an acute rehabilitation hospital. The goal of the acute setting was to allow him to progress to the next phase.

For some patients, the next phase meant going home; for others it meant moving to another facility. This time period is referred to as the post-acute rehabilitation time frame. Bryn Mawr is a specialized acute rehabilitation hospital, but there were options after that phase. Some of those options depended on funding, insurance coverage, and family preference or availability. We had briefly discussed facilities that Taylor could possibly go to, but for our family that was not an option. *Taylor was coming home.*

I attended my first support group meeting for loved ones of survivors a few months before Taylor's discharge. I had also seen many survivors walk into their own support group, so I had some idea of what a survivor might look like a few years out. In the group I attended that evening, there were about ten participants; two were mothers fairly close to my own age. Everyone had a chance to share his or her story and we were encouraged to speak from the heart.

A gentleman who appeared to be in his late fifties or early sixties facilitated the group. His brother was a state trooper who had been shot in the head during a routine traffic stop many years before. The parents of these two men had passed away many years earlier and now this man cared for his brother at a distance. The survivor lived on his own in a setting for disabled individuals, but was unable to manage many of his day-to-day affairs like shopping, paying bills, and other necessities.

Another mother's son had been injured several years before in a biking accident. The son had gone through an acute rehabilitation facility and then came home. After a brief time at home, the family had made the excruciating decision to put their son in a long-term setting with other survivors. This setting was a community based post-acute rehab, and it gave everyone a different kind of opportunity. Both these families had been dealing with their tragedies for years, and yet the rawness of the emotions they felt were still very apparent. As I sat and listened, I tried to comprehend and process anything that I might be able to learn from them. What I did learn was that taking Taylor home was not going to be easy, and recognizing that fact would be part of getting through it.

Keith and I woke up early on the morning of April 15. Taylor's discharge date had been moved up two days to make things easier for everyone. Keith went over to the rehab to gather some of Taylor's belongings that had not been taken home previously. I tried to wrap my head and heart around the adjustments that were about to occur. I wanted to remember this day, and I would try to hold on to each moment of it. I finally mustered up enough courage to face the events that were about to unfold and walked through Bryn Mawr's doors for the final time as the mother of a patient. I was profoundly satisfied that love had led us to this place where medicine, compassion, and a drive for excellence in care coexist.

As I walked into the Maple Unit for the last time, I took a deep breath and I said a prayer for every person who would come to occupy the rooms, and for every person who cared for or loved them. I wished with all my heart that such a place never needed to exist, but I was deeply aware of what its existence had meant to us.

265

Some of the final procedures had to take place while Keith and Taylor were waiting. Freda, our beloved nurse, was gathering Taylor's discharge papers and list of medications. Taylor's medication ritual was as follows:

In the morning, Taylor would take Lexapro, Geodon, and Buspar to help his depression and mood disorder issues. For his seizure-related issues, he would take Dilantin and Keppra.[30] He also continued to take two medications for his asthma. At midday he took only one medication, and in the evening, he would take the same drugs he had in the morning except for the Lexapro. We knew the medications and dosages were subject to change and that it was essential that the medicines be administered correctly.

Freda took the time to go over each detail of the list with us, accurately and carefully. She copied the medication chart for us, which made it easier to follow. The chart showed what time each medication was to be given, what it was for, and how many milligrams were in the dosage. She and Nick reminded us that they were only a phone call away if we needed some reassurance. Their words "Do not hesitate to call" were genuine and heartfelt. Dr. Lynch and Dr. Hertz spoke their final words of wisdom to both Taylor and us. Dr. Lynch came in to remove the feeding tube that had remained in Taylor's stomach until now. Keith would be with him for this moment, and I felt relieved that I did not have to be present for it.

Nick had explained to us and to Taylor that the removal of the tube would hurt. There was a small tube on the outside of Taylor's stomach northeast of his belly button. The tube was held in place by a small inflated balloon-like device. Dr. Lynch asked Taylor to sit upright, take a deep breath, and tighten his muscles as if he were doing a sit-up. As Taylor did what he was told, Dr. Lynch wrapped the tubing around his hand and gave it an aggressive pull, and then you heard a loud POP! The tube had been removed; the removal was painful, but Taylor was

---

[30] Dilantin is the brand name of phenytoin, an antiseizure drug that has been used since the mid-1950s. Keppra is the brand name of a newer drug used alongside Dilantin to treat tonic-clonic seizures, the type that Taylor had.

happy to have the tube gone. It was the last of the tubes to be removed, and that was wonderful to see! Taylor would later relay to us that the removal of the tube felt as if someone had punched him in the stomach, which was similar to how Nick had said that it might feel. The hole left by the tube was covered with a small bandage after this final tube had been removed from Taylor's body.

What had occurred over the last several months was remarkable. Over the final month, the fine-tuning of Taylor's rehabilitation goals was accomplished as much as possible. We were going home with a person who was far more improved than the person we came in with. Much of what rehabilitation focuses on is specific to the therapies available.

In physical therapy, Taylor had completed the process of safely, slowly, and independently walking up and down stairs. He still needed someone with him, but he was able to complete the actual process of walking on his own. A few days earlier, Taylor, and Lauren, his physical therapist, and I rode the elevator down to the main floor of the rehab and taken a somewhat long walk to some public stairs. Up to this point, Taylor had worked only on short flights of stairs in an enclosed stairwell, with no one other than his therapist and sometimes family around.

I could feel his anxiety as he looked at the set of two flights of stairs in the open staircase. *He was afraid and so was I.* I knew that he was safe; Lauren was right there with us and nothing was going to happen, but for Taylor these stairs represented much more. Falling had robbed him of almost everything, and now someone was telling him he had to climb both upward and downward. As I stood next to him, the upward part of the exercise was manageable. We arrived at the top and he needed to rest, but I could sense his dread as he peered down the stairs. I was afraid with and for him. He asked me whether we could go down another way. I knew there was an elevator close by, but I also knew that both Taylor and I had to do this exercise. We took one step at a time and before we knew it, the challenge had been met!

In relation to walking outside, Taylor had learned to follow the directives of the therapist; he came inside when he was asked to and he walked safely on a variety of surfaces. Taylor's left foot had a strong tendency to drag. Walking on smooth surfaces was easier than on those that had a rougher texture, like grass or concrete. He was given several sheets of exercises to continue to perform at home, and we were shown how to execute each exercise correctly. It was important that the core of Taylor's body continue to be strengthened. There had been so much work put into his ability to simply hold himself upright, and we didn't want that ability to decline.

In occupational therapy, Taylor had begun to understand the concept of rituals: activities of daily living like changing his clothes daily, preferably in the morning, were practiced over and over again. He had been brushing his teeth and using mouthwash two to three times a day, an improvement over the multiple times that he had been doing these things over the previous weeks. He willingly participated in the schedule of showering every other night, and making sure that he was clean. Each day and routine followed a pattern. Step by step, self-care and other routine tasks were carried out with as much consistency as possible. It was through multiple executions of the same patterns that he would remember things. A major part of what we needed to do for him was to keep those patterns in place.

In regard to speech therapy, Taylor understood that he should eat three meals a day. He would pay attention to chewing his food completely and clearing his mouth of "hidden" food after meals. Taylor had to be made aware of the importance of consuming food safely. Part of what he struggled with was allowing food to sit inside the pockets of his cheeks, where it could present a choking hazard. He had worked on eating slowly, taking small bites, and not speaking while he was eating.

Such behavioral goals as not asking to leave the rehab multiple times a day or not asking to go to the bathroom several times an hour had been achieved. Taylor was actively working on not interrupting and expressing himself respectfully. He had willingly explored and participated in activities like making special treats for our dog Ginger, and writing me a card of appreciation.

All this activity took a substantial amount of determination and focus on Taylor's part. Setting his mind to something was like throwing a box of ping pong balls in the air and accurately guessing where they might land. Each task that Taylor was able to complete successfully was an accomplishment that deserved celebration. The culmination of his hard work, the love that others poured into him, his first-rate medical care, and the unseen elements of faith and hope had led him to where he was. This was his moment to shine, even if he did not fully grasp what a beautiful ray of light he emitted. *Taylor was alive.* Taylor was going to walk through the exit doors of the rehab. Taylor was going home while other patients had to be transferred to long-term nursing facilities. I was proud of Taylor. I was also proud of each and every person that had helped bring him to this point. A concept that is difficult to grasp is that the drive and determination that was inside Taylor prior to his fall played an active role in his recovery. Along with that, so did his injury. There were many patients whose injury had forever stolen their abilities; and no matter how much determination lay inside them, it could not compensate for what the injury had done.

Before we left, I ran down to the cafeteria to say goodbye to some of my favorite workers. As I waited for the elevator, I crossed paths with an internal medicine physician who had worked closely with Taylor's case. He told me something I will never forget. He looked me in the eyes and said, "Nicole, I want you to remember something. Taylor has had a remarkable recovery. It has taken place for many reasons, but you and your dedication to him is one of those reasons. I do not believe Taylor would be where he is without you. Your love for him is something we all felt, and it was a pleasure to have you among us." That was my good-bye party. This quiet, often stoic man spoke to me when I needed it most. I would etch his words on the tablet of my heart, and I would need to read them again and again.

Before our conversation ended, he added one more thing. He said, "Don't forget—I don't think Taylor should play video games at home. They could trigger his seizures."[31] It made me laugh out loud to

---

[31] The doctor was referring to a condition known as photosensitive epilepsy. Video games that feature rapidly flashing lights or alternating patterns of different bright colors can trigger seizures in patients with this type of

think that Taylor would not be playing any video games. Taylor *would*, however, want to go outside and play in the woods.

The time had come, and it could not be put off any longer. Keith and I loaded our car and we helped Taylor get in. As we drove away from Bryn Mawr Rehabilitation Hospital, the sun was shining, and I understood a new part of our story had begun.

Taylor was smiling as we drove down the road. I was in the back seat and I was thankful that Keith was behind the wheel. Twenty-two years before, we had brought our first bouncing baby boy home from the hospital and now we were bringing him home again. Taylor had been given a new beginning; he was alive, and that is what mattered most.

Halfway through our trip, we stopped at a full-service rest area. Taylor and Keith went into the bathroom and when they came out, Taylor knew exactly what he wanted to eat. There was a Burger King in the plaza, and he and I walked up to the counter. I could feel everyone watching us. With some coaching from me, Taylor slowly placed his order for a cheeseburger, French fries, and a Coke. Placing an order was a big deal for him, but he remembered his manners. He said both "Please" and "Thank you" to the cashier. He ate the burger like a champ, but was unable to consume the fries.

When we finally arrived in our small town, things appeared as they always had, but everything had changed for the people in our home. We drove down the picturesque streets and reminded Taylor of various spots he had previously enjoyed. He took it in with little excitement or animation, but he was happy to be home. He would say once in a while, "I remember this." Our house is outside the town center, and we had to literally go over a creek and through the woods to get to it. In my mind, I envisioned what it would be like welcoming Taylor home in another scenario. This homecoming would be private, quiet, and lovely in its own right. There would be no fanfare, no balloons, and no shouts of celebration.

---

epilepsy. See for example Epilepsy Foundation, "Triggers of Seizures," http://www.epilepsy.com/learn/triggers-seizures (accessed February 6, 2015).

Our neighbors, who were close in age to Tanner, Avery, and Taylor, had made a simple but impressive sign that read, "Welcome Home Taylor." Those words said enough and they read beautifully. As we pulled into our driveway, Taylor's face broke into a grin . . . it was reserved, but it was present. After six long months, Taylor was going to walk through the open doors of his home. We were not sure that this moment would ever happen, and now that it was taking place, we knew that it was a priceless gift.

We opened the front door and our German shorthaired pointer, Ginger, greeted us. In Taylor's absence, Ginger had shredded his sheets by digging at them. She had endlessly whimpered and whined, and now she examined her buddy slowly and methodically. I hoped her instincts would guide her in the right way, because there had been some discussion that her rambunctious nature might be too much for Taylor. Taylor was happy to see Ginger, but his reaction was contained and reserved. He just did not have the energy to express more than a small amount of emotion. After just a few minutes in the doorway, he asked, "Will Avery be coming home today?"

Avery was in university, which was a little over an hour away. It touched my heart that he was one of the first people that Taylor thought about. I was, however, still saddened by the level of disconnection that seemed to be present in the relationship between Taylor and Tanner. Taylor had spent the last few years before his fall cheering on Tanner at every possible sporting event that he could attend, and now he seemed unaware of the relationship between them.

Prior to leaving, the therapists at Bryn Mawr helped us determine that at least initially, one of us needed to sleep near Taylor. We had a mattress pad with an alarm on Taylor's bed, a monitor with a camera in his room, and alarms on the doors. All these safeguards were essential, but our home is large and Taylor needed to be closely monitored. For the first few nights, I slept next to him in his bed. After a few nights, we put a single mattress on the floor and set up a schedule for sleeping in Taylor's room. If Taylor woke up in the night, he had a routine that he had to follow. Because I was so drained, the routine was most unwelcome in the hours I was supposed to be sleeping. Taylor would first awaken and ask me to turn on the light; next he had to put on his slippers, and then we would walk together to the bathroom. Once he finished, he would wash his hands. Each task in the series took several minutes. Every small step involved was in slow motion, and my mind and body screamed for rest. It was a major adjustment being in charge of Taylor's care and safety twenty-four hours a day, and my body was rebelling; I just wanted to sleep.

Our first few days at home were fairly quiet. There were a lot of people who were anxious to see Taylor, but we had to schedule visits carefully. In his mind, he wanted to see everyone and catch up, but in reality he could not handle a high level of commotion.

One of the most helpful gestures toward us was when a close friend whose daughter had lost her battle with leukemia a few years earlier had set up a meal schedule for us. Her understanding of what it meant to care for someone who was so dependent due to illness prompted this favor, which also brought our community together. Every Monday, Wednesday, and Friday she arranged for people to drop off meals at her place of business, and Tanner picked them up on his way home from school. This kindness was a tremendous help. It alleviated the drain on energy involved in both planning and preparing meals each night. It also meant that there was food available for those who happened to be visiting.

On Saturday, April 21, one of Taylor's closest friends was home from college for the weekend. We were excited about seeing her, and having breakfast with her and her mom. They came over with a breakfast casserole and before we had even put the first bite in our mouths, Taylor had a seizure. We had specific instructions as to which type of seizure warranted a call to 9-1-1. This was one that did. We had to pay attention to the severity, the length, and the type of seizure that had occurred, but at this point seizures were not routine and we had been instructed not to treat their occurrence lightly. There was nothing routine about such an occurrence and we still did not fully understand seizures. They were new and scary to us.

This was the first time that Tanner and Keith had witnessed an "event." In the medical world, seizures are often referred to as events, and that term always sat well with me. Taylor hated the word *seizure*, so saying *event* made it seem less ominous. Seizures are frightening, and the fact that they just occur like some monster suddenly knocking at the door is very unsettling.

The paramedics arrived, and I met them outside. I explained to them as calmly and quickly as I could that Taylor had previously suffered a brain injury. They would not be able to rush into our home and create a lot of commotion as Taylor would not respond well to that. In my panic, I had to be calm and I needed to tell them effectively that Taylor would need them to be calm as well. The stretcher was left outside and they came in to assess the situation. They took Taylor's vital signs, talked with him, and then called the physician on duty in the emergency room. I spoke with the doctor and we all felt comfortable with not sending Taylor to the emergency room. Of course, we were given more directives about what to do if it happened again. Part of me felt unsure about calling 9-1-1, but all of this was new to us. Were we supposed to call an ambulance every time a seizure occurred? Which symptoms would warrant a trip to the hospital? The doctors informed us that for now, making the call is what we should do, and we had to get over the fact that we might feel apprehensive about it. Until the nature of the seizures could be better understood, we had to have them documented and monitored in some fashion.

As soon as the seizure had begun, and before it went into full swing, Taylor indicated that he did not want his friend to leave. He was making motions with his hands and trying to speak through the jerking and spasmodic motions of his mouth. He was trying to say his friend's name, but "Ka," "Ka" was all he could get out. Between the waving of his arms and his utterances, I was able to determine that he was telling me that he did not want Kollie to leave. *This recognition broke my heart.* He needed to see his precious and dear friend. He had no recollection of her visits or the times they had shared at Bryn Mawr, and his heart was not in a place to see her leave right away. So, I told Kollie and her mom how much we wanted them to stay. "Breakfast at the Bingaman's" was proving to be far more than they had anticipated.

After the EMTs left, Taylor sat down and we all ate. No one but Taylor felt hungry, but after the first bite, the food tasted good. It was warm and comforting, and I recall thinking how fantastic it tasted. As soon at breakfast was over, Taylor was ready to rest. Our friends left and we settled Taylor in for naptime.

As Taylor slept, Keith and I explored our feelings about the new changes in our life. I wrote later that day:

> *During Taylor's nap, Keith and I took some time to discuss how very sad we are. We shared how heartbreaking all of this feels, and how much we miss the son we had before. We also discussed how much we deeply love Taylor, and how thankful we feel for his life. We are fully aware that we could have lost our son on Thanksgiving Day. We grieve the part of him that we did lose. But we still have Taylor here. He is different and requires more care than we ever imagined, but we are thankful for his life.*

Taylor slept for most of the afternoon and woke up with a sudden urge to find his favorite belt, and we did find it. We were experiencing an extraordinary transformation in Taylor because he was starting to remember his life prior to the accident. Being home triggered a number of responses to the familiarity of his environment. He clearly felt a totally different level of care and comfort in the daily presence of his family, some friends, and his beloved dog.

Prior to coming home, I had imagined that it would feel better for me as well—*but it didn't*. I was now juggling Taylor's schedule with friends, physicians, medications, routines, and life in general from 7 a.m. to 5 p.m. on my own. It was a heavy responsibility. When he napped, I was figuring out how his outpatient therapy would work, trying to catch up on other matters, and going through the motions of my newfound occupation. I was not only Taylor's mother, but I was also his driver, his chef, his nurse, his companion, his secretary, his advocate, and his friend. I was on call twenty-four hours a day. It was exhausting.

When Taylor's friends would come to visit, I often wanted to ask if they would mind if I went to take a nap. Unfortunately, I was not at the point where I felt comfortable leaving him to rest. Instead, I would often be able to grab a quick shower, catch up on some phone calls or paperwork, or just sit still for a few minutes. A few of his friends were nurses, and that felt like a special treat for me. I knew that they could handle any unusual situation that might have arisen.

Looking back at that time, I realize now that I was continuing in a pattern that prevented me from truly feeling the level of loss that had occurred. It was like trying to process an incredibly challenging diagnosis while training for a marathon. I was going through the motions of what needed to be done. I would have to take time to actually feel what was happening, —but for now, my emotions simmered on the back burner. I recall crying every now and then, or talking with a friend about how bad all the changes felt, but as time went on, I realized that the real grief had not yet surfaced.

Those were still the early days, and taking care of Taylor and staying on top of what he needed meant that I would have to put my own grief on hold. It was not until months later that the magnitude of our loss would hit me, and in truth, I am grateful for the delay. I could not have been present effectively for Taylor and felt the full pain of what had happened to him.

Chapter Twenty-one
If Only
Mid- to Late April into Early May

After the initial week home, Taylor and I settled into a predictable routine. His outpatient therapies would continue at Health South Rehab, which was adjacent to Geisinger Medical Center, the hospital where he was initially treated, but it was *still an hour from our home*. The rehab worked out his schedule to make it as convenient as possible for us because the drive was less than appealing. Taylor would attend occupational, speech, and physical therapy sessions three days a week for a total of nine sessions. Our intention was to make the time we did travel there as beneficial as possible. Even traveling was difficult for Taylor. The things we don't recognize that require energy from our brain actually happen all day long without our being aware of them. For Taylor, this fact meant that mentally preparing for therapy depleted him as well as the actual therapy itself.

The appointments were not scheduled too early, as Taylor could not be rushed or hurried in any way in the morning, and by the afternoon he was exhausted. When developing the schedule, we tried to find the sweet spot when he could be most successful. We would leave around 8:45 a.m., and during the commute, the radio was turned off and we rode in complete silence. Taylor was going to have almost three full hours of therapy, which would require all his mental and physical energies. I felt it was important for his brain to be quieted and disengaged beforehand.

The silence was not something I favored, but over the course of the last several months I had become accustomed to it. I had spent many hours alone or sitting next to Taylor while he was unable to respond. It gave me a lot of time to think, which may or may not have been productive depending on the hour or the day. The quiet drive did serve as a time of peace and allowed me to map out tasks that still needed to be completed. *There were times when the silence felt like a reminder of the loneliness that plagued me.*

The back-to-back appointments would prove to be challenging for Taylor, but everyone made a conscious effort to make the schedule work. It was comforting to be welcomed by friendly therapists and staff at his first appointment. I felt overwhelmed as I met everyone; I wanted to remember their names and the role that each of them would play in this next phase of his recovery. We had met so many people over the last few months, and that trend would not be stopping anytime soon. In order for Taylor to feel secure and to thrive, he would need to have a sense that I felt confident in where he was and who would be helping him.

The orders from Bryn Mawr for therapy were clear, but more broad than concise. Taylor's first session would be full of assessments. It would be necessary for me to attend Taylor's sessions with him, at least until he became acclimated to the new people and new environment as a whole. The orders provided a general outline of Taylor's present condition and some goals for continued direction. As time progressed, the idea would be that each therapist would learn where he was mentally and physically and how best to treat him. There was the same team approach that had been in place for him previously, which we had valued.

At a facility like Health South, each patient is met individually and goals are set within each particular form of therapy. In regard to his physical, speech, and occupational therapies, Taylor was invited to give input about his goals. Taylor was not able to identify his goals clearly, but he did want to get stronger. He wanted parts of his body to work better, and he knew that a part of that meant building up his strength. He still required considerable prompting to answer questions, especially when the concept behind them was open-ended. His perception of reality was often inaccurate, so that when asked to identify his goals, he was still focused on tasks like driving and working. He wanted to get back to both activities, but did not understand that they were far from the first issues at hand.

The therapy team communicated to him effectively that his thoughts, feelings, and ideas mattered in this process. At the end of a week, the team had a meeting. This meeting gave them time to discuss any concerns that I had expressed and any challenges they would have, as well as other vital issues in regard to Taylor's progress.

The physical therapist needed to address his balance, strength, and endurance. I was pleased to see that Health South had some pieces of equipment that Taylor had not previously used. One of the pieces that immediately caught my eye was a treadmill. This particular treadmill had a harness apparatus that could be attached to Taylor as well as safety rails that could be used for extra support. It would be a piece of equipment that Taylor would develop a love/hate relationship with. However, he was initially excited to see the treadmill. The gym area was smaller than the one at Bryn Mawr, but there were fewer patients being treated simultaneously. I felt that the lower level of distraction would be more appropriate for Taylor at this juncture in his recovery. The physical therapist that Taylor worked with was a soft-spoken man named Brett. He immediately related to Taylor by discussing sports. My first impression of him was that he reminded me of a younger, more conservative version of my dad. I liked him and I knew that Taylor would like him as well.

In occupational therapy, Taylor needed to work on fine-tuning his eye-hand coordination, working on improving his activities of daily living (ADLs) and improving his own awareness of personal safety. A warm, friendly therapist by the name of Stacey greeted us. She had a soft-spoken demeanor and I could tell immediately that she had a compassionate heart. She made both Taylor and me feel comfortable from the start. Her smile was her greatest asset and it was well-matched with the twinkle in her eyes. One of the first things she asked me was whether I could explain to her the types of activities that I thought might keep Taylor engaged in his therapy. She wanted to get to know him as an individual and learn what different avenues of therapy he might or might not enjoy. I told her that Taylor had always been a very hard worker and someone who liked to play hard too. I explained his love for the outdoors, including fishing and hunting. I also explained that he had been good at his job, and for the most part seemed to enjoy what he did for a living, working in the heating, ventilation, and air conditioning (HVAC) field. These details helped her understand that Taylor was a person who liked to get things done, and that he enjoyed working with his hands.

Speech therapy was once again proving to be challenging. Taylor and his previous speech therapist had worked out a rhythm that played out successfully while he was at Bryn Mawr, but he was never one who liked to read or write. For whatever reason, it seemed like patients identified this aspect of therapy with classroom-based learning. I knew his therapist would have to be exceptionally creative for it to go well, and even then it might be a struggle.

Taylor had clear communication deficiencies. The primary goal of speech therapy was to address his executive functioning, reasoning, problem solving, and memory skills. Those were just the basic components in his plethora of deficits. In my mind, success in this arena was one of Taylor's most difficult hurdles. As we met with the speech therapist for the first time, I couldn't help thinking that she would remind Taylor of an old-fashioned schoolteacher; and knowing his personality, I feared there would be a struggle. One of the more burdensome aspects of this whole process was realizing there were times that Taylor's "clicking" with someone did not depend on whether they were a pleasant or intelligent person, and I knew from the initial meeting that speech therapy would take more encouragement than the other areas.

Even though I had spent a considerable amount of time alone with Taylor over the last few months, as I watched him grow and learn to do new things, I remained fascinated by the process involved in his recovery. The brain is what allows us not only to be who we are or express how we feel, but it is the organ that makes the organs of our body as a whole work together. Everything we do depends on our brain to make it happen. It was exhilarating to see new growth occur or a new concept take hold.

One of the most important events in the first week of outpatient therapy was a general assessment. Various tools were used to measure Taylor's physical strength and cognitive abilities in an array of areas. A simple weight-bearing tool was placed in his hand to measure the amount of gripping strength that he had. The strength was measured by having Taylor complete a repetitive squeezing motion. Taylor's endurance level was assessed by charting how many repetitions of a movement could be completed, then matched with the length of time he could give to a particular task. He was asked to read simple words and phrases, and recognize any patterns he saw in them. This information would prove to be invaluable in a few weeks. These assessments would be used as an initial starting place or baseline; the goal was to see his scores improve.

The real work began after we settled into the dynamics of the schedule, which therapy was best to have first as well as last, and finally getting better acquainted with one another. As time went on, I did not attend all the therapy sessions because I wanted Taylor to gain some independence. We started by having him stay by himself with Stacey in occupational therapy. He was most comfortable with her, and the activities he did were challenging, but not as frightening or frustrating as the other arenas of therapy. One activity he enjoyed was an adaptation of dot-to-dot drawing. This was a timed activity and Taylor seemed to like the process as well as the challenge. As with everything, he started small . . . his first worksheets had fewer than fifteen dots to connect; in time that number would increase.

An interesting pattern began to emerge more strongly at this time, and it often showed up while at therapy. The technical term is confabulation, a word widely used in psychology circles. As Taylor began to relate to Brett and Stacey, he was fully aware that he was meeting them for the first time. As a young man prior to entering high school, Taylor had played and loved baseball. When he was about thirteen years old, he had a bad experience with the game and made the decision that he would rather devote his time to hunting and fishing. His baseball career had ended. It had not been an easy decision for him, but one he appeared to feel confident about.

In ninth grade he played football. He ended up breaking his arm early in the season and decided that after that, he was no longer going to play. His sophomore and junior years, he explored the idea of wrestling, but it too was short-lived. Ultimately, Taylor did not like being tied down to schedules and practices for sports that he was not sure he would have any actual time to participate in when it came down to the hour of the actual game or match. With hunting and fishing, he could set his own rules and control his success in a way that felt comfortable to him. At the time, that attitude seemed reasonable to us. Enjoying the outdoors was not a school-sanctioned activity, but it served many of the same purposes.

As Taylor related to Brett and Stacey, he seemed to spin stories of a new life for himself. Suddenly he was a star running back, champion wrestler, and home-run hitter. He had a sports career in high school that no one but he remembered. I was not sure how to deal with these stories because the things he was saying seemed real to him. In terms of baseball, Taylor had been a solid and dependable player when he had been in elementary and middle school. He was always chosen for the Little League All-Star team and was a successful base runner, hitter, and position player. After middle school, however, Taylor never played organized baseball again. Some of the stories he told were based on true events but others were not.

In relation to wrestling and football, it seemed as if he were remembering either what he wished he had been, or what his younger brother Tanner had been. Either his memories were murky or he was blatantly lying. Having relatively limited experience in the mental health field, as well as witnessing similar things in his recovery, I began to research what these tall tales meant.

Another story he told repeatedly concerned a therapist at Bryn Mawr. This particular therapist was a strikingly lovely young woman. She had fair, milky-white skin; beautiful long blonde hair and a smile that radiated from within her. She epitomized natural beauty. She was firm but soft-spoken with Taylor and despite her youth, she seemed to be a tremendous asset to the team. One word that always came to mind when I interacted with her was *reserved*. She was terrific with Taylor, but did not yet appear to be as comfortable in her role as some of the other therapists.

As Taylor began to recall some of their time together to his friends, he would say, "There was a pretty girl who came in everyday to help me shower. She always wore black leather chaps, and she loved to wash my body. Sometimes she would shower naked with me!" He would always smile and express joyful animation about his time with her. Not for one second did a part of me think there was a shred of truth in this story! This was the brain injury talking, and Taylor might have imagined this scenario to be true. He was, after all, a testosterone-filled twenty-two-year-old man! I would remind him that this therapist actually wore khaki pants and that she was there to teach and assist him, but he would grin and then laugh and say, "No, she was hot and she had a crush on me!" Maybe this fantasy was how he survived; it was not unusual or unheard-of and it certainly did not offend me. I had already witnessed the staff members who devoted themselves to helping people recover from traumatic brain injury develop and maintain thick skins.

A friend had relayed a personal story about an experience she had with a patient she had helped years before. She was a young physical therapist and had been assigned to a man who had been around Taylor's age when his accident occurred. One day she was helping him with his activities of daily living and it was time for him to shower. The man looked at her as she was assisting him and asked, "Does your boyfriend know you are doing this?" When she told me, I laughed and could easily relate to the story. There is often a common thread among people who are the same age and who have damage in the same areas of the brain. Taylor's thoughts about his therapist were nothing new to the team who worked with him.

In regard to these new stories he was telling, they were plain and simple confabulations. The Memory Disorders Project at Rutgers University defines confabulation as follows:

> Confabulation is a memory disorder that may occur in patients who have sustained damage to both the basal forebrain and the frontal lobes . . . Confabulation is defined as the spontaneous production of false memories: either memories for events which never occurred, or memories of actual events which are displaced in space or time. These memories may be elaborate and detailed. . . . It is important to stress that confabulators are not lying: they are not deliberately trying to mislead. In fact, the patients are generally quite unaware that their memories are

inaccurate, and they may argue strenuously that they have been telling the truth.[32]

Taylor was not intentionally spreading false information. He was sharing what he remembered about his prior life and his recovery. The doctors explained his confabulations as filling in the gaps where there were empty spaces in his memory while he was unaware of it.

Other recurring patterns of behavior were emerging as well. In some aspects, our lives were beginning to feel like the Bill Murray movie called *Groundhog Day*. This is a film in which a weatherman finds himself living the same day over and over again. For example, Taylor ate Lucky Charms cereal every day for breakfast, and it was problematic if we ran out. He needed to have designated shower days, so we stuck with the bathing schedule that he had followed at the hospital. Taylor still needed to be monitored and assisted in the shower, so either Keith or I would help him. We had to remind him of the various steps and the order in which they occurred. It would cause a lot of confusion if Keith or I had deviated from Taylor's known pattern, and we were aware of his need for consistency. He needed to perform the steps involved in the same order every time, which is how he was relearning them.

He woke up at 6 in the morning on his therapy days, showered, ate, returned to the bathroom to brush his teeth and wash his hands multiple times, and finally would be ready to go. This routine was a slow-moving process and Taylor required constant prompting. Taylor's behavior included a lot of repetitions; he needed to have things go in just the right order as they had previously.

About midway through his therapy sessions, he needed a snack, so I always packed something for him to munch on and water to drink. When he was finished, he really liked to go to Subway for a sandwich. Taylor was still very thin, so anything he wanted to eat made us feel

---

[32] Memory Disorders Project at Rutgers University, *Memory Loss & the Brain,* Glossary, "Confabulation," http://www.memorylossonline.com/glossary/confabulation.html (accessed February 7, 2015).

relieved. On the days we went to Subway, he always ordered exactly the same sandwich as he had the previous time. If I suggested something different, he would politely tell me that he already knew what he wanted. These visits were another good form of therapy for Taylor: waiting in line, ordering each item, and carrying the task through to completion. His mind needed the steps of ordering to be the same each time.

From time to time, there were students preparing to enter various fields of therapy who came to Health South as interns. A couple of weeks into Speech Therapy a young female student joined us. She was good for Taylor; he wanted to impress her, thus making him work harder. This student was a lovely young woman and I knew her presence would be helpful to Taylor's will to engage in his sessions.

On May 1, I wrote:

Today in speech, Taylor worked with his therapist and her student doing an activity with animals. Taylor had to group them together in groups of three consisting of a mother, father, and baby animal. For example, the word groupings were: mare, stallion, *and* foal; *or* hen, rooster, *and* chick. *Taylor had to choose from multiple words which ones belonged together. This was not an easy task for him. This process of sorting was something that his injury had made difficult for him. The medium used for this activity was something similar to flash cards.*

Taylor then had to answer some questions that related to his cognitive understanding. Taylor concentrates very hard and tries to give his full attention to the task at hand. He was extremely perplexed by one question today. The student asked Taylor, "Can someone paint an eagle?" He kept discussing that the eagle would have to be so still and remain that way if someone were going to paint it. When the therapist showed him a painting of an eagle, he still was unable to sort out what the phrase, "painting an eagle" meant. He was stuck on the concept that a live eagle would not tolerate being painted on by a human.

285

His mind was picturing a man with a paintbrush holding a live eagle and attempting to paint him.

These types of exercises shed a lot of light on Taylor's thought processes and the fact that he took in everything in the most literal sense. His concrete thinking would cause issues as time went on, but the insight was invaluable to me.

At some point around two weeks into May, we began noticing some changes in Taylor. His appetite had not yet come close to fully returning, but now it was decreasing instead, and he was vomiting frequently and having copious diarrhea. He also seemed to be getting less and less steady on his feet. Initially, we were not overly concerned with the vomiting, and we attributed the decline in his strength to the fact that he was not having physical therapy as often as he previously had. But as the days passed, we grew increasingly concerned. On one particular Monday, his therapists expressed concern as well and sent a message to his neurosurgeon.

Around that time, Taylor had been looking forward all week to attending a local fundraising event to benefit his medical fund. That morning he woke up and appeared to be doing a bit better, or so I thought. When he awoke from his nap in the afternoon, however, he was worse. He was so weak he could hardly stand. I called Dr. Taggart and extra time was set aside for his appointment the next day. We were fortunate that he had an appointment already scheduled!

Tanner turned seventeen years old on May 22, the same day as Taylor's appointment. After six months of so much attention being poured into Taylor, my desire was for Tanner to have a special day. I wanted him to be the primary focus, and to feel loved and celebrated for who he is. Tanner was generous and unselfish in regard to Taylor, but I knew he needed to be acknowledged too. He and Avery had been through quite an ordeal since November. They were growing heroes in my eyes and I wanted so much more for them than to be surrounded by pain, illness, and struggle, especially on an occasion like a birthday. I wanted them to feel and take in the idea of the power and importance of their presence, especially to me.

Unfortunately, Tanner's birthday did not go as planned. Taylor seemed to be entering a quick decline. A few days earlier, I had spoken with Kristine at Bryn Mawr, who told me urgently that these new symptoms were not normal. As a result of the concerns expressed by her and the therapist, an appointment was scheduled immediately. So on May 22, Avery met me at Geisinger and we took Taylor for a CAT scan prior to meeting with Dr. Taggart. Over the span of twenty-four hours, Taylor had become so weak we could not leave his side.

As I reflect back to that time, I wonder why I was not more alarmed about his growing deterioration. I don't know whether I was in denial or just too blind to see what was in front of me. I was unaware of my own exhaustion and I did not want Taylor's homecoming to be unsuccessful. I was his main caregiver and if he suffered a decline, *did that mean I was incapable of giving him what he needed*? One of the things I learned about myself is that I am not a mother with an affinity for drama. Real life offers enough tumultuous emotions, and I was thankful that any internal hysteria I felt was kept at bay. The "silent scream" remained an internal struggle.

Taylor had been having routine blood work since his homecoming; up until just days before, it had been fine. Suddenly, evidence of some sort of bacterial growth appeared. At that time, Dr. Taggart discussed some best- and worst-case scenarios with us. As Avery and I sat with Taylor in the small patient room of the clinic, Dr. Taggart explained that the worst-case scenario had arisen. All this happened within a matter of days. It is an overwhelming task to piece it all together, so I am reflecting with as much accuracy as I can.

The scan revealed that Taylor's body was resorbing his bone. Dr. Taggart showed us the scan and described his replaced bone as something that resembled Swiss cheese. The holes in the bone should not have been there. Resorption is not unheard of; in fact, we had been distinctly told that it could happen. Resorption is far more likely in younger patients like Taylor; it was one of the risks involved. Taylor's body was not accepting his bone as it should.

This resorption essentially meant that his body was rejecting the bone that had been removed and frozen, then replaced in Taylor's head. The bone would have to come out and that needed to happen as soon as possible. There was a sense of urgency in the room that day. Avery was intelligent and well-spoken for a twenty-year-old. He asked the doctor whether there were other options that we could explore. *And there were not.* He also asked what would happen if we did nothing. The answer was simple and horrifying, Taylor would continue to decline rapidly. Avery and I tried to think of any questions that Keith and Tanner might have, and Doctor Taggart understood that more questions might arise.

I remember sitting in the cold white room that day. The clinic was quiet. Taylor and I had been at the hospital for the entire afternoon, and Avery had come in time for the actual appointment. As the situation unfolded, it took more time than we anticipated. All the other patients had finished and the doctors were in their offices doing their work. *The silence surrounded us.* I was stunned that yet another crisis was happening; at the moment we were told, I did not have the luxury of crying or releasing any type of emotion. Avery and I had to be calm and keep our emotions hushed for the sake of Taylor. We had to be okay so that he would know that he was going to be okay. I wanted to scream at the top of my lungs, "WHY IS THIS HAPPENING NOW? I don't want us to go through this again!" But instead my eyes filled with tears for a moment and my voice had a brief quaver in it, but then it was business as usual. This should not be happening, and especially not on Tanner's birthday.

The plan was to make a special synthetic bone for Taylor to immediately replace the bone that was being removed. This type of custom-made piece generally required a month to produce, but Dr. Taggart worked her magic and a rush was put on the order for Taylor's synthetic bone. It was quite a process, which involved using the scan to build Taylor's new bone in a way that would fit its location exactly. In the first days of June, we got a call to schedule the surgery; the piece had arrived. Surgery was scheduled for June 7.

The specific bacterium that was growing was still unidentified, but Dr. Taggart was more than ready to remove the old bone, put in the new one, and pick up where Taylor left off.

If only life were so simple.

Chapter Twenty-two
The Way the Cookie Crumbles
Early June 2013

Taylor and I had been home for roughly seven weeks. For the first few weeks of that time, he had been able to enjoy visits with friends and family. Several of these people were seeing him for the first time since his fall. During his stay at Bryn Mawr, we had had a limited number of visitors, so Taylor was more than ready to see people. We knew the importance of his reconnecting with people he cared about and those who that cared about him.

With each person, there would often be a flood of memories that accompanied their visit. Each time Taylor was able to remember part of his past was like seeing another room of his memory open. Sometimes it would just be a quick glance inside and at other times, details would come flooding back to him.

Our house became a place of many revolving doors; I had a day planner that was packed with names, dates, and engagements of all kinds. Taylor had numerous appointments in his schedule, and even tasks like routine blood work were time-consuming. On the days that he had therapy, we tried to avoid adding to his schedule to avoid utter exhaustion. Taylor usually rested for three to four hours after coming home from Health South. The staff at the rehab reminded me that he still required a great deal of rest, which is a significant factor in healing the brain. Taylor had two good time periods in the day; one was shortly after he woke up. He usually felt more sociable and energetic than he did in the early afternoon. The other good time occurred around 5 p.m.; Taylor would hit a spot when social interaction seemed more productive and meaningful to him. There were times, however, when he "zoned out," and I struggled to suggest politely to his visitors that the visit should end.

As the most common audience, I was always honored to be a part of Taylor's reunions. I often stayed in the kitchen area while visiting took place in our adjacent dining room. Sometimes Taylor and his friends would go to chat in his bedroom. It was exhausting, but absolutely worth it to see him so happy interacting with old friends. Many of Taylor's friends had been hurting because they were not able to see him for months, and the first time they got to see Taylor was always poignant.

Understandably, many friends were apprehensive or timid about their initial reunions with Taylor, but we tried to prepare them as best we could on what to expect. Taylor's friends were mainly young people in their twenties who had never experienced anything close to traumatic brain injury. The friends who saw Taylor while he was at Bryn Mawr also offered guidance and feedback throughout his social circle. As the frequency of visits increased, we were all able to see that the visits benefited everyone involved. The interactions played a role in everyone's healing.

The person Taylor's friends were coming to see was profoundly different from the person they had known just months before. The friend they called Bing had undergone a tremendous change. His injury left his body intact, but much of his personality had transformed. I often wondered how Taylor's friends perceived him, especially the young men who tended to be more reserved with their emotions and thoughts. At the same time, not many of the young women shared more than pleasant conversation. Taylor remembered each friend who came and we tried to keep the visitors to those from his innermost circle of friends.

One of the most honest interactions that took place was with one of Taylor's best friends from middle school. This friend's name was Jon. As youngsters, Jon and Taylor had played baseball together, but they also shared many more adventures over the course of their lives. When Jon first came to see Taylor, his love and concern were apparent. They had shared countless memories and many of their middle school days had been spent together. There were snow days, creek side days, holidays, endless bike rides and sleepovers. Due to Taylor's injury, however, he had no internal filter when he spoke. I had never known so much about his friends and graduating class as I learned when visitors would come.

Taylor had lost all inhibitions when it came to expressing his thoughts or memories. His injury had taken away the censor in his mind that reminds us that something is inappropriate, rude, or too private to share. Taylor's long-term memory was better than his short-term memory bank. I learned whom he had had a crush on, whom he had kissed on the bus, etc. When Jon visited, every experience that he and Taylor had lived needed to be relived and spoken aloud. It was part of Taylor's healing.

Jon, with his shy demeanor and sly grin, would be one of the first friends to be embarrassed but not mortified by Taylor's recollections. Taylor wanted to tell stories and he was not going to be stopped!

Jon was a person who made Taylor's face beam and the connection between them was evident. With some of his more recent relationships, it was as if his mind had to search for shared experiences, but with Jon the memories came back naturally. Taylor began to reminisce about many escapades I did not know had happened. His mind was almost on overload as he went through a virtual Rolodex of memories. I learned that he and Jon had skipped school and sat outside of the Burger King one day, while an old man yelled at them. I learned that they lived out the saying "boys will be boys," but the most interesting thing I learned was about their time at the creek.

Poor Jon! These recollections were gifts to Taylor. They made him laugh in a genuine way. I knew Jon must have been embarrassed for me to hear about the time they pooped while swinging in midair on the rope swing, or the day they got in trouble with a neighbor for being where they shouldn't have been. I heard about firecrackers and fish and the endless games big boys can play. For me to see Taylor laugh while reliving these moments *was beautiful*. Jon had no idea what his visiting meant, but it pulled Taylor out of the foggy cave of his memory. On another note, Jon was getting married soon and really wanted Taylor to be a guest on his special day.

Sometimes the visits were painful to watch. Taylor had another close friend named Trevor, from whom he had been inseparable for years. He and Trevor had both attended a tech school for HVAC together; after graduation, they had both landed jobs with the same company. A few months before Taylor's accident, they had both purchased Harley motorcycles as a new hobby, which was one of many things they enjoyed together. Taylor and Trevor shared a friendship that ran deep on many levels. They had hunted, fished, been young together, and now grown up as friends. As Taylor emerged from the state he was in, which continued to be similar to a haze, he did not seem to recognize the depth of closeness he and Trevor had shared. I don't like to assign labels to friends, but I know that Trevor was one of Taylor's dearest and closest friends. Taylor seemed unable to recall the bond that they had shared. In some aspects, he was devoid of feeling that level of emotion. This change was heartbreaking to me, and I know it was to Trevor as well. Would Bing ever remember the friend that "Trev" was to him?

Over the last few weeks Taylor had been gaining back bits and pieces of his life, but with his upcoming surgery, who knew what might happen? *I hated to see him enter the operating room again.* I dreaded what it could all mean, but I tried to believe the worst-case scenario would not be ours. In fact, I fully intended to take Taylor to Jon's wedding. I will never forget Jon's fiancée asking me with tears running down her face whether we could be there.

A company in Nashville, Tennessee, that specialized in making the required piece for Taylor's skull had completed manufacturing the prosthetic replacement. A 3-D imaging process using a CAT scan was used to create the synthetic bone piece; it had been designed specifically for Taylor's skull. Dr. Taggart had placed a rush on the order and it was now ready to replace Taylor's natural bone. The surgery was scheduled for June 7. Taylor's procedure was the first case of the day for Dr. Taggart.

If Taylor had not experienced such a noticeably rapid deterioration, perhaps we would have felt more apprehensive about the surgery, but we were in a position where we knew it was urgent to intervene. Early in the morning of June 7, Keith, Taylor, and I woke up and drove to Geisinger Medical Center. Before we left, Taylor told our dog Ginger he would be back in a few days, and we headed to the hospital. We drove in separate cars, knowing that things might not go as expected and we wanted to be prepared just in case.

Before leaving the house, Keith took a photo of Taylor and me. Taylor's face appeared crooked, and his eyes looked as if keeping them open was a tremendous strain. He was thin and had a frail appearance. Looking back on the photo, I was able to see how bleak things were.

Keith and I were able to stay with Taylor in the preoperative waiting area; while waiting, we had a visit from a special friend. One of the nurses in the pre-surgery section was a friend from Taylor's graduating class in high school. She not only came to see Taylor, she also informed us that she would be the nurse escorting him back to the operating room. The thought of someone familiar being with Taylor gave us tremendous comfort. He was childlike in his vulnerability, and needed the security this friend represented. Taylor was still confused about the state that he was in and he was rightfully afraid.

Fortunately, he was not able to comprehend the level of seriousness that his condition presented. In those particular moments, his lack of understanding was both a curse and a blessing. We would have given anything for him to be more aware. This accident had stripped so much of who Taylor was away from him and us, but Taylor did not know that yet. *Would this operation bring more of him back? Would our son really ever come home? Had Tanner and Avery lost the big brother whom they had always known?*

Taylor had come so far with an extreme amount of effort and energy; *I could not bear to see him lose any of that progress.*

The anesthesiologist came in to discuss her role in the procedure and the medications she would be administering, and Dr. Taggart went over the plan with us a final time. Those who interacted with Taylor that day prior to the surgery found him to be sweet, pleasant, very quiet, and far younger in development than others his age. As always, I was impressed by the staff's level of care for him.

Taylor was taken back to the operating room and we were told that it would take about four hours for his surgery to be completed. As he was rolled away on the gurney, his friend Kaylee was next to him and he was smiling. His smile was slight and full of the innocence his heart held. Kaylee's presence meant the world to us in those minutes. As he disappeared from our sight, we each took a deep breath while a few tears fell. Neither of us said anything. It hurt too much to speak the words that were reeling through our minds. There were a lot of "what if's" and "Please, God" thoughts.

Because we had been in this situation before, we were fully aware that the surgery might take longer than anticipated. Keith and I went to the cafeteria, had a cup of coffee, and planned our morning of waiting. We would not be alarmed if the clock turned past the designated finishing time; surgeries often take longer in the operating room than planned. I comforted myself with the oatmeal that had become all that my stomach could hold during the first month following Taylor's fall. It was still warm, gooey, and sweet enough to taste, but did not stir my stomach to the point of nausea.

Several hours went by; when the fifth hour approached, we asked whether someone could tell us how the surgery was going. There was an electronic board that gave us information through a number that had been assigned to Taylor earlier in the morning. The board indicated that he was still in the operating room, but that was the extent of the information. About thirty minutes later, a nurse called from the room and said that Taylor was still on the table and that Dr. Taggart would call us as soon as she could. She told us that there had been some complications and that we would be given the details as soon as possible.

I pictured my son covered with a sterile blue blanket in a cold room full of strangers who I hoped would know how precious he is to me. I could not stand the idea of Taylor's not being all right. My words to Dr. Taggart prior to the surgery had been simple; I asked her to take care of our son and she assured us she would. She was a mother whose own kids had eaten Lucky Charms for breakfast that morning. I knew she would fight for Taylor. I knew her heart would beat with the love and care that a mother's heart does . . . *but would that care combined with her skill be enough?* It bothered me that Taylor could not have someone he loved there holding his hand even if he were unconscious. I prayed that he would feel our love. I prayed that he would fight for me, for his dad, for Tanner, and for Avery. My heart screamed in refusal to let him drift any further away.

The nurse was limited in what she shared. But what she did have to say was not good. I covered my mouth so that my cries would not be too loud and the tears formed in my eyes. As I spoke with her, I had to calm myself. *What had gone wrong? Was Taylor okay?* I begged God and I did not make any bargains with Him, I had nothing more to offer. I wanted my son to survive, and I could not stand to lose another piece of him.

We were in a large waiting area with many other families. The waiting area for day surgery patients is the same as for those who are being admitted overnight, so there were several people in the designated space. As I stood trying to comprehend what the nurse was and was not saying, I was frightened. The nurse offered me calm and comfort on the other end of the line, and we prepared for a longer wait. She simply kept to the fact that complications had occurred. My hands trembled with the same amount of intensity as they had on the morning in February when Taylor had had his first seizures.

Keith's twin brother and his wife came to sit with us and helped pass some time. We sat in silence, but their presence was soothing. I called the high school so that Tanner was made aware that Taylor was still in surgery and that he should drive over to the hospital after school. Avery sent a text that he was coming over after his classes.

The waiting room phone rang again and we were paged. This time, the nurse explained that before the initial incision had been made on Taylor's head, Taylor had begun to seize. She said that it took a while for the seizure to stop and the team had to wait to make sure they were clear to start again. I don't know much about being a surgeon, but I certainly understand enough to know that you cannot perform surgery in the area next to someone's brain while they are seizing.

The day before this procedure, someone told us that compared to what Taylor had been through, this procedure would be a "walk in the park." The moment the comment was spoken, it provoked anger in me. *How could they know that?* Dr. Taggart certainly took it extremely seriously and nothing she said indicated that it was going to be routine. I think the person intended for their words to provide reassurance, but I would have rather heard something like, "I know this must be really scary and hard, but Taylor is strong and he has come through so much, let's have confidence that he will get through this as well." This was turning out to be anything but a walk in the park. Unfortunately, when families are dealing with multiple layers of struggle and trauma, those around them should weigh their words carefully.

The wait continued, and finally the nurse called to inform us that the surgery was over, and as soon as Dr. Taggart had made sure that Taylor was settled back in the intensive care unit, she would come talk with us. The nurse said that it had been a long and difficult ordeal for Taylor, and the doctor did not yet want to leave him.

The surgery was supposed to go something like this: Taylor's own bone flap, which had been frozen for two months and then replaced in his head in February, had to be removed due to the complication with resorption. Following its successful removal, the new synthetic prosthetic piece would be put in its place. The wound would be reclosed, Taylor would be sent to the ICU for a night or two, and then he would be able to return home after a few days in a step-down unit. *That is not what occurred.*

After Taylor was settled in, Dr. Taggart came to find us. We spent enough time with her to understand her demeanor, and she was fairly familiar with ours. As she walked towards us down the hall, she held out her arm to take me in for a side hug and said, "I am sorry, kiddo, this is not how it was supposed to go." I heard the angst in her voice and the exhaustion from which she spoke. She had referred to Taylor as "her boy" during our appointments. Her deep regard for Taylor was apparent. I was able to recognize her struggle within his problems. She explained what had happened during surgery.

After getting Taylor quiet following the initial seizure, the surgery began. When Dr. Taggart made the first incision, Taylor began to have another sort of convulsion on the table. The anesthesiologist was able to get it under control, and the team proceeded to remove the original bone flap. The flap was far more deeply infected than anticipated, making it more difficult to remove. With the deft hands of

Dr. Taggart, it had finally been taken out. The bone was covered by infectious material. Resorption meant in this circumstance that the infectious matter around the bone was causing it to dissolve.

After the bone had been removed, the convulsions and seizure-like activity started again. Dr. Taggart had to take special care while carefully and precisely cleaning the area underneath the bone. This area had to be washed with extreme care because it had to be sterile in order to stop the infection from causing further destruction.

Basically, Dr. Taggart and her team worked when Taylor's body had calmed. The details of the infection were still unclear, but it was certain that the cause of Taylor's deterioration was the infectious organisms growing and brewing inside his head. The surgical team was not able to attach the prosthetic piece to Taylor's remaining skull. The infection would have to be resolved; and for now, he would again be without protection on the left side of his head. *Things continued on a downward spiral.*

Taylor was returned to the ICU, still heavily sedated. He had been given a high dose of sedatives and antiseizure medications, so he was unconscious. When we initially saw him, we were absolutely stunned by his appearance. He was hooked up to a ventilator and looked very similar to what he had on the day of his fall right after surgery. There were tubes everywhere, and his entire face was swollen and puffy. His head was fully wrapped with a lot of white gauze. We had become too familiar with the appearance of his long incision and not being able to see it initially was a relief.

Taylor was spiking a high fever and things looked rather bleak. The initial goal was to stabilize him. Late in the evening, he appeared to settle down and while his body reached a calmer place, the lab worked to identify the cause of the infection. Keith and I were given the impression that things were stable, so we went home to rest and Avery stayed by Taylor's side for the night.

Taylor began to seize again around 11 p.m. He entered into a state of nonepileptic seizures that were difficult to identify. This activity was called rigors. In this case, Taylor's body was very rigid but

299

trembling and shaking with phenomenal force. The activity occurring was so strong and severe that his body was jerking up and off the bed for several minutes at a time. Keith stayed up all night texting with Avery, and I slept on and off. I had taken a mild medication to help me sleep because I knew we were in for a long, exhausting series of days.

Avery sat with Taylor, and in his words, Taylor shook like something from the movie *Poltergeist*. The doctors were relieved that the shaking was not seizure-based activity, but it was nonetheless extremely concerning. Numerous physicians and nurses observed Taylor, and some of the younger and less experienced staff members told Avery that they had never seen anything like it. Some of the more experienced staff did not make light of it with Avery, telling him that Taylor's rigors were difficult to watch and that it was one of the worst cases of this type that they had observed. Avery relayed to me that throughout the evening; he heard a lot of "Wows!" combined with numerous discussions and expletives about what was occurring.

By early morning, I arrived back at the hospital. Avery and I hugged and he caught me up on what had happened, and then returned to his apartment to rest. Taylor's body was more controlled at this time and the convulsions were occurring far less frequently. Their cause was still not identified. The doctors thought that as Taylor began to become more aware, the rigors would lessen and they did. He remained febrile and we knew that past a certain level, these fevers could present a whole other world of problems.

As the day went on, we learned a little more. Whatever the infection was, it fulminated when Taylor was cut open. The unidentified culprit had spread to Taylor's bloodstream and he was battling sepsis. Sepsis meant that the infection was spreading throughout Taylor's body. The staff had narrowed the origin of the infection to a "cluster" of disease organisms that it might belong to and it would take a day to determine a closer specification. Taylor was given a strong dose of antibiotics and everyone hoped the drug would help. When the doctor spoke of sepsis, I felt nauseated. I knew what the term means and I knew it might end in the most horrific way.

As we stood in Taylor's room that day, the looks on everyone's face were very grim. I asked the doctor at what point should we be afraid. *How were we to know that the level of seriousness had shifted?* He answered, "You should be both worried and extremely concerned now. This is not good." The infection was taking a hard toll on a body that had already been through a war . . . *and Taylor might not be able to fight it off.* He had come so far, and now there was discussion of redoing all the procedures that we had already been through.

Keith spent that night with Taylor. He sat in his room in the ICU next to his bed on a metal folding chair. He did not sleep at all. When I came to relieve him the next day, he looked absolutely drained. The infection had been identified and was attributed directly to the *E. coli* infection that Taylor had suffered in February. The theory was that since that time, the bacterium had been silently multiplying inside Taylor's head. Depending on the specific strain that was identified, we could be in serious trouble, and we were told that Taylor might not survive. It was the strain of the bacterium that was worrisome, and Taylor needed a lot of reserve energy to fight this off. *Would his body be able to fight again?*

I wondered whether I would ever be able to breathe easily again in my whole life. Would my chest always be filled with this pounding and panic that comes with watching your child in a helpless state? Would the fear ever stop? Would this crisis be averted only to be followed by another? I can think of only one phrase to define myself at that time: *uncomfortably numb.* Not only did Taylor have to find his strength—I had to find mine too. The nurse brought in a reclining leather chair for me and we got acquainted. He said, "It looks like you will be stuck with me for a few days." I smiled and nodded, closed my eyes, and let the tears fall.

Chapter Twenty-three
Will This Nightmare Ever End?
June 11–June 16, 2013

Taylor remained in the intensive care unit as the days passed. The unit was on a different floor than the one we had previously been assigned to, which made us especially thankful when we saw familiar faces. Many of the staff members we knew from previous hospitalizations dropped by to say hello, to check on Taylor's progress, and to remind us they still cared. A circle of love had been created at this hospital and had grown since the day of Taylor's fall. Geisinger represented not only a place of physical healing, but also a place of genuine care and concern.

By day four, Taylor began to improve enough that the staff discussed transferring him out of the ICU. The antibiotics were taking care of the symptoms and the ominous threat of severe danger was subsiding. Before he could be moved, however, the second of two important steps had to occur. The first step was taking Taylor off the ventilator, which had already taken place. Prior to the removal of the ventilator tube, I learned an interesting fact from a well-respected doctor whom many nurses referred to as "Pappy." Pappy explained that the timing of disconnecting a patient from a ventilator is one of the most important decisions that a doctor can make. If the patient is not ready and cannot breathe on his or her own, early removal of the tube can be disastrous. On the flip side, if the tube is kept in for longer than necessary, there is an increased risk of infection. Removal must occur at just the right moment. Thankfully, Pappy and his staff had taken Taylor through that step successfully, and he was breathing sufficiently on his own.

Second, Taylor needed to have a PICC line put in. A PICC line is a peripherally inserted central catheter; these lines are used to give patients much-needed medicine, often in a home setting. The nurses and Dr. Pappy explained to us that the PICC line would deliver the strong dosage of antibiotics to Taylor's body. This news was intimidating because we would now be in charge of giving Taylor his medications. The team assured us that we would be properly trained and that we would have a nurse to help us on Taylor's initial release home. The antibiotics would be given for at least four weeks. The dosage was stronger than the amount that could be given orally, which was part of

303

the need for the PICC line. The formula for helping Taylor to overcome the infection over the long haul had been carefully discussed and decided on by Dr. Taggart, the internal medicine specialist, and an infectious disease team. In order for Taylor to reach the point at which the prosthetic piece could actually be placed, he had to be clear of all infection.

On day six, we moved to the Special Care Unit. Taylor's head was once again in a vulnerable position; he was sporting a large soft spot, and was sick and profoundly weak. We had spent time on this unit in late December and again in February, and the nursing staff once again warmly embraced us. Taylor was becoming more alert and had begun eating again, which started with a cold, tasty, and nutrition-packed item called a Magic Cup. He ate three on the first day of being allowed to take in food by mouth. He could have been a poster child for these cups; he really enjoyed them and we appreciated both their caloric and nutritional values. I was relieved beyond words that he was eating. I did not know whether I could bear to see him revert to taking in nutrition via a feeding tube.

Taylor remained incoherent and was unaware of what had transpired in the days prior. We dreaded telling him that the surgery had not gone as planned. As I looked at him lying in the hospital bed on June 12, I remembered a conversation that had taken place a couple of years ago in our kitchen. I was sitting on the counter with my legs dangling off to the side when Taylor walked in looking very grown-up. He was then a senior in high school and thinking a lot about his future plans. Suddenly a realization hit me. All those women who had been mothers long before I was, who had told me how quickly time would pass, *were right*. My "little boy" had become a man. The transformation hadn't taken place overnight, but it felt as if it had. I started to cry and explained to Taylor that despite how proud I was of him, it was difficult for me to see him grow up so fast. Taylor had always been sensitive and he looked out the window and away from me for a few moments. His cheeks flushed and I could see emotion flood his face.

Turning back to me, I saw the tears in his eyes. He hugged me and said, "I love you, Mom. I am not sure I am ready to grow up either." He was never a man of many words in moments like that, but I had a sense of comfort from him . . . *and I missed that young man.* Taylor had been strong and independent. Now, I found myself looking at him and barely recognizing him, while feeling overwhelmed with grief. I was again responsible for his care; his independence was gone. And while there were times I longed to return to the days when he sat on the counter mixing brownie batter and licking the beaters, this situation was not the same. *I wanted my son back.* I desperately wanted Taylor to have some concept of what was happening to him. I wish I could explain how hard it is to lose bits and pieces of someone you love and watch them lose themselves while they remain unaware of their loss. It felt as if we were navigating Taylor through a horrendously heavy and oppressive fog that he was unable to see.

After a few days in the Special Care Unit, Taylor was moved to a private room on the neurology floor. Each time he was transferred represented a change in his progress, and another change in how to best care for him. The initial move from the intensive care to the special care unit was a positive step. It meant that he was coming out of the dire straits he had been in physically. The transfer from Special Care to the neurology floor took place because that is where his current needs could be best addressed. The room was quieter, and he was gaining his strength for the next phase. Each of these moves became more and more distressing for me. Day after day and night after night were spent in the hospital. *I wanted us to be home again.*

The issue at the forefront of our minds was the question of where Taylor might go from the hospital. When someone enters the hospital and there is a possibility of an aftercare plan outside the home, the patient is assigned a social worker to help the family make arrangements. During this time frame, a newly assigned social worker arrived with every new room or floor assignment. That was very frustrating. The first two social workers had known us, but now we had someone with whom we had had no prior contact, and it did not feel good. This social worker had no knowledge of Taylor's back story and no personal connection with us. It was a stressful time. My patience grew thin and my emotions were frazzled.

Taylor was once again without his bone flap and his progress had not only halted, but reversed. Because of these changes, there was discussion about sending him back to Bryn Mawr or to another rehabilitation setting. Due to insurance issues and thinking about the big picture, a number of things went into determining what would be best for Taylor and for all of us. Taylor had a hard time staying on his feet and moving from point A to point B. His seizures were not yet controlled and were occurring quite frequently.

He was responding well to the antibiotic treatment, but the infection remained difficult for his body to fight. It required a lot of energy for him to get better, which consumed much of his reserves. Dr. Taggart explained the infection to us as something similar to a fire that had been silently smoldering for weeks and had suddenly flared up. The embers were still hot and now things could easily get out of control. This leg of the race felt terrifying; and planning Taylor's care over the next several weeks was overwhelming to imagine and comprehend.

One day, the newly assigned social worker came to discuss placing Taylor in a nursing home for a few weeks. Dr. Taggart wanted to save his rehabilitation days in an acute setting if he needed them, and there was concern about his safety at home.[33] I remember standing in the hall having a discussion with the social worker and Dr. Taggart. Taylor had just experienced another seizure; the nurses were with him and the friends who were visiting had stepped out into the hallway with us. I was so angry and frustrated by the idea of putting Taylor in a nursing home. Dr. Taggart and the social worker explained that caring for Taylor at home would be very hard on me, and the rest of our family. They were concerned about my ability to care for him when Keith was at work and Tanner and Avery were not home. They knew that Taylor's condition

---

[33] Most insurers approve only a certain number of days per case, and Dr. Taggart wanted Taylor to use the days when they would provide maximal benefit.

had been a long haul . . . we were eight months into the world of traumatic brain injury and those eight months had been a relentless series of crises. Taylor was a big guy, and he had several medical conditions that required strict supervision. The hospital team was trying to protect me and wanted me to comprehend that his care would be a major undertaking. They wanted us to be aware of our options and asked me whether I would at least go to visit some nursing homes in our area that had rehabilitation units.

I was very distressed and angry over everything that had happened over the last few weeks. My faith had hit a wall and I was certain God was punishing us. I wasn't sleeping; my eyes and body were tired; and I could not stand the thought of more bad news. I stood in the hall with Dr. Taggart; I was crying and asking, "How could this happen to us? Was I doing something wrong? Why were we going backward and not forward?"

A couple of weeks before when I mentioned Taylor's infection to a friend, they said that perhaps it was because I was not giving God enough public praise or not saying on Facebook that Taylor's recovery was a miracle. Those words rang in my head . . . at that moment, the suggestion that somehow I had caused any of this haunted me. And when the person uttered those words out loud, I stood in front of them, clenched my jaw, and did not respond, but internalized every word. They could have beaten me to a bloody pulp and it would have hurt less than their careless words. If I had any part in Taylor's deterioration, then I wanted to disappear. Later that same evening, a close friend came to get me. It was my first night out since Taylor's fall. I openly wept with her when I simply wanted to be enjoying my time. *Instead I hated myself.* The notion that I had failed Taylor assaulted my mind and heart. She reminded me that when we are vulnerable, we tend to believe things that are not true. I had been a wonderful mother to Taylor; I was doing my best in a situation for which there was no formula. I could not afford to listen to the kind of negativity that self-blame and accusation carried.

During this hospital stay, another person said to me, "Your faith used to be so strong. You were unshakeable. If you want Taylor to improve, maybe you should . . . . " So many things were running through my mind. I felt like I was failing Taylor...*was all of this to remind me that I was not doing it right? Was I letting Taylor down? Was there some sort of lesson that God wanted to teach me?* I did not understand the place these people were coming from. They hugged me, they claimed they loved our family, but inside I felt as if we were being further destroyed. Was there some pendulum of punishment swinging toward me, punishing those I loved most? Were the words of these few people what others were thinking as well?

I reluctantly made arrangements for a tour of a local nursing home facility. I knew some of the staff there, as well as one of the directors. It was a good place that I am sure was full of the right mix of care and love, but from the moment I walked in the doors, I felt sick. I couldn't picture sending Taylor there. I had to find a way to make it work for him to be home with us; we had done it up to that point and we could continue to do so. It touched me when Dr. Taggart shared her concern. At the time I was not able to admit it, but I was worn down in many ways. I was emotionally spent and many of the things I had once leaned on now felt hollow. But Taylor would not be staying anywhere but home. Period.

I posted on Facebook on June 14:

We are sad, tired, frustrated and more. Yet we continue to find the strength to do what we need to do. Taylor is deeply loved. And I stand in awe of what true love can compel people to do. We are still hoping for that happy ending that puts all fairy tales to shame, but right now it feels like we are in the teeth of the big bad wolf.

Chapter Twenty-four
Lemonade Stands and Harley Rides
Mid-June – July 2013

On June 17, eight months after Taylor's fall, following another lengthy stay in Geisinger, we once again returned to our home as a family. We fought through another series of days and countless hours wondering whether Taylor would survive, and my emotions were both numb and raw. Each one of us had reached a breaking point and it showed in our demeanors. We vacillated between genuine sadness, anger with a razor-sharp edge, or expressions devoid of all emotion. It was a lot to handle, but we were doing our best. Despite the circumstances, I was proud of my family for continuing this long journey together.

We were collectively exhausted, worn down, and ready for some sort of long summer vacation, but that wasn't in the cards for us. I didn't care about going to the beach or seeing a new city, but I desperately yearned for a moment of calm that lasted for more than a few hours. I would close my eyes and picture myself in a place of peace and solitude. I could hear the gulls and the gentle crash of the ocean right before it touched my toes with its warmth, and I missed the tranquility that came with the place where I had found the most comfort. *I was drained.* I was depleted of hope inside my heart of hearts; my soul had trouble finding rest; and my head was full of questions that might never have answers.

Years ago, someone told me that they believe each person has a place in nature where we feel most connected to ourselves—where we know ourselves to be the most whole and complete version of our inner person. For me, that spot has always been the ocean. In those days, I longed to look at the sea. I would have been satisfied with a mere glimpse of the way the light hits the water and sparkles perfectly, or just a few moments to breathe in the salty air as it comes off the water, and perhaps an afternoon to sit on the old porch of the weathered house where our family spent a week for many summers. I struggled with wanting normalcy; with needing peace and quiet, but not the kind of stillness that came with my twenty-two-year-old needing to nap much of the day while I watched and listened to him through a baby monitor. I was beginning to miss the way that life once had been on a much deeper level; I became increasingly aware that the map of our future was changing drastically.

310

As I thought of the place where I felt most complete, I remembered how my boys had each slipped into their realm of comfort in that spot as well. For quite some time, my dad and stepmom lived in a small town called Gloucester Point, Virginia. I had finished my last year of high school there and the area held fond memories for me. Over many summers, an acquaintance of my parents had allowed us to stay in their summer home on the York River. We had a sort of barter system with them; my dad would repair something or paint a deck, or complete some general upkeep on their house so that we could have a week there as a family.

The boys had spent many days at Gloucester Banks fishing from the pier, doing cannonballs on the jellyfish, and soaking up the summer sun. When they were toddlers, I had bathed them in the old claw-foot bathtub at night and I can still smell the Baby Magic wash I used on them. In the morning, we ate too much French toast and bacon, and for lunch I often delivered peanut butter and jelly sandwiches to the pier. In the evening, we would once again gather around the huge table on the screened-in porch. We would have a fish fry or eat some of my stepmother's famous Southern cuisine. There was sweet tea, bacon, grits, butter, poor man's lasagna, and more love than my heart could hold around that table. *I ached for that place. I longed for more than a memory of it.*

I always felt that the beach house and the area that surrounded it is the most magical place on earth. We had no part in owning it, but it felt like part of me. Because the family so graciously allowed us to stay there year after year, it felt like it was ours for that time. We created a treasure house of memories and I cherish each one of them.

I learned that it was a very meaningful place to Taylor as well. Taylor had a young lady he was interested in for a period of time before his fall, and mentioned that it was his dream to get married at the beach house. He wanted to say "I do" at the end of the pier. He wanted a wife. He hoped for a family. I never knew all of the details he shared with her, but I knew his young and tender heart had held a lovely dream. He shared bits and pieces of that dream with me and I treasured his thoughts.

When I close my eyes, I can still see the sun hitting his back, or watch him run and jump with great exuberance into the water in a jackknife or cannonball position. I can see him cleaning fish; and see him on our last visit, sitting with his best friend Trevor at the end of the pier while the rest of the world was getting ready to sleep. Trevor and Taylor were laughing and sharing life underneath a blanket of stars. They had been boys, and now they were becoming men. I recall one day of that vacation when Trevor and Taylor sent the youngest of the crew, Tanner, out to the Yorktown beach to meet girls. All these memories make me smile. I can see Taylor holding onto my little nephew Will, and holding him up on the skim board while Will smiled with delight. I can see him and my beloved niece Ellie searching for shells in the sand on that perfect summer day. Life was beautiful then. *It did not feel that way anymore.*

For now, Taylor had made it through another battle. He reminded me of Rocky in the 1970s movie . . . he had been down for the count, lying on the mat, with all odds against him. He was fighting his way back despite being unaware of all that he had endured. He was fighting for himself. He was fighting for his return to us and to the life he once had.

I felt like more of a coach than his mother. I felt like I too had taken every blow on his body, but my pain went straight to my heart. The image of my own body lying there, trying to open my eyes despite all the bruising and damage came to me. And I felt as if every time I would lift my head and think that maybe I could go another round with him, the steel-toed boot of traumatic brain injury came and kicked me alongside the face. The times that I allotted to cry or get angry were brief. Keith, Avery, and Tanner were gone on the weekdays; for the most part, it was Taylor and I. I was pummeled by the reality of all that the fall had encompassed. *Taylor had fallen away from us.* Parts of him were still left at the bottom of the stairs, and I now knew they might not come back.

Following his discharge, Taylor's nursing and therapy staff came to our home three days a week. Taylor was too feeble to participate in therapies outside the home. The nursing team was assigned to check his sutures, draw blood for lab tests, and complete tasks like taking routine vital signs. They also made sure that the PICC line was working properly. The young nurse who was assigned to us had a calm demeanor and pleasant laugh, which Taylor and I both appreciated. She was a new mother, and her tenderness showed. Physical and occupational therapists were assigned to us as well, and it was nice to have Taylor in safe hands for forty-five minutes of the day. It was also gratifying that though weak, he could still work on his recovery. When the visiting nurses were present, I could do things like shower, go to the bathroom, make a phone call, or just sit and stare at the blue sky—which was a gift I appreciated.

I was increasingly unsure of Taylor's future, and how it would affect our family. In my mind, I had a series of snapshots of the last eight months and I was afraid to envision the next eight. I had come to understand that to survive this part of the journey I would have to take life one day at a time. If I reflected too much on the past or worried about the future, I became overwhelmed. It was a matter of simply doing the best I could to get each of us through the next day.

Months earlier, some of Taylor's friends had begun a wonderful display of support in starting "Team Taylor." The idea behind Team Taylor continued; T-shirts that said, "Team Taylor: Beating the Odds, One Step at a Time" were worn with great pride. Our plan was to continue to help Taylor beat those odds no matter what came our way. When I was out and about, seeing the shirts always gave me a sense of a greater good and reminded me of the support that was present.

Also in the early months, there had been some fundraising events for Taylor and times when people gathered just to help us out and show support. All the funds that were raised covered costs that otherwise would have added another strain on our already fractured family. I had not been working for seven months at this point, and up until recently, even though I wasn't collecting a paycheck, our benefits package was covered. My employer carried all the health benefits for our family unit and that was something we literally could not afford to lose.

Even though I was not paid for the first six months of my leave, there was no charge for keeping our family insurance benefits. In the second juncture of my leave, we were required to cover the expenses of our health, dental, and vision insurance. In order to keep the benefits, we had to pay for them. It was hard to think about the financial aspect of things, but it was hard not to as well. There was no way for me to focus on the impact that these costs might have had on us financially. I had to continue to trust that we would be okay. We were beyond grateful and would forever feel indebted to the circle of love that had formed in our home town. This support was revealing itself more and more, and it felt very timely.

As we settled in at home, anxiously waiting for Taylor's infection to clear up so that his prosthetic piece could be put in his head, our community continued to rally around us. A few months earlier, a local motorcycle chapter had organized a benefit ride and I was honored to be asked to say a prayer, then watch the group ride in unison on the designated morning of the ride.

As stated before, prior to his fall, Taylor had purchased a Harley-Davidson motorcycle, and had made big plans to ride with friends. As a mother, I did not like the idea and worried about living in a state that has no law in place regarding wearing a helmet. It had been a bone of contention between Taylor and me, and it was certainly not the only bone of its kind. I had worried so much about his Harley, his tendency to have a lead foot on the accelerator, and the general dangers that come with the territory of "boys and their toys." Taylor was a responsible young man, but he was flawed and imperfect. *How did he become so damaged in his own home?* My mind still had a hard time grasping it all.

As I looked out on the faces of the bikers, many of whom were familiar, I felt loved. Taylor was someone they cared about. Our family mattered to them as well. They were hurting with us and for us, but they were also cheering us on. I wished that I could explain to Taylor in a way that he could grasp, how many people were rooting for him. I wanted him to know that his life and his recovery affected many people. I had mixed emotions that day, but I most profoundly recall that none of what was happening yet felt real. I still waited for the moment when I opened my eyes and realized it had all been a horrible, inexplicable nightmare—but it was life . . . real life. *I wasn't going to wake up.*

Our town of Mifflinburg has the most Norman Rockwell-type Fourth of July celebration I have ever seen. When we first moved here, I could not believe that something so nostalgically lovely and simple still took place. There are various events scattered about the local park throughout the day. There are races for kids and adults, and in the evening, games like bingo are played under a pavilion while a band performs on stage and food vendors sell goodies. There are cake wheels, ice cream, and sodas for sale. The Boy Scouts and church groups all sell special treats, and people come together to celebrate our nation's independence. July 4, 2013, will be forever etched in my memory.

The next town over, which is called New Berlin, hosts a famous turtle race. The race is for kids and it is always a highlight of the day. One of Taylor's little buddies had a brilliant idea! He placed a removable Team Taylor decal on the shell of his turtle. His mother sent me a photo early that morning of her sweet boy and his turtle. I never knew I would root for a turtle to win a race, but I cheered him on from afar. The turtle didn't win that day, but this little man captured my heart.

Later on that evening, a group of Taylor's friends had organized a lemonade stand where they sold fresh-squeezed lemonade, Team Taylor bracelets, and T-shirts. The lemonade was sold in special orange cups that said "Team Taylor" on them. I wanted Taylor to come and sit with me for part of the event, but he was still too weak. He had to wear a thick rubber helmet, which made him sweat and embarrassed him as well. I went alone because I knew that experiencing the support of our community would boost my spirit. I watched as Taylor's friends gathered for him, and I also watched as many people that our family knew stop by to offer their support. His friends all wore their shirts and smiles, and seeing them come together for "Bing" meant the world to my aching heart. There were many times I wanted to stand up and hug those who came and bought lemonade, but the rawness of my emotions held me back. All of this was not too much to handle or endure, but it was increasingly difficult.

The song I often sang to Taylor in the corridors of Bryn Mawr ran through my mind:

I know you are stronger than this.
I know you are braver than this.
I know your future is brighter than this.
Come home, Taylor,
Come home.

Taylor technically *was* home, but my heart still ached for that part of our family that was incomplete and missing.

Taylor's social interactions were occurring more frequently, but with them came more challenges. One of the major struggles that we faced was that Taylor had no concept of nonliteral language, such as joking, teasing, or sarcasm. When he and I went to Geisinger for his therapy sessions, I would often try to stop at some place familiar to him on the way home. It was good for him to have small doses of life in other settings and I hoped it helped his cognitive growth as well as his ability to relate to others. At one point, we stopped at a local store and someone mentioned in conversation with him that maybe they should just lay a sheet of steel on Taylor's head and attach it with a hammer and nails. Surprisingly, Taylor did not respond in any way in that immediate moment, but the aftermath of the conversation stunned me. Taylor was angry and afraid. He felt genuinely threatened by this man's words, even though they had been truly said in jest. Taylor stated that he could never go in that store again and was afraid of both the man and his words. This man and his business had been very generous and loving toward us, but Taylor could not grasp that truth either. Taylor had a very concrete way of thinking; it was literal in its most basic sense.

Another time, someone referred to another friend as a couch potato. Taylor's mind was churning; he was picturing two things in his mind. His first thought was of an object called a *couch*, and his second thought was of another object called a *potato*. And then the process began . . . trying to determine what exactly a *couch potato* might be. He never reached the conclusion. His mind stayed with the literal meanings of the spud and the sofa; the two had no apparent or reasonable connection in his mind.

Keeping up with Taylor's communications was another full time job. I jokingly dubbed myself his press secretary. One fact that is always hard for survivors of traumatic brain injury and their families to deal with is when someone thinks that the survivor can simply figure something out. This is how a professional best explained it to me: "Just like you cannot tell a person who has been paralyzed to get up and walk, you cannot tell a person with a brain injury to think straight." Taylor's brain was broken, and I was beginning to comprehend the reason that TBI is referred to as the invisible injury.

Being assertive in regard to Taylor's needs was challenging because I certainly did not want to offend anyone. It was even more problematic because so much of this circumstance was new to me. There was so much territory that was uncharted and misunderstood, and I had to be Taylor's protector and advocate. I was discovering that in loving Taylor, I might suffer the pain of being misunderstood. The whole situation we found ourselves in was endlessly heartbreaking and at times felt increasingly isolating.

Chapter Twenty-five
Holding On to Hope
Late July into August 2013

There was no question about how excruciatingly deep my love could or would go for my defenseless son. The question was whether my spirit could survive the ever-changing process of treatment and recovery from traumatic brain injury.

How could I maintain the balance of being tough and tender? How could I successfully carry the weight of my pain along with the burdens that Taylor now carried? These are questions I asked myself, and my expectation of my responses was high.

Although I loved the comfort of our home, having Taylor there had become more challenging than ever. Once again he had no bone on the right side of his head, which is hard to imagine and describe. The upper right side of his head was completely depressed. The area over his right eye had a definite dent, and his appearance at times alarmed people. The location of the missing bone flap was a profound deformity, but the helmet hid it sufficiently. It was not new to us because we had seen it throughout December, January and part of February, but it was not something our eyes easily adjusted to. This soft and unprotected spot left Taylor even more vulnerable. He was ambulatory but quite unsteady. Taylor was unaware of the dangers that might occur because he was unable to recognize his own state of physical frailty.

It was rare that someone left Taylor's side over the next few weeks. The times that were manageable came about because of good planning and simple tools. When his friends had rearranged his room, they placed a recliner in it and mounted his television on the wall. Taylor watched little or no television because he had no attention for most of the programs, but he did love to watch the country music television station. I became more familiar with Jason Aldean, Carrie Underwood, and Eric Church than I had ever imagined I would be, and Taylor liked the sound of the familiar tunes. The recliner was a safe place, and as the baby monitor was on, I could be further away than a stone's throw if necessary. When Taylor was up and about, however, one of us had to be very close by. Keith, Avery, Tanner, or I accompanied him to the bathroom, assisted him in the shower, and stayed close to him throughout the night. We drilled into Taylor's mind the importance of wearing his helmet, and he was good about putting it on when he moseyed around the house.

Taylor's closest friends came by, and their company boosted my morale as much as it did Taylor's. For some reason that I was unable to pinpoint, I struggled when it came to allowing my own friends to visit. I had a small circle of people who stopped by to visit or help me. In part, my emotional distance was the result of total exhaustion. At the beginning, middle, or end of the day, I had nothing to give. I wasn't sure how all of this tiredness affected my relationships and what kind of friend I had become, but I knew there had been a drastic shift. Something had changed inside me, and I wasn't ready to expose that new person. I was more broken than I had ever felt in my life, and I needed to find my footing in my new role. I was in extreme emotional turmoil and keeping up with my old friends was not something I was able to manage. I knew they missed me, and some of them expressed frustration with the distance between us, but it had nothing to do with my not wanting them around. It had everything to do with feeling overwhelmed and misunderstood in my grief. I simply had no energy to talk, explain, or address my own feelings. In fact, I longed for someone to come and take me out for a relaxing dinner or a cup of coffee. I wanted to be held, hugged, and reassured, but my pain was too raw to share with anyone. I desperately needed social interaction, and yet I was not in a position to step out of my comfort zone. I also had little to no free time.

Letting Taylor's friends into our world was a less arduous task. A few of them were people I had known for several years. They had been involved in church activities, clubs, sports teams, or were simply a part of his social circle, and I had developed a genuine closeness with a couple of them. One of the most precious of the bunch was another girl named Shelby. Shelby was now a registered nurse and she was the epitome of the expression "heart of gold." When she visited, I found a quiet joy and peace that came along with her presence. Over the years, Shelby and I had developed a friendship apart from her relationship with Taylor, and she was a light to me in what was an extremely dark time. Shelby is a creative person, and she always had an activity or something helpful planned. One time, she brought a four-ingredient dinner for her and Taylor to cook for our family. Another time, she brought a wooden sign with water balloons attached to it, and she and Taylor went into the yard and attempted to pop the balloons with darts. Taylor's interest and energy was short-lived, but these activities sparked something in him and stimulated his mind. Shelby's presence was like warm sunshine on a chilly spring day.

If Taylor was done socializing with a visitor, he had quite an interesting and humorous way to explain that the visit needed to end. He would abruptly stand up, turn toward his room, and say, "Thanks for coming, you can leave now." And then he would walk away. He did not know how to move to the level of conversation where he could politely say, "I am tired and I need to rest." This abrupt dismissal often happened when Shelby visited, and after I would tuck him in, the two of us would dissolve into giggles over Taylor's frank expression. He enjoyed seeing people and cherished their visits, but he lacked the social skills that directed his manners and other cues that he had once been aware of. His way of saying "See ya later!" was Taylor's way of taking care of himself and addressing his needs. It was part of what his therapy team referred to as problem solving. The problem from Taylor's perspective was that he was tired. He wanted to take a nap. His solution was cut and dried, or black and white; tell the visitor to go home.

One Monday morning, our normal visitor, nurse Jessica, came and checked Taylor's sutures and his PICC line, and completed other parts of her morning routine. A few minutes after she left, it was time for Taylor's shower. Despite all the interruptions and changes, we made every attempt to stick to a routine. I always brought my cellphone with us into the bathroom just in case I needed to make a call.

I wrapped the area around the PICC line in a towel, along with the airtight extra-cling plastic wrap that had been suggested to us to keep the area dry. I turned on the water in the shower and helped Taylor finish getting undressed. He stepped in and seated himself on the new bench that had been installed. I held the shower wand in my hand and made sure he was washing himself properly. Taylor still did things very methodically, one step at a time in the same order, as this patterning is how he relearned things. The warm water ran over his body and I knew it felt good to him. He could wash himself, but I still needed to assist him.

Believe it or not, we also washed his head. We had to be careful, but the incision area still needed to be kept clean. We used baby shampoo and a washcloth, and rubbed the area with a gentle motion. I was standing halfway in and halfway out of the shower, but fully clothed. I always waited until Taylor was done showering before getting dressed for the day because I inevitably got wet. On this particular day, I would become drenched with water and the salt of my tears.

Without warning, Taylor's left hand began curling in a half-grip position and I noticed a twitching motion spreading on his left side. The twitch that I saw originated in his cheek area. *A seizure was starting.* I cannot recall exactly how it traveled, but I knew I had to get him out of the wet shower stall and away from the metal holding bar. The surface around us was unforgivingly hard. I dropped the shower wand, turned off the water, and shimmied myself behind Taylor. I was telling him everything was going to be okay, as he was entering another arena of consciousness. This was the worst seizure I had witnessed, and I was afraid. Instinctively, I knew that it was the type of seizure I was most worried about occurring. I had no firsthand experience of what was coming, but I knew it was different from his previous episodes.

I slid my body behind him so that my chest was against his back. I put my arms beneath his armpits and secured my own body against the wet slippery surface of the shower. I spoke to myself along with Taylor, "It's okay. God, please help us. Breathe." My voice trembled, but I maintained my composure. I felt like everything was happening in slow motion. My inner alarm was screaming, and I implored myself to remain calm. I reached out of the shower with my right arm and threw the towels from the rack onto the floor while holding Taylor with my other arm. He was convulsing and I needed to get him on the floor, but I also had to protect his exposed head.

Somehow, I managed to lower him to the floor and push the towels underneath his head with my feet. I looked down at Taylor; he was naked, convulsing, and the seizure was increasing in intensity. I quickly grabbed my phone and pressed the button to call the last person I had spoken to, who happened to be his nurse, Jessica. I explained he was seizing badly and it wasn't stopping . . . thankfully, she was not too far from the house and said she would come back. I pulled a group of towels out of the linen closet and put them around and over Taylor. His nakedness bothered me; I felt as if I were seeing some part of him that he never intended for me to see. He was so thin and looked so helpless.

When I touched him, his body felt cold. *He was unconscious, and I thought he was going to die.* After all that he had overcome, I was going to watch him leave us while lying on the bathroom floor, and I was powerless to save him. The fear and absolute panic that flooded my entire being startled me.

And then the seizure began to slow down.

After a few minutes, Taylor's eyes peeked open and he mumbled something to me. His mouth seemed to be full of marbles; I could not understand what he was trying to say. He attempted to get up, but there was no way we could manage that. His left side was entirely incapacitated and his right side was not strong enough to make up for the deficit. After a few minutes, which seemed like forever, Jessica entered the house, found us in the bathroom, and helped me get Taylor back to his room. She took his vitals, we called the doctor, and the day continued. Before leaving, Jessica asked whether I was all right. I obviously wasn't, but I did not know how to put it into words.

These frightening episodes were going to be part of our lives for a while. I was not sure I could get used to them, nor did I want to. *Were these monsters going to keep popping up, shrieking at us from some unexpected place, seizing Taylor's body and our hearts?*

That afternoon I cried. I lay on my bed and soaked my pillow with tears while peering at the small screen of the baby monitor. Every time Taylor flinched, so did I. There was a part of me that felt destroyed and yet another part felt strong. I had successfully helped Taylor through a terrifying seizure. He was resting and appeared to be okay. Despite my inner panic and absolute feeling of no control, I had maintained my calm.

323

There was not an ounce of hysteria present, and I had handled the ordeal to the best of my ability. There were no doctors present at the time and by the time the nurse arrived, the storm had passed. Even though I frequently felt that I could not deal with what was in front of us, I *was* dealing with it. Taylor was not in immediate danger, the crisis of the moment had ended, and that is what mattered.

It would be several months before I could escape the image that crossed my mind when I recalled that day. I had to learn how to cope with the mental pictures and keep the anxiety that tried to invade my heart at bay. As a family, we knew that we would have to educate ourselves and understand what having the threat of seizures in our lives meant.

The types of seizures that Taylor was and would continue to experience varied. Unbeknown to me, there are multiple classifications of seizure types. We continued to keep track and pay attention to the smallest of details in regard to these awful events. We charted specific facts, and knowing that we had to keep track of them helped to keep us calm. We noted:

1) How long they lasted; we had to time them as best we could.
2) What happened during the seizure; in other words, which parts of Taylor's body were involved. Some seizures affect the whole body; others manifest with just a twitching motion, or what appears to be "zoning out" on the patient's part.
3) How Taylor felt afterward; whether he could speak clearly, and how long he slept.

We knew that Taylor was having tonic-clonic seizures, formerly defined as grand mal seizures. These seizures are the most brutal and frightening when witnessed and experienced. Fortunately, they occurred less often than the others. The most accurate description of them comes from the Epilepsy Foundation. In a tonic-clonic seizure,

. . . the tonic phase comes first: All the muscles stiffen. Air being forced past the vocal cords causes a cry or groan. The person loses consciousness and falls to the floor. The tongue or cheek may be bitten, so bloody saliva may come from the mouth. The person may turn a bit blue in the face.

After the tonic phase comes the clonic phase: The arms and usually the legs begin to jerk rapidly and rhythmically, bending and relaxing at the elbows, hips, and knees. After a few minutes, the jerking slows and stops. Bladder or bowel control sometimes is lost as the body relaxes. Consciousness returns slowly, and the person may be drowsy, confused, agitated, or depressed.

These seizures generally last 1 to 3 minutes.

A tonic-clonic seizure that lasts longer than 5 minutes needs medical help. A seizure that lasts more than 10 minutes, or three seizures without a normal period in between, indicates a dangerous condition called convulsive status epilepticus. This requires emergency treatment.[34]

While combatting these seizures, we noticed that they normally lasted for more than five minutes and would often piggyback. Taylor sometimes lost consciousness, but most times he did not. More frequently than not, his seizures started in his upper body and affected his left side far more profoundly than his right. They were hard to define in a clear-cut manner because they were so different each time.

The other type of seizure that occurred frequently is the partial seizure. Noticing their occurrence is often something that requires a keen eye, and the only way to diagnose them accurately is through working with a specialist who can observe them as well as monitor them with electroencephalography (EEG).

Once again, according to the Epilepsy Foundation,

---

[34] Epilepsy Foundation, "Types of Seizures: Tonic-clonic Seizures." http://www.epilepsy.com/learn/types-seizures/tonic-clonic-seizures (accessed February 9, 2015).

These seizures usually start in a small area of the temporal lobe or frontal lobe of the brain. They quickly involve other areas of the brain that affect alertness and awareness. So even though the person's eyes are open and they may make movements that seem to have a purpose, in reality "nobody's home." If the symptoms are subtle, other people may think the person is just daydreaming.

Some people can have seizures of this kind without realizing anything has happened. The seizure can wipe out memories of events just before or after it. Some of these seizures (usually ones beginning in the temporal lobe) start with a simple partial seizure. Then the person loses awareness and stares blankly. Most people move their mouth, pick at the air or their clothing, or perform other purposeless actions. These movements are called "automatisms" (aw-TOM-ah-TIZ-ums).[35]

What we frequently witnessed with Taylor was that the seizure began as a small twitching motion of his mouth. He would then begin to drool as his mouth continued to jerk toward one side. His hand would stiffen, the stiffness would spread through his arm, and eventually the whole arm would jerk or thrash. Given the time and the circumstance, Taylor would try to get up. The activity that accompanied the seizure often lasted 3 to 5 minutes; depending on the day and how Taylor felt, he would need to rest afterwards.

As a result of these episodes, we had to call the ambulance on several occasions, and once Taylor had to go to the emergency room for treatment. The complicating factors included knowing when to call for help; and how to understand whether he needed immediate treatment or whether the seizure was par for the course of his injury. What we consistently did was communicate with the doctor about the seizures, and most of the time they required a follow-up visit. But taking Taylor to the

---

[35] Epilepsy Foundation, "Types of Seizures: Complex Partial Seizures," http://www.epilepsy.com/learn/types-seizures/complex-partial-seizures (accessed February 9, 2015).

emergency room and putting him through all the commotion that went on in that location was often not the right solution for him. This problem was something that we were going to have to learn to live with and deal with. Taylor was under continuous care, and we trusted his physicians and their team.

The surgery to replace the bone flap was tentatively scheduled for the end of August, and we hoped the outcome would be successful. As a family, we strived to hold on to *hope*, and the word itself was a common topic around our dinner table. How can you keep hope alive when everything around you feels so uncertain and fragile? My conclusion was that we had no choice but to believe that things could and would get better. We knew by now that nothing was guaranteed. And a shred of hope is better than no hope at all. There were times when it felt as if no hope remained in us. Our grief brought us to a place where letting go of hope felt easier than holding on to the fear of losing more.

Years ago I had been given a small figurine of a little boy holding a balloon that said, "Hope." I thought of that figurine and what it really represented . . . if I let go of hope, I would be left empty-handed. I had to release my doubts, my fears, my hurt, and my frustration into the hands of something larger than myself. I had to trust that somehow within all of the pain, there was light, life, and good to come.

Chapter Twenty-six
Riptide
August 22–August 30, 2013

After three lengthy months and ten long weeks, Taylor returned to Geisinger on August 22 for surgery to have the prosthetic piece placed into the right side of his skull. This would be the second attempt, but Dr. Taggart felt confident that the infection was completely gone and the surgery would be successful. By now, Keith and I knew the routine and we prepared ourselves while allowing cautious optimism to take residence in our mind. Our hearts were still weighed down and heavy, but we kept on going. We forged ahead not only out of love for Taylor, but also out of love for each other, for Avery, and for Tanner.

Taylor got settled in the pre-surgery area; we spoke with Dr. Taggart along with the anesthesiologist, and watched as our son was once again rolled away on a gurney to the operating room: an image we knew well, but still something consistently heartbreaking. At the end of the day, you never know what will or could happen during surgery.

Deep breaths; falling tears; embraces; pushing fear aside. I drank coffee and once again ate the hospital cafeteria oatmeal with brown sugar and raisins. We had lived through this scenario before. *Would this time bring a happier ending?*

Life has a way of surprising you, and there is no real way to control the future. Sometimes life hands you something that you never saw coming, and whether that something is good or bad, there are times when you have no choice but to embrace it. *Embrace the pain. Embrace the fear. Embrace the light. Embrace the dark. Embrace the hope. Embrace the love along the way, and let it embrace you.*

Ten months earlier, prior to Taylor's fall, we had three sons who were strong, vibrant, and full of life. Our lives were far from free of worry or care, but we had no idea what kind of turmoil we would soon face. Within our family over the course of the last ten years, we had been through a lengthy illness with Keith; the passing of Keith's father; the sudden loss of my half-sister as the result of a complication during childbirth; and the random act of violence that had ended the life of my stepbrother. Those were the tough times that stood out the most, but in the midst of those stressful events were the everyday issues we all face at one time or another.

We were familiar with sorrow and loss, but we were not familiar with how long grief can last and what it means when it is ambiguous, unending, and hard to define. It is like the undertow of the ocean, with its ability to sweep you away and render you helpless. You spin and spin, and just hope as the force of the water works against you that you come out on top, but you are always left exhausted and gasping for air. The reality was that we had not yet reached the depth of our pain and sadness; we were too caught up in tending to the minutiae surrounding Taylor's current state.

Taylor had been twenty-one years old the previous November, wrapped up in trying to make decisions about his future, his career path, and searching for that special someone to share his life. On the weekends, he helped his dad around the house, spent time with his buddies, and most recently had been gearing up for his favorite season of all—the season within a season, *hunting season*. Recently life had seemed somewhat burdensome and complicated for Taylor, but he had a way of getting through it. He was figuring out his path and discovering more about who he was as a man. *So much of his life was just beginning.*

I wondered now whether Taylor would ever experience falling in love, getting married, and having children. That gift seemed stolen from us as well. We stood on the cusp of many things unknown.

At the same time, Avery was nineteen and had been at university, just settling in to his sophomore year and pursuing two majors, elementary education and Spanish. He was feeling excited about the course of his life, as he enjoyed his space away from home and the change in atmosphere from high school to college. He was discovering who he is and dreaming about what might be ahead. He was happier than I had seen him in a while, and he wore that happiness well.

Tanner, my Tanner-man, as I liked to call him, was busy being the baby of the family. He had just finished his junior football season, which was one of the most important things on his radar. He liked learning songs from YouTube on his new guitar and was doing what most sixteen-year-old boys do—growing up and separating from their parents. He was a conscientious student and all-around hard-working person.

I was proud to be the mother of such a neat trio of people. Each one of the boys had unique passions and pursuits, but they were brothers and their bond had become strong over the years. I was endlessly drawn to items that came in threes or had a threefold design . . . jewelry pieces, stained glass designs, etc. Three represented my three sons, and one of them had almost been stolen from us.

Fast forward to a place we had never dreamed of being, and each one of my sons had distinctly changed and grown up. I had a history of being proud of them. They were good kids—not perfect, but good. They were interesting and delightful people with generous and caring hearts . . . but critical moments also define people, and I was in awe of our sons. Taylor is not the only hero in this story; his brothers are also heroes in my heart.

Over the last several months, not only did I witness the sheer strength and determination of Taylor, but I also watched the unyielding and relentless love of his brothers. They refused to abandon him on any level. Despite their own pain, grief, frustration, anger, and turmoil, they stayed by Taylor's side. At times, their own friends quietly slipped away, unsure of how to handle the burden that Avery and Tanner now carried. And they were often left alone. Avery and Tanner's eyes had been exposed to many things; they had become more opinionated than ever about circumstances that could place people in danger. They were upset when they saw someone riding a motorcycle without a helmet, or a child on a four-wheeler who rode by waving and smiling, wearing nothing to protect his or her head. They saw firsthand what can happen as the result of being intoxicated and driving, or of losing control of your car by speeding. They worried about seizures and infection, and they had each slipped into new roles. Spending weekends at Bryn Mawr gave them lessons about life that they would never have learned otherwise.

They knew what it was like to be exhausted. They knew real and raw emotions that could not be hidden. They had heard the sounds that no child should ever have to hear from his mother—the cries that release themselves without warning despite the efforts to hold them in; the cries of anguish, despair, and gut-wrenching agony that come from a place of absolute fear. They were now familiar with the tired eyes their father wore day after day, and they did not shy away from the pain of their parents . . . they stood by us, just as they had with Taylor. They made it clear that we would not be expected to do this alone.

Avery changed his education major at university to biology with a pre-medicine focus and kept the Spanish major. He handled each event in Taylor's treatment by learning everything he could about TBI. He soaked up the information we were given and longed to understand what he could in regard to the aftermath of Taylor's injury. He made friends with some of the physicians, many of the nurses, and dug deeper into the causes and effects of traumatic brain injury. He was almost always our hospital night owl, and endured some hours with Taylor that were as critical as they can get. He kept up his studies; he never gave in and did not even once paint himself as a victim of some horrible event. He never said, "What happened to Taylor was horrific and excruciating, but I am hurting too." I knew he felt alone and at times invisible, and it broke my heart to see it. I knew how much he missed his brother even if he was not able to say it.

Avery hugged me tightly hundreds of times; he let me cry on his shoulder and rarely would he let his own tears fall. He was a rock. His strength was undeniable, and his life was proof of his love for his big brother.

Tanner took a different path in his coping, but his loyalty was richly present as well. He is three years younger than Avery, and five years younger than Taylor. I think his age and peer group made processing everything that occurred more difficult. Later, one of his teachers told me that seeing Tanner in school was agonizing for her. She knew he was operating in crisis mode and he was not going to let his guard down in the crowd of high school students. Some were aware that this situation was excruciating for Tanner, but he was not the type of person to let anyone know just how hard it was. That was something he never even shared with me.

Tanner had always been the kid with the smile on his face; he had a warm and welcoming presence, and took pride in helping others. He had a hard time with the attention that we were getting as a family, the pain that I was in, and the level of intensity that never seemed to stop. Where Tanner had once been soft and sweet, he became a bit harder and rough-edged. It was too much for his shoulders to carry alone, and I think at times he struggled with not knowing where to turn with some of his burdens. As his mother, I wished he could still crawl up on my lap and bury his head in my shoulder until he was certain that I could make everything all right.

Tanner's seventeenth birthday had passed by. He got his driver's license with little fanfare. His last year of high school was coming and it was hard for me to balance all that was ahead. I worried about missing out on many things with him, and I desperately wanted to stop time. I know that Tanner and Avery suffered not only the loss of Taylor, but also the impact of my not being as emotionally present as I had been before. This injury stole many things not only from Taylor, but also from those who loved him most. I strongly believe that Taylor had a protective heart toward his little brothers and I knew their pain would bother him *if he could see it.*

Tanner remained fiercely protective; he was not going to allow anyone to hurt Taylor on his watch. From the earliest hours, he was like a German shepherd on guard duty. These dogs are known for their bold, confident, and fearless demeanor. They are extremely vigilant, quick to learn, and highly intelligent. They are calm in their home environment, but just like Tanner, fiercely reactive when someone they love is threatened. This description fits Tanner well. If he needed to speak up along the way, he would. He did not get sidetracked by who someone was or what title they might carry, or the thought that he might hurt their feelings. He trusted his instincts and his instincts were to protect Taylor. He is one of the most courageous people I know. He gave new meaning to the word *brave.*

I believed that Tanner's soft side would come to the fore again. But for now I had to understand that as the only female in my house, I cope with things in a much different way from the men around me.

The surgery on the morning of August 22 went well. The successful result allowed some of our fears to dissolve and dissipate—at least temporarily. Taylor spent one full day in the intensive care unit, transferred to the Special Care Unit for two days, and then went to another floor for 24 hours. He was then discharged home with the prosthetic piece placed safely in his head.

We scheduled in-home therapy to start again, and fortunately we had the same outstanding crew of nurses and therapists to help us through the first harrowing weeks. The goal was to get Taylor back to Health South for his outpatient therapy.

It seemed like things were moving in an uphill direction. This reprieve from the crisis mode of previous months was necessary. It was almost September and the countdown to when I would have to return to work had come. I wondered if that would ever be a possibility.

One day at a time, one task at a time. I looked at my lists day after day, and reminded myself that things would work out, *they had to*. And I had to believe that they would.

Chapter Twenty-seven

The Invisible Illness

September 2013

Before we knew it, ten months had passed since Taylor's injury. Tanner, the youngest member of the Bingaman crew, started his senior year of high school, which generated a sense of excitement. Our middle son, Avery, had begun his junior year at Bloomsburg University, which was only a little over an hour away. The close distance was a blessing during such an uncertain time.

Taylor was doing well since his most recent surgery and the seas were calmer and smoother than they had been in a while. His seizures were far less frequent, and the vomiting and constant stomach-related distress had also slowed down dramatically. Taylor's body was accepting the newly placed prosthetic bone flap and the infection appeared to be gone. In general, Taylor was showing improvement. He was still weak and had lost a lot of momentum, but we were picking up the pieces and more determined than ever for him to keep progressing. Forward motion remained an arduous process because traumatic brain injury in itself slows down everything. However, we continued to forge ahead with hard work and tenacity.

That September, we still had very little that felt positive to us despite Taylor's progress. I was preparing to return to work while Keith was trying to adapt to the countless changes in our lives. We were having a hard time coping with the new situation and the profound grief that had become a constant and unwelcome presence in our lives. I am not sure that anyone outside our household knew the level of pain that our hearts endured, but each day it became harder to live in an atmosphere in which joy suffered such constant depletion.

I felt within me that my happiness was slowly suffocating. No matter how hard I tried, it felt almost impossible to remember what being happy felt like. The idea now seemed like something from the past that was so far out of reach it was almost unattainable. I tried to tell myself that nothing is hopeless, but it felt like all hope had abandoned me. My inability to see beyond my grief was expanding. My sadness was as certain as the sun's rising and setting. This sorrowful mood was a heavy and challenging weight to bear.

The isolation and depression that had been creeping up on me over the last several months was taking its toll. There were times when I was constantly with people—therapists, nurses, doctors, Taylor's friends, and kind-hearted people—but at the end of it all, I was more alone than ever. No one could see how much strength it took for me to function. I had no choice but to keep encouraging Taylor, to take care of others whom I loved as best as I could, and to keep it together when all I really wanted to do was fall apart all over the place and have someone recognize the depths of my despair so that in recognizing it, perhaps they could fix it.

Around this time, Taylor and I went to see my family doctor, the wonderful Maggie Smith. I have always thought of her as having the same kind of poise as Princess Diana. She exudes elegance, sophistication, and class while tending to her patients with a gentleness and compassion that has been part of her practice since the time I met her over 20 years ago. We made the decision to appoint her Taylor's primary care physician, because we knew her well and she had known Taylor since he was in kindergarten.

Taylor and I went to her office so that he could have a general checkup. The idea was to get baseline measurements for the time when Dr. Smith would take over some of Taylor's more general care. Dr. Smith had been the doctor for all three of our sons when they were little boys, but she had not cared for Taylor since his adolescence, when he changed to a male doctor in another practice.

I could tell that what had happened to Taylor had shaken her. As we sat in the examination room and she spoke with him in her customary demeanor, I felt as if I might fall to pieces. Years ago, I had gone to see Dr. Smith with a tired voice and broken heart, and I explained that the unexpected losses of my stepbrother and half-sister, as well as some other hurdles in life, had become too much for my heart. She was wonderful in encouraging me to take an antidepressant and helped me see that the medication could be a wise tool to manage a trying time. At the end of that visit, years before, she hugged me tightly and said, "You have been through a lot and I am sorry." I knew that she was aware that this journey with Taylor would break me in ways that life had never done before. I could barely look at her, because she was someone who knew how much I loved each of my baby boys, and she had been an important part of their growing years. It relieved me to know that she would be part of Taylor's continuum of care because I trusted her. The visit was nothing more than routine, which was perfectly fine with me.

By now, autumn was in full swing and it was time to get back to the activity that centered our family at the time—football. My heart was pleased to have something else to focus on. Tanner had played for the Mifflinburg Wildcats since eighth grade. He would be the first to say that he was not a star athlete, but he loved the game and that love showed. He was a captain and a well-respected player. Tanner was one of the smallest guys on the team, but his determination and dexterity allowed him to have a decent amount of field time. I never imagined being so thankful for something as simple as his starting a game or going for a drive down the field. It brought our family together and gave us something to look forward to every week. Keith, Avery, Taylor, and I would sit together in the bleachers and cheer for Tanner, which was a welcome familiarity.

In the most recent years, Tanner and Avery had been the closest of the three boys. The bond they shared had started when they were very young. Taylor had entered kindergarten a few months after Tanner was born, which meant Avery and Tanner were together at home with me. Avery was my sidekick during Tanner's infancy. He helped me bathe him, change his diaper, and hold him whenever possible. Avery fell into the role of big brother easily. He liked the shift from being the baby to now being one step up on the ladder.

As more time passed, Avery and Tanner shared more common interests like reading books, playing video games, traveling, and listening to the same types of music. They also shared an enthusiasm for learning the Spanish language, which allowed them to communicate with each other in ways that the rest of us could not. The bond between Avery and Tanner that had been formed when they were younger grew even stronger.

While the boys were growing up, I sensed at times that Taylor desired a deeper connection with his younger brothers, but they were different individuals. Taylor was far more into hunting, the outdoors, and country music than either of his brothers had ever been. They had the same parents, but like many siblings, they were formed from different molds. As their mother, I celebrated their individuality while valuing the activities and interests that brought them together. I knew that they loved one another and would do anything in response to that love.

As individuals, we always peer through the lens of our own perspectives, and as I watched the lives of my sons unfold, I was able to see that while brothers are your first and hopefully forever companions, sibling relationships are not built on perfection but rather on reality. My perspective was that Taylor desired some of the closeness that the other two shared, but he showed more outward commitment to his own friends and hobbies.

Avery and Tanner had craved Taylor's approval and acceptance, but he was not the kind of brother to lavish open praise or love; he was more of a silent supporter. Each of the brothers accepted their respective relationships at the time, but it also seemed like they would have welcomed more. We used to joke that Taylor's "I love you" took the form of a wallop on the arm at the dinner table or by cheering the loudest at a sporting event. He was not nearly as affectionate as the other two even with me, so it was clear they spoke a different kind of love language.

Following Taylor's accident, I endlessly wished that he could be fully present to experience and feel the depth of love that his brothers had for him. Some of the lyrics of a song by Mumford and Sons titled "Timshel" ran through my mind often. For me, the song reflected much of our situation and the relationship that these brothers shared.

And death is at your doorstep
And it will steal your innocence
But it will not steal your substance

But you are not alone in this

339

And you are not alone in this
As brothers we will stand and we'll hold your hand
Hold your hand . . .

And I will tell the night
Whisper, "Lose your sight,"
But I can't move the mountains for you.

My instincts and what I witnessed day after day told me that Tanner and Avery would move any mountains that they could for Taylor. I was certain that just like Keith or me, they would have done almost anything to ensure that this event had never occurred.

Collectively, we needed what Friday nights offered us. Our family had spent hour after hour together over the last several months, but we needed to spend time together enjoying something pleasurable rather than enduring the agony of a hospital waiting area or room. We geared up for Tanner's final football season with great anticipation and I refused to focus on the sadness that it had to come to a close. Instead, I would measure every moment and savor the memories that the games would bring. Hearing *"Tanner Bingaman, with a carry"* over the loudspeaker became sweet music to my ears. As I cheered for him, I momentarily forgot the chaos that filled our agenda.

Months before, within days after Taylor's fall, Tanner's coaches had come to the hospital to sit with us. I admired that their love for Tanner extended far beyond the football field. I would imagine none of them had ever known anyone whose brother had a fall that resulted in a devastating injury that left him in a coma. It was awkward and uncomfortable, but they came and their presence mattered. Sometimes when there is nothing left to do, we have to understand that simply *being there is enough.*

Taylor loved going to his former high school to watch the game on Friday nights. He could not wait to wear the jersey with the number 31 and the name BINGAMAN on the back representing his all-time favorite player. He would tell us that he should go out on the field and play. As a family, we found this attitude especially funny because Taylor

340

always did like to live vicariously through Tanner. Tanner had taken chances and risks in sports that Taylor had never taken, and it was easy to see that there were times when Taylor wished he could go back in time. On game night, we would sit up in the corner bleachers with our dear friends and Taylor would cheer for his baby brother and the Wildcats. Initially we were concerned that the lights, the clapping, and the yells of the crowd would be too much stimulation for Taylor, but he tolerated it.

We quickly discovered, however, that Taylor was not a fan of the high school band. The pounding of the drums along with the sounds of the other instruments combined was too much for him. He experienced sensory overload. He would quickly become angry and agitated, which was further fueled by his medications. He was taking a high dosage of Keppra to keep his seizures at bay, but we were not aware of the level of agitation that Keppra can cause, particularly at higher doses. At the time, we attributed the agitation directly to his injury, but the medicine enhanced it. He managed to stay throughout the band's performance, but by the end, he was ready for it to be over.

At the beginning of the season, the coach's wife called me and told me that the football team wanted to do something special for our family. A group involved with the team collectively planned to have a "Team Taylor" night. In honor of Taylor, they would sell camouflage shirts with the "Team Taylor" logo on them. The money raised would go directly into Taylor's recovery fund. They would also spread the word among the students and fans that there would be a designated "Camo Night" in support of Taylor.

At halftime, the cheerleaders slipped on their Team Taylor camouflage shirts and invited Taylor to come on to the field. I wanted Taylor to be able to look up and see all the love that covered the bleachers, but Keith and Avery became the voice of reason. In my heart I probably knew it would be too much for Taylor, but I was still in some level of denial. Keith and Avery were able to nudge me into realizing that it would be too much stimulation for Taylor, which the cheerleaders graciously understood. Over the loudspeaker, the announcer explained what the crowd full of camouflage shirts represented, and Taylor stood in an upper corner of the bleachers and waved for a moment. Our family felt the love and support that was present in the stadium, and as I told Taylor, "This is all for you, buddy," tears ran down my cheeks. It was for us too; our community was embracing our struggle, and it was simply beautiful.

Taylor remained completely unaware of all that his injury would come to mean for him. Later, he would need moments like this to reflect on and remind him that his life still has purpose and meaning. Taylor truly did not grasp the seriousness that his injury involved. He was ten months out from his fall, but in those ten months he had been in a coma, had undergone multiple surgeries, and was still in a mental fog. The best way to describe it would be to say that he was still "waking up." He was just learning the words *traumatic brain injury*, but lacked the ability to recognize their true definition. We could not tell him, you may not work again, you probably won't drive again, and your mind has been stripped of several years of learning and processing thoughts. He would not be able to understand that his injury had changed his physical body, physiological functioning, and intellectual abilities . . . not to mention all of the minor details of his being that were affected. Taylor was not yet at a point where he expressed or seemed to have many feelings in regard to his injury or impairments. It seemed to take all his energy just to wake up and function throughout the day.

The football team also reached out to us on a personal level. Previously, I had been proudly involved with its Booster Club. I loved helping with the meals, planning fun things for the boys, and having input in reference to something that meant a great deal to Tanner and the team. I was surprised by how tough it felt to give up my role in the club. But when we could, and when Taylor's mind and body allowed, he and I would go in and help serve the players at the pregame meals. The players and coaches had to adjust to the reality that Taylor had no mental filter but lots of game advice—which often proved an embarrassing combination. Taylor would suggest who should play which position, and his vision of the team was limited to Tanner and Tanner's best friends,

Nazar and Devin. In Taylor's mind, the three of them could accomplish anything. It was a good lesson in a safe place for Taylor to relearn some basic "people skills." I was the little bird chirping over his shoulder, reminding him of what is and is not acceptable to say and do. It was a powerful life lesson to witness the acceptance that this group of young men offered Taylor. Taylor needed as much safe socialization as we could offer him.

The games were also a place where friends in the community or former teachers could come to say hello. It was the place where many people were able to see Taylor for the first time since his fall. It was not easy to feel as if people were watching and satisfying their curiosity about how he would appear, walk, talk, or act, but there was a sense of security present. I knew that the people who watched us also cared about us. Their curiosity never felt intrusive or cruel, but it is an undeniable part of human nature.

One week, Taylor spoke of wanting to see his middle school gym teacher, so we spread the word, and prior to the start of the game, the former teacher came and found us in the bleachers. It was a profound moment for me because he was the first teacher that Taylor had remembered while he was in rehab. I witnessed how Taylor's memories come back to him and how he had to sort out where they belonged. Most of us are unaware of the processes involved in memory and the ability that our brain has to categorize and file its memories in chronological order. When Taylor had been a student in this teacher's gym class, the teacher had made him feel good about himself, and Taylor's mind had retained that kindness. It was a gift of vast proportions that may be hard for an outsider to understand. One factor that has proved true time after time is that Taylor can remember feelings associated with a particular person. Whether positive or negative, former situations that had generated strong emotions carry enough force for memories to resurface.

On another game night, Taylor and Keith got up to go to the restroom. Keith proceeded ahead of Taylor, trying to pave the way for him to get down safely, but all the background noise made it hard to hear what was happening. As Taylor was coming through the bleachers, he

343

said, "Excuse me," to a young man we didn't know. The young man didn't move; he didn't say "no" to Taylor, he just ignored him. Taylor spoke a second time and again received no response. Taylor lacked the dexterity to maneuver the stadium steps well, so moving around on them was always a precarious feat. He ended up tripping a little bit, which not only scared him but also made him angry. He responded with "What the hell is wrong with him?" in reference to the teenage boy, who for some reason was acting stubborn toward Taylor. I knew it was nothing personal—the boy's behavior was apparently typical for him, but this was not the time for that kind of display.

The situation could have quickly escalated. Taylor's injury combined with his medication meant that he had a short fuse, and he was annoyed and afraid, which was clearly a bad combination. Taylor was relearning social cues and how people interact. His mind was not able to comprehend that even though he did his part and said, "Excuse me," he was not guaranteed a polite response. This incident was part of the gray area that Taylor's black-and-white thinking did not accommodate.

These kinds of moments were isolated, but they reminded us that not everyone would have empathy for Taylor. That evening most of the people in the bleachers around us could see what was happening and everyone was holding their breath. Keith managed to get Taylor down the steps, and all was well, but the episode was something Taylor's mind replayed for weeks to come. It produced ongoing fear and anxiety in Taylor. After they got down, Avery went over to speak to the young man, and when Keith and Taylor came back, we had to use some simple distraction techniques to get Taylor seated without further incident.

Taylor's brain held onto upsetting and unsettling moments in an uncanny way. This characteristic made certain social scenarios awkward. Taylor could not grasp joking, sarcasm, or teasing, and he most certainly had no understanding of blatant disrespect or rudeness. Taylor felt afraid and vulnerable, and he did not have the wiring in his brain that enabled him to sort out those kinds of feelings. There was a real sense of paranoia present, and it hid itself just enough so that others could not see it. But for Taylor, it was a hard battle. His body and mind were both exposed to the weaknesses and deficits that were constantly present, and he worried about his own safety.

He took the words and actions of others at face value; it was something that required constant addressing. This was quite a challenge with people whose personality traits include joking, sarcasm, and teasing as a means of communicating, because Taylor took everything literally. I noticed that people in their nervousness would find it hard to communicate and say something instead that they thought would make Taylor laugh or smile, but which often backfired.

These situations were not only frustrating to me, but became increasingly hard for me to address. I found myself feeling like an old schoolteacher with a knuckle-cracking ruler in my hands. I was becoming the person that people dreaded to see coming. I had to educate people in order to protect Taylor, which was burdensome. My own self-esteem was suffering, I felt like a turtle that wanted to hide in her shell. Publically, people would say how fortunate Taylor was to have me advocating and defending him, but privately I sensed there were times when the reality of what Taylor's injury had done to his personality had a negative effect on my relationships with people. It felt at times as if life had become a series of awkward moments. No one wants to tell people how to relate to a friend they have known for years.

I learned how to communicate with Taylor during my time at Bryn Mawr and by immersing myself in learning what damage to the brain actually means. As his mother, I put myself in a position to learn more about traumatic brain injury and what it means to *his* personality and *his* ability to communicate and relate to others. There is a lot about brain injury that is hard to swallow, and one of the biggest problems is the ways in which it changes the person who had been present before. I followed countless blogs online, spoke with other survivors' families, and shared a home with the living example of what TBI means, so it was easier for me to understand. Most importantly, as Taylor's mother, I felt an inner guide regarding *his* needs.

Living in the Northeast close to New York and Philadelphia means that our area is home to a lot of Phillies and Yankees fans. The old

345

Taylor loved to banter back and forth about fan statuses. He would have shot right back if someone had teased him for wearing an Atlanta Braves hat. The new Taylor had no concept of that type of teasing. His mind kept it simple—he loves the Braves. He wore the hat Avery had signed for him with great pride. And when he was teased about his favorite team, he became defensive. The battle felt unending. The old ways of relating to Taylor could not continue. People often had a hard time with this fact and felt that it was something that Taylor should learn to accept. Others understandably got their feelings hurt, and we all learned that loving and relating to someone with a traumatic brain injury takes a thick skin. The difficulty was that Taylor often held in his feelings until he was in a safe place. But he needed to address them, *no matter what*. It was so strange because he did not have a filter, but also was somewhat aware of not wanting to say something that would hurt someone. And yet he was hurting.

I tried to communicate both privately and publically what Taylor needed from others. I discovered that most people among us truly wanted Taylor to be able to feel safe, and I found that some people just could not comprehend what Taylor's injury really means. It was a difficult position for me to be in. It meant speaking up for Taylor whether or not I felt uncomfortable. It was always meaningful to me when someone said, "Please don't apologize for what this injury has done."

While new personality traits were surfacing in Taylor, I also had the unpleasant reminder that I needed to return to work in a relatively short amount of time. One of my closest companions frequently mentioned that November was right around the corner. She cautioned me to stay on track in regard to securing caregivers. She would advise, "Nicole, I know you don't want to think about this, but we can't afford not to." She spoke in a gentle but authoritative tone. As a longtime friend, she seemed to have an inherent sense of what I needed. I valued the word *we* in her references. It was a clear indication that she was not going anywhere. She was in this with me, and I loved her for that.

While still at Bryn Mawr, we had begun the process of obtaining funding for Taylor's daily care. The Pennsylvania Head Injury Program

(HIP)[36] was a resource that might have been helpful to us, but the funds for that had been unavailable for quite some time. Their people were wonderful to work with. They were compassionate and sincere, and their knowledge was beneficial.

Recovery from head and brain injury is costly. Statistics about the costs incurred are alarming and certainly true. For example, both Taylor and I had not received paychecks from employers for ten months. This meant that our family of five now had one source of income when we previously had had three. We had paid out of pocket for health care and dental coverage for six of those ten months. Those things combined with endless trips to the hospital, eating meals at the hospital, and various new expenses like equipment, medications, doctor co-pays, and special food added up to a lot of extra costs. It was not something we liked to discuss or dwell on, but the financial pressure was ever present. Most of the time I avoided focusing on that end of things, but there were times when my head would pound. If I took too much time to ponder the financial implications of Taylor's care, I was left feeling as if the world had stopped spinning. I worried about what his expenses meant for our ability to help Tanner and Avery with furthering their education, and how it would play out in our future. We had a beautiful home and we discussed selling it should that became necessary. We felt as if we were sinking in so many ways. I had to put a lot of the financial pressure on the back burner. It was just not something that I could focus on for any length of time. I also had a hard time caring about money when it felt like so many other matters were on the line. I knew one thing without a doubt. *I knew that I would give every dime I ever had and every dollar I would ever earn to wipe this entire nightmare away.*

---

[36] The program was created in 1988 by the Emergency Medical Services Act of 1985. According to the HIP website, "The goal of the program is to help individuals with a traumatic brain injury (TBI) live independently in their homes and communities." Pennsylvania Department of Health, http://www.portal.state.pa.us/portal/server.pt/community/head_injury_program/14185 (accessed February 11, 2015).

After lengthy discussions with our case manager at Bryn Mawr, some of the therapists at Health South, and the Head Injury Association of Pennsylvania, we went with a program through the Department of Public Welfare called the waiver program. The waiver program had various segments, and clients would be appropriately assigned to the correct waiver, but funding for that had been frozen as well. The best route in regard to Taylor was a program called the COMMCARE waiver. This is a waiver specific to diagnosable traumatic brain injury survivors;[37] in Pennsylvania, it is run through the Area Agency on Aging. We were on a waiting list, so for the time being, it meant that Taylor's in-home care was a cost that we would have to cover when I returned to work. The going rate for such care was between $8.50 and $10.00 an hour. We were thankful that there was a waiver program that was specific to Taylor's case and his needs, but acquiring the approval was going to be a time-consuming and lengthy process. The ball was rolling, so to speak, but it rolled at a sloth's pace. We were told that the funding could take months to obtain, and that there would be no retroactive benefits.

The first task that had to be done in terms of the waiver was the application itself. The process involved securing medical, financial, and personal information about Taylor. Every detail had to be accurately documented, and if it had not been, the forms would be returned. The program was not available to everyone simply because they had a brain injury; other criteria had to be met. Approval hinged on the level of care required and the most effective way for the state to fund that care. Once the application was submitted, the Department of Public Welfare forwarded the information to the Area Agency on Aging. The agency office would send out a representative to evaluate and determine the level of care that Taylor needed. The care evaluation was tied into funding in-home care at various levels ranging from an aide to a nurse, or even a referral to a nursing home or long-term care facility. From there,

[37] Pennsylvania Department of Human Services, COMMCARE Waiver, http://www.dhs.state.pa.us/fordisabilityservices/alternativestonursinghomes/commcarewaiver/index.htm (accessed February 11, 2015).

evaluations would be sent to another agency and funding would be determined.

At one point during this lengthy process, I got a phone call that Taylor had been approved for waiver services, but within a few moments of call one, another call was received and the approval had been misread. *I was devastated.* He had actually been denied, which meant we would have to appeal and start the process all over again. This decision tied into funding and the Area Agency on Aging's goal to place Taylor in the program that would be most beneficial to him. Because funding was unavailable through the COMMCARE waiver, the department had tried another waiver service. This was all happening behind the scenes, so I was not aware of the logistics surrounding the decision. Following a series of anxiety-filled phone calls, one of the directors ended up calling me one Friday evening. She herself had a child with special needs, and explained to me more about the ins and outs of the approval process. Once I understood that the idea was to place Taylor in the *right* program, which might take more time, I was able to regroup.

The details of everything that had occurred over the last several months overwhelmed me. I admit that sometimes I sank into a pool of despairing thoughts.

> *I can't do this.*
> *I am failing as a mother to all of my sons.*
> *I am not a good wife.*
> *Will this struggle ever stop?*
> *Why is all of this so hard, and is there a way to make it easier?*

I would not allow myself to wallow in the frustration and tiredness that all these complications brought with them, but it was wearing me down. Sometimes late at night, the unending scenarios of "what if's" assaulted me, but I was generally too exhausted to entertain them. My prayers were brief but sincere, "God help me. God help Taylor. God help us." The next morning, I often woke with the same thoughts, but the day itself was too busy to lend itself to too much concentration on anything other than Taylor's needs.

Some people saw me as a rock, but I knew that the pounding waves from the constant storm were wearing me down. There were times when I wanted to let go and simply let the raging storms take over, but I knew that I had to dig deep and find my strength to fight. If Taylor could make it through countless surgeries and fight for his life, I could manage to hold it together as his mother. I felt overcome and disorganized, but somehow we had gotten this far and I trusted that everything would come together. In the beautiful words of Paul McCartney, I had to "let it be."

Chapter Twenty-eight
Winds of Change
Early October 2013

I woke up one morning and remembered a poem I had written years earlier. I wrote it when Taylor, Avery and Tanner were not-so-little boys, but still young and fairly innocent. I looked outside one day and realized how quickly each of them had grown and was simply astonished. Immediately, I sat down to write.

My recollection was of a time when they were tow-headed blue-eyed kids filled with wildness; they captured the phrase "adventure brothers." Their afternoons were spent riding their bikes along the driveway of our first home, playing in the leaves while our golden retriever, Lacey, watched over them with loyalty and pride.

It may sound strange, but since Taylor's fall, I thought of Lacey frequently. She was the kind of dog every little boy should grow up with. She slept with Taylor on a nightly basis and her commitment to him was unmatched. I would weep from a place deep within and whisper to the wind that had carried her away, *"Can you believe what has happened to our boy?"* I longed for her to sit at my feet again and look at me with her loving eyes. I could not stand to think of the way her tail used to wag when she saw Taylor, or the image of them sleeping together every night . . . it broke my heart. Lacey had died in my arms a few years earlier of nothing more than old age, but all that was happening with Taylor made every loss in my life feel more profound. Her memory haunted me as much as the memory of my dreams for Taylor. To think of her too long brought a level of emotional torture that I could hardly endure.

I became obsessed with finding the poem that I had written years before. Surprisingly, it did not take me days to find. I recalled that it was tucked in a Bible that my dad had given me, and there it was, waiting for me. *The way things used to be.* Something had torn up my baby boy from the inside out, and I felt as if I should have appreciated and treasured every moment with everyone I loved more deeply. I ached physically for what had been, what should be, and what was supposed to come.

How could I have taken the value of life so lightly? I had no idea when I wrote the poem that the pain of your children growing up too quickly is nothing compared to the idea that they might not grow up at all, and that their dreams may not come true. My hands trembled while salty-tasting tears ran down my cheeks as I read about what once had been.

Autumn winds
Reminding my heart of three little boys
Playing in newly fallen leaves.
Fresh breezes blowing,
On rosy cheeks
While clean, cool scents sweep
Through the air.

They move together
Laughing
Playing
Living
Loving life.
These brothers expressing loyalty
In yellow, orange and red,
Fallen leaves.

Autumn sun
Shines golden rays on three
As they ride bicycles swiftly down
The lane.
Racing with laughter.

Lacey's high -pitched bark
Cheers them on.
And I watch with immeasurable joy
My beautiful princes
Learning
Sharing
Cherishing life.

Chapter Twenty-nine
Growing Complications
Mid-October to Early November 2013

It was the middle of October and soon I would celebrate my forty-third birthday. I knew the day would not be easy because celebrating anything at this point was challenging. Every holiday or birthday was now marked with a profound sense of sadness, loss, and reminders of the contrast between what had once been and what now is. Days that were supposed to feel notably good were instead filled with a new kind of pain.

A few weeks earlier, a photographer had called and offered a family photo session free of charge in honor of Taylor's recovery. She found our family's story to be inspiring and wanted to do something meaningful to give back to us—a gesture that was incredibly generous coming from a complete stranger. Just three years earlier, we had had a family photo shoot at the same time of year. As the date for the new session approached, I grew increasingly anxious.

I thought a lot about the day that had taken place three years before. Taylor was nineteen at the time and being his silly self during the shoot. He was never a fan of having his picture taken, and like me, he had to work hard to have a photo of himself that he felt good about. He was not photogenic in the usual sense, but he was ever so handsome! Taylor had a bright, beautiful smile; he was strong and stood tall. He had the most wonderful thick hair and his cheeks matched his jawline perfectly. My stepmom used to say, "Taylor is such a hunk!" Taylor had to make an effort to be comfortable in front of a camera, especially when it came to posing.

Keith, Avery, Tanner, and my mom had all been present on that day three years ago. That year, my birthday wish had been to create a memory, so family pictures were scheduled. It had been too long since we had had them done, and I knew the importance of capturing our togetherness while we could. I asked the boys not to get me any gifts other than to show up for the occasion with smiles on their faces. It turned out to be a both pleasant and memorable afternoon. During the session, all three of my boys picked me up to lie sideways in their arms, and we laughed as we tried to strike a pose. That photograph would become one of my favorites. I had it framed immediately along with another beautiful photo of the five of us. If I close my eyes, I can still go back to that day and vividly hear my family laughing together.

Now it was a new day and another year. The photographer arrived and set up her equipment. There was an indefinable feeling in the air. It was a heaviness that hung like a black cloud over us. For me, I felt like this day could have been so much different. There was an acute awareness that Taylor had survived something terrible. He was with us, and we still had three sons. I was mindful that our family size could have been forever changed and there could have been no going back to the "five of us." But despite the number being the same, there remained a palpable emptiness. The pain of the absence of who Taylor had been stung as much as death; it just stung in a different way. My thoughts kept flashing back to other times when we sat or stood in front of a camera and I felt broken. The snapshots of yesteryear played like an unending movie, and this scene was unexpected. All five of us remained present, but one of us was in so many aspects *gone*.

I wanted the day to be unforgettable and it was. We were creating fresh memories with the new Taylor. We have all heard the phrase "the new normal," and we were most certainly discovering ours. The photographer was terrific and ended up falling in love with our family. She too is the mother of three sons, which allowed for an instant connection between us.

There were photos taken that day that spoke more than words ever could. They told the story not only of a person who had survived, but a family that had as well. Survival had not been without hardships and great obstacles. The photos captured many things. They revealed the anguish, love, despair, exhaustion, joy, humor, and compassion that was present but most of all . . . they captured a strongly bonded family. They captured *my family*, surviving with Taylor.

The photographer posted the following on her blog after our session:

Where to start? A few months ago I came across a Facebook page for a local family named Team Taylor. Taylor suffered a traumatic brain injury last year, and his mom documents his progress, trials, and successes through the Team Taylor page. The more I read about Team Taylor, the more I felt the need to do something . . . something meaningful...for this family I was praying for every day. Nicole, Taylor's mom, has three sons. They have roughly the same age gap between them as my boys do. Of course I was drawn to this family!

Life can change in an instant. One of the main reasons I am in love with photography is what it can do for a person's soul. Capturing that moment you can never get back. In the spirit of the Olivia Act, named for a girl who was killed in the Sandy Hook shootings last year, I wanted to capture the family who was capturing my heart.

Words cannot come close to describing how beautiful and miraculous this family is! The love between each of them . . . you can feel it in these photographs. I could have spent all day on that porch . . . talking to Nicole about this & that . . . listening to Avery and Tanner playing their guitars (you would not believe the talent these two have vocally AND instrumentally!) And, Taylor made me laugh with that gut-busting kind of laughter. These conversations I will never forget. From making fun of my "Ford" vehicle, to welcoming me to "the gun show" by showing off his muscles, Taylor made me truly smile.

Watching the three guys with their mom & dad was emotional. You see, I can see us in them. I can see my three boys. I hope and pray they are as close as these three brothers. Taylor, Avery, & Tanner are the ultimate role models. My boys love superheroes like Batman, Superman, & the Green Lantern. There are three real life superheroes living right here among us.

Working through their session had my nerves a mess! I truly wanted this family's amazing strength and love to show through. Nicole told me her motto is "Love Wins." She couldn't be closer to the truth. Through tears and laughter . . . Love really does win.

357

These moments on film would forever reflect part of our story. Not only was the session a gift, but so was the life of each person who was present. I was filled with gratitude and thankful for being able to focus on creating a space for new memories.

Unfortunately, there were still issues that demanded attention and there was no time to really slow down. Our lives and family structure had changed dramatically from three years ago. The gift of enjoying the new moment was followed by the awareness of decisions that had to be made and more work that needed to be done in regard to Taylor.

Many years before, I had gone through the strenuous process of finding and then leaving Tanner at an in-home daycare center when he was four years old. I thought the days of that type of anxiousness were over. *I was wrong on many levels.* Returning to work meant finding full-time care for Taylor during the day. I took the planning and scheduling one day at a time, but it produced great angst within me. I felt overwhelmed by all that would have to fall into place in order for me to return to work. So many pieces of the puzzle had to come together and I was uncertain as to how the pieces would fit. Keith constantly reminded me that it was going to work out, but the noticeable palpitations in my heart said otherwise. *I wanted to scream at the world.* I felt as if my frustration was invisible and that was partially because it was hard for me to share my feelings with anyone. Most of the time, my stomach would simply churn and eventually . . . my eyes would begin to water.

How could there be more stress, more responsibility, and more pain ahead? *Hadn't there been enough? Would I ever have a moment to simply be still again?* I yearned for time to sit and mend some of my brokenness, but life continued to pummel us, which meant there would be a minuscule amount of down time. Every ounce of energy our bodies had was being poured into Taylor, his recovery, and planning for his needs—but as a family, we needed to recover too.

I was scheduled to return to work on November 11. We had to get serious about who was going to stay with Taylor and on which days. We were down to the wire, but plans were still being finalized. My friend

Michelle had come sporadically on Wednesdays over the last couple of months so that Taylor and I could get used to being apart. It was never an issue of trusting whom Taylor was with; it was always fear of the unknown. Michelle was one of the safest options we had. She loved Taylor with a genuine hard-to-find kind of love. She is gentle and patient, but prodded me as a friend to do what had to be done for Taylor. As she arrived one day, I left to run errands but ended up just driving around alone. I cried. I took long country back roads that led nowhere; I even got lost a couple of times. I felt aimless, sad, and isolated. I rolled the windows down, took in the fresh air, and tried to allow myself the freedom to feel and really think about the past eleven months.

Taylor's physical care was in the forefront of planning. He was on numerous medications; he had established both seizure and mood disorders with all the symptoms that those diagnoses encompass. He had control of his bladder and bowels, but there were still occasional episodes of incontinence that could be quite embarrassing for him. He continued to be unsteady on his feet and had numerous cognitive impairments that proved to be challenging time and time again. He imagined things that did not exist, remembered events that had never taken place, and exaggerated things that had occurred. He still continued to move in slow motion, and being with him required a level of patience that few understood or could handle.

Life with Taylor meant that molehills often turned into mountains. And these mountains would be climbed over and over again in his broken mind. For example, at therapy he had been struggling. He didn't like some of the exercises he had to perform; he was tired of going three days a week, and he wanted to be finished. Other families had warned us about this behavior and encouraged us to try to make him stick it out for as long as we could. The smallest thing became an excuse for him to try to avoid going.

One particular event really threw him for a loop. Within the context of the session, the therapist said in jest, "I am going to have to duct-tape or staple your hand to the table." (Taylor is the definition of fidgety and she was referring to his inability to sit still.) Taylor didn't joke. Understanding those kinds of statements was something he had not yet learned to do, so instead he took them literally. This was part of the way his brain translated figures of speech. He took every word that was spoken in the most concrete or literal sense.

I was relieved that he did not respond in anger right away, but as soon as we left the session . . . *he exploded.* I had not been present in the room that day, which meant I had to find out exactly what had happened. Taylor had some underlying fears that readily surfaced when he felt threatened.

Taylor relived and replayed the scenario at least one hundred times before meeting with the therapist again two days later. He and I came up with a plan and we rehearsed what he would say. He walked in that day and there was no time for pleasantries—he had to cut right to the chase with what he needed to express.

As we previously had rehearsed, he said to the therapist, "I do not like joking or teasing." I placed my hand on his arm to remind him of my presence and explained to the therapist that her comment had made Taylor feel unsafe and afraid of coming to therapy. Talking about his feelings was also challenging for him because it added another layer of vulnerability. The therapist was crystal-clear in her apology and later told me that she knew as soon as her words had come out of her mouth that they might have a negative effect. We also discussed that when someone says they are sorry, we should forgive them. Taylor apologized as well for getting mad. The therapist took complete and full responsibility, which was important. The session went well and Taylor came out smiling. This was a small but critical victory!

How would his caregivers handle these situations? Taylor was unable to voice his feelings and fears with everyone, so I worried that he would not let people know when he was frightened or frustrated. Along with that, I expected that his recovery would continue and that his caregivers would actively pursue his rehabilitation with him. This expectation meant a certain commitment to his needs, and understanding how the "new Taylor" operated. We did not want Taylor to be merely accompanied or looked after; we wanted his progress to continue. On a personal level, I knew that balancing work and Taylor would be a huge adjustment. I did not know whether I was prepared to juggle everything. I worried that I could not handle work responsibilities and the demands of my child with TBI at the level that I expected of myself.

My FMLA leave was almost exhausted and the decision was certain that I had to give returning to work a try. I had been off just shy of one year. My job provided all our family's health benefits. Keith's employer did not offer health insurance, which was one of the primary factors in our decision that my returning to work was not really negotiable. I put off a lot of the final details for as long as I could. It was very hard for me to visualize how Taylor would get through a day without me. That probably sounds self-absorbed, but I had been with him since the first day of his accident. We had an established routine and he was still fragile in many respects. I was also scared as hell of what might happen to him in my absence.

It was time to spread my motherly wings and let go on some level. Others reassured me that Taylor would be okay. I told myself that I too would survive and that nothing about this decision was written in stone. I had to attempt to return, one day at a time, one foot in front of the other. Life hands us many things we don't necessarily want to do, but we have to do them regardless. I should have known that lesson better by that time, but I didn't.

I thought about the times when Taylor was an infant and I first left him in the care of others. Then, he was in a familiar place, our church nursery. I would stand outside the door when he was about nine or ten months old, and he would cry with vigor until he lost his energy and finally gave in to staying. My last glimpse of him was always that of his arms extended, mouth open, and screaming with fear over my not being next to him for an hour or so. It took weeks for him to accept the ritual. Weeks of my standing outside the nursery door wanting to run in and rescue him, but understanding that healthy separation is not the end of the world. It just feels like it sometimes.

I also remembered various times when we left Avery or Tanner with family or friends for a night out or a short weekend away, and how despite my uncertainty and their absolute resistance, they were fine. The transitions were not easy, but eventually things came together. Over the years, I recalled a song from the boys' childhood. It was from a read-along story that beeped to tell you when to turn the page. The story described various scenarios about when mommies have to leave their little ones. The boys would put the cassette in their Fisher-Price cassette player and listen to it from time to time. *"My mommy comes back, she always comes back, my mommy comes back to get me. My mommy comes back, she always comes back, and she never will forget me."* The catchy tune always made leaving easier. I can still recite it word for word, which makes me laugh with the knowledge that the song greatly comforted me too.

In caring for Taylor, we knew that we would hire people that he was comfortable with and had previously known. The thought of a stranger from an agency tore me up inside. All that I could imagine was Taylor being yelled at or somehow misunderstood during the course of the day and wounded emotionally. I also worried about abuse. I don't know why these thoughts plagued me, but my once-strong and very independent son was in a position in which I did not know whether he could protect himself. The thought of a stranger caring for him filled my heart with intense terror. There were times when images would come to my mind of Taylor being harmed; and if I allowed them to, the thoughts haunted me. I knew that in order for me to go to work, Taylor had to be in the hands of people I trusted implicitly. The threatening thought patterns had the ability to paralyze me and allow me to reason why my return to work was not feasible, but I felt that it really was best for everyone involved. The decision to return was largely based on the needs of our entire family.

Two long-time and trusted family friends offered their days off from work to be with Taylor. One of them even changed her schedule to provide the day when we needed care. She was a registered nurse with years of proper experience. The other friend was a mother of four children, three of whom were boys close in age to our own sons. The third person was a close friend of Taylor's, a recent graduate of Penn

State with a degree in elementary education who had some flexibility in her schedule. The final person we hired was my sister-in-law, who had loved Taylor since he was in diapers. This care was a tremendous blessing to us at a tumultuous time, and each of these strong women brought something special to Taylor's recovery.

Keith arranged with his employer to work four ten-hour days instead of five eight-hour shifts. This arrangement allowed him to be home with Taylor on Friday, eliminating the need to find someone for the fifth day. The pieces were coming together and I felt like I could at least breathe instead of being overcome with panic.

It was not going to be easy to care for Taylor in this way. There were many fears, feelings, and scenarios everyone would have to work through. Taylor's care would turn out to be one of the most challenging aspects of navigating our new lives, especially from my perspective. I had to learn to be the liaison between Taylor and his caregivers, which would at times be a tricky tightrope to balance.

In my mind, Taylor was already so broken by the fall that I felt that it could not get much worse. I had let go of many of my fears and learned to live in a state of acceptance versus constant worry. He had survived and endured so much. I felt confident that we would get through this phase. Others had been broken too, and none more so than those who lived with Taylor. It would require a lot of inner strength for our family to release the reins of Taylor's daily care into the hands of those who might not do things the way we would necessarily do them. We were letting others into our home and our day-to-day lives, and giving them control in a situation where control already felt limited. Emotions were at such a high pitch, and it was hard to talk about certain things with everyone. The necessity for caregiving in general added a new layer of stress.

All in all, it shaped and changed our relationships, and as one caregiver told me, "You cannot spend significant time with Taylor and walk away the same person." Our relationships with those who were willing to take on this role would be challenged. I was raw with emotion, and fully aware of some of the side effects created by having a child with a devastating diagnosis. I wanted and needed absolute security in regard to Taylor's care. Each of the caregivers, with the exception of the nurse, was walking into a situation they had never encountered and so was I. I was growing more restless as the days approached, but I knew the transition had to take place.

I took the ladies out for dinner one night and we tried to come up with various plans. What were some things that could be done to make this schedule work? What were their concerns and fears? As we sat around the table and discussed these details, I felt like I was having some sort of business meeting. It was awkward for me, but I wanted everyone involved to be reassured and comfortable in their new roles. After eating and socializing, I asked each person to write down what they felt would be the most challenging aspect of Taylor's care and any concerns or fears that they might have.

Everyone wrote down that they were worried about Taylor's seizures, and what to do when and if they took place. Another person wrote that she was afraid that Taylor would not like being with her, and still another was worried that the caregiving would have a negative effect on our friendship. Each of these uncertainties broke my heart, but they made complete sense to me. It made me sad that we were sitting around the table having to talk about these matters instead of what our conversations had once been about, but I appreciated their candidness in sharing. The contrast between what once had been and now is stood out that evening.

I hated traumatic brain injury that night. I hated the staircase in my house. I hated the fact that instead of feeling like things were getting easier, the stress and struggle involved had merely shifted. This injury found its way into every nook and cranny of my life . . . there was no part of me that felt angry with Taylor, but I despised this situation from day one and I had a feeling we had not even reached the middle yet.

A few days later, just before my scheduled return to work, my dad flew up for a visit. For the last few years, he and my stepmother had been living with and caring for my grandmother in Georgia. She was in her nineties and her health had been deteriorating for some time. This made my dad's ability to get away challenging, and we had not seen him since the early days of Taylor's accident. He had not seen Taylor awake and out of the intensive care setting.

Taylor and "Pawpaw," as the grandchildren knew him, shared a wonderful bond. My dad had always been a kid living in an adult's body; as the old adage says, "he enjoys being a boy!" He was full of countless stories of adventure and the sea, and he captured the hearts of my sons from the first time he held them.

Taylor had been asking for Pawpaw for a couple of months, and that alone was heartbreaking. Over the course of the last year, the reality that my family was scattered over the map in places too far away for frequent visits had burdened me deeply. I not only wanted their presence and support, I needed it. I needed it more than anyone would ever imagine, and it was so painful to acknowledge that I rarely allowed myself to do so.

To hear from Taylor that he wanted to see his Pawpaw cut me apart inside. I wished I were like Jeannie on the television show from the late 1960s, having the ability to grant a wish with a mere nod of my head. I was thankful that Taylor mentioned his wish only periodically, rather than the endless obsessing that sometimes took place. At times, I wrestled with bitterness about how far away everyone was. I wanted my family to live just down the road; I ached for Sunday meals together and some type of weekly ritual that would allow me to feel safe and secure in the nest that a family can provide. I felt as if my roots had been cut off and were now exposed. When my dad came that November, it was one of those "just in the nick of time" moments. Taylor's desire to see him coupled with my own was too much to bear. My father's presence brought comfort and joy. On the other hand, not having people there when you need them produces some kind of underlying resentment. There was a part of me that seemed to scream from inside, *"Can't you see how much I need you?"* but those words were part of the silent scream. All the cries and thoughts that I held inside that I was not brave enough to release ran through my mind instead and further bruised my heart.

My dad has always been the kind of man who is comfortable with his emotions and has never been ashamed to cry. For some reason, throughout this ordeal he rarely did. This trial that I imagined would break him made him strong in front of me. I saw his eyes fill with tears and his sadness was present in his quietness. It was written on his face, but he did not break down. I do recall a time a few days after Taylor's fall, when he and I were in Taylor's room in the ICU. Our eyes met and I knew his thoughts. He knew that Taylor might not live, and he knew that it would destroy me. I have had that look as a parent, wondering how in the world I can fix something for my kids with the knowledge that at times we can't solve the problem. His look will be forever etched in my mind; it was a look I had never seen before and it allowed me to see right into his heart.

I realized that neither he nor my mom had a moment with me when the dam broke and the tears flowed like a raging river. I wondered whether that is a part of a parent's protection. I imagine that if they had broken with me, my pain would have amplified too. It is a curious thing how emotions and our unknown ability to control them work.

In the depths of my sorrow, I wanted someone to stop this horrible nightmare. My heart demanded that it all go away, but it never did. No matter how many times I felt like I could not face another day, the next day came—and along with it, the heavy weight that it brought.

When I was around my dad, I wanted to be a little girl again. I longed to feel safe. I wanted to climb on his lap and have him hold me tight. I wanted him to promise me that things were going to be okay. I wanted to be twelve years old sailing on the Chesapeake Bay and hear him call me "Pumpkin" from the bow of the boat. I wanted happiness, *not this ordeal*.

I pictured Taylor at around age three having a horsey ride on my dad's back, grinning from ear to ear. My mind flashed through years of seeing Taylor fishing on the dock, reeling in the fish one by one with Pawpaw, while the golden sun danced behind them with dreams yet to come. I could see Taylor as my little boy, then growing into a teenager and now a young man . . . *before it had all come to a sudden stop*. I

366

wanted to be back at a place in time where none of this misery had ever happened. I wanted to redo my life so that I could somehow provide an escape to the outcome in front of us. I felt as if every dream I had for Taylor had been thrown into the sea and washed away in the tide. There was nothing I could do to save them. What would happen to my son's future now that its plan had been stolen from him?

Being with my dad reminded me of so many times past and the emotions associated with them; it reminded me of magical memories, memories that despite their beauty caused me great pain. It reminded me that Taylor's fall was something that I never saw coming and was totally unprepared for.

During the visit, my dad and I were able to sneak away one afternoon and have some time for just the two of us. I was hurting a lot, and for the most part I was unable to voice the pain that I was feeling. But it was nice to go to the thrift store and grab a coffee together. My dad and I have always been close, and I have always felt that I could be open with him, but this situation was different. If I had let out any of the hurt, I think it would have washed over both of us like an unexpected tidal wave. Keeping it in and close allowed me to contain it. It gave me control in the midst of so much chaos. But by not sharing it, I also robbed myself of the comfort that can come when you let someone know the depth of the wound in your heart. I was just not ready to expose how horrific this all felt to me.

There were moments of tremendous joy during our time together. It was not the kind of joy with confetti flying around in your thoughts, but it was a quiet, assured peace and beauty that comes with really seeing a snapshot of people, togetherness, and love.

There was pleasure in seeing my dad interact with Taylor, Avery, and Tanner. His love gave something to each one of us. Perhaps in a time of so much loss, his presence was just enough of a reminder that not everything was gone. I noted the gift that each second, minute, hour, and day together held. And I became more aware than ever that people we love will not always be with us.

The visit was uncomplicated and full of ordinary things. We took Taylor to his therapies, and it was rewarding for my dad to see how hard he was working in physical, occupational, and speech therapy. Taylor felt proud of himself and enjoyed sharing the progress he had made. Taylor would pass by us while moving down the hall; he would have a grin on his face and say, "Watch this, Pawpaw." My dad enjoyed interacting with part of the "village" of caregivers that made up Taylor's care.

One of the daily rituals that occurred was that Taylor would stand in front of my dad and flex his arms. Taylor loved to show off his muscles. Each time he did, my dad would give a loud reaction. He would growl like a tough dog, or yell "Oh man, Taylor, they are huge!" Taylor would laugh, grin, and take it all in. His Pawpaw was a hero to him, and now, he felt the tables turn—he was a hero too. And I was able to see how extraordinary Taylor really is.

Part of me understood how much sadness my dad must have felt not only to see Taylor's suffering and hurt, but also to see me, his daughter, suffer so deeply. That week I talked a lot with my dad about how afraid I was of everything. This pain was pulling me apart inside and parts of me hoped that by sharing it, it could somehow be fixed. My dad offered his quiet reassurance and acknowledged that the situation was horrible, and that it had us somewhat trapped. He reminded me that he didn't think it would always feel this difficult, and to get through it the best way that I knew how. He spoke to me of his deep faith and the knowledge that when we can no longer hold ourselves together, there is Someone greater than us Who does. He encouraged me to pray and to trust that the struggle would not continue so fiercely.

When Taylor's accident happened, I imagined my pain had reached its peak, but the truth was that the woe inside me was growing. There is a vast difference between what the moments of crisis bring and the feelings that emerge once the dust has settled.

Chapter Thirty
The Abyss
November 12, 2013

The day broke like an unexpected storm in which I felt like lightning was striking my every move. Even though it had been brewing for some time, when it arrived in its fullness, I was unprepared. There are moments in life that you can't skim over, go around, or skip; these moments are times that you have to simply get through. And that is what I intended to do: to get through the next series of events the only way I knew how, one second at a time. The storm that had come would bring dominating and forceful emotions. This was not going to be a disturbance we could hide from; Taylor and I would have to face it and all of the raging feelings it brought, but we would not face it alone.

I cannot say, "Fortunately, Taylor felt the emotional impact of my return to work less than I did," because part of the tragedy was that he was unable to feel and experience what was really happening. But in that instance, I don't know whether I could have handled any kind of heartfelt objections on his part. His emotional numbness played the role of silent partner to my own struggle.

Everyone else in our family had gone back to their daily routines. Tanner was in school, Keith was at work, and Avery was attending full-time classes at university. Now it was my turn to reenter the real world although I was not ready for that daily ritual. For Taylor, his routine would be uncertain and we knew that for now there would not be a return to anything.

I gave myself some sort of pep talk about putting on my big-girl pants and doing what had to be done, but every fiber of my being resisted the change. No part of me was ready to leave Taylor, but I tried to prepare him as much as I could for the transition. I told him that this time apart from me could be beneficial, and I attempted to encourage him, but I didn't really buy the lie I felt I was asking him to believe.

I had an innate sense that I knew what was best for Taylor. He had changed so much in every way. Reading him took paying attention, being aware, and being in tune with his needs. Hesitation coursed through my body, but despite my lack of readiness, I had to pass on the torch.

The first morning that I returned to my office was a Tuesday, the day following Veterans Day, which I would vividly remember because I felt like the holiday bought me an extra day with Taylor. If there was relief in returning to some type of normalcy, I didn't feel it. In the early days post-accident, I craved that normal lifestyle, but over time I had forgotten what normal meant. There were rarely any days that passed that did not encompass traumatic brain injury and all the fallout that it leaves in its path. *Normal* had taken on a new meaning; it meant a day without some sort of crisis brewing.

In the place of what used to fill my thoughts was now dread, more sadness, and a tinge of fear. Oddly enough, I was not a person who was prone to excessive worry, and I was still in a position where my heart was not guided by "what if"-type scenarios. What actually was occurring held enough power in my life. The element of fear that was present was not enough to paralyze me. I had learned over the last few months that I could roll with the punches and that they were not easy to anticipate, so it was better to simply let them come and then cope with them to the best of my ability.

Kellie, my sister-in-law, was the designated caregiver for that particular day, and leaving Taylor with his aunt provided an element of peace. Kellie was nervous and that was not only expected but okay; it was not a situation that I wanted anyone to go into with light feet. My feelings were similar to those that arise when a mother leaves her young child with a babysitter, but there were more complexities and layers to my anxiety. There was a part of me that still rebelled against the whole idea that Taylor's accident had happened, and again I wondered how in the hell we had ended up here.

Kellie came that morning and there were few words exchanged. When she hugged me briefly, I found comfort in her assurance. I felt that as a mother, she had some notion of how hard this had to be for me and she expressed her sympathy in wanting to mend the situation. No one could repair our current position, but compassion and kindness carried a lot of weight in this new world. I had been with Taylor for almost a year, and in those 365 days, I held no regret. I knew that I had loved him fully and fearlessly; I had helped him and held nothing back. Day after day, I had been the person whom I would have wanted next to me if I had been in his situation. There was something about leaving him that morning that seemed wrong, unfair, and cruel on top of everything else, but there was no getting around it.

As I was driving down our lane that morning, all the makeup I had previously applied was washed away within seconds. I considered my co-workers close friends, but my return to the office was going to be quite difficult for everyone. Two friends in particular had more than a special place in my heart. I knew that they would be there for me as much as possible. These friends were my *Ya-Ya Sisterhood, my girls*, and our friendship had been tried, tested, and proven. Over the years we had laughed, cried, and supported each other through other rough times. This situation would be no different. They would be present for me; *I just had to let them.*

As I walked into the office that morning, a silence fell. It fell into the space that surrounded me and it fell upon my heart. The black cloud of sadness seemed to be hovering over me as my marker. The silent scream was back. Every part of me hurt so much, and there would be no relief from the inner ache that was now present.

The best way to describe my experience that day would be stunned silence. My coworkers had not been around me that much and no one quite knew how to handle the fragility of my emotional state, including me. Over the next few weeks, some profound conversations would take place and I would treasure them. But first we had to get through day one. I was told later that during the first day I appeared to be in some sort of shock. Every action, word, and breath that came out of me showed that I was not at all okay. I could not see it, but I felt it within. I had reached some kind of breaking point, but breaking down wasn't in the plan, so I had to keep moving.

I felt the awkwardness that my presence brought to the office. I interpreted the silence of my colleagues to mean that my presence was unwanted, and in part, that was true. Those who loved me wanted me to be where my heart already was, *with Taylor*. What I needed was a lot of reassurance coupled with heaps of hugs, but what I got initially was silence. I had become familiar with it on some level; I was in this new situation in which people became uncomfortable around me. I had already witnessed the myriad ways in which people did not want to say the wrong thing, or did not know the right thing to say, as well as all the emotions involved.

Throughout the morning, I made a few calls to Kellie and I found relief knowing Taylor was doing okay. There were numerous trips to the bathroom where I could release some of the tears I could no longer contain. The sobs that I was trying so hard to hold in seeped out and I hoped that no one could hear me through the thin walls. I covered my mouth with my hands and tried to stifle the noises that came from somewhere deep inside me, each one representing the ocean of grief that I was swimming in. I stood for minutes at a time in the empty bathroom in a stall feeling lonely, afraid, and abandoned. I felt as if I were watching a sad movie about someone else's life. Being at work reminded me that this nightmare continued, and that instead of waking up, I was just plumbing another depth within the abyss of struggle it represented.

My presence felt like a burden to others and I wasn't ready to share the ocean of grief that washed over me. I had been forever changed as a person, and there was no going back to who I had been before. A year earlier, working in this very same building, I thought I had known struggle. Now struggle, sadness, loss, and worry had become embedded in me. The definitions of each of those concepts had been changed. I was now aware of them in their starkest form.

Just before Taylor's fall, I had begun to dabble in painting. The pictures were of simple things on tiny canvases: trees, birds, and happy scenes. It was a relaxing form of art and I was satisfied exploring this creative side of myself. I had given my supervisor a small painting of a rope swing with a yellow sky in the background and tiny purple flowers dotting the grass. I saw it in her office the day I returned and I knew the person who painted that, who had felt that kind of brightness, *was gone.*

Once again, I saw clearly the before and after of my entire life. It reminded me of when I had had my children. After giving birth to each one, I had a distinct sense that they had always been there. Taylor, Avery, and Tanner were not just a part of me now, but they always had been—they had just not yet been born. They represented an unknown joy waiting to be revealed; an incredible force of love and light that could not have just come into being . . . but it did. That feeling was something that always fascinated me.

Taylor's accident felt like an eruption of the opposite force. During the course of his life, all these beautiful dreams had been building for him. He represented so many wonderful things to me: his infancy, boyhood, and manhood were all leading up to something special and profound to a mother's heart, even if they seemed ordinary to the rest of the world. I had looked forward to watching each part of his life unfold: his finding a companion, having children, seeing him blossom into more of a man . . . and then, this nightmare came and he fell away from all of that. With every second of his fall, those dreams, abilities, and all the hopes of those things fell with him. A year later and it still haunted me that as his mother, I should have been able to protect him. I felt that I should have sensed that he was in danger, and that feeling was a horrible monster to face. I had to remind myself that there was nothing that I could have done to prevent his injury, but I didn't always believe it.

There were a few times over the past year when I had felt as vulnerable and defenseless as I did in those hours when I returned to work. Every part of me screamed, *"I cannot do this. I don't want to do this. I should not have to do this."* The loudest voice in my head said the same thing over and over again: "I miss Taylor. I miss my son." And yet he was still here. I hated that aspect of traumatic brain injury—that so many people seemed to say, "You are so fortunate to have him with you. Taylor is such a miracle." But he was gone in so many ways, and that was hard for people to truly comprehend.

I thought briefly of Keith, Avery, and Tanner. How had Tanner returned to the crowd of high school students in the weeks after Taylor's fall and gone through each day without breaking down, running away, or releasing his pain on some poor unsuspecting soul? How had Avery walked through a campus of peers who were unaware of the weight he

374

was carrying? Was his response to someone's "Good morning" ever, "No, it isn't a good morning. My big brother is all but gone and there is nothing good happening for me." Did Keith ever go into the bathroom at work and weep, or did he sit at his desk and want to crawl under it because a violent wave of grief had unexpectedly assaulted him? The night that Taylor fell, our family fell with him. We just fell in different ways.

Keith fell into a frozen grief. It was the kind of anguish that can almost immobilize a person, but life doesn't allow it. He was able to do what was familiar, but you could see every drop of hurt and turmoil he experienced. His agony registered in the pallor of his face, the new and more profound wrinkles on his brow, and the sadness in his eyes. He fell into a pit of silent despair. I wondered if and when he would emerge. He was going through the motions of living, but simply living seemed to drain him of everything else.

Avery fell too. I could see this situation was destroying him. His big brother was gone in an instant, and Avery was trying desperately to believe that he could somehow bring him back. If the big brother had so significantly changed, then what was Avery's position? What did this mean for his life and his future plans? I had a sense that he was swimming upstream, and no one could relieve him. The harder he worked to fix matters, he found that the struggle around him seemed only to intensify. All his efforts were intended to bring his big brother home to us, and suddenly he realized that the brother he had was gone and that nothing could change that awful truth.

Tanner tumbled too. He lost friends as he wandered into his new role and tuned into someone that I hardly recognized. The outgoing, laid-back young man who had been the baby of our family had been transformed. His entire outlook had changed. Where he had once been soft and tender, there were walls going up all around him. Tanner had never had a mean bone in his body, but suddenly his anger was palpable. He was never unkind or cruel, but the little boy who used to melt when you hugged him or loved to cuddle had a new hardness to him. His jaw was set in a new way and his demeanor had changed. His brother's fall had shaken him; I wanted the good, tender heart inside him to return, but for now he had to wrestle with his frustrations and his loss.

I cannot tell you all that Taylor's fall encompassed for me. I have felt it, but I am sure those around me could tell you much more about how I coped. I like to think that I was strong and that I felt a sense of strength in my brokenness. But I was also broken. I know I was shattered into a million tiny pieces by all that has happened, and to this day, I am not sure I will ever be completely whole again.

Returning to work was not something that anyone felt I should have to do, which complicated things. I had some sort of expectation regarding my return, but in truth it was just my need to have this huge desolate spot inside of myself filled, *and nothing could do that*. I wanted to be welcomed back in a tangible way, but how should that welcoming have played out? I can't explain what I needed, because to this day I don't know. There had been a distinct shift in my entire life, and some part of me needed to address that among my workplace family.

Over the next several days, those closest to me in the office had to navigate some treacherous waters. If I were to make it through this transition, I had to be somewhat honest as to where I was in it. Everything about it hurt. I felt as if my emotional skin were being ripped off, layer by layer, leaving me further exposed to the brutality and pain of life. Everything hurt me. Someone not saying hello; someone ignoring me because they didn't know what to say; someone saying the wrong thing because there was no right thing to say—all of it hurt. And I felt it. I felt the extent of what I had been through more than ever before.

I distinctly remember that at one point people were discussing the upcoming holiday season. There were conversations about what people would be doing as Thanksgiving and Christmas approached, what gifts to buy, and the like. I found myself wanting to stand up and scream at the top of my lungs: *"How can you talk about such trivial things? I MISS MY SON. Nothing else matters!"* I was not at all proud of these emotions, but I felt them. I think that a part of me wanted to know what it felt like again to have a life that includes dreams of happy holidays, but my life felt like happiness might never show itself again. I felt abnormal and selfish in my anger. At this time, Taylor was restricted from flying, and because of this restriction, we were not comfortable driving more than a couple of hours from our home. I longed to be able to get on a plane and see my father in Georgia for the holidays, or spend a weekend with my brother in Richmond, but I felt tethered to our home. I was in need of some respite, and it felt like it might not come.

My grief, which had been stifled for so long, suddenly burst out through every pore and at times it could not be stopped. It assaulted me without abandon and it roared in like a hurricane, causing everything else to disappear beneath the sea of sadness that I was in. I felt as if I wanted to disappear, go away, and give up the struggle. To say I was in a "bad spot" would be to understate the condition that I was truly in. My heart was full of despair, I had no hope at all, and underneath the surface that others could see was a sorrow of such depths that I was not sure that I could ever resurface. What kept my heart intact in those times was the fact that I could not stand to see anyone I love suffer any more, and my disappearing would cause them great suffering.

I did not quite understand why these feelings revealed themselves the way they did, but for the first time in a year, I was away from Taylor for an extended period of time. I was away from the other family members whom I felt the need to nurture and protect, and I was alone with myself. Now I had to take care of me, and that was a shift in what had been happening over the last several months.

My office family began to see how unsettled I was, and each in their own way tried to be present for me. One of my dearest friends, named Tracy, listened daily and wrapped her warm arms around me while sharing words of wisdom and honesty whenever I needed them. She has a way of communicating that is genuine, plainspoken, and goes straight to the heart of the matter, and it worked for me. She doesn't candy-coat things and I didn't want them candy-coated any longer. I was dealing with high-voltage emotions, and it was increasingly impossible to contain them all the time. I had been gracious toward the injury, but I now felt my heart sliding into madness. Stuffing the millions of thoughts that swirled through my head day after day was toxic to me. Tracy recognized my struggle. I could curse, cry, and question whatever I wanted to in her presence. Not once did she say, "How could you say that or feel that way?" Instead she said, "Of course you do." She reminded me of how much she loved me, what an amazing mother and wife she thought I was, and she believed in me as I questioned all that I ever had known to be true.

Kelly, another treasured friend and co-worker, was an added pillar of strength. I could be honest with her too, and that was the best gift that she continuously gave me. I was tired of pretending to be okay and I wasn't even aware that I was pretending. Kelly had loved Taylor since he had been a little boy, and she was working through her own feelings regarding his fall.

We had a unique bond based on many things, but our trust and friendship in each other had been well established. Kelly cautiously shared her grief with me. She missed Taylor too, and that felt like a truth that held great love. Kelly would often reminisce about her memories of Taylor. Her favorite story concerned an incident that occurred when we were neighbors and our kids had played baseball together. She told of first meeting a much younger Taylor, who came over, knocked on her door, and said, "I am sorry." Taylor had said something mean on the bus to her stepson, and he and I had marched over to Kelly's house to apologize. She remembered what a nice little boy Taylor had been; this reminiscence led into story after story, and those recollections were healing. They brought laughter and tears to both of us. I could see that Kelly also missed the person whom she had known and considered a friend in Taylor, and it made me aware that even though people might not share it with me, they too missed the person who Taylor had been. *I was not alone in missing my son.*

I also had a new desk partner who was much younger than I, and was full of good energy. I felt bad that she was partnered with me at such a challenging time, but she was a burst of sunshine and light. She displayed maturity far beyond her years, and was a true friend. She listened and expressed sympathy whenever I needed it, and she shared sweet stories of her delightful daughter, who was not yet two years old. I nicknamed my new desk partner "Little Miss Sunshine," because that is what she brought into my daily routine. In her I was able to see joy, life and light in a way that felt unobtrusive to my suffering.

Tuesday, Wednesday, Thursday, and Friday all came and went in the office. I was like the Little Engine That Could, reminding myself of what I thought I could do. My co-workers held me up and gave me courage. They reminded me that I was going to be all right and that every part of how I felt was normal. They loved me and accepted my pain, but it took hard work. It took my being okay with not being okay, and it meant they had to be comfortable with what I was feeling on that day because I was and still am on an emotional roller coaster.

Taylor's transition was not as difficult. He accepted the shift in our schedule and he was still exhausted almost all of the time. He almost always woke up early to see me off, and then his day began. At least two days a week he had therapy, so that helped to fill the eight-hour day. Other routines were established; many of them at the time revolved around food. Taylor did not have a lot of stamina, but he loved to go to familiar places to socialize. He and his caregivers would go for lunch at local spots: Chilly Willy's, Subway, and the Carriage Corner became fast favorites. After lunch, Taylor would often need to be tucked in for a nap and spend the next few hours resting. Often he was resting peacefully when I came home. We were stretching to find ways for Taylor to improve, but for now he was still working hardest at recovering. It was a simple time along the path of his recovery, and that made everything else less brutal.

One day, a co-worker stopped me and casually asked how I was doing. As we talked for a little bit, he told me something that I had not thought about before. He explained that when I returned, he could see that I had changed. The person who had been full of laughter, smiles, and warmth had become isolated and full of heaviness and sadness. He simply wanted me to know that he missed the "old me" too. It was said in an eloquently simple way, but I heard his words and I felt the kindness in his heart. My friends were sorry for me; they missed my old life and

379

my old self too. I hoped that that old self would come back. More than that, I hoped that more of Taylor would return to us.

Over the course of the first weeks and months, work proved to be a challenge of vast proportions. There were multiple phone calls from caregivers, texts or calls from Taylor, insurance battles and doctor's appointments that had to be scheduled. There were seizure episodes, and on Taylor's "off days," there was worry. Most of all, there remained a level of sadness that surpassed anything I had previously known.

There were times when I called Avery, and in between catching my breath, sobbed into the phone about how much I missed Taylor, how full of sadness I was, and that I wanted to speak with someone who missed him too. Some mornings I called Keith, who was not able to talk very long or frequently at work, but I needed just a moment. Sometimes I did not say anything for several minutes, only cried. He knew what I wanted to say and I just needed him to know how badly I hurt. There were days and moments when it took all of my strength to stay at work, to stay at my desk, instead of standing up and screaming, *"I cannot do this anymore."*

I started a daily ritual with my mother by calling her every morning. We would chat for a few minutes before I began my workday. She shouldered whatever emotion I was feeling at the moment. I needed her to be present; supportive; loving; and accepting toward me, and she was. There were times when I hesitated to burden her with my thoughts, but I could not allow them to stay hidden.

Returning to work remains one of the greatest obstacles that had to be overcome, but I am proud of myself for doing it. It was a very real way to put the love I have not only for Taylor, but for Keith, Avery, and Tanner as well into practice. When I look back on my childhood, I remember so well the mantra of the Little Engine That Could. I learned the author's lesson well: "I think I can. I think I can." And I did. I have continued to do it. I know that if not for our caregivers, my coworkers, friends, and family, this little engine would not have made it up that hill. Leaving Taylor was a daily act of trust, courage, and commitment to our family as a whole. I was doing what I had to do for everyone's lives to be more secure, but that doesn't mean that I don't continue to wrestle with the decision. I am aware that while returning to work alleviated some burdens, it created countless others.

In the first days back, I was keenly aware that I was taking things day by day, and often minute by minute. My goals of continuing to work expanded to taking the job a week at a time. I have not been able to move out much further than the weekly scenarios, and I feel like continuing to work is something that might not be possible. Each day brings challenges, and as you can imagine, some days the challenges are tougher than others. There are some times when I am just not sure I can manage it all. I do find a way, but getting through it is not always easy. I want to handle all of the frustration, grief, and pressure with evidence of grace and dignity instead of what so often feels like a series of endless struggles. If people could see the image of myself that I see, they would see a mother lying on a cold concrete floor, waving a white flag of surrender in the air, pleading to the powers that be: "Please make a way so that I don't have to do this anymore. I don't feel strong enough." And then people would see the frustration subside, the tears dry up, and I would repeat the same thing the next day. It goes without being said that some days present less frustration than others, and I appreciate it when those days occur.

The frustration involves issues that you would and would not imagine. It involves random calls or texts from Taylor full of heightened sadness or agitation. It involves a caregiver who has just witnessed her first seizure. It involves the appointment I forgot to make, or the call from the one doctor I truly do not care for; a man who talks to me like a child and makes me aware that Taylor's care is nothing more than a bother to him. It involves a snowstorm, which means I will be late to work and I have very little time to spare. It means crying through a staff meeting while a PowerPoint presentation is taking place, with my tears running for an hour like an open faucet with no one noticing, and trying to time how often to wipe my face and nose with my sleeve because I have no tissues. It involves not being able to suppress a surge of sudden overwhelming sadness, and it involves pretending to be okay while desperately wishing life felt normal again.

What allows me to sustain my present position is certainly an inner strength; I won't deny that I could not do all of this on my own. There is the presence of Something that has been with me since the onset of this journey, and long before that; Something profoundly larger than myself and unseen but clearly felt. On the bad days, I miss Taylor even more. I miss being able to share with him the story of what has happened in our world. I miss the son that we had before, and I miss his presence. But perhaps what I miss the most is the day when my heart didn't have to feel crushed by the weight of it all, and a day free of any kind of sadness and pain.

I have recently embraced this new thought: in the worst and most challenging of times, your strength must prove to be greater than your struggle. I choose to believe that amid all the turmoil that adversity brings, there is a far greater force. That force is love; and ultimately, love wins.

Chapter Thirty-one
The Truth Shall Set You Free
December 2014

As I write these words, it has been two years and one month since Taylor's fall. The situation remains heartbreaking and exhausting. So much has transpired, I feel like this book could go on forever and I am sure it could. A lot of people in the world might know what it's like to experience this kind of ordeal far longer than our family has, but there are countless people who have no idea what traumatic brain injury requires families to endure. What puzzles me is how little I knew about traumatic brain injury prior to Taylor's accident. It seems as if there is a silent veil over situations similar to ours. An essential aspect of traumatic brain injury that outsiders should comprehend is that its effects are endless in multiple ways. One of those ways is summarized by the type of loss that traumatic brain injury represents. *Ambiguous loss* is a phrase that I have become very familiar with; it is a loss in which closure is more difficult to attain or define.

Ambiguous loss occurs in such situations as a child's disappearance; a soldier declared missing in action; or with such a diagnosis as traumatic brain injury. All these situations are extraordinarily different but have the same impact on the person's loved ones. Ambiguous loss means that there is no end to the grief, the loss, and the struggles associated with what is taking place around you. It is like looking down into a well that dried up long ago and not being able to see its bottom. Instead of families having closure, they must learn to live in the shadow of an ongoing *continuum of grief*. Ambiguous loss is a difficult concept to explain, and often in a family such as ours the greatest source of heartache. It is imperative to find a core of inner peace when dealing with ambiguous loss, or it may consume you. *The key is to not allow that to happen.*

When I fast-forward a year from where this story closed in the last chapter, I am not even sure where to begin. I know you are all wondering how we are coping today, and perhaps what Taylor is doing at this very moment. I sometimes wonder what truly is going through his mind every second of the day. He will tell me certain things, but he may not ever be able to explain to me what he cannot fully comprehend.

384

There are conclusions that I fear he will never reach. His injured brain makes it hard for him to nail down any concrete ideas or concepts.

As Taylor's mother, I am incredibly grateful for his progress and yet I still mourn the profound changes in his and our lives. These changes are ever present; and even two years later, unwelcome surprises occur. There are days when I feel lost in the cycle of our circumstances. My career, caregiving, keeping track of Taylor's schedule, and having some kind of life of my own are all areas that I am still working to balance. I'm unsure whether this new life will ever be something I can fully manage in the way I desire.

At times, I feel that I do remarkably well, but at other times I feel like I am barely keeping my head above water. There are times when my bucket cannot hold another drop, and when that drop comes, the spillover feels like a torrential downpour.

On those days, I still feel as if I am drowning in the pain and responsibility of it all. Traumatic brain injury has that effect again and again. We are faced with situations that seem impossible, but we must continue to navigate them.

There is a voice that often creeps into my head when I am feeling low. It is the voice of *failure*. Wearing so many hats, juggling numerous balls, balancing multiple plates, eventually takes its toll. Instead of cutting myself a break and accepting my humanness, I join the thoughts of self-abasement. Not being able to manage it all is not acceptable, according to my standards. But I am learning that maybe I can't do everything or perhaps I am not able to do everything well. This new life requires more focus on details—all of them. It means that I am going to have to trim some unnecessary responsibilities and focus on what matters most.

When things go awry with Taylor or he experiences unnecessary hurt, I feel like I should have better control of his life. When I feel the changes in the relationships with my other sons, who are equally important to me, I think I should be more present for them. Unfortunately, my marriage has suffered too, and so have my friendships. The injury has even spilled over into my profession, and at times I feel pretty defeated. Everyone in my family copes in various ways, and I know that I am particularly hard on myself. One of a mother's jobs is to make life easier and better for her children, but what if you can't? What if there is no remedy or cure? I think the solution, if there is one, is finding a way to be my best self, and resting in the knowledge that I am doing the best that I can in the circumstance. I think it is imperative to hear the voices of those who love and believe in me. Caregiving takes a toll that is hard for outsiders to understand; it wears away at inner reserves, so as caregivers, we must learn to be gentle with ourselves.

As for Taylor, he no longer attends physical or occupational therapy because according to insurance guidelines, he has maximized his potential. I strongly disagree with that assessment, and I am certain that without Taylor's determination, his progress would come to an abrupt stop. He participates in weekly art lessons and he appreciates the company of his instructor. Taylor is drawn to her energetic and creative demeanor. His weekly sessions involve going to her studio and making art for an hour or so. He seems to enjoy it, and we feel that it is a step in a new direction and stimulates more cognitive growth. He also goes to the gym at least twice a week. He is limited as to what he can do and his workouts are fairly repetitive, but nonetheless they represent forward motion. He has a circuit that he walks; he works on an elliptical machine and lifts small weights. The hope is that these activities create new pathways in his brain and opportunities for further healing in his mind. He has not been permitted to swim or jog yet, due mainly to the possibility of seizure activity and the jostling that can occur when jogging. We are uncertain whether these activities will ever be approved. He also has a maximum weight limit, and has to be aware of avoiding excess pressure on his head.

From time to time, he attends sessions with a neuropsychologist who has been a phenomenal addition to his care team. Taylor was tested a year ago; at that time, we were told his emotional and cognitive functions are those of a nine-year-old child. We felt the interpretation was spot on, and that it aligned with his behavior. This information was gathered through testing methods that are widely accepted.

As parents, we often discuss our child's achievements and accomplishments as a cornerstone of our parenting. When I sat with the psychologist that morning, I had images of "My Child is on the Honor Roll" bumper stickers flashing through my mind. I remembered how proud I had been when Taylor was ahead of his class in math and reading; now all of that had changed. He was impaired, not only physically, but also even more profoundly in terms of intellect and cognition. What kind of bumper sticker did families like ours make? How do you share the kind of humble progress that occurs in Taylor's world?

I have never been ashamed of Taylor, but there have been times when I am made to feel like I should be. He has been treated poorly on occasion on the basis of his appearance alone. Taylor can get lost in trance-like stares, and even though he is not looking at a particular person, his stare can feel uncomfortable to others. People have asked him, "What are you looking at?" or "What is your problem?" I try to shield him from these behaviors, but I am not always successful in my attempts. His new youth and innocence, coupled with the lack of a mental filter and inhibition, can make these kinds of situations nerve-wracking.

On November 9 of this year, I shared the following story about my day out with Taylor:

> Today was not the easiest day for me, and I hope the reasons why are something you can understand. For the first year we were home, we kept our outings to places within our community and of course the hospital. With the passing of time, Taylor is able to get out to other places. Taylor has some quirks, and physical things that make the idea that he is different stand out, but not in a way that screams at you and even if they did it wouldn't matter. I suddenly have situations with Taylor that I

387

was never educated about or prepared for. Parts of those things are how some people's responses to him really sting.

He was feeling social and wanted to talk to a girl who was wearing camouflage in Michael's (he can't resist a girl in camo), and as soon as he complimented her shirt, she needed to get away and fast. It was apparent that she perceived him as some kind of creep, even though I was standing close by. Then in Pet Smart, he wanted to talk to another lady about her puppy, which he thought was a pit bull. She was having no part of that conversation. Finally he wanted to talk to a sales associate in Dick's Sporting Goods, but after his "Can I help you?" the associate didn't want to hear Taylor's answer because it involved listening for more than a few seconds. Taylor speaks slowly and can ramble, and listening requires extra patience.

All of these people were clearly uncomfortable with or annoyed by Taylor. Part of me gets it, but another part of me felt really hurt and as if we had something to be ashamed of. I am sure that I was feeling extra prickly by this point, but then we got to the register, and this lady who looked nothing less than picture-perfect was staring at Taylor. I felt like I wanted to hold up a sign that said, "I am so sorry his differences offend you!" or say, "I am sorry that he doesn't fit into the mold of your idea of what people should be." Truthfully, I am sad and sorry that this happened to my son or could happen to anyone for that matter. Why was I feeling the need to apologize for our pain?

I wanted to release the sadness inside of me, but I couldn't. I know that people who appear or behave differently than what we are used to can be disturbing and sometimes even scary, but Taylor wasn't doing anything other than making conversation. These responses made me feel like I wanted to crawl into a dark hole and disappear. If one of them would have asked what was wrong with him or something along those lines, we both would have shared. I guess that is part of why they call brain injury the invisible illness.

When we left Dick's, a young couple was entering and looked like they were just enjoying their day. I thought, "That should be Taylor. He should be with some sweet girl instead of me." We should not have to be figuring all of this out on the fly. It is easy to say to someone in my shoes, how someone responds to Taylor is their issue, but when someone acts rude, etc., it becomes our issue as well. It hurt me. And I just prayed and hoped that it did not hurt Taylor.

I did not want to bite anyone's head off. I did not want to tell them that they were being rude. I simply wanted to tell them a bit of our story, so they would understand that just because someone looks or acts different it doesn't mean it is contagious.

Among his new attributes, Taylor has gained a lot of weight over the course of the last year, creating another constant battle for him. I attribute the weight gain to many things, which we are working together to control. Taylor's indicator of satiety (the inner sensor that tells the brain that the stomach is full) is basically nonexistent. This is not a surprise because this sensation is governed by hormonal and neurological signals. Both of these are out of alignment for Taylor. Food brings Taylor a sense of happiness, and helping him learn to say "no" or walk away from a favorite food is challenging. Taylor weighs over 200 pounds; and if it were not for constant intervention, that number would rise at an alarming rate.

Taylor's body is not badly proportioned, but he is large. We notice that the more weight he puts on, the less steady he becomes on his feet. There is an area on the right side of Taylor's face where you can see a dent about the size of a small woman's palm; and because his facial muscles were cut multiple times, there is an area that appears as if the side of his face is permanently pinched. His gait is slow, and some times more than others, you can see the weakness of his left side. As the day progresses, Taylor will often shuffle instead of lifting his feet. His tiredness shows in every part of him: slurred words, slow responses, and the like.

Taylor takes pride in his self-care. He showers routinely and he can do it from start to finish on his own, which he was not able to do a year ago. He needs reminders at times about the order of things or what tasks to complete in the shower, but he has made impressive strides. His favored scent is Old Spice Swagger, and a result of his injury he rarely deviates from the products he uses. At times, his injury manifests itself in obsessive-compulsive tendencies; Taylor's hands are kept clean to the point where they are often cracked and bleeding due to excessive washing. He maintains good oral hygiene and likes to smell nice for the ladies; however, there are times when his appearance is a bit disheveled. This unkempt appearance is in stark contrast to the man he was before his fall. Taylor always took pride in being well put together and he still does, but putting himself together is hard for him. Sometimes he wears mismatched shorts over longer pants, and he is forever cutting his sleeves off his t-shirts. Just last night, I looked at him and had to suppress a giggle. He has a new way of styling his hair, which actually goes back to when he was in about seventh grade. He loads it with gel and then goes "rock star crazy." He can't quite pull off the look any more, and I was trying to explain to him that perhaps we could come up with another hairstyle.

The most notable change that I observe in Taylor's physical appearance is his countenance: Taylor often looks angry or mean. When I come in the door at the end of the day, I try to remember to smile at him and hug him. My smile results in a reciprocal response from him. And I love that smile. His affect is often flat, however, and even though he may be smiling inside, his face doesn't reflect it.

A few days ago Taylor asked me, "Do you think I am ugly because I know you think I am fat?" This kind of direct conversation is typical; we rarely have to wonder what is on Taylor's mind. I responded, "Taylor. I think you are a handsome, strong, truly amazing young man." To which he replied, "Thanks, Mom, because I thought you thought I was fat." Balancing how to speak the truth in love about his physical shell and protect his tender heart is difficult. I always keep in mind that

Taylor's self-esteem is fragile and that my role is to build him up, *there has been enough tearing down.*

Another side effect of Taylor's injury is that he experiences frequent deep depression and a strong sense of loathing for his current life. Fortunately, we are able to talk Taylor through these times, but they are excruciating to endure. Recently, he told me how much he hated having seizures. We discussed the fact that they cause unexpected fear and embarrassment along with other emotions. At the end of the conversation he confessed, "There is something good about my seizures, Mom. If I have one that is bad enough, it could kill me, and I would like to die."

My response was simple and to the point, "I would be so sad if you died, buddy." I have made peace with the fact that Taylor struggles with his new life, and that from his perspective, he sees leaving the earth as a gift. Suicidal ideation is something we were told to expect, and I try to be thankful that Taylor can express his feelings rather than stuffing his frustration. The scenarios of our days are anything but typical now, but they are often similar in the way in which they unfold.

There are a lot of issues about being Taylor's mom that I find heart-wrenching. I try not to let them steal the joy that I have also found in who he now is, but at times they do. Even as open as I have been about things that we deal with and the thoughts that haunt us continuously, there are a few things that I feel I am not permitted by some unwritten rule to share. I am finding the courage to reveal a bit more of the pain in the closing of this book. My heart pounds as I think about being so honest, and I want my forthrightness to be met with the knowledge that I cannot change our truth. Just as I have learned to embrace what is, I hope others can embrace our process and feelings about it.

Taylor and I were at a field hockey game a few months back, and he was sitting with a friend of his, playing with her baby girl. He was smitten by the natural charm of this mother and her beautiful baby, and he glowed in the awareness that the sweet baby was also taken with him. The sun was setting behind the three of them and I took a photo. A close friend who is an astute observer of both Taylor and me later spoke to me about what the picture meant to her. She hugged me and said, "If I were you, I would really wrestle with the fact that this should be Taylor's real life."

When I look at Taylor's friends, I see a lot of life changes happening for them. They are getting engaged, some are already married, and others are having their first babies. His buddies from work and school are settling into better career paths because time has given them the skills and education to have more opportunities, and some of them are wrapping up their master's programs and preparing to venture out into the world in a new way.

Being in your twenties is a time when people's lives are full of excitement, change, and new beginnings. Once the dust settles for many twenty-somethings, their future begins to take shape. Taylor has lost his career, which is a permanent loss because of his injury and what his work involved. He desperately wants to be in a relationship, and finds himself confused by the thought that no one seems to reciprocate his desires. He is currently "in love" with one of his best friends, but would also quickly latch onto a nice girl whom he considers attractive and shows him attention. Last week he told me that he was going to buy his "big sister, best friend" an engagement ring, and he could not understand why this gift is not appropriate.

His reasons were, "We have been like best friends since I graduated; my arms are bigger than her boyfriend's; I am a gentleman; and I will treat her right. And most importantly, I love her." Ultimately, for Taylor this attraction is about the fact that she is such a force of love in his life and she has a radiant inner beauty. Sadly, his attraction to her is also another avenue that feels like rejection. There is the element of not wanting to hurt Taylor, but also the element of shying away from him because the situation is uncomfortable. This is something that we have approached with his neurological psychologist, but getting to the root of these issues is often challenging because Taylor does not have an accurate perception of how off-kilter his interpersonal skills really are. In our area, which is fairly rural and remote, we do not have the types of support systems for TBI survivors that may be available in larger cities. This relative isolation makes networking about these issues less than ideal, and meeting others in the same boat as Taylor is hard.

Taylor's relationships are subjects that have caused my heart a great deal of distress. I am certain that his friends have suffered too. I deeply appreciate those who have stood with us over the last two years, but I contemplate a lot of turnover regarding his friendships. Sharing the sadness about the shift in things is a lesson in bravery, because it hurts so deeply and exposing the wounds takes a lot of courage.

Taylor was a loyal friend before his accident and continues to display that trait, but in a different way. He has misconceptions of relationships and the boundaries that come with them, but those who work with him to deal with the issues find that though challenging, a healthy relationship with him is both doable and rewarding. Sometimes it feels as if I am simply waiting for everyone to abandon him, and even though I know in my head it doesn't mean that they don't care, my heart feels devastated to see any further blows come to Taylor. Over the last several months, I have seen people slowly fade away and it never becomes any easier. I have this image of Taylor standing there looking at someone as they depart. I never knew how much I could hurt for another person. I think at times I feel it more than he does.

Taylor can spew hurtful things; he can assume the worst; and in general he suffers from confusion about how some people feel toward him. At times, he even forgets those who matter most and who love him most deeply. These problems can be resolved, but I have found they cannot be ignored. If something is avoided, it festers for Taylor; and I think many people tire of the way that Taylor's mind plays things over and over again like a broken record. When these situations cannot be addressed, Taylor is stuck with sorting them out on his own, unaware of why others may feel alienated from him.

During the first year following his accident, Taylor was shown a tremendous amount of love. Even though the rehabilitation hospital was three hours from our home, his good friends made time to come see him, and I will always value the role they played in his recovery. When we returned home, our house was full of his friends; keeping up with all of the visits was hard, but well worth it. I know that people have their own lives and time changes things, but just as Taylor has fallen away from us, his friendships have changed as well. At times when I share truth, I feel people's walls go up and their automatic defense mechanisms turn on, so I try to share only a diluted version of the truth. I tiptoe around the hurt and silently nurse the wounds it has created. I care deeply about his friends and I do not want to create more sorrow for any of us.

Losing the closeness once shared with friends is a reality for most traumatic brain injury survivors, and because of Taylor's age, it is even more apparent. Taylor also lacks the ability to relate to others on the level of intimacy that is required in deeper relationships. I am not assigning blame, but it has felt like another cruelty to have to pretend that it isn't happening. I tell myself at times to keep smiling and maybe it will hurt less, but it remains a deep wound that most people are unable to see.

Taylor always enjoys getting out with the guys, grabbing a bite to eat, or just hanging out with his peers. His friends offer him something that we cannot provide, and their presence, no matter how little or often, will always be a cherished gift. Balancing the feeling of gratitude with the pain of the struggle intensifies the emotions. But in my heart of hearts, I would love to wrap my arms around each person who has made Taylor a small part of their circle, and express the gratefulness I feel for their presence. At the same time, I see myself screaming inside, "Please don't abandon your friend. You have no idea what your presence means."

Our small tight-knit community has been good to us and welcomed us into much of their lives and world. But in contrast to that, there is also the truth that Taylor spends ninety percent of his days and evenings with his caregivers or his dad and me. The reality of his isolation makes me feel like he has been forgotten. I remember one particular day when I was consumed with an inner panic, a certainty that Taylor had been left behind. And while life continued for everyone else, my sweet son was nothing but a memory and he didn't have to be. He could be part of the present and future of his friends, not just their past.

Such an undeniable sadness gripped my heart in those moments. I reached out to one of his closest friends, and felt like pleading with her to not forget my son. Upon hearing my voice, she began to cry. She welcomed my emotions, she accepted my struggle, and she wept with me for our Taylor. She chose not to downplay the cruelty of it all, and instead of causing me more sorrow, she had given me the sweet balm of comfort and acceptance of the truth.

It was one of the lowest moments, realizing that after Taylor lost so much of his life, I couldn't stand to watch him lose any more. After such a great deal of pain, suffering and struggle, there was more to come. Letting go of what I cannot change, deciding what to fight for and speak about, led to a small death within my soul. I watched another inner light go out, and I knew that part of myself had been forever altered.

The length of time involved in Taylor's recovery has been surprising. I believe people have grown tired of what traumatic brain injury has meant. I am tired too; one day this unwelcome presence invaded our lives and nothing has been the same since its arrival. Only part of me understands the distance the injury created between Taylor and his peers. The other part of me is a broken mother who wants her son to have all that he can despite this cruelty.

If I were to have one wish that could be granted for Taylor, it would be for him to find a new place where he can belong. I long for him to have less pain, less isolation, and just to be more welcomed into the circle of other people's lives. Welcoming him means accepting him, and accepting him means dealing with some of the complexities of brain injury. I am acutely aware of the challenges, and I know that they can present obstacles that may be too hard for some to get beyond.

The absence of some friends has profoundly affected his recovery, along with my ability to show grace and forgiveness when I feel that he has been slighted. There is no blame to be placed; it is so complicated, with so many layers and perhaps none of us know how to properly get through them. But from my perspective, Taylor needs his friends, and while their lives continue, he misses them.

My frustration does not take away from the friends who are present and those who despite the struggle try their best to stay. I just can't make excuses for people when I see Taylor's absolute joy in his friendships and what the presence of others means to his recovery. Not having his peers around cuts deeper than many of the wounds associated with his injury. It is a cruelty that can be avoided and that makes it more frustrating. To negate this truth would be an injustice to stories like Taylor's, so I tell it in the hope that it is understood. The loss of relationships is a devastating aftermath of an injury for people like Taylor.

Another source of continual turmoil is associated with Taylor's caregiving needs. We have been very fortunate in that we have had capable and caring people to spend their days with Taylor. Each person involved has been exceptional. That being said, the emotional tightrope that has to be walked is hard. I would describe his caregivers' roles as challenging. I have no earthly idea of why his condition is so full of mazes and maps, but perhaps because of Taylor's age, his personal issues, and all of the dynamics combined, it has been one of the most stress-producing aspects of this ordeal. One thing that makes it difficult is that it is new to all of us. For those who were simply his friend or "fun" aunt before, they now have to entertain him for eight hours at a time. They had to learn the delicate balance of his moods and his new interpretation of the world around him.

As the coordinator of his care, I have felt every bump in the road. Fortunately, we have had two of the same people for a year, but unfortunately, three have left due to getting new and rewarding jobs. Just last week, my Tuesday and Thursday caregiver resigned, as she was presented with a great professional opportunity, and I am panicked about what her departure means for Taylor and us. Because she was so exceptionally good with Taylor, it was hard to see her go. How long can this road continue? What is next? I wish that those closest to us could walk the road for a few days and understand how tender and on edge it seems that everything is, because at times I feel isolated and misunderstood. The constant pressure never seems to let up. I have reached out to other families to try to improve how we do things, but most of them either do not rotate caregivers, or one of the parents, spouses or another family member has taken on that role full time.

My friends tell me that I deal well with all this commotion, which is why people are surprised when I express how bad I am feeling. I have never felt safe or comfortable with anger, so feeling chronically angry is new for me. More than anything I am angry at Taylor's injury, but the continuum of chaos it creates stifles my ability to cope at times. After two years, things are supposed to be better and they aren't. They are different and challenging in new ways.

One morning recently, my mom and I were discussing the fact that I need to implement some self-care in my routine. Having to tackle so many new roles is wearing me down and affecting my ability to enjoy life and my other relationships. I have felt a bit like a drowning person and that no one really notices enough to throw me a life preserver. Everyone seems to be cheering, "You can do it, Nicole!" but there are days when I am left gasping for air, trying to rise above the currents swirling around me, and feeling wiped out in the process. These emotions ebb and flow, but at the same time they feel permanent and unyielding.

This is the dimension of caregiving that is hard. I glean enough information from other TBI families to know that we are not alone in the absolute distress that comes to pass. These times call for us to sink or swim; it is one or the other. This is where character is built, but am I strong enough to go this distance?

Over the last two years, I appeared strong through everything, and now I feel tired and weak. When the conversation with my mom was finished, after many tears, some shouting, and everything in between, I walked away knowing that I will have to work harder to take care of my needs.

Later that day, Taylor and I kept an appointment with his neurologist-surgeon at Geisinger for a follow-up visit. He had been asking a lot of questions recently about the night he fell. He claims to have memories of it, but his recollections seem to be more like filling in the gaps. Admittedly, his memories are haunting and chilling to me. This was the night that Taylor lost the life he once had, and he deserves answers to some questions.

I worked up the courage to discuss with his surgeon some facts about the night he fell, and to clear up any gray areas that I might have. In the beginning, I did not care how Taylor got to the bottom of the stairs. I cared about the fact that he might not survive. All my energies were focused, not on why or how his accident happened, but on bringing him home as much as possible.

Over the last year and a half, I have met many families who dealt with preventable accidents and other simple instances of happenstance. Some brain injuries occurred because of failure to wear a helmet while riding a motorcycle, or a new driver's inability to navigate treacherous roads in bad weather. Some injuries were the direct result of one poor decision resulting in a change that would haunt many for the rest of their lives. Other injuries were as unusual as that of a man whose head collided with his water ski while enjoying a sunny afternoon on a lake, or as cruel as that of a woman whose skull was crushed by a large rock thrown intentionally from a highway overpass. There were even those injuries for which there will never be an answer. Some recoveries were inspiring, while others came to a sudden halt with no forward motion.

No one deserved the predicament they were now in and might seemingly remain forever. In the case of Taylor's rehabilitation facility, no matter how you arrived there, you were broken and they were there to put you back together as much as they could. One family did not deserve better care than another, and we all mattered equally. People celebrated baby steps and commiserated about setbacks. The staff members at Bryn Mawr were extraordinarily special because they never placed blame on a survivor or their family. They gave instead healing, hope, and goodness. There were different pieces to the puzzle regarding the night of Taylor's fall, and all of them came together to create a terrible outcome.

Taylor had always been tired in the weeks prior to Thanksgiving of 2012. As I stated in the early chapters, he worked atypically long hours performing a physically demanding job. Because he was young, and strong, he was pushed to his professional limits. He was excessively sleepy and he should have rested more. He had been cranky for a long time, and it had affected his mood for many months. My last e-mail from him was an ongoing discussion regarding a change in his career, and it was to be a positive step in his life.

Along with his job, Taylor was frustrated about some aspects of his personal life and his relationships within our family unit. Taylor was at a low point and had been working through some difficult emotional elements that are not unusual for someone in his twenties but are painful nevertheless. He was good at hiding his discontent among his peers, but those closest to him understood that he was in real pain. He was fighting hard to find himself and find his way to a good life, but it wasn't easy. His self-esteem was suffering and so were his relationships. In fact, relations had been strained between Taylor and each one of us in his immediate family. We had all been worried about him. Suddenly we were outsiders looking in, and it seemed as if Taylor had forgotten those who truly mattered most. I know that twenty-one-year-olds are not typically wrapped up in their younger siblings or their mom and dad, but we missed him. I was always able to see the love inside that Taylor had for us. Taylor was uncomfortable with the level of emotion he felt, but it was there and it was part of his tenderness. Looking back, he was in a much more fragile place than anyone knew.

Did these pieces play a part in the puzzle? I truly don't know. But I do think Taylor had less regard for the fragility of his own life. The final piece is something I have struggled deeply to address. Taylor was with his friends in the hours leading up to his fall. They were gathered for Thanksgiving Eve, and they were socializing and drinking. Sometime around 48 hours or so after the fall, one of the doctors met with us and went over some facts. This type of discussion is routine following an accident; there were no drugs in his system (no surprise there), but there was alcohol. Had a non-alcohol-related neurological event happened inside his brain prior to his fall? It is possible, but no one will ever know because the source of the damage could not be pinpointed after the fact.

We knew he had been drinking. At the time, his blood alcohol level was just one number on a list of many others factors that had been explained. I was not looking for something to blame; I was looking for a way out of the nightmare we were in. I wanted Taylor to wake up, to survive, and to be okay; I did not have energy to address much else.

On a December day two years later, I asked his neurologist-surgeon to make clear how much Taylor had had to drink and whether his alcohol level could have played a role in his fall. And it did. That is the cold hard gut-wrenching truth. When I first started writing this book, I did not know the full significance of what I am writing now. Perhaps I could not have handled that reality because whenever Taylor's drinking was mentioned, I felt defensive and irate within myself. It produced a reaction I was not prepared for; it still does. The notion that any of this pain may have been preventable haunts me.

Taylor had had too much to drink the night he fell and his drinking played a part in what occurred. That does not change my love for him, and I hope it won't change the hearts of others toward him either. Sometimes good people make bad choices. When the doctor told me the details, she did not belabor them or discuss them in depth. She simply stated the truth: Taylor had drunk more than he should have. He did not drive that night, but nonetheless he put his own life in danger. I know that because he almost died, and perhaps had that one element changed, this book would not have had to be written. Sometimes good things come together and something wonderful occurs, and at other times bad things collide and a nightmare results.

There are many reasons why this issue is hard to address. It causes every fiber of my being to tremble, and yet it is a fact that I cannot ignore. I wrestle with wanting to gloss over it, but in my heart I think that would be cowardly. Taylor's actions played a part in his fall, and we will never know what might have been had he made a different decision. At times, people suggested to me that if Taylor had been drinking he *deserved* his injury, and that it should be a lesson to others. This attitude adds such heartache and pressure to an already pain-filled situation. Taylor got together with his friends for an enjoyable night of reconnecting and reuniting with those who were off at school or other places. It was a well-intentioned group with the simple objective of having fun together. No one ever would have imagined the outcome, and had they imagined it, the night would not have ended as it did.

All the opinions and feelings of other people sit on my shoulders like a thousand-pound boulder. Will people judge Taylor and take the view that "you made your bed, now you get to lie in it"? How many will turn their backs on him, and how many will say, "I told you so."? I hope the answer is zero. The fact that Taylor was intoxicated when he fell is part of a multi-faceted puzzle with many pieces—some of which still remain unknown.

I have been unable to write for close to a month. The book is coming to an end and I am afraid. I fear that the truth will cause more pain. I fear that Taylor will lose more than he already has. I wonder whether the consequence of sharing the truth will be worth it. I worry that instead of creating understanding for the wounds we carry, my words may stir up more turmoil, but ultimately I have to share the truth I have. I have to practice my own form of bravery. I have to believe that expressing the truth will set us free from some of the hurt and that maybe it will somehow free others as well. Taylor is an amazing person who along with many others would give a lot to ensure his accident had never happened. But it did.

Chapter Thirty-two
The Greatest Lessons of All
January 1, 2015

This is the final chapter of my book, but it is far from the end of our story. If I were to write another book, I could title it *1,000 Lessons I Learned Along the Way* and still not cover all the territory involved in traumatic brain injury. Since the first second of Taylor's fall, the universe has been teaching me new things. The first lesson was that our family is stronger than we ever imagined and love one another more than we ever realized. Our love had been present before, but this crisis catapulted us into the deeper depths of not only despair but also love. Love that is about far more than emotion and feeling, this love is defined in constant action . . . a driving force that doesn't quit. This love says I will be present for you even when you are unable to be present for yourself. It is unyielding and powerful.

This love can fight through the nights in the intensive care unit when you are told your son may not survive. This love can help you return home and research acute rehabilitation hospitals despite the exhaustion of a twelve-hour day at the hospital. This love can stand up and say, "I will give thanks for this moment, no matter how much it feels like hell." This love can be quiet even when you want to scream because there is no noise allowed in the recovery room. And this love can find its way to the chapel, and even though there may be no words to say, this love can sit, and feel, and trust. This love stands up in the middle of insurance denials and endless runarounds, and it does not wave a flag of surrender but instead claims, "I can stand my ground for as long as I need to until this is made right." This love declares I will not leave you, Taylor, even when it is hard to stay, I will be here. This love is full of fight, strength, and courage, and is both soft as a kitten and fierce as a lion. But this love does not always come easily.

Some of the lessons learned brought with them tremendous struggle while others felt rewarding and victorious. As I am writing this, a fire is roaring in our wood stove, and I am looking at my bare Christmas tree. The fabric garland and the rusty jingle bells have been taken off, but one ornament remains hanging among the lights. It is a small wooden sign that Taylor helped to make. The sign reads, "Love Wins."

You may recall that "Love Wins" was one of the phrases that we hung in Taylor's hospital room in the weeks after his fall. The phrase was typed in large font on a simple sheet of paper, hung with a family photo that had been taken the year before—but other than those simple words, his room was bare. The thought was adopted from another family who had endured great sorrow and loss. Tanner called it to our attention, and we loved the meaning it represents.

As Taylor's mother, it has been challenging for me to see beyond the pain that this has caused not only for Taylor, but also our whole family. As you are already aware, it has shaken each of us to our innermost core. There have been times when I was certain I would be stuck in the black pit of despair forever, but I wasn't and neither was anyone else. When our hearts revisit those feelings, I remind myself that they come to an end and we move on. That being said, the aftermath of Taylor's accident on my other sons has torn me apart inside, and has brought me to my knees with undeniable force. Not only has Taylor suffered, but at times those around him have endured a much greater agony.

Can you find light in darkness? Is there joy in times of great sorrow? Are you able to laugh on the same day as you have previously shed a million tears? Will you recognize the gift of life in the presence of potential death? The answer for me is yes. Some days my "yes" is said with confidence and other days with defeat, but I know that I believe in the power of our ability to press through whatever we face.

I have had many occasions over the last two years when I am incredibly aware that life, even with its moments of great distress and sorrow, is still profoundly lovely, magical, and full of opportunities. I am aware of the drops of dew on the spring grass, the pink hue hidden in the sunrise on a cold winter's day, the gentle warmth of the sun on my back in midsummer, and the changing of leaves as autumn finds its home in the mountains.

I am more aware of touching, seeing, feeling, tasting, smelling, hearing, and my own ability to take it all in. I have told myself on particularly painful days that being able to feel, comprehend, and understand sorrow is a gift in itself. I am now filled with the knowledge that the absence of these things may mean that life has ceased. I would rather feel pain than be lost in a bottomless void of nothingness.

When Taylor's body erupts in a seizure and he begins to shake, *I hate it*, but I must embrace the gift that comes in my being able to be present with him through it. I recognize that he could be trapped in this world without me, without us, and without love . . . and that would be most excruciating. I am acutely aware that the alternative to all of this may have been his death. The whole of his person, gone forever, except for in our memories.

Taylor's issues on certain days seem crueler and more prominent than others, but he possesses some remarkable qualities that make me look at the world in a different light. He finds great joy in the simple things. When he is happy or surprised by a moment of good news, he will tuck his elbows close to his side, open and close his fist, and while pumping his arms back and forth, he yells, "YES! YES! YES!" with as much enthusiasm as a child who is getting a new puppy might exert.

He manages to work through his frustration and that is awe-inspiring to witness. Taylor cannot have certain belongings that he used to be able to use freely. Things like car keys, some of his hunting equipment, and other potentially dangerous items must be kept under lock and key or outside our home. This restriction is always a sore spot for Taylor, but he sorts through it, and sometimes we can find an alternative. For example, Taylor used to have an extensive firearm collection for hunting. On Christmas, he was disappointed that he did not receive more hunting paraphernalia and openly expressed his dissatisfaction. Today, we went to Dick's Sporting Goods and shopped. He had to be told again what is off limits and why, and we looked into some other options. For Taylor, it is about relearning the rules of life and renegotiating some of the boundaries. We decided on a pellet gun, some paper targets, and some other fun items. The day started off with his feeling frustrated about the limits placed on him, but by the day's end, he came into the house and proudly proclaimed, "I am one lucky boy!"

Taylor takes great pride in his recovery and celebrates his success when given the chance. He loves to flex and show his biceps, trapezoids, and abdominal muscles. We recently returned to the hospital where he had spent months recovering. This was his first time returning since his discharge a year and a half earlier. Taylor embraced every doctor, nurse, therapist, secretary, and nursing assistant that he could. When I asked if he remembered them and in some cases he didn't, he would say, "No, but that's okay." Then he would wrap his huge arms around them and hug them, saying, "Thank you" or "Love you." Taylor recognizes what these people did for his recovery and has enough awareness to know what they mean to him. For those he was able to recognize, his demeanor, words of thanks, and warmth expressed the level of gratitude he felt.

This Christmas, Taylor decided to give two funny gifts. Keith had been roaming around the house singing, "I want a hippopotamus for Christmas, only a hippopotamus will do" for a month, and Taylor, taking the song literally, wanted to find him one. He took great joy in finding a small lifelike replica in a local store, keeping the gift a secret, and then wrapping it and holding onto the surprise and joy of giving a humorous gift. He laughed deeply and fully as his dad opened the hippo, and said, "Well, you got what you wanted." For Tanner, Taylor's heart was set on finding a monkey because Tanner insisted he wanted a live monkey as a gift. Taylor wanted to get him a live one, yet he knew that would not be possible, so he settled on another replica and took such pure delight in granting these wishes.

From time to time, we will meet with friends who have suffered crushing losses. Taylor is always mindful of their situations and wants to ease their pain. He remembers what they have been through and respects their grief. He relates to sadness, and will do what he can to ease another person's burden.

He has regular heart-to-heart conversations with the mother of a friend from his high school years, whose son committed suicide several years ago. He feels her sadness and he wants to help her. He participated in a fundraiser to raise awareness of the importance of suicide

406

prevention, and he encouraged those in his circle to be a part of it. He ponders with thoughtfulness the sadness associated with other friends who have lost siblings and children.

Perhaps one of the greatest moments of seeing Taylor's excellent spirit shine through was when we visited another traumatic brain injury survivor's family. This was the first time that Taylor had joined me in this fashion, and I felt that he was ready. I had gone to the hospital other times on my own to meet with families whose loved ones were suddenly in the throes of traumatic brain injury, but Taylor had not. During the ride over, Taylor was feeling blue and then had a stressful session with his neurologist-psychologist that involved some reality checks. Taylor cried during the session as he shared how difficult his day-to-day struggle was, and as we headed over to the rehab hospital, I knew he had to get into a different mindset. Switching gears can be hard for Taylor.

On the ride over, I talked to him about how the family might want to ask him some hard questions, and that he should share with them openly and honestly. I also asked him what he thought they needed from us. We discussed hope and encouragement. Their survivor was almost killed in a horrific intentional act of violence when some teenagers threw a rock from an overpass that landed on her car, causing extensive damage to her frontal lobe. This family is precious, loving, and strong, but I knew the toll that rehab, brain injury, and the thought of a lower level of functioning being your new life can take. I wanted to give them a glimpse into where they might be able to go with their loved one. I wanted Taylor to give them hope.

As we entered the room, the survivor's husband and parents received us warmly. They had some firsthand knowledge of what it must have been like for Taylor to get to where he is in his recovery, and they made him feel significant and important. Taylor spoke words of love and encouragement to them, and they poured their own goodness right back on us. At the close of our visit, Taylor indicated to me that he had brought them a gift—three "Team Taylor" bracelets. He took them off and gave them to the family members one by one as their survivor slept quietly. Taylor told them that she was going to improve, and that he would pray for her. When we left, he said, "That poor lady, Mom. She is so broken." Bearing witness to that level of compassion, love, and goodness in the human spirit is a rare gift. This is what the phrase "Love Wins" means, and this is an example of beauty in the face of tragedy.

Life is beautiful, even when it feels ugly.

One of the greatest pleasures I have on many nights is tucking Taylor in. Taylor is now twenty-four years old. He is six feet tall, and weighs over two hundred pounds. But he is once again my little boy. Keith and I take turns with the bedtime routine, and it is something we both find rewarding. Usually between nine and ten p.m., Taylor starts getting tired. He will climb into Keith's side of the bed and stay there while giggling. Those of you with children of your own can picture the scenario. Taylor wants to fall asleep in our bed, and he hopes he won't be moved. He settles in underneath the warm blanket, but for obvious reasons he can't stay there. So eventually he gives in and is ready to be tucked into his own bed. The routine of getting to bed is time-consuming. Taylor moves slowly while going to the bathroom (he has to pee before bed and will not go to bed until he has done so); then he washes his hands, brushes his teeth, puts in his retainer, and finally is ready for the tucking-in part. We settle him and his faithful companion (our dog Ginger) underneath the covers, and they are almost ready for sleepy town. He looks sweet and innocent, and you can see that in his mind he is nowhere near twenty-four years old. The final task is when he applies his lip balm, which is part of his bedtime ritual. After I turn out the light and say our "I love you's," he reminds me that if I want to rub his back while he falls asleep, I can. He almost always calls us back in to ask us one more random question before drifting off. Keith and I both treasure these tender moments.

Taylor's "Yes" continues to be expressed by using the phrase "I can" or "we can," and his "No" is expressed as "we don't have to." There is some kind of communication barrier that inhibits a straightforward "yes" or "no" response.

Taylor has found a renewed sense of laughter, a real sense of kindness, and a spirit of triumph from overcoming hurdle after hurdle. His ability to push through physical, emotional, and even spiritual challenges is absolutely astonishing. I believe that Taylor is where he is because of who he is at his core. The part of him that was always there and still is, is part of what has made his recovery work.

Taylor's life brings joy and inspiration to others, and I am proud to know him. I am proud to be his mom. And as much as I hate that this injury happened, I stand firm in my refusal for it to steal more from our lives. There are days when defeat feels much closer than victory, but the victory comes when we face the next day together as a strong family. Victory lies in not quitting and moving ahead day after day.

I still often wonder what Taylor's future holds. Will he get married? Is being a father even physically possible? How long will he live? Will he work again? The answers to these questions have a direct effect on my future as well. I feel like I do not see many of his previously held dreams coming true, but maybe he can create new dreams.

I have had the honor of meeting other heroes and overcomers along the way. Each traumatic brain injury survivor and family has a special place in my heart. I have been witness to such incredibly strong people, facing horrible losses and circumstances and still shining brightly. I have witnessed agonizing recovery scenarios. I have seen some beat the odds, though others have not been as fortunate. But each one of them is like a shining star, beaming rays of light to the world that they are in. The lessons I have learned as I have delved further into what traumatic brain injury means have altered and changed who I am as a person.

I miss the old Taylor terrifically. I miss the person that he was so much that it produces a physical ache in my body at times. I miss his grin, his gait, the way he held his shoulders. I miss the way he smelled and expressed himself. I miss his abilities and wonder whether I will ever see him do a flip off a pier again, or reel in a fish with a calm twinkle in his eyes. I miss his really knowing me, and who I am, and the bond we share. Taylor was bright, handsome, and full of so much promise . . . and now much of that has changed. One thing remains the same—he is still so very amazing to me.

In the lyrics to one of my favorite Ben Howard songs are the words, "Gracious goes the ghost of you, my dear." I feel at times that we are living with a ghost of Taylor, and in some ways ourselves. I remind myself that in order to fully move on, to bring the most healing that we can have, we must embrace the changes that have come. We cannot afford to fight them. In releasing the struggle, we can also overcome some of the pain, and perhaps we can find wholeness in ourselves that we imagined to be lost. If I could have one more moment before Taylor's fall, I know what I would say to him . . .

I am so very proud of you and I will always love you. I am grateful for each impression you left behind. This is the song my heart has written for you.

In your birth,
I see you as a little gem,
first entering my broken world,
coming to revive my belief in humanity,
And the possibility of what my life could be.

Your cheeks were pink and rosy,
each offering their own sweet
baby scent to me.
The nurses said you were
exceptionally big,
tipping the scales past nine pounds,
but your fullness
fit in my small arms,
Perfectly.
You were my firstborn,
I felt you were
all mine,

but was willing to share you.
You showed me a love that I did not know myself to be
Capable of.

As an infant,
You grew
not too fast,
not to slow,
But in a way that felt right.

We shared many firsts;
I remember,
your first step.
Watching you walk was a beautiful
swirling blend of
fear and delight.
Our little beagle puppy
watched you.
I sat across from you
on the warm linoleum and cheered you on.
And then clapped
When the five-step mission was complete.

Two years later we gave you
a baby brother.
You wanted a puppy or an Elmo instead.
But once he came
you were almost as in love with him as me.
He was yours,
but you were willing to share.
We named him Avery, and you called him
Avery-doodle.
You sang to him,
And made sure that everyone knew

411

Who he was.

Two years later,
Baby boy number three arrived,
But you would always be the first of the
Bingaman Boys, and you led the way
Well.

The first day of school came.
You were ready to go.
A shining five-year-old,
wearing nautical gear
and sporting a
jungle backpack,
with a wonderful smile.
I promised myself I would reflect your joy.
You were unafraid,
walking away with confidence
I was fighting the urge to stop time.
I wanted to hold you close to me,
And never have to let you go.
I smiled until you were out of sight,
then the tears fell.

A few months later
we made a vegetable rainbow
in kindergarten class.
Together,
for what I imagine would be
Always.
Other mothers told me how quickly time
Would pass,
But I had no understanding of that concept.

The years were filled with
beach memories,
baseball games,
trips to Atlanta,
Sunday morning Children's Church,
making brownies,
holidays and everyday events,
like
playing with the cousins or the brothers in the yard.

Living life
while loving you,
and our family.

You often walked in the shadow of your dad
Throwing his clothes and boots on once,
And crawling into our bed with them
Still on.

When you were about twelve years old,
We shared
a meteor shower viewing,
that you
Excitedly
told everyone about.
In that same year,
We watched
"Little Women" on PBS,
which you made me promise
not to tell a soul you enjoyed.
I rejoiced that you liked
PBS beyond Big Bird.
It was our secret.

In middle school
you dabbled in art,
and felt proud of your drawings,
and the things you created.
Your design was chosen for the cover of the
Art Show Invitation
That love slowly slipped away,
but the treasures remained on the shelf,
in my closet,
and most of all
Within my heart.

I can see you at your
Sweet Sixteen party,
Jumping in the pool
At the YMCA,
Laughing with your friends
And later saying,
"Thanks, Mom, for the best party ever!"

There were prom nights,
Homecoming dances, and
You being crowned the
Sweetheart King.
We picked up Mallory,
And you nervously told her how pretty she looked
In her black dress,
You wore a shirt from
American Eagle,
And looked as handsome as ever.

The summer of your junior year
You would experience your first love,
And I would wonder how others would compare.

I enjoyed each moment of watching you mature,
And they made me proud to be your mother.
You were a good person,
And a good boy.

You truly brought
More than
Sunshine to me.

More days passed
And suddenly they had become
Years.
You grew up
with a desire to work
And earn money.
Your were passionate about
Big trucks
That made loud noises.
You never tired of
hunting,
fishing,
and your dog.
You were intelligent about the great outdoors,
And that stood out to me.

I was grateful
That somewhere in all of your manhood
You kept a space for me.

Before I knew it
you became an adult,
and people always said
that we should be proud of you.

We were so proud of you,
And
we still are . . .

I anticipated with joy
what time would reveal for your future.
I knew it would all work out,
The way it was supposed to be.

I never imagined the struggle
That would come to be,
Yours, mine,
And our family's.
The story is being written
And the end remains unseen.
The impressions you left behind
play beautifully in my mind.

For as long as I live and breathe
There will never be,
A single moment in time
When you are not loved
By me.

Part VI: Taylor's Brothers

Two Years Later
By: Avery Bingaman

Taylor and I were brothers; we still are brothers, this is something no event has the power to take away from us. We got into trouble, we scrapped; he knocked people down a few pegs when they picked on me because the only person allowed to pick on me was—yep, you guessed it—he himself. We enjoyed nature together, we played sports together, we made small talk, and we exchanged hearts in conversation about girls and all the other things that trouble teenage boys. What existed in our brotherhood was far from perfect, but love resonated from every angle and direction of our relationship. Every relationship hits a rough patch at one point or another, and ours has been no different. In order for you to grasp where Taylor and I stand today, it is imperative that you have an understanding for where it was prior to November 2012, prior to the evil presence that snatched my brother away—a presence that only occasionally gives back fractions of the pieces it took away.

During the months precluding his accident, Taylor and I drifted apart from each other. The divide was by no means to that of non-communication, or anything of the ugly sort. However, our relationship was nothing to brag about. I had found my friends, he found his. He took his road and I took mine, and we ended up in completely different places. He was in a rough spot at the time-- and as I slowly emerged from my own, it just didn't work out for us to have a strong relationship. Did that stop us from hanging out, laughing, occasionally crying, and all the best things relationships hold? Of course not, we were just different.

Different. What a powerfully simple word to describe what our lives became that Thanksgiving Day. Returning home from college, the first people I cared to see that day were my old high school friends. Tanner and I drove to a friend's house, played some games, caught up, and came home early that morning. Taylor was not home yet, and being restless teenagers, we set up shop in his bedroom to play video games on the tube. After several short hours, we heard the front door open, accompanied by some rustling outside his bedroom door—no big deal. A few minutes later, we heard the real crash. To this day, two years later, I truly haven't the slightest idea why Taylor even started to go downstairs because his room is upstairs, but no matter how many questions I ask, it

419

will never change reality. I used to suppress the idea of one decision holding the power to change your life, but now I've shaken off the ambiguity and know it's a very real thing. That step, I promise you, changed Taylor's life for the worse. Brain injuries exhibit a ripple effect, and the cyclical pattern has a way of persistently creating more ripples, more pain.

As you know, Taylor took a tumble down the flight of stairs that still haunts my parents' home. Tanner and I stormed out of his room, peered down the steps, and saw him lying there . . . motionless at the bottom of the stairs, and bleeding ever so slightly from his head. We cautiously but quickly walked downstairs to see how badly he was hurt, but from our observations, nothing severe happened. Blood from a cut clumped his short hair together, but he maintained breathing on his own and appeared simply out of it as if asleep but unconsciously agitated. After some debate and not being able to wake him, we handed the power to the team behind the infamous number 9-1-1. I absolutely hate having to dial it, and that Thanksgiving morning was only my second time. While at my Grammy's as a youngster, I managed to call for the police because she had forced me to take a nap. I don't regret either instance. However, I do regret my ignorance and naiveté about brain injuries, and the possibility of one not even crossing my mind when Taylor fell.

The early morning hours after Thanksgiving droned on to my dismay. After The EMTs trudged in, slapped Taylor on the gurney just like any other job, off they went to the hospital, leaving me to examine the incident. What does one do in this situation? The feelings and happenings of that night are forever scorched into the confines of my memory, but as I try to describe them, the words would be unspeakably inadequate and insufficient. Nevertheless, off went Taylor, flying in a helicopter whose sound still makes me cringe to this day.

When my parents found out, their reactions appeared at different ends of the spectrum. Dad's calm manner and collected character showed through as usual, but you could tell he still had not gathered his senses since being woken up. Mom on the other hand poured immediate tears, not necessarily tears of sadness, but of anger. Each one of them cried the

420

same series of words, "How could you do this, Taylor?" Was it his fault? No, of course not; but her sentiments remained uncontrollable in such a situation; mother's instinct.

Allow me to fast-forward a bit to save repeating what you already know. Where are we now?

Post-surgery, the entirety of my family's situation spiraled downward towards a black pit holding demons Dante didn't face. I once maintained the mindset that every spiral has a rock bottom, but the bottom of this particular one proved nonexistent as it widened into an opening abyss that grew increasingly deeper with each passing moment. Taylor spent some significant time in the ICU, both immediately after and later on in the story, which I am sure you now know. My time with Taylor came late that first night in the ICU. I'm usually awake during the day, but I live most of my life in the late night and early morning hours, and since I lived closest to the hospital, it made sense for me to be on the night's watch. One of the only times in my life I embrace having an abnormal sleep schedule was during this time when I wanted to be at Taylor's side.

One of the conversations that commonly replays in my head is one with a doctor whose name I cannot recall. It took place a few weeks after the accident, as the medical team continued the process of bringing Taylor to a more stable state. I remember sitting in a room with my parents as Tanner sat in school. The doctor, looking me in the eyes so genuinely, and asking how I was. I was speechless, so I just sat and cried. I felt the most hopeless of hopes stand over me, drive its nails into my shoulders, and keep me from ever believing in a return to normalcy. The doctor paid attention in her psychology classes because she read me like a book—a feat most people who know me cannot claim. She assured me that no matter how I reacted the night of The Fall, the outcome would have been exactly the same. The damage occurred during the impact of skull with floor, not in time that followed.

The doctor also encouraged me to consider dropping my classes for the semester and taking family time. After a lot of internal struggle, I couldn't bring myself to take a leave of absence. School was the only place I went where no one knew my name or what my story entailed, I embraced it. Was it the right decision? I believe so. However, it matters not at this stage, but I paid for it both that semester and for the ones that followed. I can live with the decision I made.

Sitting quietly in a room with an unresponsive someone you love brings out a whole new set of emotions you would think you were incapable of feeling or enduring. Many times I sat alone with Taylor, thinking about the lone bellow of the hospital corridors. Other times, I had a friend or family member by my side.

My best advice for finding comfort in this kind of situation: talk to someone more or less removed from it. My comfort was found in a friend I hold most dear to my heart. She listened during my atrabilious moods. When I sulked in anger, confusion, helplessness, and even when I put forth shades of falsified happiness- she listened. Find strength in the people around you, and feed off of it when you've none of your own.

I can honestly say that I have made and lost more friends in the past few years than in the previous eighteen. The things I dealt with allowed me to weed out the people who didn't want the best for me, and who practiced absenteeism when I needed them most. The weeding started immediately. Now it's apparent that some people have no idea how to react to a given situation, and it shows through their words and actions. Ultimately, it's up to you how you react to them, up to you how you want your garden to look.

I spent a whole lot of time with Taylor when he moved to the Special Care Unit. He lay there breathing but emotionless for the most part. I frequently cozied up on a chair and did a little bit of studying, reading, or writing. Times were lonely; sitting in a dark room with no one to talk to at three in the morning wears on you after several weeks of it. There was one particular nurse who worked in the SCU, a lady by the name of Heather, an absolute gem. She was there if I cared to talk about what was happening to Taylor; she was there if I wanted to talk about travel, and to spark laughter in a time when my heart required a smile. I've met and dealt with enough nurses to know the best from the worst, and Heather was among the greatest. It's important to find comfort in those who care for your loved one, and she showed both Taylor and me so much compassion and love in times when we needed it the most. We shared conversation on a lot of heartfelt topics, she kept me in check with the reality of the situation, while reminding me that hope should not be disregarded. She made sure I took care of me just as much as I tried to be there for Tayl.

You hear people telling you to take care of yourself, or your worth to your loved one plummets. It becomes an annoyance and a hassle listening to it day in and day out, but in my experience some of these people know what they are talking about. Every one of my family members and friends close to the situation admits they hit a breaking point at one point or another, and they took a temporary—and occasionally permanent—leave. I hit more than one wall along the way; at times I pulled my hair out at 5 a.m., waiting for Mom to relieve me of my shift. This period lasted several weeks, leading up to the other winter holiday forever tormenting my memory.

The day came that I thought I had prepared myself for, but clearly I was wrong. After Tanner and Mom had scoped out some rehabilitation facilities for Taylor, we were essentially cornered into a situation where only one place wanted to deal with Taylor . . . Bryn Mawr. What a blessing that turned out to be. That December, the day came and Taylor was going to be moved. It hurt because he wasn't going to be twenty-five minutes away, he was soon to reside in a temporary home two hours away. I remember the transport team loading him up, my internal pleading for Taylor to open his eyes, to give me a thumbs-up, for anything to let me know that he was still in there somewhere. Nothing. They loaded him up, made him as comfortable as he could be on a rock-hard bed, and I stood in the hallway crying with Mom. I'm generally not much of a weeper; a few times in the initial stages I let the tears flow freely, but I usually bottle them up. Not this time, I felt like I had lost him all over again.

In order to save time and get into the heart of what I want to talk about, I'm going to hit the fast-forward arrow again and trust that Mom covered Bryn Mawr with the passion and love it deserves. I'm going to pick up with Taylor's homecoming. Pardon my lack of remembrance for the exact date, but that entire year fused into one miserable continuum.

The day Taylor returned home marks a significant point for our relationship: the downward trend. We had our moments at Bryn Mawr when his uncontrollable tongue lashed out at us, but for an injury like Taylor's, you just have to tough it out and hope it gets better.

"Hope remains hopeless; the joke is that it's always there." This line from The Milk Carton Kids has resonated in my life, but not because it's what I wanted to believe; because it was a forcing of the heart. Needless to say, hope fell upon deaf ears. It didn't improve for Taylor and me. For some reason he never wanted my help, advice, or assistance, unless in a position where a physical constraint limited him. Only then did he ask for help.

Tanner and I are in a tough spot, because no matter what changes Taylor's brain undergoes, we always play the same role with him: little brothers. Any of you with siblings know about the ongoing hierarchy accompanying brother- and sisterhood. This characteristic isn't something foreign or present only in the millennial generation; its presence thrived as a commonality throughout history. Whatever phenomenon explains the brain barrier that tells the older party he or she is in charge was heightened to the extreme at some point during Taylor's trials, exhibiting the generational hierarchy persistence.

We've all been around someone whom we never please, and this is where Taylor and I stand now. Does he love me? Yes, it shows for the first few minutes or maybe an hour if I'm lucky when I go to my parents' house. Sometimes it lasts a bit longer if I've returned from abroad, or my parents have company; nonetheless, being the little brother means that everything I say is null and void. Do I love him? Of course I do, but that can't mask the loathing sentiments I feel towards parts of the new and unimproved Taylor.

To begin, my Grandbunny (Mom's mom) visited one week to help out with Taylor, give us her love, and provide a light in one of the times we needed her most. I have a very loving and ever-growing relationship with her that I'll forever treasure. The two of us relaxed in the yard on this particular day; for the life of me I can't remember what sparked Taylor's anger, but he became livid. Unfortunately, this anger was directed at yours truly. He stomped over to us, told me to stand up and get ready, because we were going to fight and he intended to "beat the shit" out of me. One word someone might use to describe me is "quippy." Within me resides a clever bone, possibly even snide at times, but it's part of how I deal with the everyday mess of this conflicted world we live in. So naturally, after Taylor approached me, I just sat chuckling to myself. I stated simply that I would not recommend keeping that promise, because it would end with his hindquarters making a new friend in our yard. After a few more exchanges, he stomped inside, certainly unsatisfied. My grandmother, a psychiatric nurse throughout her life, assured me I did the right thing.

The first several months that Taylor was home, I often felt like I was the only one who stood up to him. Everyone else tried to cater to his every whine and whimper—everyone except me. One of the things I feel most important is to push his independence. In my ways, I tended to be quite brash at times. The episode in the yard marked the beginning's end for us, or at the very least, a sharp decline.

Another story I'll share with you shows a more general trend as opposed to one specific time or place. This trend stems from a fault I find within myself that I worked extremely hard to alter—all for nil in this instance. Throughout high school, I never developed the ability to take people for what they are presently, and always found myself delving into and holding onto the past. That's a quick recipe for unhealthy friendships across the board, so I put a lot of effort into finding myself, getting in touch with what I truly care about, and seeing people for who they are now as opposed to digging up and examining the past. As you've probably heard, someone with a brain injury often lives in the past. Why? It makes sense for Taylor, and in his mind he hasn't anything to look forward to in the grand scheme of things. The past is concrete, the past is funny, the past is an easy conversation-starter. In his mind, the past is all Taylor has any more. He hasn't the ability to think critically about something or reflect vividly on what he has now. He lives for the moment through his storytelling. His insistence on staying in the past remains hard for me to swallow, because it feels as if everything my parents and family have done for him goes completely unnoticed, when he still lives for everything that happened prior to the accident. After working hard to overlook the past, I find myself constantly backsliding from what I worked hard to achieve in order to please him. I don't blame Taylor, at all. If my future was picked up and tossed in a meat grinder, I'd revert to the past for internal peace as well. It's the natural thing to do, but innate sucks at times.

Myriad discrepancies wreak havoc on our relationship, but this one speaks the loudest. Taylor and I often lack the ability to connect on any level. What do I like to do? I'm a sports fan, watching games, playing them, reading about them, etc. I love travel; I've been lucky enough to travel and to see places and things many people will see only on the *National Geographic* channel, and it helped define a lot of who I am today. I enjoy music, every aspect of it: listening, writing, creating, and going off to concerts with Tanner and Mom at the last minute when one of our favorites plays somewhere in the area. I enjoy reading and getting lost in someone else's world, because I want to forget mine for a little while. I truly love learning, and embraced the mindset that one can never know too much, factually speaking. I enjoy chatting over lunch with my Mom, or learning how to cook something new with her. In a world gone mad, seemingly simple hobbies help me maintain my sanity.

Of all of the things I've mentioned, if Taylor likes one of them, it is on the complete opposite side of the field. He is narrow-minded and disregards the fact that I love culture, learning, and travel. That usually turns into name-calling, and his telling me I'm going to contract X disease because I'm going to Y place. Can this negativity create some very interesting, unforgettable conversations? You bet; however, I'd trade it all to have the brother back that I got along with no matter the situation. The one who called me when in need, and the one who asked me for advice despite the fact I'm the little, less-experienced brother. I can't think of anything I wouldn't surrender in order for him to have his old life back.

Everyone swears by a silver lining amidst the most brutal of storms, and Taylor and I have ours. Amid the constant struggle and cloud of misunderstanding that hazes our judgment and burns our eyes, we've had some truly enjoyable, genuine, and heartfelt times. For instance, when the five of us sit together as a family, we generally erupt with a few long-lived moments of uncontrollable laughter. Taylor enjoys being the center of attention, which is fine by me because I'm usually pretty reserved and don't mind playing some background music. When we start laughing as a family, it is a task to maintain it. Admittedly, the subjects of our jokes may be borderline inappropriate to the easily offended, but we're a family and what happens under our roof stays there. Prior to his fall, Taylor had a wonderful ability to imitate people, especially those he disliked. Although the true talent got lost at the bottom of the stairs, the comedy behind it all has not faded in the least. He often tells stories of times he got in trouble at school, or stories about some of the guys he worked with, or one about a girl that we never dreamed of hearing about. When Taylor's brain focuses on this creative area, we have a blast. The end result is surely a world of stomach pain followed by shortness of breath, and tears due to extensive laughter. If only this good humor described every moment we spend together.

I find Taylor more pleasant when I've a friend or two over. Taylor enjoys being the focus of every eye in the room coupled with the attention my friends give him. The friends I've brought around him are wonderful, even if it is not easy to expose them to what he offers. If I invite some friends over to play guitar and just catch up, or I bring a friend over that I just need to sit down and spill some of myself to, it proves to be a difficult task when there's someone in the room who wants in on every moment. My family and I often make the correlation that Taylor is like a kid, and it's just an accurate way to depict it. He wants to be around you when company is present, even when you want to spend time with your visitor. He wants in on every secret; to be included. The desire of inclusion is an innate quality of human being, but with Taylor there is no limit or boundary he is unwilling to cross in an effort to achieve it. To get privacy or peace usually takes the involvement of a third party to occupy Taylor.

Before the accident, I could look at him a certain way or motion my hand in a specific manner and he'd understand that I needed some alone time. It's no less than a grueling task trying to find where to draw the line, because he isn't going to remember the complexity of what surrounds a friendship when you're in your early twenties. I want to be able to share that and discuss it with my friends without having to entertain him. This is part of the reason I find myself not going home nearly as much as I used to.

I made an effort to go home every other weekend my first year of college. I missed home, I missed my Mom and Dad, Taylor- who was at home most of the time, and Tanner was still in high school. I lived with my best friend at the time, but sometimes you need home. Since the accident, it's gotten harder and harder to enjoy home. I'm not sure whether I successfully shut myself down emotionally and drove away any of the feelings affiliated with home--maybe, there's an underlying cause, but the enjoyment I get from being there is severely minimized in comparison to the time preceding the accident.

I've one more thing to talk about turning off: your religious ears. After Taylor's accident, I faced insurmountable amounts of religious opinions, prayers, and ideas. The overall conservative values of my hometown made it a general trend, and it was often the first response when people heard about Taylor's fall. They mentioned that they pray for me, or that God will help Taylor through it. I've no problem with this approach, as I've been exposed to it for the better part of my life; nonetheless, I assure you these things occasionally go against the grain of the hurting party.

Admittedly, with some anger and disgust I took to social media to make a statement regarding Taylor's accident. Several people responded that there was no denying that God saved Taylor's life the night he fell...not quite. Tanner saved Taylor's life. Dr. Kirkland saved Taylor's life. I saved Taylor's life. We are not Gods. I wasn't mad at anyone for this, I was hurt. Hurt by the fact that they could so easily disregard the fact that it wasn't their brother, their son. It's a whole different demon you face when it's your loved one- it's easy to play it off and put it on the supernatural when you're looking through the glass.

The main difference between a doctor and a god is simple: the general public surely places the blame on a doctor if something goes wrong, but not a god. A god gets the credit for saving lives, he or she also gets it for stuffing them up. In response to my comments, these people who vouched for the idea that their god saved Taylor also gave the same god the entire glory story when Taylor made a positive stride. If you're anything like me, this anecdote will cause you to put several white-knuckled creases in the binding of this book. You want to see credit given where it's deserved, to the right persons. For instance, my Mom, who always found love for all three of her boys, even when her heart felt empty. For my Dad, who put in a ten-hour workday and then came to Geisinger to sit and visit with his eldest son who didn't have the mental capacity to give a care whether he was or wasn't there at the time. Give credit to the physicians and their assistants, to the therapists, to the amazing staff in the emergency room and ICU during one of the most critical times. For Taylor's few good friends, who have been his friends for several years and not left his side to this date (early 2015).

If you're on the outside looking in on a situation like ours, here are the best things you can do: offer an ear instead of a slew of words if you're unsure what to say; wrap your arms around someone hurting; or simply tell them that you remain awestruck and sorry. This approach goes much further than words or actions that you may not realize are more harmful than helpful. Why? What I dealt with was already surreal, I don't want anything else intangible or unfactual. I want love, and to appreciate the palpable people doing their best to bring Taylor back.

I heard everything; from ideas that his fall was a part of God's intricate master plan to the notion that it was my family's past transgressions which had spawned a divine punishment. If I had allowed them, these things would have driven me up a wall. I went through a phase where I nearly let them. I hated hearing anything about a higher power, because what I knew and accounted for was the fact that three people played an initial role in getting Taylor to a hospital, and then the doctors took it from there. To this day, the concept remains a raw wound that's easily reopened. Neither fault, nor hindrance, I am comfortable with the way my brain works.

I remember my Uncle Kerry looking at me and telling me that not a soul would care if I ran down the hallway, flailed my arms in a crazy manner, and screamed obscenities at the top of my lungs. His comment was a bit of advice that I still keep close to my heart. It's a reminder to do what I need to do to see that I make it through a given situation. No one on the outside looking in is going to hold something against you when you're in a stressful environment, and if they do, then chances are you'll have been graced with their dismissal from your life. At the end of the day, I found it most important to stay true to my own mind, and follow what I saw in it formerly. A time like this isn't one for finding yourself or getting in touch with other parts of yourself, it is about keeping yourself together when you need to most; about being there for your brother and hoping your decisions make an impact in the long run. Most importantly, it's about giving your family someone to lean on when you know they are at a caving point.

We all have experiences we feel are sure to crush us, but that's okay. It's essential we don't let them define who we are and stay true to ourselves. I assure you that during this time of my life, emotions have never run higher. You, like me, may find yourself in a spot where you can't be a friend to someone because you feel as if the problems he or she comes to you with are loaded with a mundane insignificance. Yet out of this, true friends will understand. What you must focus on is taking care of you and those around you. I also highly recommend that you place a piece of your heart in the care of someone removed from the situation, who doesn't see the repercussions that it has on your family on a daily basis. I made the best friend I've ever had by opening up, being myself, and sharing my thoughts and feelings on a regular basis. Was it easy? No, I'm an introvert. Nevertheless, it was worth it and I'm thankful for it every day.

Don't let fear win, divide up your heart and give pieces to the listeners. Take snapshots of the moments, even the vicious ones, and hang them inside your skull. Lend a shoulder to the family you've been given. Providing yourself with outlets, ways to escape, and people to lean on will help you beat the odds one step at a time. Even though every step may send a throbbing pain directly to your heart or mind, the important thing is that you keep trudging through the muck.

Tug Life
By: Tanner Bingaman

As individuals, we bear many things heavily. Comparatively, some heaviness is more burdensome than others; some individuals encounter heavier things. The heaviness, the pain, takes shape as a sword, piercing and slicing, exposing more tender tissue with every pass. The heaviness is like a stone tied to the ankles, muscled on only by those strong enough to overcome its load. I have heard pain is meant to be embraced, that we must use the fires of pain to ignite our healing. All pains are different, and time does not heal all things, but it can lighten the load.

The sword pierces the heart and ravages the mind, but with time the edges dull and the entirety of the sword, the whole of the pain, may be grasped. The pain can be managed. Even if we haven't the strength to crawl with the weight of our stones, rain will fall and slowly erode away the stone's layers. Friends and family feel the sting of a sword and the weight of a stone together. It is together that we can overcome. Together, we'll keep tuggin' along.

Taylor's fall has bred a lifetime of emotions, bringing with it depths of sadness I once viewed inconceivable. This is truly the pain of a lifetime. I feel honored and grateful to be able to share this story: Taylor's story, our story.

I do not always find it funny the way things change, but it is intriguing. The stairs of our safe log home used to represent at the worst the possibility of a naggy contusion. As a child I would run them, propelling myself like a cheetah through my hands and feet, and occasionally I would slip. The stairs were the cause of many bruised shins growing up. I used to hate when that happened; nothing seemed worse at the painful moment than the fresh welt. I am now aware of the depth of innocence in this association with those stairs. They are no longer so blissfully ambiguous.

When Taylor crashed down those stairs, I hadn't the slightest recognition of how drastically my perception of them would change. As Avery and I tended to Taylor's stiffened body, lying still on the hard tiles, I hadn't the capacity to imagine such a demon as traumatic brain injury. As I hoisted Taylor to an upright seated position to set his back against the nearby couch, I couldn't, in my wildest of dreams, have formulated a more fantastical being. As Avery dialed 9-1-1, and Taylor's body began to give the slightest of tremors, I didn't know of the pain that would come to reside in our hearts. I didn't know those stairs were capable of such bruises.

Now I know the stairs are a mountain; an unrelenting and treacherous mountain, one that even the most experienced of climbers may never scale. One that now Taylor and those closest to him have been challenged to climb. We've been placed at the bottom with a paper-bag lunch and a set of freshly bloodied shins. We have no ropes, no harnesses, and not a single karabiner. We've been asked to carry ourselves up and to bring Taylor back with us. There is no way to prepare for such a task.

After the initial fall, things began to change quite rapidly for us, while they seemed to stand rather still for Taylor. For a short time, my contact with the outside world became limited to those who visited the hospital. I wanted so badly to get away from it all, yet couldn't leave the hospital without the thought of Taylor's battered head and corpse-like body running through my mind. I spent two weeks in the waiting room and at Taylor's bedside before I was willing to return to school.

For the first time in my life, I knew what it was like to feel like an outsider, as if I didn't belong. The hospital was a place of sorrow and longing; sorrow for what had come to be, and longing for a glimpse of good to sprout through the rubble. With that said, the hospital had also become a safe haven of sorts. As I sat next to Taylor's coma-stricken body, I did not feel the need to fight tears or suppress laden thoughts into neglected corners of my mind. This, however, was not the case with the outside world.

On the first day returning to school since Taylor's fall, I truly felt as if all eyes were on me; I was sure the world was watching my every step. It also seemed as if the world was at a loss for words. Those who managed to muster up a comforting phrase or two were answered with a quiet response. What is one to say to a friend that has recently been confronted with the most painful circumstance of his life? They knew not what to say, and I hadn't the desire to answer.

434

Eventually, school came to be a place of relaxation. As the weeks wore on, the readiness of thinking to ask how our family was coping dwindled. This is not to say that our town didn't care; Mifflinburg responded, in many aspects, in a manner one could only dream of in such a situation. Nevertheless, while in school, I did not want to think of reality, Taylor's stricken state, or the fog of misery life seemed to be doused in at the moment. I was glad not to be pestered with questions regarding his, or my, well-being. When peers or teachers asked how Taylor or the family was doing, I felt no guilt in feeding them a line of verbal manure, saying things were coming along fine, "all things considered." I became a world-class liar in the first weeks of his fall.

Other attempts to provide comfort came from those who visited while Taylor was in the hospital. There are those who really do bring healing to the table, and those who oppose the healing process. Within days of Taylor's fall I had heard something to the extent of, "He is going to wake up and be himself, and everything will be okay," about a thousand times. For a while my family and I clung to farfetched hopes of this kind; they were simple-minded reassurances and what we most desperately wanted. Those statements, those false hopes, did nothing but cause a temporary uplifting, and then a consequential downfall. When the medical truths rang out, and the facts were faced, mental hell broke loose, letting reality sting like alcohol over a mangled wound. These attempts to give shelter were hopeless shots in the dark toward a miracle; they landed far from their target.

In one specific case, a man who was not well acquainted with the family came to visit as we congregated in the hall outside Geisinger's ICU (as the waiting room was under construction). At this moment, the hall was quiet. There were more than a handful of us seated there, but there was not always a need to create chatter. At times, it only felt right to submit to silence. The man walked in, politely introduced himself to those he hadn't previously met, and plainly asked, "So, to my understanding the situation is pretty hopeless, right?" I could have broken his jaw and felt no remorse. His words burned me up, maybe because I feared he might be right, but I had no place in my mind for pessimism at the time.

Luckily, the majority of the company did not come to add weight to the sorrow. There were visits from grandparents, aunts, uncles, cousins, friends, and coaches. I wish Taylor could have been consciously present to witness the love pouring through the hospital doors and into the waiting room. Certain people would come and create a diffusion of sorts, releasing positive energy into tender crevices of a dreary circumstance, providing momentary solace. People simply came to offer a warm embrace, and some would go so far as to provide a meal or gas money toward our daily commutes to the hospital. Shelby, a longtime friend of Taylor's, went to great lengths to establish Team Taylor and express her care for our family. It was empowering to witness the rally of a tiny Pennsylvania town that showed, and continues to show, great support for our family.

Our in-home family dynamic began to change as well. About three weeks in, our family seemed to be closer than we had been in some time. When struck by a deep pain in the midst of another, we realigned as a family to soften the hardness. As we came together, it felt like harmony had been restored. I often wonder whether my family would be a single unit as it is today had Taylor not fallen, but I question whether we needed such a gut-wrenching blow to wake us from an apathetic slump. That sense of revitalization, it's not always present anymore.

It is dumbfounding how rapidly life can change. Within a month's time everything was made new; a new schedule, a new state of mind, a new Taylor, a new family, and a new me. A completely new set of priorities came about because others were shattered. New is not always better.

I cannot recall a more specific date, but at some point during the first month Pawpaw (my maternal grandfather) looked to me and said, "That's what you will need to find." At first I was confused. Pawpaw is notorious for saying things out of the ordinary. Generally they are profound or extremely funny, sometimes both, and tend to leave one lost in a sea of thought. He was pointing at the New Balance shirt I had on.

"That's what you will need to find: new balance." The advice was sweet, like fresh Costa Rican mangos after a day's play on the beach, providing the energy boost needed to push just a bit further onward, past the floating driftwood and skittish land crabs. Since receiving it, I have tried to find and apply the essence of balance to any aspects of my life I see fit. This approach does at times include a balance of the unbalanced. I remember thinking only Pawpaw could supply such a proverb under the dire conditions in which we dwelt. The advice felt pure, and it seemed to be a guiding hand for the transition to Bryn Mawr in the next phase of Taylor's journey.

Bryn Mawr is characterized as a place of progress to me. It became a place of progression through resilience and hard work, mainly on the part of my mother, Taylor, and the medical professionals of the Maple Unit. My weekend home became the halls of the facility and the living quarters close by, where Mom stayed during Taylor's time there. Bryn Mawr is where I witnessed the rebirth of my eldest brother. It was nothing short of watching the emergence of a person in a twenty-two-year-old body from a coma to an infantile being, and then through various stages of child development.

The first momentous occurrence that sticks out in my mind was the first time Taylor laughed after his fall. Dad and I were driving to Bryn Mawr, and Mom called to inform us that Taylor had a dangerous series of grand mal seizures and was being moved to nearby Paoli Hospital. Taylor was pretty well out of it when we got there. Seizures seem to temporarily strip their victims of any desire to engage in activity and cause general tiredness. He was agitated, but not yet extremely active.

As the day wore on, Taylor began to regain a bit of strength. Instead of seeming like he needed a daylong nap, he became more like an uncoordinated bull wearing puffy protective gloves. The staff of the hospital seemed ill-informed about his state and ill-informed about TBI in general; they were not much help in caring for him. He had been transferred due to legal niceties regarding adjustments of neurological medicines post-seizure, and because Bryn Mawr serves as a rehab facility and cannot provide the care given by a standard ICU. With that said, it turned out to be more of a hassle for all involved than a relief that Taylor would be in good hands.

Taylor was restless and hard to manage. He kept wanting to take off his gloves, and rightly so, because they were obnoxious and annoying. We would take them off now and then to let his hands air out, but he had to be closely watched when they weren't being worn to keep him from picking at the sutures on his head.

At one point while his hands were cooling off, he stuck his index finger in his ear in search of gold, or maybe gum or something (when we were kids Dad used to act like he pulled the pack out of our ears whenever he surprised us with Bubblicious Gum). Taylor must have been shorted because he removed his finger and was left with nothing more than a generous coating of earwax. He took a long look at his finger as if deciding what to do with his find, and then graciously offered me the earwax by sticking his finger toward my face. I sniffed at the offering and then pretended to lick at it, making noises as a dog does when lapping up water. Taylor found this gesture hilarious and broke into the most pathetic yet heartwarming laugh. He was laughing for the first time since surfacing from his coma and it seemed like an enormous milestone. Hearing his laugh was worth the stressful hospital situation.

Another moment worth mentioning is when Taylor said his first word. Taylor's speech therapist thought Taylor was close to getting out some words, for he had been making low groaning noises as if attempting to spit out something more coherent during the past few days. Avery, Mom, and I were taking turns wheeling Taylor through the halls of the ground floor and sat down to rest for a while. Taylor was fidgeting in his wheelchair and wanted to be tilted forward so his feet could touch the ground. Avery adjusted it for him, and Mom urged Taylor to say thank you. After about thirty seconds, Taylor managed to squeeze out a soft, almost inaudible, "Thanks." For a moment, I was ecstatic; to hear even a single word come out of Taylor's mouth meant a new world of hope had emerged. The celebration was short-lived.

A younger brother shouldn't have to celebrate his older brother's "first word." To hear Taylor speak again was a relief, but it bred a harsh realization. For the first time I began to toss around the idea that from now on, I would be a younger brother by nothing more than age. The job descriptions were changing; I was to look after Taylor now. He was more or less an infant trapped in a twenty-two-year-old body. As a child I envisioned a simple life for myself . . . I wanted to be a farmer, claiming the cows across the street from our home were mine. Acting is not my forte; it is too dramatic, but I have become an actor as best I can, allowing Taylor to maintain his standing as the older brother.

Looking back, I find it odd that we did not jump for joy when Taylor spoke for the first time, but our reaction also makes sense. Taylor could speak before, and though we knew a TBI could strip its victim of all previous abilities, we expected progress to be made. This is still the case. I expect progress, and as Taylor progresses, the celebrations are short-lived while regression is accompanied by a regret that seems to be fed by a desperate yearning to thrive once again in previous abilities. The harvests of progress are taken for granted and then sought endlessly after when they go sour. It's a shame we find ourselves grateful for rain only during drought.

Taylor pushed on and on at Bryn Mawr, making remarkable strides. He started with close to nothing, at the mere capacity of a baby, with no promise of betterment. For the first days, he plainly stared into an abyss in his wheelchair while restlessly moving his legs back and forth, but this meant he had opened his eyes and was beginning to move his limbs. Then he began to write, mainly nonsense words and phrases, but occasionally emitted a coherent sentence. Slowly, he began to take food by mouth and worked away from reliance on his feeding tube. He started to verbalize words and finally sentences. Every threshold broken was momentarily celebrated, and then used as a basis for how to breach the next.

Sometimes the building up was a destructive process. I remember well a period during Taylor's stay at Bryn Mawr wherein I was not a preferred visitor. This discovery was hard to swallow. Taylor was entering a very aggressive stage of recovery that entailed many outbursts and malicious actions. During this time, the bulk of his anger seemed to be directed at me. When I entered a room, he immediately began yelling, cursing, and spitting good for nothings in my direction. For a few weeks, my name became "f-----g faggot." He hadn't even remembered my real name yet, and now he was creating less desirable ones for me.

I think I handled his abuse well, but it did hurt. It was hard to be ostracized from his good graces. I wasn't even tolerable. When I remember this phase now, I think of the grandmother of Taylor's first roommate at Bryn Mawr. Her grandson remained in a vegetative state for the entirety of Taylor's stay; it was heartbreaking. She once said to Avery, as Taylor was throwing a verbal tantrum, "I would give the world to hear my grandson curse me out."

Taylor began to emerge from his state of constant aggravation within a few weeks of its start. A more pleasant and child-like person took the place of the persistent vilifications. This change was a relief, for Taylor was soon to be homebound. The staff at Bryn Mawr sent us off better than I feel any other facility would have. It was nerve-wracking to contemplate caring for Taylor at home, but it marked the next phase of this story.

The person we brought home was different, through and through, from the one who had lived in our house before. My oldest brother was now much like a child. I went to visit Bryn Mawr the day before Taylor was to return home. He had received a dancing chicken from a friend as a care package. The hen sang in a high-pitched voice and squawked up and down. Now and then she'd say, "Oops, there it is," and a plastic egg would pop out.

Taylor pressed the chicken's start button time and time again throughout the day. With every dance the hen did, he would dance along. Before his fall, he would not have been caught dead acting in such a way; he was a kid again. A forgetful kid who was unsteady on his feet, couldn't dress himself, forgot the names of more objects than he remembered, and remained thoroughly confused about his condition.

Taylor was fragile when he returned home. He had to be guided while walking, and always had two spotters for stairs. He required long periods of rest and couldn't focus to save his life. I had to learn to suppress sarcasm, which comprises the basis of my humor, as he couldn't comprehend word play of any sort. There had also never been a previous need for me to help him shower nor requests to tuck him into bed. When he returned from Bryn Mawr, these things became regular occurrences.

Despite his fragility, Taylor was excited beyond belief to be home. Anyone and everyone he knew or ever had known, he felt the need to invite for a visit. Various acquaintances and friends were in and out of the house throughout the first month of his return. People promised to make regular visits and maintain friendships, despite the changes that had come. Some relationships were salvaged, but even more relationships were tarnished beyond repair.

I wish I could have known who would remain and who would stray; I could have saved the whole family a lot of heartache. There were times when I found myself lost in dark fogs of rage, too angry to think straight because of the pain people have caused through not being there for Taylor. I cannot say what I would have done in the shoes of his friends, but I can say I hope I would have acted more like some and less like others. It hurts when you're forced to find out who your friends are.

As I learned about brain injury, I became more aware of possible consequences of my own actions. Before Taylor's fall, I had regularly partaken in using alcohol. I was never one to care about legalities; I got drunk simply in an attempt to have fun. The fact that Taylor was drinking the night he fell combined with exposure to alcohol and drug-related injuries through Bryn Mawr drastically changed my views on the use of these substances.

It took a long while before I felt I had established a new balance between expression of my opinions and tolerance of others'. While my views were changing I did fall, though not entirely, out of relationships with some close friends. I was excluded many times from weekend activities and nights with the boys. Even if they were just hanging out to play video games or sit around a fire, I was not always invited because they knew they might want to get drunk, and I would not have been comfortable with that. This exclusion hurt something fierce.

I think both sides were at fault. I should not have expected them to be able to empathize, but they could have met me in the middle; it felt like they wouldn't even consider my side of the story. Alcohol can create a barrier between friends and loved ones. When it did so for me, I felt defeated. I feel comfortable with light use of alcohol, but I don't believe I will ever reacquire the mindset of a drunkard.

Tragedy pulls some people apart and brings others together; the same happens within the individual. Taylor's injury matured me. I went from being a regular high school kid to feeling surrounded by a malicious set of mishaps that forced me to change. I began to read more often and put more time into writing music. I felt like more of an introvert than I previously had, spending great sums of time sitting quietly to simply think about the world around. Family became a priority, and for once it wasn't taken for granted. It was due to a strike of tragedy that I matured to fit a character possibly more like that of an older individual. I loved these changes about myself, but not all the changes were for the better.

Before Taylor's accident, I cannot recall having experienced anxiety to any great degree. I had always been a relaxed and laid-back person. About the time Taylor began his rehabilitation at Bryn Mawr, I started waking during the night in pools of sweat and feeling extremely anxious. Some nights, I would wake up short of breath or feeling as though I would never again think clearly. I'm not sure if this was because of the stress I was facing that I never had before, but I do not believe it was a coincidence.

I remember waking one evening, soaked in sweat and short of breath, feeling like the world lay on my chest. I stood from the bed and staggered upstairs, trapped in a clouded mind. There were hundreds of screaming thoughts crashing through my head, but I couldn't grab hold of a single one to make sense of it. In this moment, it felt like the weight of the past months had snowballed into a persistent entity and taken residence upon my soul. I wandered the house in a haze until I ventured outside to our stone driveway. Standing in my boxers, I fell hard on my knees. Under my breath and looking to the night sky, I begged for the madness to stop; for my mind to feel at ease, for Taylor to be whole again, for our family to feel peace. I pleaded in this fashion for what seemed like hours before the anxiety began to dissipate.

I saw no grand silver lining, no ray of hope that broke through the darkness, but since that night I have felt relieved to some degree of my anxieties. I no longer wake in the night to a relentlessly-screaming mind.

Things were getting better. Taylor, despite many bumps along the way, kept moving forward. As weeks turned into months since his return home, hope grew steadier. Taylor had changed so much; he had been stripped of nearly everything, but somehow he managed to continue forward. His persistence was undeniable and his steady progressions gave room for thought that all might be well someday.

Home started to feel a little like home again, but things were still not easy. I would come home to see Mom exhausted from the day's errands; she was bringing Taylor to therapies, administering medications, furiously trying to find ways to lighten the financial load of medical bills, and still searching for energy to show love to Avery, Dad, and me. There were days she would come to me sobbing, expressing how sorry she felt for not being there for me as she wished to be. Taylor was the center of attention, but this did not hurt me as she feared it might. I felt she was doing the best she could to balance a ridiculously out-of-balance situation.

It was fascinating to see Taylor's lost abilities slowly resurface. His speech was becoming less monotone, more characterized, and his vocabulary was returning. He began walking more steadily and having better overall balance. I enjoyed sitting in while his friends would visit as he tried desperately to make them laugh, which usually worked. He would recall embarrassing stories about whoever was visiting and recount them to anyone willing to listen. The return of part of his humor was most refreshing.

The boyish, arguably repulsive nature of his humor had not much changed. I would do anything I could to expose his laughter. I feel no shame in peeing off the porch in the freezing cold or racing through the house in the nude like a wild man if it makes someone chuckle a little. I'll puff up my hair or hike up my shorts to the nipples and walk into his room when he's had a bad day to cheer him up. Taylor finds these things quite comical, and it brings me joy to give him the gift of laughter.

I could mark Taylor's first months at home with only deceptive notions of optimism, but I would be excluding many parts of the whole. Taylor's injury left him with a very literal and one-track mind, making it extremely easy for him to fixate on a single idea. Anything he heard that he deemed dangerous or worrisome became the most prominent thought on his mind for weeks to come. He would harp on things endlessly and could not be reasoned with.

Taylor's mind was not only fixated; it held a constant potential for storm. It is a disheartening experience to witness a seizure. The seizures take him by surprise, like a crack of thunder, and leave him thoroughly exhausted. I did not know what exactly to expect, for I had not seen any of the seizures he had while at Geisinger or Bryn Mawr. When he seizes, it is as if someone places a hooked finger into the edge of his mouth and yanks backward, forcing his head to turn sharply toward his right ear. His balance leaves and his shoulders often twitch along with his wrenching head. He is always trying to push out words, but the most that usually emerges is a faint gurgling as he chokes on saliva. He looks terrified. Seeing these convulsions has taught me how instantaneously life may be ripped from our grasp. Life is so often more fragile than we are willing to admit. I never thought I would be able to bear watching these terrors take my brother in their clutches, but I have.

Even with the road bumps along the way, things still seemed to be progressing. The new life we had been given seemed to hold more promise and I was growing optimistic about Taylor's future. Every month great strides were made, and I thought nothing could stop Taylor from moving forward. I was wrong.

During Taylor's stay at Bryn Mawr, we had been informed that many TBI survivors reach a peak in their recovery somewhere between one and a half and two years post-injury. This timeline was not frightening to me; I saw it as just another challenge Taylor would overcome, but battles with time are not often won. As the two-year mark approached, Taylor's progress came to a halt; he had reached a plateau. This plateau is where he is stuck today, and it is heartbreaking.

As a college student, I look forward to returning home between long weeks of study. Seeing Taylor is satisfying after weeks of mental strain. We catch up on what he has been doing, go for walks, and always seem to get lost in a fit of laughter at some point or another. Then the shine wears off and the emotional weight of reality sets in. I see that Taylor is stagnant in regard to progressing and showing no signs that this may change. He still requires caregivers, cannot entertain himself, and is unable to comprehend his daily challenges logically. He has not made notable progress in over six months. We just passed the second anniversary of his fall. I hate the idea that Taylor may never be independent again, and so does he.

The most heart-wrenching part is to know that my parents feel encaged in this new life while Avery and I have set off. We are starting lives away from home, doing what we are meant to do as sons: spread our wings and move on. My parents are left with the baggage of their altered son, knowing well that he will likely never be able to lead a life on his own.

When I returned home for the first time after the start of my first college semester, I sobbed. On the drive back to school, I felt heartbroken for my mother, father, and Taylor. They, pulled down by the tragedy that struck Taylor, may never again move forward. They are laden by an injury that persistently challenges all hopes of venturing beyond, wherever that may be. They are caught in the very essence of nostalgia. Though I feel ever-connected to Taylor's injury, I have means to escape the hell. I often wonder: if Taylor's injury does not have to define everything I am, why should it have to define him and my parents? To deem it destiny that he would fall and be forever condemned to a life of dependence is not comforting; it does not seem fair. I have learned life is not always fair.

At Geisinger Medical Center, there are automated robots programmed and wired to carry basic medical supplies to various units of the hospital. The robots are referred to as "Tugs." They regularly passed by us en route to their destinations, and sometimes we placed objects on the floor for them to navigate around, just for fun. One evening in the hospital Mom's brother, Uncle Eric, drew a cartoon version of a robot and captioned it "Tug Life." We are living the Tug Life.

The hospital trips, the constant worry, the fight against change, the sorrow and the sobbing, and the screaming to the stars above; that is the tug life. Picking up your brother's stiff body from the cold floor, watching his head swell to the size of a basketball, realizing that any moment could be his last, your last; that is the tug life. Holding your crying mother as she shakes and pleads with God to bring her son back, and hearing your father wail through the night just to wake to his pale and exhausted face in the morning; that is the tug life.

Every tug life is different, every one unique, but they share a basic principle; every tug has its loads to carry. When you've got only four wheels and one gives out, it makes for rough rolling; imagine trying to carry the weight, bear these loads, with a set of faulty wires. Taylor faces the world with a set of faulty wires, but he keeps on. Day in and day out, he keeps on. I guess that's what we all do, because sometimes it's all we can do; keep on tuggin' along, one day at a time.

Afterword: Team Taylor

Team Taylor was organized by Shelby Hackenberg, a close friend of Taylor's, in the days shortly after Taylor's fall. She came to talk with our family one night in the ICU waiting room and described a remarkable plan: to gather love and support for our family and for Taylor as we faced this unknown crisis. Taylor was still lying unresponsive in a coma, which was an intensely frightening time for us. We began to understand that the road ahead would be both long and treacherous. Shelby wanted to form a team of supporters and was willing to do everything that organizing it would involve. As time went on, we realized that Taylor's accident would mean months of changes for us. We discovered that traumatic brain injury would affect our family in many ways, but Team Taylor was there to help us through that time.

The Team Taylor Facebook page is a way for people to read updates about Taylor's progress via social media as well as a place where people could turn to help us. Team Taylor T-shirts were sold in the early months; over time, there were numerous fundraisers and displays of community support. Shelby led the team and found ways for people who wanted to help to be able to do so. She is a person of great integrity with formidable organizational skills that were an asset to the team she led.

Shelby was awarded the Medical Advocate Award through the American Red Cross for the work she did for Team Taylor in March 2014. The award is a great honor and beautiful recognition of the love of a special friend.

With the passing of time, Team Taylor has come to mean many things. The people who make up the team are people in Taylor's community; people in the community in which Nicole grew up; and others spread across the United States. Team Taylor T-shirts have been shipped to Texas, Georgia, Illinois, Tennessee, Minnesota, Alaska, New York, New Jersey, and Vermont as well as Australia and New Zealand. People of all ages and from all walks of life proudly wear them. We strongly believe the shirts represent not only Taylor but also other survivors of traumatic brain injury. Team Taylor remains dedicated to spreading awareness of traumatic brain injury and its effects as well as supporting the Bingaman family.

APPENDIX

Rancho Los Amigos (Revised): 10-Level Scale of Cognitive Functioning

Level I– No Response: Total Assistance
- Complete absence of observable change in behavior when presented visual, auditory, tactile, proprioceptive, vestibular or painful stimuli.

Level I– No Response
- Patient appears to be in a deep sleep and is completely unresponsive to any stimuli presented to him.

Level II– Generalized Response: Total Assistance
- Demonstrates generalized reflex response to painful stimuli.
- Responds to repeated auditory stimuli with increased or decreased activity.
- Responds to external stimuli with physiological changes generalized, gross body movement and/or not purposeful vocalization.
- Responses noted above may be the same regardless of type and location of stimulation.
- Responses may be significantly delayed.

Level II– Generalized Response
- Patient reacts inconsistently and non-purposefully to stimuli in a nonspecific manner. Responses are limited in nature and are often the same regardless of stimulus presented. Responses may be physiological changes, gross body movements, and/or vocalization. Often, the earliest response is to deep pain. Responses are likely to be delayed.

Level III– Localized Response: Total Assistance

- Demonstrates withdrawal or vocalization to painful stimuli.
- Turns toward or away from auditory stimuli.
- Blinks when strong light crosses visual field.
- Follows moving object passed within visual field.
- Responds to discomfort by pulling tubes or restraints.
- Responds inconsistently to simple commands.
- Responses directly related to type of stimulus.
- May respond to some persons (especially family and friends) but not to others.

Level IV– Confused/Agitated: Maximal Assistance

- Alert and in heightened state of activity.
- Purposeful attempts to remove restraints or tubes or crawl out of bed.
- May perform motor activities such as sitting, reaching, and walking but without any apparent purpose or upon another's request.
- Very brief and usually non-purposeful moments of sustained alternatives and divided attention.
- Absent short-term memory.
- May cry out or scream out of proportion to stimulus even after its removal.
- May exhibit aggressive or flight behavior.
- Mood may swing from euphoric to hostile with no apparent relationship to environmental events.
- Unable to cooperate with treatment efforts.
- Verbalizations are frequently incoherent and/or inappropriate to activity or environment.

Level V– Confused, Inappropriate Non-Agitated: Maximal Assistance

- Alert, not agitated but may wander randomly or with a vague intention of going home.
- May become agitated in response to external stimulation, and/or lack of environmental structure.
- Not oriented to person, place, or time.
- Frequent brief periods, non-purposeful sustained attention.
- Severely impaired recent memory, with confusion of past and present in reaction to ongoing activity.
- Absent goal-directed, problem-solving, self-monitoring behavior.
- Often demonstrates inappropriate use of objects without external direction.
- May be able to perform previously learned tasks when structured and cues provided.
- Unable to learn new information.
- Able to respond appropriately to simple commands fairly consistently with external structures and cues.
- Responses to simple commands without external structure are random and non-purposeful in relation to command.
- Able to converse on a social, automatic level for brief periods of time when provided external structure and cues.
- Verbalizations about present events become inappropriate and confabulatory when external structure and cues are not provided.

Level VI– Confused, Appropriate: Moderate Assistance
- Inconsistently oriented to person, time, and place.
- Able to attend to highly familiar tasks in non-distracting environment for 30 minutes with moderate redirection.
- Remote memory has more depth and detail than recent memory.
- Vague recognition of some staff.
- Able to use assistive memory aide with maximum assistance.

- Emerging awareness of appropriate response to self, family, and basic needs.
- Moderate assist to problem solve barriers to task completion.
- Supervised for old learning (e.g., self-care).
- Shows carryover for relearned familiar tasks (e.g., self-care).
- Maximum assistance for new learning with little or no carryover.
- Unaware of impairments, disabilities, and safety risks.
- Consistently follows simple directions.
- Verbal expressions are appropriate in highly familiar and structured situations.

Level VII– Automatic, Appropriate: Minimal Assistance for Daily Living Skills

- Consistently oriented to person and place within highly familiar environments. Moderate assistance for orientation to time.
- Able to attend to highly familiar tasks in a non-distraction environment for at least 30 minutes with minimal assist to complete tasks.
- Minimal supervision for new learning.
- Demonstrates carryover of new learning.
- Initiates and carries out steps to complete familiar personal and household routine but has shallow recall of what he/she has been doing.
- Able to monitor accuracy and completeness of each step in routine personal and household ADLs, and modify plan with minimal assistance.
- Superficial awareness of his/her condition but unaware of specific impairments and disabilities and the limits they place on his/her ability to safely, accurately, and completely carry out his/her household, community, work, and leisure ADLs.

452

- Minimal supervision for safety in routine home and community activities.
- Unrealistic planning for the future.
- Unable to think about consequences of a decision or action.
- Overestimates abilities.
- Unaware of others' needs and feelings.
- Oppositional/uncooperative.
- Unable to recognize inappropriate social interaction behavior.

Level VIII– Purposeful, Appropriate: Standby Assistance
- Consistently oriented to person, place, and time.
- Independently attends to and completes familiar tasks for 1 hour in distracting environments.
- Able to recall and integrate past and recent events.
- Uses assistive memory devices to recall daily schedule, "to-do" lists and record critical information for later use with standby assistance.
- Initiates and carries out steps to complete familiar personal, household, community, work, and leisure routines with standby assistance, and can modify the plan when needed with minimal assistance.
- Requires no assistance once new tasks/activities are learned.
- Aware of and acknowledges impairments and disabilities when they interfere with task completion but requires standby assistance to take appropriate corrective action.
- Thinks about consequences of a decision or action with minimal assistance.
- Overestimates or underestimates abilities.
- Acknowledges others' needs and feelings and responds appropriately with minimal assistance.
- Depressed.
- Irritable.

453

- Low frustration tolerance/easily angered.
- Argumentative.
- Self-centered.
- Uncharacteristically dependent/independent.
- Able to recognize and acknowledge inappropriate social interaction behavior while it is occurring and takes corrective action with minimal assistance.

Level IX– Purposeful, Appropriate: Standby Assistance on Request

- Independently shifts back and forth between tasks and completes them accurately for at least two consecutive hours.
- Uses assistive memory devices to recall daily schedule, "to-do" lists, and record critical information for later use with assistance when requested.
- Initiates and carries out steps to complete familiar personal, household, work, and leisure tasks independently, and unfamiliar personal, household, work, and leisure tasks with assistance when requested.
- Aware of and acknowledges impairments and disabilities when they interfere with task completion and takes appropriate corrective action, but requires standby assist to anticipate a problem before it occurs and take action to avoid it.
- Able to think about consequences of decisions or actions with assistance when requested.
- Accurately estimates abilities but requires standby assistance to adjust to task demands.
- Acknowledges others' needs and feelings and responds appropriately with standby assistance.
- Depression may continue.
- May be easily irritable.

- May have low frustration tolerance.
- Able to self-monitor appropriateness of social interaction with standby assistance.

Level X– Purposeful, Appropriate: Modified Independent

- Able to handle multiple tasks simultaneously in all environments but may require periodic breaks.
- Able to independently procure, create, and maintain own assistive memory devices.
- Independently initiates and carries out steps to complete familiar and unfamiliar personal, household, community, work, and leisure tasks, but may require more than usual amount of time and/or compensatory strategies to complete them.
- Anticipates impact of impairments and disabilities on ability to complete daily living tasks and takes action to avoid problems before they occur but may require more than usual amount of time and/or compensatory strategies.
- Able to independently think about consequences of decisions or actions but may require more than usual amount of time and/or compensatory strategies to select the appropriate decision or action.
- Accurately estimates abilities and independently adjusts to task demands.
- Able to recognize the needs and feelings of others and automatically respond in appropriate manner.
- Periodic periods of depression may occur.
- Irritability and low frustration tolerance when sick, fatigued, and/or under emotional stress.
- Social interaction behavior is consistently appropriate.

CPSIA information can be obtained at www.ICGtesting.com
Printed in the USA
LVOW12s2205100615

442029LV00003B/208/P